Ethnography Unbound

Ethnography Unbound

*Power and Resistance in the
Modern Metropolis*

Michael Burawoy • Alice Burton • Ann Arnett Ferguson
Kathryn J. Fox • Joshua Gamson • Nadine Gartrell
Leslie Hurst • Charles Kurzman • Leslie Salzinger
Josepha Schiffman • Shiori Ui

UNIVERSITY OF CALIFORNIA PRESS
Berkeley   Los Angeles   Oxford

University of California Press
Berkeley and Los Angeles, California
University of California Press, Ltd.
Oxford, England
© 1991 by The Regents of the University of California

A different version of Joshua Gamson's chapter appeared in *Social Problems* 36, no. 4 (1989).

Library of Congress Cataloging-in-Publication Data
Ethnography unbound : power and resistance in the modern metropolis /
  Michael Burawoy . . . [et al.].
     p.   cm.
  Includes bibliographical references and index.
  ISBN 0-520-07320-7.—ISBN 0-520-07322-3 (pbk.)
  1. Ethnology—Field work. 2. Participant observation. 3. Social
action—California—Case studies. I. Burawoy, Michael.
  GN346.4.E84   1991
  305.8—dc20   91-8552
                                                                   CIP

Printed in the United States of America
9 8 7 6 5 4 3 2 1
The paper used in this publication meets the minimum requirements of
American National Standard for Information Sciences—Permanence of Paper for Printed Library Materials, ANSI Z39.48-1984. ♾

For Carol Hatch—Twenty-Two Years
Participant in and Observer of Berkeley Sociology

CONTENTS

PREFACE

This was almost the preface to a cookbook instead of a collection of ethnographies. The volume grew out of a graduate sociology seminar in participant observation. When the seminar ended, we decided to continue meeting informally over dinner to revise and rework our research projects into a book, and the menu became a barometer of our progress. When the writing was going well, we ate take-out. When we were having difficulty, however, the meals were sumptuous, and there were times when some of us wistfully considered abandoning the social sciences in favor of the culinary arts. But we helped each other through those rough spots, and two years (and many meals) after entering the field, we emerged with this collection of essays.

In truth, when we began the seminar in fall 1988, we were probably more qualified to be cooks than ethnographers. Only one of the twelve, all of us graduate students at the University of California at Berkeley, had ever done participant observation before. We had merely two weeks to select our sites and begin research, a time constraint that permitted neither a leisured nor circumspect entry into the field. Moreover, during the course of the seminar, the scope and direction of many of the projects changed. At the end of the semester most of us felt that our projects were far from complete, but by that time we had become committed to our research.

So we agreed to meet weekly at the home of Michael Burawoy. Perhaps it was the informality of the setting, perhaps the conviviality of the gatherings, or perhaps it was a growing interest in and dedication to one another's work. Whatever the reasons, we were fortunate to be graced with a highly collaborative and collegial working relationship. This spirit had been evident during the seminar, but it deepened over the course of our evening meetings. Rather than the posturing and jockeying for status that commonly characterize seminars, it was the norm for us to present unfinished work, to offer ideas and theories only half-formed, which in turn allowed us to benefit from each other's rigorous and constructive feedback.

Perhaps those inclined toward participant observation as a technique of research are also more inclined to a participatory approach to learning. Certainly there was a congruence between our own interactions and those we had with our subjects. As Burawoy argues in chapter 1, the process of working alongside those we study necessitates a dialogue between observer and observed. While much sociological work may appear seamless—the researcher invisible behind the scenes—there is in fact always a relationship between ourselves as researchers and our subjects. Participant observation brings this conversation to the fore. For that reason, he argues, participant observation is paradigmatic of all social science and not merely a quaint technique at the margins.

Participant observation also generates rich and detailed data about everyday life. These studies, for example, attempt to convey the flavor and texture of life in the San Francisco Bay Area and specifically, as the book's title suggests, how people's daily lives are disrupted, threatened, and impinged upon by forces outside their control. In his discussion of the extended case method in chapters 2 and 13, Burawoy explains how we were able to extrapolate outward from our particular sites to explore the more general themes of power and resistance, and how from there we were able to reconstruct existing explanatory theories.

Thus, the significance of the studies resides in both their particularity and their generality. Chapters 3 through 12 deal with five features of the modern metropolis—social movements, work organization, immigrants, education, and knowledge. Each chapter concludes with methodological reflections that call attention to distinctive aspects of the research process. In chapter 14 Burawoy offers an account of his experience as teacher of the seminar.

Sadly, two members of our seminar, Carol Heller and Ann Robertson, couldn't continue with us. We missed them as our collaboration developed, and we thank them for their many contributions during the first semester. We also thank Nancy Scheper-Hughes for an inspiring talk about her field work in Brazil; Judy Stacey, Rick Fantasia, Nina Eliasoph, Paul Lichterman, Carol Stack, Bob Freeland, Ida Susser, and one anonymous referee for their comments and help on different parts of the manuscript; Amy Einsohn and Andrew Alden for sharpening the essays by their copyediting; and Naomi Schneider, whose enthusiasm for the project gave us the confidence to pursue it to the end.

ONE

Introduction

Michael Burawoy

This book examines the way in which everyday life in the modern metropolis is continually eroded, distorted, overpowered by, and subordinated to institutional forces that seem beyond human control. In part 1 Joshua Gamson and Josepha Schiffman thematize the importance of power in new social movements (an AIDS activist group and two peace groups), particularly the way civil society is not outside but traversed by regimes of micro-power. In part 2 Alice Burton and Ann Arnett Ferguson criticize the exclusive focus on hierarchical control in studies of work. Instead they underline the importance of horizontal ties for creating the conditions of resistance to bureaucratic control in a welfare agency and for maintaining alternative organizations such as a baking cooperative. In part 3 Leslie Salzinger and Shiori Ui downplay what is conventionally stressed in the literature on immigrants, namely their cultural background. Instead they highlight the way in which state and economy have shaped and limited strategies for occupational advancement among refugees from Central America and Cambodia. In part 4 Leslie Hurst shows how the separation of family, school, and classroom contributes to the breakdown of teaching of lower-class teenagers, and Nadine Julius shows how restoring connections between teacher, parent, and student can improve education. In part 5 Kathryn Fox shows how the state, through its laws and regulations and through its control of funds, constrains ethnographic outreach work among drug users, while Charles Kurzman studies the autonomy of academic ethnographers to adopt different values and interests.

All the studies examine how power and resistance play themselves out in social situations that are invaded by economic and political systems. They highlight what Jürgen Habermas calls the colonization of the lifeworld by the system.[1] In the face of commodification through money and administration through power, everyday life loses its autonomy and shared purpose. But their analyses do not simply record this colonization, they also explore resistance to it in the forms of negotiated orders, alternative institutions, and social movements.

If the students share a substantive theme, they also share a common research technique—the technique of participant observation, or what some call the art of ethnography. Participant observation is usually viewed as one among a number of techniques of social research—archival, survey, demographic, and experimental. What distinguishes participant observation is the study of people in their own time and space, in their own everyday lives. It is often referred to as natural sociology, studying subjects in their "natural habitat" as opposed to the "unnatural" setting of the interview or laboratory.[2]

According to convention, each research technique has its own advantages and its own distinctive biases, ways in which it distorts the reality it seeks to comprehend. Thus, the advantages of participant observation are assumed to lie not just in direct observation of how people act but also how they understand and experience those acts. It enables us to juxtapose what people say they are up to against what they actually do. The dangers of participant observation are said to derive from the same source as its virtues. Too close contact with the participants can lead to loss of objectivity or to contamination of the situation. The problem of objectivity is compounded by the problem of validity, namely, intensive research limits the possibility of generalization. It is sociology's "uncertainty principle": the closer you get to measurement on some dimensions—intensity and depth—the further you recede on others—objectivity and validity.

As a technique of research there are courses on participant observation as well as excellent books that outline ways of countering or compensating for its pitfalls.[3] They take the aspiring participant observer through entry into the field, being there, and finally leaving. They describe field notes and how to analyze them systematically. They distinguish between overt and covert participant observation, conducted in open or closed settings. They consider the range of membership roles from full participant, at one extreme, to participant-as-observer to observer-as-participant to complete observer at the other extreme. They discuss the ethical dilemmas of entering the lives of others and then of broadcasting the information collected there. This book is different. It is not a cookbook; it does not provide any recipes. If it demonstrates, it does so by example. Each study presents its own unique constellation of problems, and only in their afterwords do the authors discuss the dilemmas they confronted in their studies.

This book is intended less as a contribution to the technique of participant observation and more as a contribution to the methodology of social science. We seek to unchain ethnography from its confinement as a quaint technique at the margins of social science.[4] In our eyes participant observation is the paradigmatic way of studying the social world, and from this point of view anthropology becomes the paradigmatic social science. By "paradigmatic" I do not mean that participant observation is the only technique or necessarily the most appropriate technique of social research, but rather that it best exemplifies what is distinctive about the practice of *all* social science. Situated at the crossroads of the humanities and natural sciences, social science combines both understanding and explanation. Understanding is achieved by virtual or actual participation in social situations, through a real or constructed dialogue between participant and observer, or what we call the *hermeneutic* dimension of social science. Explanation, on the other hand, is the achievement of an observer or outsider and concerns the dialogue between theory and data, or what we call the *scientific* dimension.[5]

From this standpoint there are two reductions we seek to avoid. The first is the positivist reduction that reduces social science to the natural science model and suppresses the hermeneutic dimension. In this view the interaction of participant and observer is a source of "bias"—a nuisance to be minimized rather than the distinguishing feature of all social science, indeed without which there could be no social science. Rather than allowing us to regard ourselves as inextricably part of the world we study, positivism demands we aspire to the position of the neutral outsider. The second reduction we seek to avoid is the humanist and, more particularly, the "postmodern" suppression of the scientific dimension. Here scientific theories are exposed as simply another world view, this time that of the observer, in no way superior to the world view of the participant. Social science is reduced to a dialogue between insider and outsider aimed at mutual self-understanding—"the comprehension of self by the detour of the comprehension of other."[6] In the words of Alain Touraine, sociology becomes a "discourse that interprets other discourse, an ideology criticizing other ideologies, all the while remaining blind to effective behavior and situations."[7] Explanation loses any distinctive meaning. Defending this reduction, Clifford Geertz says our business is limited to the "understanding of understanding."[8] This leads social science down the path of textual analysis, where it merges with literary criticism.

For us participant observation has the distinct virtue of highlighting the limitations of both forms of reduction. It brings together both the perspective of the participant who calls for understanding and the perspective of the observer who seeks causal explanation. It necessarily combines both hermeneutic and scientific moments and thereby casts exaggerated light on the tensions and dilemmas that are definitive of all social science.

Let me deal with the hermeneutic axis first, that is, the problem of understanding. Like natural scientists, social scientists face the task of interpreting data. However, they differ from natural scientists in that the data are themselves constituted by a community—the community of participants. In the social sciences there are not one but two interpretive tasks, what Anthony Giddens calls the "double hermeneutic."[9] Data are the preconstituted theories and concepts of participants, and their meaning can be gauged only in relation to the context of their production. What respondents say in interviews is shaped by the context of the interview. Whether a death is counted as a suicide depends on how and who and in what circumstances the death was registered. This context dependence of meaning, or what Harold Garfinkel calls indexicality, requires careful examination of the situation in which knowledge is produced, which in turn requires actual or virtual participation in the lives of those one studies.[10]

But how does one conduct such a situational analysis? In order to appreciate the self-understanding of the participants, some advocate that observers strip themselves of their biases in order to become like their subjects. Ethnographic work is then a feat of empathy in which we immerse ourselves in the community we study. Others argue the opposite: that objectivity comes only from distance. Herbert Gans, for example, embraces the image of the participant observer as a marginal person—detached and emotionally removed.[11] From a different standpoint Geertz makes the same point: "Understanding the form and pressure of, to use the dangerous word one more time, natives' inner lives is more like grasping a proverb, catching an allusion, seeing a joke—or as I have suggested reading a poem—than it is like achieving communion."[12]

We advocate neither distance nor immersion but dialogue. The purpose of field work is not to strip ourselves of biases, for that is an illusory goal, nor to celebrate those biases as the authorial voice of the ethnographer, but rather to discover and perhaps change our biases through interaction with others. Thus, an "I-You" relation between observers and participants replaces a "we" relation of false togetherness and an "I-they" relation in which the I often becomes invisible. Remaining on the sidelines as a marginal person or positioning oneself above the "native" not only leaves the ethnographer's own biases unrevealed and untouched but easily leads to false attributions, missing what remains implicit, what those we study take for granted. The practical consciousness of everyday life—whether of oneself as social scientist or of those one studies—contains a great deal that is tacit, what Peter Winch calls nondiscursive, and therefore not explicitly articulated.[13] The pursuit of nondiscursive knowledge, that is, knowledge that is assumed rather than unconscious—both the observer's as well as the participant's—calls for participation but not immersion, observation but not marginality. Once more this privileges participant observation.

Dialogue between participant and observer poses the question of power. Insofar as the relationship between participant and observer is that between power unequals, to that extent the dialogue is distorted. Recently anthropologists have become sensitive to the way power differentials affected the study of colonial societies.[14] Classical anthropologists too easily bracketed the domination that made their field work possible. Coming in under the auspices of a colonial regime to study preliterate societies, anthropologists were not compelled to be responsive to the interests of those they studied—people who would never read or even be aware of the books that were written about them. Following recent trends in anthropology, we too are sensitive to inequalities of power between participant and observer. But being sensitive to power inequality doesn't remove it. Although many of us had considerable loyalty to the people we studied, and revised our papers in the light of their comments, nevertheless in the final analysis what we wrote was outside their control. This is not to justify either complacency or paralysis but to recognize the limits of responsiveness. As Michel Foucault has taught us, social science as we know it today rests on an irreducible level of domination.[15]

I now turn to the scientific dimension of social science, the dialogue between theory and data whose goal is explanation. Participant observers can be distinguished from those whom they study by their participation in the academic community. Indeed, the academic community gives them the reason for being field workers in the first place. Although social science depends on lay concepts as the foundation of its analysis, it also tries to go beyond the lived experience of participants. We are interested not only in learning *about* a specific social situation, which is the concern of the participant, but also in learning *from* that social situation.[16] In contrast to the participants, we want to be able to make causal claims that have validity beyond the situation we study. It is the task of *methodology* to explicate methods of turning observations into explanations, data into theory.

What methods are available, then, for moving from the data of participant observation to the level of social theory? One can attempt to make generalizations across different social situations, looking for what they have in common. This is a process of induction associated with *grounded theory*. Alternatively, one can try to uncover the tacit understandings, the taken-for-granted knowledge that underlies competent performances of those we study. We can set about revealing the non-discursive knowledge that makes social action at all possible. This is the project of *ethnomethodology*. Both grounded theory and ethnomethodology are methods that use participant observation to develop micro-sociology.

While we have drawn on these microsociologies, we are more concerned to examine what they bracket—the institutional context that shapes and distorts what happens in the lifeworld. In this connection there are also two approaches. On the one hand, what we call the *interpretive case method* regards the micro context as a setting in which a particular "macro" principle, such as commodification, rationalization, or male domination, reveals itself. The uniqueness of each situation is then lost as it becomes an expression of the whole, of some essential defining feature of the totality. While we are concerned with a single principle, that of domination and resistance, nevertheless we also pursue a different strategy we call the *extended case method*, which examines how the social situation is shaped by external forces, or, in the terms of C. Wright Mills's sociological imagination, tries to connect "the personal troubles of the milieu" to "the public issues of social structure."[17] The extended case method thus bursts the conventional limits of participant observation, which stereotypically is restricted to micro and ahistorical sociology. (If one wants to do research of a macro or historical kind, one had better leave the field site for the archive, the survey research center, or the institute of demography.) We challenge the conventional correspondence between technique and level of analysis and argue that participant observation can examine the macro world through the way the latter shapes and in turn is shaped and conditioned by the micro world, the everyday world of face-to-face interaction.

But such an outward extension calls for a particular mode of theorizing, described in chapter 2. In traditional ethnography, participant observation tends to produce detailed descriptive accounts that have no obvious relevance beyond the immediate situation. When traditional ethnography makes good its theoretical claims, they usually concern what Erving Goffman called the "interaction order" in settings of "co-presence."[18] Such theorizing emerges directly out of the data. It is very different from the extended case method, which is realized not through induction of new theory from the ground up but through the failure and then *reconstruction of existing theory*. But what existing theory? We search for theories that highlight some aspect of the situation under study as being anomalous and then proceed to rebuild (rather than reject) that theory by reference to the wider forces at work, be they the state, the economy, or even the world system.

As the following chapter makes clear, our intent is not to reject bad theories but to improve good theories. We don't believe there is a final truth which once arrived at gives incontrovertible insight. Nor do we start with a tabula rasa, as if social science begins with us. Rather we seek to place ourselves in a wider community of social scientists by taking the flaws of existing theory as points of departure. This is not a token recognition that perfunctorily appears at the beginning of an article, but a deep engagement with the ideas of others.

Thus, in our view participant observation is not only a paradigmatic technique for studying others; it also points to a distinctive way of understanding ourselves. The dialogue between participant and observer extends itself naturally to a dialogue among social scientists—a dialogue that is emergent rather than conclusive, critical rather than cosmetic, involving reconstruction rather than deconstruction.

TWO

Reconstructing Social Theories

Michael Burawoy

In the social sciences the lore of objectivity relies on the separation of the intellectual product from its process of production. The false paths, the endless labors, the turns now this way and now that, the theories abandoned, and the data collected but never presented—all lie concealed behind the finished product. The article, the book, the text is evaluated on its own merits, independent of how it emerged. We are taught not to confound the process of discovery with the process of justification. The latter is true science whereas the former is the realm of the intuitive, the tacit, the ineffable, in short, the "sociological imagination." In this chapter I try to break open the black box of theory construction by regarding discovery and justification as part of a single process.

One of the most appealing features of Glaser and Strauss's exposition of grounded theory is the way they bring order to the process of discovering theory. They too deny that the only true scientific process is "verification." They too refuse to insulate the "process of discovery" from the "process of justification." But where Glaser and Strauss are concerned to discover new theory from the ground up, we on the other hand seek to reconstruct existing theory.[1]

Grounded theory approaches social phenomena from the standpoint of their *generality*. Whether we study peace movements or AIDS activism, a baking collective or social workers, domestic workers from Central America or refugees from Cambodia, grounded theory treats each case study as a potential exemplar of some general law or principle that applies across space and time. Here, theoretical advance is the movement toward greater generality; that is, the inclusion of more phenomena under a single covering law. In pursuing generalizations, grounded theory remains at the same level of reality. By contrast, the extended case method attempts to elaborate the effects of the "macro" on the "micro." It requires that we specify some *particular* feature of the social situation that requires explanation by reference to particular forces external to itself.

But how does one decide what is particular and has to be explained? We look for what is "interesting" and "surprising" in our social situation. That is, we look for what is unexpected. Initially, it is not important whether our expectations derive from some popular belief or stereotype or from an academic theory. What is important is that to highlight the particularity of our social situation we self-consciously and deliberately draw on existing knowledge to constitute the situation as "abnormal" or "anomalous." That is to say, in the first place we treat social phenomena not as instances of some potential new theory but as counterinstances of some old theory. Instead of an *exemplar* the social situation is viewed as an *anomaly*.

Grounded theory moves from substantive theory, developed for "an empirical area of sociological inquiry," to formal theory, which pertains to a "conceptual area of sociological inquiry."[2] For example, Glaser and Strauss studied dying as a nonscheduled status passage, and in developing substantive theory they compared hospital wards where patients died at different rates. To then develop the formal theory of status passage, they would compare dying with becoming a student or entering a marriage. They proceed from the ground up through a theoretically guided process of constant comparison to develop transhistorical and trans-spatial generalizations.[3] We, on the other hand, move from anomaly to reconstruction. We begin by trying to lay out as coherently as possible what we expect to find in our site *before* entry.[4] When our expectations are violated—when we discover what we didn't anticipate—we then turn to existing bodies of academic theory that might cast light on our anomaly. But here, too, the focus is on what that theory fails to explain. The shortcomings of the theory become grounds for a reconstruction that locates the social situation in its historically specific context of determination.[5]

Rather than theory emerging from the field, what is interesting in the field emerges from our theory. Rather than seek ever more general theories that cover diverse sites, we move from our own inchoate conjectures to the existing body of literature in search of theories that our observations show to be anomalous. Rather than treating the social situation as the confirmation of some theory, we regard it as the failure of a theory. But failure leads not to rejection but to rebuilding theory.[6]

We, therefore, agree with Karl Popper's critique of induction and verification.[7] We also follow Popper's own logic of scientific discovery in emphasizing processes of conjecture and refutation. Where we depart from him is that we use counterinstances to reconstruct rather than reject theory. That is to say, instead of proving a theory by corroboration or forsaking a theory because it faces falsification, our preferred approach is to *improve* theories by turning anomalies into exemplars. In a sense we take Popper to his logical conclusion. Instead of abandoning theory when it faces refutation, we try to "refute the refutation" by making our theory stronger.[8]

If counterinstances are something not to be avoided but seized upon to reconstruct our theories, then one can go beyond Popper and think of falsifiability not simply as demarcating science from nonscience but as a criterion of theory choice. We look for theories that are refuted by our observations, but, of course, we don't choose any theory. We look for a theory or body of theory that we *want* to improve, a theory that is of interest, and then show how it is challenged by the social situation we are studying. This approach, therefore, leads us to strengthen preferred theories.

So far I have restricted myself to one sort of theoretical failure that prompts the reconstruction of theory—the existence of anomalies or refutations—but other types of failure call for reconstruction as well. *Internal contradictions*, highlighted by empirical studies, can also stimulate reconstruction. Alvin Gouldner's study of a gypsum plant led him to highlight a latent tension in Weber's theory of bureaucracy between promotion based on expertise and promotion based on loyalty, out of which he constructed his different patterns of bureaucracy.[9] In the studies that follow, the focus is often on yet another kind of theoretical failure, namely *theoretical gaps or silences*. A given theory may fail to address an aspect of a particular empirical phenomenon that, once included, compels the reconstruction of theory.

The way we interrogate our field notes depends on whether our goal is to reconstruct existing theory or to discover new theory. Thus, Glaser and Strauss are very concerned to develop concepts, categories, dimensions, and sampling that are grounded in the data and reflect the data's complexity and richness: "In short, our focus on the emergence of categories solves the problems of fit, relevance, forcing, and richness. An effective strategy is, at first, literally to ignore the literature of theory and fact on the area under study, in order to assure that the emergence of categories will not be contaminated by concepts more suited to different areas."[10] They ransack the data for emergent categories; the focus is on organizing and reorganizing, coding and recoding of data.

In pursuing theory reconstruction, on the other hand, we conduct a running exchange between field notes and the analysis that follows them. The conjectures of yesterday's analysis are refuted by today's observations and then reconstructed in tomorrow's analysis. But there is a second running exchange, that between analysis and existing theory, in which the latter is reconstructed on the basis of emergent anomalies. Analysis, therefore, is a continual process, mediating between field data and existing theory.

Although we take a respectful view of existing bodies of theory, we don't mean to imply that one has to have read "the literature" before beginning field work. To be sure, knowledge of the literature is not the contaminating influence that Glaser and Strauss attribute to it, but neither is it a sine qua non of research. We can start, as I suggested above, with our own conjectures to highlight what is surprising, but there does come a time when we turn to some existing literature with the goal of improving it. We begin by experimenting with a number of different theories, perhaps, that highlight different aspects of the social situation as anomalous. Over time, if we are successful, we will home in on one particular theory that calls for reconstruction.

In the following discussion of the studies in this volume, I try to show how the process of theory construction evolved, in each case contrasting it with grounded theory. For those accustomed to thinking of the scientific process as a linear movement in which a theory or hypothesis is presented and then tested, my exposition will appear unflattering to the authors. On the other hand, to those who think of the scientific process as inscrutable, as tacit, personal knowledge, I hope to convey the logic underlying the extended case method; in chapter 13 I systematize that logic. In their afterwords, the authors reflect on the research process, highlighting those features they found particularly salient. Here I write as a participant observer of the seminar, describing how the authors made sense of their data—the way they built and rebuilt theories.

"NEW SOCIAL MOVEMENTS"

The literature on "new social movements" is almost the prototype of the generalizing mode. From Robert Park to Neil Smelser the goal has been to pursue the most general, transhistorical theory of collective behavior.[11] Not surprisingly, critiques of this generalizing mode have come from historically minded sociologists such as Charles Tilly and his collaborators, who have located social movements in specific contexts of urbanization and industrialization.[12] More recently European theorists, always more sensitive to historical context, have sought to specify the peculiarities of what they call "new social movements" (NSMs), which mobilize primarily middle classes to defend an augmented civil society against state and economy.[13] In this volume Gamson and Schiffman take this literature as point of departure, using their case studies to highlight specific silences in the way theories of NSMs treat power.

Joshua Gamson began his study of the AIDS activist organization ACT UP by walking into one of its meetings. The scene, with its progressive left politics, was quite familiar and unexciting, but the actions the members planned and, even more, the ones they fantasized captured his interest. Members were spending a great deal of energy devising ways to reappropriate symbols of blood and death—symbols the media had mobilized against people with AIDS (PWAs) and gays. Gamson noted how these symbolic dramas were attempts to reclaim power through an inversion of their meaning. But he was puzzled: Was this gay activism or AIDS activism? Who was the audience for any given action? He went to a national conference of AIDS activist groups in Washington and returned convinced that these strategies to reclaim power were typical of groups trying to combat the stigmatization of PWAs and gays.

But what was the significance of this distinctive symbolic politics? Gamson became a man in search of a literature and a theory that would shed light on this peculiar form of expressive politics. He turned to theories of the new social movements. ACT UP showed all the marks of a new social movement, yet theories failed to illuminate what he was observing. In part this was because what was new about the NSMs remained obscure or unconvincing. His first insight was to distinguish between movements oriented to strategy and those oriented to identity. Certainly both threads could be observed competing for prominence in ACT UP, but why this concern for identity? At this point he began to focus on the way gays and PWAs confronted mechanisms of domination, particularly their invisibility. They had to face strategies of "normalization," power exercised over everyone by labeling a particular group as deviant. Here lay the dilemma faced by ACT UP: open resistance drew attention to stigmatization and thereby reinforced it.

Having extended out in this way, the explanation stalled once more. After all, normalization, as Foucault insists, can hardly be regarded as new, yet the resistance was new. What was it about the contemporary political order that accounted for this particular response? Casting around for comparison groups, Gamson decided that in the past stigmatized groups had resisted differently because normalization was coupled to the state. He argued, therefore, that the distinctive symbolic politics of ACT UP was a response to a specific form of normalization in which the state became less visible.

But at this point he halted. Because of his highly unusual experiences in the field, Gamson was uncomfortable with turning his extension into a generalization: that what new social movements shared, what made them "new," was their response to new forms of invisible domination. With only one case to go on, he did not feel able to define the scope of his reconstructed theory of NSMs.

Josepha Schiffman found herself in a different quandary when she began her study of SANE/Freeze. Her goal, as she laid it out in her original proposal, was to examine the way peace organizations resolved internal conflicts—did they resolve their differences through peaceful, democratic means or in a coercive, authoritarian manner? However, she was not anticipating what she found: a moribund organization that was primarily involved with the Democratic election campaign. There was a limited, overworked, and somewhat inexperienced staff and a board that had nearly dissolved. Peace issues were rarely discussed. Her project inevitably shifted to examining this apparent state of decay.

The most obvious explanation was that this very active and vibrant social movement had succumbed to bureaucratization—it had simply played out Michels's iron law of oligarchy. Delving into the history of SANE/Freeze, however, suggested that the organization had gone through similar periods of decline in the past. So she countered the argument that all social movements have a similar "natural history" with an argument specific to SANE/Freeze, namely that its radical goals were at odds with its reformist strategies. Furthermore, its futuristic and utopian aims of international harmony provided the basis of a vibrant social movement only in the wake of concrete experiences of the dangers of war—after a nuclear scare, fallout episode, or international conflagration. But such a theory could only be evaluated by undertaking a historical analysis, and she was, at least for the moment, confined to field work.

This was the unsatisfactory state of affairs at the end of the semester. Schiffman returned to the field after Christmas to discover that her hitherto moribund organization had now sprung to life. The national elections were over and the organization had joined the coalition of the Bay Area Peace Test (BAPT), which was planning its annual spring action at the Nevada Test Site. Schiffman now became interested in the dramatic differences between the politics of SANE/Freeze and BAPT and how both contrasted with the "consciousness-raising" politics of Beyond War (BW), another peace organization with which she was familiar. She felt as though she was beginning her project all over again.

Why should the peace movement adopt such different and unconventional strategies for achieving its goals? Like Gamson, Schiffman turned to the literature on new social movements, but she problematized it in a slightly different way. Where he saw new social movements as a response to the invisibility of domination and strategies of normalization, she saw them as responding to the penetration of the state, particularly the nuclear state, into private realms. In this view, NSMs define themselves as carving out arenas of civil society autonomous from the state. But how does this explain the very different strategies of BAPT and BW? This silence in the literature became her puzzle.

She turned to the conceptions of power that informed the strategy and organization of BAPT and BW. Both were opposed to institutional forms of politics, but for very different reasons. BAPT saw power as a relationship of domination that pervades all arenas of social life. Participation in state politics only reproduces that domination. BW, on the other hand, saw power as a neutral energy that operates outside institutions of the state. International peace will come about through personal transformation, through "right thinking."

Schiffman goes on to conjecture that similar bifurcated tendencies can be found in other new social movements, such as the ecology and women's movements. In declaring themselves to be organizing in "civil society" and opposed to institutional politics, they turn toward anarchistic confrontation or consciousness-raising. Thus by locating the peace movement in its context of determination, namely the state, Schiffman reconstructs the theory of NSMs and thereby sheds light on other contemporary movements.

REORGANIZING PRODUCTION IN A SERVICE ECONOMY

Everett Hughes's pioneering work on occupations represents the best of the Chicago School's grounded theory. He saw his mission as drawing out commonalities between the most disparate occupations: "[W]e need to rid ourselves of any concepts which keep us from seeing that the essential problems of men at work are the same whether they do their work in some famous laboratory or in the messiest vat room of a pickle factory."[14] Hughes was particularly interested in how professionals and service workers negotiated their relationship to their clients, how they dealt with problems of visibility, mistakes, and power. Although Hughes had great insight into the matrix of roles that defined work situations, he did not locate that matrix within its historical context. Nor did he examine how and why the matrix changed, over time and between workplaces, or the consequences that change might have for collective resistance. While both Burton and Ferguson in this volume examine the relations between producer and consumer, they do so by locating them within the changing context of the welfare state on the one hand and the contemporary capitalist economy on the other. Moreover, they are interested not only in the way these wider systems structure the possible forms of work organization, but also in the circumstances under which workers organize themselves collectively against those systems.

Alice Burton enlisted as an intern with a labor organizer of a union of local state welfare workers. She was interested in the relationship between union organizers and rank-and-file membership, but attending union meetings only brought her in touch with union activists and staff. Nevertheless a pattern began to emerge. Union officials often divided along the lines of the two groups they represented: social workers (SWs), who dealt directly with and often visited families with dependent children, and eligibility workers (EWs), who were confined to the office and processed applications for welfare. The EWs were more militant than the SWs but at the same time were more hostile to their clients. Nor was it difficult to see why. Social workers advanced their interests through the autonomy they exercised in dealing with their clients. They pursued their grievances on the basis of their professional prerogatives. The EWs, on the other hand, were subjected to intensive surveillance. They had no autonomy to manipulate the work context and so instead confronted the state in militant but usually unsuccessful strikes.

So what? Burton had an answer but no question. The division between EWs and SWs seemed quite "natural" until she turned to the literature. There she discovered a very different perspective, one that portrayed state workers as potential carriers of labor radicalism. According to James O'Connor, for example, welfare workers would forge an alliance with their clients based on their common interest in the expanded provision of social needs.[15] Burton's observations challenged this argument: the militant workers, the EWs, turned out to be those most hostile to their clients, while the most sympathetic workers, the SWs, were neither militant nor radical.

What began as a question—why the EWs rather than the SWs were inclined toward collective mobilization—now became a puzzle: where did O'Connor go wrong? Burton's study suggested that O'Connor's mistake was to *impute* to state workers and clients a common interest in the expansion of welfare, an explanation that failed to take into account the way work organization structures interests. Therefore, Burton introduced an auxiliary hypothesis into O'Connor's theory, positing that day-to-day relations of EWs to their clients engender antagonism, not solidarity, just as the work autonomy of SWs engenders professionalism rather than militant unionism.

Her analysis led her to spend more time examining the workplace. In the second semester she undertook intensive interviews with welfare workers about their work and how it had changed over the last two decades. O'Connor's anticipations were based on the radical labor-community alliances that sprang up in the early 1970s. Why was O'Connor correct then but wrong now? What had happened to the organization of work? Burton traced the history of the division of case workers into SWs and EWs. She discovered that, following the early struggles, the welfare system began carving up each client into a set of distinct problems and distributing these to different workers. By fragmenting welfare work and by fragmenting clients, the system effectively undermined any solidarity. The state's strategy of divide and rule, budget cuts, and union busting took the wind from the sails of labor radicalism. Thus, Burton's observations of grievance meetings led her to enter into a dialogue with and eventually reconstruct O'Connor's theory so as to accommodate and interpret the historically changing forces shaping public sector unions.

Ann Arnett Ferguson also studied collective organization of workers, but of a very different kind: a bakery cooperative producing healthy food, which she felicitously calls Wholly Grains. Cooperatives have often developed out of social movements, and Wholly Grains was no exception. Most of its members were white middle-class exiles from the student movement of the sixties for whom Wholly Grains, always teetering on the brink of bankruptcy, was more appealing than career paths in the state sector or the corporate world. Ferguson wondered what it meant to work in such a cooperative: was it any different from other small enterprise? She became interested in the "empowerment" of its members—their sense of fulfillment through participating in a community with others—a characteristic that the members valued in the collective and the standard by which they evaluated its operation. She was struck by how jealously they guarded collective decision making, yet she couldn't discover its mechanisms. Indeed, the secret of the operation seemed to be the absence of rigidly enforced rules. But this fluidity also made the collective vulnerable to usurpation by individuals in structurally powerful positions. Anticipating this possibility, the collective, somewhat half-heartedly, tried to organize a rotation of members through different "shifts." Certain groups, though, particularly the drivers on delivery, seemed exempt from rotation. Ferguson was also struck by the unwillingness of anyone to assume the role of coordinator. This, she determined, was at least in part due to the members' unwillingness to deal with the imbalance of power between shifts, such as between the "delivery" and "wrap" shifts.

After circling around this complex of problems, Ferguson looked for a theoretical point of entry—a key that would unlock what she was observing. She turned to the longevity of Wholly Grains, then thirteen years old. Certainly the literature suggested that cooperatives should be ephemeral organizations, unable to withstand the inevitable internal tendencies toward bureaucratization or external pressures to place profit before collective decision making. So how had Wholly Grains survived? Without doubt these subversive pressures existed; indeed, they led to a never-ending succession of crises. Ferguson examined three such crises that threatened the collective: the use of white flour (which would compromise the political commitment to healthy food), the development of efficiency norms, and the abdication of production coordinators.

While these crises originated in external pressures, their solution depended on the mobilization of the energies of the collective's members. In this regard Wholly Grains relied on a continuing supply of workers with ingenuity and commitment to the collective. The collective could draw on people who circulated through the relatively dense network of cooperatives in the Bay Area, leaving one cooperative for another and taking with them their accumulated skills. Wholly Grains was also able to draw on the specialized resources at reduced rates made available through the same network of cooperatives. Finally, although market forces always threatened to turn Wholly Grains into a losing enterprise, it could protect itself against competition from mass production bakeries by providing for the specialized tastes of young urban professionals. What began as an anomaly, the longevity of Wholly Grains, could now be explained. External pressures, which continually threatened the existence of the cooperative, called forth countervailing responses from the membership, responses whose efficacy depended on resources available in the Bay Area economic environment.

Wholly Grains violated theories that regarded cooperatives as unstable organizations. In explaining its longevity, Ferguson reconstructed these theories by highlighting the importance of the specific economic and political context. Extending out thereby became a vehicle for making generalizations about the conditions under which cooperatives can reproduce themselves.

NEW IMMIGRANTS

The study of immigrants was another area in which Chicago sociology developed grand generalizations. Beginning with Thomas and Znaniecki's *The Polish Peasant in Europe and America*, studies of the effects of industrialization on immigrants to the city deployed the theory of social disorganization. This was further generalized to all urban populations in Louis Wirth's classic summary statement, "Urbanism as a Way of Life," and from there found its home in theories of deviance, delinquency, crime, and youth cultures. In developing the theory of social disorganization, Thomas, Znaniecki, and their followers lost sight of the specific political and economic context within which communities were forged, both in Chicago and their place of origin.

Leslie Salzinger's and Shiori Ui's studies of new immigrants in California downplay social disorganization and focus on responses to the economic and political context of the United States. Not their countries of origin but the distinctive array of economic opportunities, which is in part shaped by their political status as immigrants or refugees, defines what new immigrants have in common and distinguishes them from earlier waves of immigration. However, when it came to comparing the different responses among immigrants, Salzinger emphasized their institutional connections here in the United States, whereas Ui stressed their different class background and political status in the country of origin.

Salzinger attached herself to two job-distribution cooperatives for Central American immigrants. She had intended to use these as sites to study how oppressed peoples develop common identities. Would the clients see themselves as Central Americans, as immigrants, as women, as poor, and with what consequences for collective mobilization? At first she found few signs of the degree of organization she anticipated. Central American women came to the centers to find domestic work and that seemed to be all. Although Salzinger noted differences between the two co-ops—the style of job distribution, the attitude of the staff toward immigrants, the affiliations of the job center—she couldn't fathom their significance. At this point she began working with her first "extension," following Sassen in locating immigrants within world economic changes that created the demand for menial domestic work.[16]

But still she regarded the women, first and foremost, as immigrants. She therefore couldn't make sense of the endless discussions of the ins and outs of domestic work at one of the co-ops. Frustration with her whole project triggered an insight that transformed the research. She began to recognize a self-conscious creation of work identity in all the talk about cleaning. This had been difficult for her to appreciate because she considered domestic work demeaning. She had assumed that it was simply the only job these women could find. Listening to them she realized that there was more to domestic work than met the eye. As an occupation it had some virtues: autonomy and flexibility, and indeed a certain satisfaction in a job well done. The switch from "immigrant" to "worker" led her to a second extension, an examination of the historical changes in the character of domestic work from servant to wage laborer.

Through the lens of "work" the two co-ops took on a new significance. At first it seemed that one catered to newer immigrants who had few skills, didn't speak English, and were paid particularly low wages, while at the other co-op women had generally been in the United States longer, constituted a more developed occupational community, and even organized English lessons and training sessions for their members. But social characteristics of the women couldn't explain the differences between the two co-ops. Instead Salzinger focused on the limited economic opportunities available to immigrants from Central America. If women were largely confined to domestic work, then upward mobility could be assured most effectively by professionalizing the occupation through credentialing and establishing an occupational community.

But why did this not occur at both co-ops? The answer lay in her third extension, examining the structure of the demand for domestic workers. She discovered that there were also two types of employers. On the one hand, female-headed households or working-class families needed help in day care for their children. They paid low wages and were not (or could not be) concerned about the status of their employees. On the other hand, richer employers were prepared to pay higher wages for workers with a more polished image. The organization of the two co-ops corresponded to these two types of employer. However, Salzinger uses the extended case method to examine not only how social and economic structures limit opportunities but also how they enable actors to reshape those limits. The co-ops were not only reacting to the labor market but, by their different occupational strategies, contributing to its bifurcation.

So what? Sassen's studies place the flow of immigrants in its widest context. New immigrants, she argues, are slotted into a "service economy" by providing for the domestic needs of a new professional class. But Sassen fails to analyze the responses of immigrants to their occupational fate. In examining these responses, Salzinger sheds new light on the structure of the lower end of the service economy. The two occupational strategies, survival and professionalization, reflect and promote two distinct tiers of employers with different household needs. Underlying this balkanization of the labor market is the historical transformation of domestic work from neofeudal servant relations to regulated, market relations of a service sector, that is, from servant to wage laborer. Moving through a series of extensions, Salzinger was able to locate Central Americans within an economic, political, and historical context which they themselves had helped to shape.

With interests similar to Salzinger's, Shiori Ui set out to examine the place of women among Cambodian refugees. She spent some time in Bay Area cities trying to gain access to families but without much success. Leaders of the Cambodian community told her that women play no significant role. Pursuing a contact from her Khmer language course, she visited the Cambodian community in Stockton where, much to her surprise, she found a group of women leaders. A tension developed between her original interest in women as family members and her discovery of an influential group of women leaders. For a time her research pursued both tracks simultaneously, until she saw a link between them.

She reconstructed her project around the puzzle of why women assumed such importance in Stockton but not in the Bay Area. She discovered that the greater leadership role for women there, as compared to the bigger cities, was tied to their employment possibilities. She found women involved in the informal economy while at the same time receiving welfare payments and learning English. A few were working in welfare agencies that dealt with Cambodians. The men, on the other hand, were often unemployed and dependent on the earnings of their wives or children.

Employment possibilities favored women and thus often gave them a dominant position within the family as well as the resources to become community leaders. But which women became leaders? She turned to the background of the Cambodian refugees, in particular their experience under Pol Pot. Many of the women had been rescued from concentration camps, where they had been forced to marry much older men, often from a lower socioeconomic background. Moreover, it turned out that the Cambodian community leaders in Stockton came from educated urban classes rather than from the rural peasantry.

How unique was this community? Here Ui turned to the literature on ethnic enclaves and compared the Cambodians to the Vietnamese. She found the Vietnamese to be doing much better, reflecting their different class background and their earlier immigration. Cambodians were coming to California as secondary migrants from other parts of the United States because of the more generous welfare and educational provisions. When they settled in the smaller communities, as many were doing, economic opportunities gave women a dominant role in the family, and some of them translated this into community leadership. By strategic comparisons first with other Cambodian communities, then with other Southeast Asian immigrants, and finally within Stockton on the basis of class background, Ui was able to extend out to the political and economic forces that gave rise to the anomalous role of women.

FROM CLASSROOM TO COMMUNITY

Education became a focus of sociological research only after World War II, when immigrant communities had established themselves. It was then that sociology turned to questions of integration and consensus, and particularly to the role of education in promoting inter- and intragenerational mobility. Riding the tide of large-scale surveys, sociologists would try to establish correlations between social origins, education, and occupational mobility, but without careful attention to the social processes that produced the effects they were measuring. This came much later, with the development of the ethnography of schooling, studies that located schools in their specific cultural and economic context.[17] The studies of junior high school students by Leslie Hurst and Nadine Julius follow in this tradition.

Leslie Hurst volunteered to tutor eighth graders at Emerald Junior High School. At first she was taken aback by the anarchy that reigned in the classroom, but soon she began to discern patterns of bargaining between students and teacher. Students continually strove to expand their rights while the teacher attempted to invoke the disciplinary order to restrict those rights. In her first presentation to our seminar, Hurst conceived of the classroom as a negotiated order. But it could have been any organization. Asked to specify what made this a school, she spontaneously responded that it served a babysitting function, keeping kids off the streets and out of the home.

From here she turned to the schooling literature to discover that it did not really address the issues she found compelling. On the one hand, schools were studied in terms of their "future" effects—slotting people into the class structure, training people for jobs, socializing people for adult life, and so forth. On the other hand, the few studies that examined the school in "presentist" terms, such as the building of peer groups, missed the specificity of the classroom as a negotiated order.

She proceeded to reconstruct the classroom as a contest between students and teachers over how much time should be spent teaching and how much simply babysitting. To highlight what others might find quite normal but what she found so interesting, she contrasted her classroom with Roald Dahl's autobiographical account of the authoritarian order of a classroom in a British public school. There the teacher commanded control over the body, mind, and soul of the pupil. At Emerald the teacher had legitimate authority only over the pupil's mind, so that body and soul could be continually mobilized to disrupt teaching. Teaching was supposedly supported by the school, which policed the student's body, and by discipline in the family, which shaped the soul or moral character of the student. But Emerald was not a middle-class school, where pupils come from a rather homogeneous cultural background and where relations between family, school, and teacher are fairly coherent. At Emerald the balance of power in the classroom and the separation of spheres undermined teaching and promoted babysitting.

It was precisely the failure of schools to deliver adequate education to African-American children that motivated Nadine Gartrell's study of an experimental after-school tutorial college for African-American students in East Oakland. Project Interface (PI) employed tutors to give extra lessons to students in small groups. It worked with what Gartrell calls an "interactive" model of education in which parents were not obligated to pay fees but had to enter into a contractual agreement that they would provide appropriate conditions for their child to work at home. The students were also contractually bound to the project.

Gartrell began her research skeptical that such a program would be effective. Theories of cultural or linguistic capital assert that instruction works for middle-class children because the form of schooling is congruent with their experience at home. In explaining the reproduction of class or racial differences, writers such as Pierre Bourdieu and Basil Bernstein paint a bleak picture because they rely so heavily on irremovable cultural obstacles.[18] Contrary to Gartrell's own expectations and those of education theory, her observations at PI and the results it achieved suggested that the project was very successful. Why? The patterns of recruitment seemed to rule out the possibility that students had been specially selected on the basis of their abilities. Instead, two factors suggested themselves. First, the higher quality of instruction at PI—smaller classes and more highly motivated tutors—could more effectively stimulate students. Second, the cooperation between PI and parents created better conditions for students to learn both at school and at home. Unable to separate these two factors, Gartrell argued that the success of PI lay in the mutual reinforcement of the separated spheres, a feature absent at Emerald. PI offered an interactive model of education—interaction among students, teachers, administrators, and parents—rather than the normal fragmentation and isolation of spheres.

In the second semester, Gartrell began her extended case method by investigating whether there was anything specific about PI that might account for its success. She interviewed six sets of parents, focusing on why they had enrolled their children in PI. The parents, she discovered, were not engaged in middle-class occupations, but all were providing their families with relatively comfortable and stable circumstances. They were determined to give their children the best possible education, propelling their children to PI and arranging the best possible conditions for study. It turned out that the stringent conditions for parental participation would have denied the vast majority of poor African-Americans access to PI. In locating the problem at the level of interaction among separated spheres, Gartrell presents a picture that is less deterministic than the cultural theories of Bernstein and Bourdieu.

But still she is not optimistic that the separation of spheres can be overcome for the majority of African-Americans who face poverty and deprivation.

RESEARCHING THE RESEARCHERS

In his article "Sociologist as Partisan," Alvin Gouldner subjects the work of Howard Becker, pioneer of labeling theory, to withering criticism for failing to locate deviance within its wider context.[19] He accuses Becker of treating deviants as victims of middle-level bureaucrats, whereas they are better seen as political actors in a context shaped by the state. Chicago School ethnography insulated drug addicts, the homeless, and delinquents from their determining context, exhibiting an anthropological fascination with the exotic and pathological. But Gouldner takes his argument one step further and asks what lies behind this approach. He comes up with the bleak hypothesis that behind the veil of "underdog sympathies" lies a sociologist trying to advance a career by establishing lucrative connections to the welfare state. In answer to the question, "Whose side are we on?" he replies that we are on our own side. Gouldner's extended case study of the sociology of deviance informs both Kathryn Fox's study of ethnographers doing outreach work among injection drug users and Charles Kurzman's study of the participant observers in our own seminar.

When the semester began Fox had already begun her study of an agency that was tackling the AIDS epidemic by bringing condoms and bleach to injection drug users. Intervention was designed according to the "ethnographic model" of bringing the agency to the streets and defined in opposition to the "treatment model," which expected drug users to come to clinics. In addition to distributing supplies, outreach workers were to gather data on the culture of injection drug users and then use the data as a means of helping them cope with the AIDS epidemic. Fox went onto the streets with the outreach workers, who were themselves ideally from the community, often former drug addicts or retired prostitutes. She began as an enthusiastic partisan of this ethnographic model, but her enthusiasm was thrown into doubt by what she saw, crystalized by the revulsion of one of the outreach workers. In a fit of rage, he condemned the project directors as poverty pimps, extracting information from the drug users for their own private ends.

At this point Fox was more interested in the expression of disaffection than its content. She wondered whether the ethnographic project spontaneously generated such dissident responses. On further investigation she found dissidence to be an important but minority response of outreach workers. Those who stayed with the project turned out to be of two types: professionals who endorsed the means and the goals of the agency but were "realistic" in their assessment of what was possible, and cynics for whom it was a badly needed job. Having developed a typology of outreach workers—crusaders, dissidents, professionals, and opportunists—Fox then tried to explain their adoption of a particular orientation in terms of their prior connection to the community, whether they had been insiders or outsiders. But she couldn't get this to work out.

Disillusioned with the ethnographic model and demoralized by her field experiences, Fox turned her study toward the agency itself. Its success depended on the commitment of outreach workers, she argued, yet this commitment was systematically eroded in two ways. First, the expansion of the agency created a confidence gap between staff and outreach worker, as staff became more concerned with garnering funds than with the mission of bringing help to a beleaguered population. Second, working under such difficult circumstances gradually ate away at the commitment of the outreach workers, and crusaders and professionals became cynics.

Fox continued her research in the second semester. Earlier, she had been reluctant to shift her focus from the outreach workers toward the wider context within which the agency had to operate. However, when she began to pay more attention to discussions among the directors, she saw how the state severely constrained their room to maneuver. On the one hand the agency had to continually garner funds from a federal institute on the basis of its research component, while on the other hand a promising means of AIDS prevention—needle exchange—was illegal. Fox moved from an analysis of immediate relations between injection drug users and outreach workers to the external forces that limited the effectiveness of such ethnographic intervention.

In her conclusion, Fox draws attention to these limitations but still defends the ethnographic model as against the treatment model, the strategic comparison that frames her study. The virtue of the ethnographic model, at least potentially, lies in its holistic regard for drug users on their own terms and in their own community.

Whereas Fox converged on Gouldner's critique of sociology from the side of sociologists in the field, Charles Kurzman approached Gouldner from the study of sociologists in their own setting. He came to our seminar armed with three ready-made theories of knowledge to be tested and explored. Would his model work for a bunch of ethnographers? He was going to observe the class to study which "knowledge claims" were successful and why. His first analysis focused on three competing theories: knowledge claims might be successful because they appealed to evidence, to commonly accepted paradigms, or to interests. Each approach shed some light on what had taken place in the seminar, but, he subsequently argued, they missed the fluidity of the seminar.

This led him to reanalyze his data and offer two conclusions. First, he found that we endorsed explanations couched in broad social and political frameworks and were hostile to psychological explanations. The proclaimed hostility to social workers or to medical models supported the view that we invoked norms in accordance with our interests as sociologists. Second, he found that we recognized the views of some participants while silencing those of others. Operating according to norms of identification with and distance from the participants, we, as he put it, gave credence to the positive but not to the negative deviants. Moreover, among the seminar participants there was an unstated consensus as to who were the positive deviants: generally those who resisted subjugation to political and economic systems.

Rather than straightforwardly adjudicate among his original theories, Kurzman had translated them into terms relevant to his observations. What struck him was the contradictory character of the norms to which we appealed. Instead of there being a single interest, which we defended as sociologists, there were a multiplicity of interests: our interests vis-à-vis those we studied, other sociologists, and even other social scientists. We are indeed on our own side, but that meant different things in different situations.

Kurzman stopped short of extending out, of locating the specific interests of the participants in the seminar in their wider context. He imposed strict boundaries on his research, devoting himself to the analysis of the seminar itself. He explicitly did not want to draw on information that he gleaned from private conversations outside the seminar, or by accompanying people to their sites. This would have betrayed his classmates, who were more important to him than the extended case method. In his own terms, he saw the members of the seminar as "positive" deviants, as people with agency of their own. Not surprisingly, therefore, he did not seek external forces that might reduce them to the effects of structures. He even went so far as to deny the importance of internal structure or hierarchy.

It is one thing to place those we study, particularly if we neither depend on them nor identify with them, in the context of their determination, denying them their autonomy. It is quite another matter to do the same to ourselves. Kurzman was trapped in what Gouldner calls "methodological dualism": "others" are dupes of social forces but "we" are rational agentic beings.[20] His study problematizes the extended case method for, according to Kurzman's theory, to the extent that the participant observer becomes an insider, sensitive to every whim of those

being studied, there will be considerable pressure to give the participants full agency and to repress the way they are constrained by external forces. Of course, in some situations participants regard themselves as victimized by external forces beyond their control. Had
Kurzman studied a course that students universally disliked but were
compelled to take, perhaps he might have been happier with the extended case method!

CONCLUSION

In order to pursue the approach we have advocated in this chapter, the
ethnographer must identify existing social theories to reconstruct.
Where do such theories come from? First and most obviously, all of us
have social theories that inform the way we organize and pursue our
lives. Participant observers are particularly aware of lay theories, or
commonsense knowledge, and this can always provide a point of departure for reconstruction. Moreover, there is a circular movement in
which social science built on the reconstruction of common sense feeds
back and transforms that common sense. Our newspapers and media
are full of watered-down social science, which in part explains why
social science doesn't appear to grow. The new theory of today becomes
the conventional wisdom of tomorrow.

Nevertheless it is reasonable to argue that the last fifty years have
witnessed the growth of the body of academic theory, whether in the
form of deductive grand theory, middle-range theory, or the empirical
generalizations of grounded theory. The generation of theory from the
ground up was perhaps imperative at the beginning of the sociological
enterprise, but with the proliferation of theories reconstruction becomes ever more urgent. Rather than always starting from scratch and
developing new theories, we should try to consolidate and develop what
we have already produced.

We should, therefore, begin to think about different ways of improving theories through their reconstruction. With respect to the sort
of field work represented in this volume, I want to suggest two alternative strategies. First, one can decide what one wants to study, immerse oneself in empirical work, and then search for theories that are
inadequate because they ignore salient issues or lead to false anticipations or have latent theoretical ambiguities or contradictions that are
revealed by the data. In each case the data call for an improvement of
the existing theory. Presumably, there will be a number of theories for
which the data would be anomalous, and so we choose the one that is
closest to our interests. Alternatively, one can commit oneself to a given
theory rather than a specific empirical phenomenon. If it is an impor-

tant theory (and why else choose it?), its anomalies are already well known, and these would suggest possible empirical foci for research. Our task is to improve the theory by introducing auxiliary hypotheses that will turn anomalies into exemplars.

Participant observers are more likely to find the first strategy attractive. For, if we approach a field site to examine the anomalies of a particular theory, we often find that the data don't address those anomalies, particularly if we take seriously the self-understanding of the participants. It is then difficult to decamp to another site and begin the field work anew. For pragmatic reasons we should, therefore, adopt a flexible approach and be prepared to shop around for appropriate theories. But there are also intellectual reasons for adopting the first strategy. Participant observers often either start out with a commitment to those they study or acquire this commitment as they prolong their stay in the field. This responsiveness to the participant is often at odds with strong prior commitments to a particular theory.

Yet there is still something to be said for the second strategy, of locating oneself within a particular theoretical tradition. Whereas the first strategy may lead to the improvement of weak theories, the second strategy is more likely to foster the improvement of powerful theories that are attractive by virtue of their power. There are intellectual gains and satisfactions to participating in and contributing to an established theoretical tradition even if it constrains the sorts of anomalies one seeks to normalize. When the preeminent dialogue is between participant and observer, shopping around for appropriate theories to reconstruct is more likely. When social scientists are more interested in a dialogue among themselves than with their subjects, they are more likely to have prior commitments to established theoretical perspectives. But in neither strategy does theory emerge spontaneously from the data. To be sure it must "fit" the data, but, as Kurzman shows, this still leaves ample scope for selection in the light of the values and interests we hold.

ONE

New Social Movements

Introduction to Part 1

"It is hard to see," writes Alain Touraine of contemporary collective action, "what unifies all these numerous conflicts that do not invoke some central values, do not combat a dominant power, but seek only to modify some relations of power or some specific decision-making systems."[1] Indeed, it has become the project of many students of social movements to find this hard-to-see unity: to make sense of "new" movements and conflicts—from feminism to ecology—that seem to share characteristics while differing in their targets. European theorists generally have seen that these movements share both a middle-class base and a shift of focal activity from "the state" to "civil society." The projects in the next two chapters attempt to challenge and refine thinking on new social movements by examining their dynamics in the concrete. Both Josepha Schiffman and Joshua Gamson examine movements categorized as "new"; both find a need to delineate more clearly particular phenomena within the greater phenomenon of new movement types, turning to the operation of power in "micro," face-to-face contexts to do so.

Schiffman begins her comparative study of two groups within the peace movement—Bay Area Peace Test (BAPT) and Beyond War (BW)—by pointing to their differences. How, she asks, do we get such different responses to the same threat? Gamson opens his study of San Francisco's ACT UP (the AIDS Coalition to Unleash Power) by pointing to its distinctive theatrical style. Why do we find activists fighting AIDS at baseball games? Why and how does contemporary activism operate in the cultural sphere? These questions do not appear to be adequately addressed by writings on new social movements. Schiffman sees a need to delineate and explain differences between new movements. Gamson suggests that what is "new" in these movements, in particular how they operate in "civil society" and the "cultural sphere," is too vaguely conceived. The studies thus attempt to ground what theory leaves blurry.

Schiffman and Gamson find the operation of power in their sites particularly striking. In ACT UP, Gamson finds, actions are often involved in symbolic inversions that attempt to replace dominant representations of people with AIDS with alternative ones. Moreover, the actions that express gay identity—an action type familiar in contemporary movements—are attempts to use labels of abnormality against the process of labeling itself. It is this process of stigmatization, seen as lethal in the AIDS epidemic, to which ACT UP in large part responds: a new form of domination in which power is carried not only by state institutions but also by everyday interactions, through the delineation of the abnormal from the normal.

Schiffman finds different notions of power—neither of which is chiefly concerned with macro-level, state power—at the heart of the different strategies of BAPT and BW. The Peace Test, while in part directing itself to state power, is focused mainly on the pervasive operation of power. Much of its action focuses on avoiding duplication of the oppressive relations against which it is fighting, and on building an alternative power structure within the group (through, for example, consensus process and "empowerment" activities). Beyond War operates on the notion that power differences are attitudinal problems and can be bridged through clear communication, an empathetic understanding of the unity of all life. Acting on this notion, it attempts to circumvent power dynamics by transforming the consciousness of individuals.

This shift in the attention within movements from vertical (state and institutional) to horizontal (person-to-person) power, the studies suggest, is crucial in understanding contemporary movements. Moreover, it helps to make sense of the odd place of the "enemy" in many contemporary movements: enemies are often difficult for these groups to clearly articulate or for an observer to infer. In BW there is a near rejection of the very concept of enemy, in BAPT a focus on the community itself (and, at times, on an abstract enemy, the "machine"). These characteristics, Schiffman suggests, can be traced to the conceptions of power under which the groups operate. ACT UP, while targeting institutional "enemies" such as the government and the medical establishment, is largely involved in activities aimed at an amorphous enemy—American society. Gamson suggests that this emphasis can be traced to domination through normalization, in which the enemy is in fact ubiquitous and invisible.

This shift to the micro operations of power, finally, helps clarify the relationship between contemporary social movements and the state. Gamson sees state institutions and actors pulling back from the stigmatization process, leaving the process itself, disembodied and less visible, the target of activity. Schiffman sees the attention of peace movement activists largely diverted from the state's involvement in nuclear issues—a very direct and visible involvement—to power relations and communication within the groups themselves. Both suggest that the fact that what unifies contemporary movements may be "hard to see" is perhaps a deeper and more literal insight than it first appears: that looking at the operation of less visible power makes the dynamics of new social movements more visible.

Joshua Gamson
Josepha Schiffman

THREE

Silence, Death, and the Invisible Enemy: AIDS Activism and Social Movement "Newness"

Joshua Gamson

Shea Stadium is packed. As the Mets play the Astros, New York AIDS activists scream and shout along with the rest of the fans. Their cheers are somewhat different than the usual: "ACT UP! Fight back! Fight AIDS!" Their banners, unfurled in front of the three sections whose seats they have bought out, shout plays on baseball themes: "No glove, no love," "Don't balk at safer sex," "AIDS is not a ballgame." The electronic billboard flashes some of their messages, as well. The action gets wide coverage the following day. Later, in a 1988 *Newsweek* article on the activist group ACT UP, a baseball fan complains, "AIDS is a fearful topic. This is totally inappropriate."[1]

The fan is right, on both counts; in fact, I would suggest, he inadvertently sums up the point of the action. He also calls attention to the oddities: Why fight AIDS at a baseball game? Why mix fear and Americana? Who or what is the target here?

Susan Sontag and others have noted that the AIDS epidemic fits quite smoothly into a history of understanding disease through the "usual script" of the plague metaphor: originating from "outside," plagues are visitations on "them," punishments of both individuals and groups, that become stand-ins for deep fears and tools for bringing judgments about social crisis. "AIDS," Sontag suggests in her essay "AIDS and Its Metaphors," "is understood in a premodern way."[2]

Yet the plague of AIDS has brought with it understandings and actions that are hardly premodern: civil disobedience at the Food and Drug Administration protesting the sluggish drug-approval process, guerrilla theater and "die-ins," infiltrations of political events culminating in the unfurling of banners protesting government inaction, media-geared "zaps," illegal drug research and sales, pickets, and rallies. AIDS has given rise to a social movement. This is not, in fact, part of the usual script.

Perhaps, then, AIDS can be understood as part of a different script as well. Much has been written in the past decade about "new social movements" (NSMs); perhaps AIDS activism follows an outline particular to contemporary movements. This classification presents its own difficulties: social movements literature has a hard time clarifying what exactly is "new" about contemporary social movements and can, through its fuzziness, easily accommodate yet another social movement without shedding new light.

In this article, I examine AIDS activism—by which I mean an organized "street" response to the epidemic—through the activities of ACT UP (the AIDS Coalition to Unleash Power), its most widespread and publicly visible direct-action group.

ACT UP, which began in New York, has chapters in Chicago, Boston, Atlanta, Los Angeles, Houston, Rochester, Madison, Nashville, San Francisco, and a number of other cities. The groups are loosely federated under the umbrella of the AIDS Coalition to Network, Organize and Win (ACT NOW). New York's is by far the largest chapter, with weekly meeting attendance in the hundreds and membership estimated near 3,000. San Francisco's chapter, with a membership of over 700, averages 50 people at general meetings. My comparisons between ACT UP chapters in San Francisco, New York, and other cities are based on a national conference in Washington, D.C., internal publications, informal discussion and interviews, and newspaper reporting.

Using data from six months of participant-observation research (September 1988 through February 1989) in San Francisco's ACT UP—general meetings, planning meetings, and actions—coupled with local and national internal documents and newspaper writings about the group, I develop an analysis intended both to sharpen focus on the struggle over the meaning of AIDS and to challenge some of the hazy understandings of social movement newness. The analysis here treats ACT UP not as an exemplar but rather as an anomaly, asking what unique conditions constitute the case and how the case can aid in a reconstruction of existing theory.

I begin with a brief review of approaches to contemporary social movements, locating ACT UP within this literature. I then turn to ACT UP's activities and internal obstacles, looking at its response to the plague script, the alternative scripts it proposes and its strategies for doing so, and the difficulties it faces in this process. I argue that asking "who is the enemy?" provides a fruitful direction for making sense of these dynamics. Examining the forms of domination to which ACT UP members respond, I argue that in addition to visible targets such as government agencies and drug companies, much of what ACT UP is fighting is abstract, disembodied, invisible: control through the creation of abnormality. Power is maintained less through direct force or institutionalized oppression and more through the delineation of the "normal" and the exclusion of the "abnormal." I suggest that this "normalizing" process, taking prominence in a gradual historical shift, is increasingly uncoupled from state oppression in recent decades. Responses to normalization play themselves out in ACT UP activities: activists use the labels to dispute the labels and use their abnormality and expressions of gay identity to challenge the process by which normality was and is defined. Finally, I point to directions this framework provides for analyzing contemporary movement.

THE THEORETICAL CONTEXT: WHAT'S NEW?

Among the shifts provoked by the rise of massive social movements in the 1960s and 1970s was a rupture in theorizing about social movements. Until that time, the dominant paradigm of collective behavior theory treated noninstitutional movements as essentially nonrational or irrational responses by alienated individuals to social strain and breakdown.[3] Many 1960s activists did not fit the mold. Neither anomic nor underprivileged nor responding to crises with beliefs, as Neil Smelser had argued, "akin to magical beliefs,"[4] they in fact came together largely from the middle class, with concrete goals and rational calculations of strategies. The predictions of classical social movement theory—who made up social movements and how they operated—had broken down.[5]

In the last two decades, attempts to retheorize social movements have moved in two major directions. North American "resource mobilization" theory accounts for large-scale mobilizations by emphasizing rational calculations by actors, focusing on the varying constraints and opportunities in which they operate and the varying resources upon which they draw.[6] This paradigm, directly challenging the assumptions of collective behavior theory, insists on the rationality of collective action. European theorists, on the other hand, have argued that rational-actor models are inappropriately applied to new groups seeking identity and autonomy. The movements of the 1960s and their apparent descendants—the peace movement, for example, or feminist, ecological, or local-autonomy movements—have been taken together by theorists as "new" phenomena to be accounted for; it is their nonrational focus on identity and expression that these theories emphasize as distinctive. They attempt to outline the characteristics shared by contemporary movements and to discern the structural shifts that might account for new dimensions of activity.[7]

With some notable exceptions,[8] American theory, with its insistence on instrumental rationality, tends to pass over these distinctive characteristics—feminist attention to "consciousness," for example, and black and gay "pride"—to which European theories of "new social movements" (NSMs) direct attention. The European literature, then, in that it attempts to explain these apparently new characteristics found also in AIDS activism, provides the stronger conceptual tools with which to approach ACT UP. Yet what is actually "new" according to European NSM theory is both disputed and unclear. Most agree that a middle-class social base is distinctive;[9] indeed, that NSMs are *not* working-class movements focused primarily on economic distribution seems to be a characteristic on which there is clarity and agreement. From here, the range of characteristics expands and abstracts: NSMs claim "the sphere of 'political action within civil society' as [their] space"[10]; they use different tactics than their predecessors[11]; their conflicts concern not "problems of distribution" but "the grammar of forms of life," arising in "areas of cultural reproduction, social integration, and socialization"[12]; they "manifest a form of middle-class protest which oscillates from moral crusade to political pressure group to social movement"[13]; they are "both culturally oriented and involved in structural conflicts"[14]; and they involve a "self-limiting radicalism" that "abandons revolutionary dreams in favor of the idea of structural reform, along with a defense of civil society that does not seek to abolish the autonomous functioning of political and economic systems."[15]

Common to this list is a recognition that the field of operation has shifted, broadly put, to "civil society" and away from the state; that culture has become more of a focal point of activity (through "life-style" and "identity" movements, for example); and that this shift has to do with broad changes in the "societal type" to which movements respond and in which they act. Common to the list is also an unclear answer to the question of how new the shift really is. As Jean Cohen points out, the theme of defending civil society does not in itself imply something new; the question "is whether the theme has been connected to new identities, forms of organization, and scenarios of conflict."[16] New social movement theorists—even those, like Touraine and Cohen, who address these questions directly—seem to be unclear on what these shifts and changes really are: What exactly is the "cultural field" of "civil society," and what do these movements actually do there? What is different about contemporary society that accounts for the characteristics of new social movements? When and how did these changes take place?

ACT UP AS A NEW SOCIAL MOVEMENT

ACT UP provides an opportunity both to examine some of these issues concretely and to offer new hypotheses. The AIDS activist movement appears to share the most basic characteristics of "new social movements": a (broadly) middle-class membership and a mix of instrumental, expressive, and identity-oriented activities. Rather than exclusively orienting itself toward material distribution, ACT UP uses and targets cultural resources as well. What, this examination asks, does ACT UP *do* on the cultural terrain? What light does its activity shed on the question of "newness"? How can a study of this group contribute to an understanding of shifts in the nature of social movements and in the nature of the social world in which they operate?

The answer begins with the group's overall profile. ACT UP/San Francisco grew out of the 1987 San Francisco AIDS Action Pledge, becoming ACT UP in the fall of that year after New York's ACT UP began to gain recognition. In addition to planned and spontaneous actions, the group meets weekly in a church in the predominantly gay Castro neighborhood. ACT UP/San Francisco is made up almost exclusively of white gay men and lesbians, mostly in their twenties and thirties. The core membership, an informal group of about forty activists, draws from both "old-time" activists (gay rights, Central American politics, etc.) and those newly politicized by AIDS.[17] Some, but by no means all, of ACT UP's membership has either tested positive for HIV antibodies or been diagnosed with AIDS. As one member said, "I'm here because I'm angry and I'm tired of seeing my friends die." The membership is typically professional and semiprofessional: legal and health care professionals, writers, political organizers, students, and artists with day jobs. ACT UP/New York and ACT UPs in other cities exhibit similar profiles.[18]

Self-defined in its flyers and media kits as "a nonpartisan group of diverse individuals united in anger and committed to direct action to end the AIDS crisis," ACT UP pushes for greater access to treatments and drugs for AIDS-related diseases; culturally sensitive, widely available, and explicit safe-sex education; and well-funded research that is "publicly accountable to the communities most affected."[19] Moreover, the group pushes for the participation of people with AIDS (PWAs) in these activities.[20] The idea here is to change the distribution of resources and decision-making power; the principle guiding actions is strategic, aimed at effecting policy changes. "People have been fighting for social justice in this country for centuries," says one member. "We're going to get aerosol pentamidine [a treatment drug for pneumocystis pneumonia] a lot quicker than we're going to get social justice."

ACT UP is also often involved in actions, however, whose primary principle is expressive. They focus inward, on "building a unified community" (the gay and lesbian community and, increasingly, a subcommunity of PWAs and the HIV-infected) and on the "need to express the anger and rage that is righteous and justified" from the community outward. They organize at times around actions in which AIDS is not the central issue or in which AIDS activism is incorporated into the project of "recreating a movement for gay and lesbian liberation." This orientation toward identity and expression, while not excluding older-style strategic action, is one key characteristic cited by students of post-sixties social movements.

Most interestingly, though, one hears and sees in ACT UP a constant reference to theater. ACT UP operates largely by staging events and by carefully constructing and publicizing symbols; it attacks the dominant representations of AIDS and of people with AIDS and makes attempts to replace them with alternative representations. At times, ACT UP attacks the representations alone; at times it combines the attack with a direct one on cultural producers and the process of AIDS-image production.

Another action principle weaves through ACT UP. As *Newsweek* put it, ACT UP has often "deliberately trespassed the bounds of good taste"[21]: throwing condoms, necking in public places, speaking explicitly and positively about anal sex, "camping it up" for the television cameras. This trespassing, or boundary-crossing—and we can include in it the infiltration of public and private spaces (the Republican national convention, for example, where activists posing as participants unfurled banners)—both uses and strikes at the cultural field as well. In this case, rather than reacting to images of AIDS, activists use a more general tactic of disturbing "good taste" and, in a point *Newsweek* characteristically misses, calling attention to the connection between cultural definitions and responses to AIDS. Boundary-crossing, along with the-atrical and symbolic actions, makes clear that ACT UP operates largely on the cultural field where theorists situate new social movements. (By way of comparison, most AIDS politics does not operate according to this description, but according to a more conventional political model. "Most AIDS politicking," as Dennis Altman describes it, "has involved the lobbying of federal, state, and local governments. . . . [This] has meant dependence upon professional leaders able to talk the language of politicians and bureaucrats."[22]) It also suggests that an examination of the specific patterns of culturally oriented actions may be especially revealing. By focusing on the cultural activities of AIDS activists as a key *distinctive* element, I by no means want to suggest that this activism is primarily cultural. In fact, treatment issues, needle-exchange programs, and access to health care are all common subjects of action. Pursuing this via ACT UP's peculiarities, I hope to generate possibilities for grounding and developing social movement theory.

ACT UP'S INTERNAL OBSTACLES

Let us examine ACT UP's distinctive characteristics. ACT UP's strong cultural orientation has already been noted. In addition, buried in its various strategies are several fundamental confusions. First, an orientation toward theatrics suggests a clear delineation of performer from audience, yet actions are often planned by ACT UP members without an articulation of whom they are meant to influence. If one wants to affect an audience—for example, by invoking a symbol whose meaning is taken for granted and then giving it a different meaning—one needs a clear conception of who that audience is. In ACT UP planning meetings, there is often an underlying confusion of audiences, and more often the question of audience is simply ignored. When activists in New York infiltrated a Republican women's cocktail party and later unfurled banners ("Lesbians for Bush," read one), the response of the cocktail partiers, a defensive singing of "God Bless America,"[23] was important not for what it showed about the Republicans' AIDS consciousness but for what it showed the activists about their own power. They were, in effect, their own audience, performing for themselves and making others perform for them. In "brainstorms" for new actions, there is almost never a mention of audience, and action ideas with different audiences proliferate. ACT UP protested Michael Dukakis's visit to San Francisco in September 1988, for example, with no media coverage, Dukakis nowhere in sight, and no one to witness the protest but passing cars. In the meetings I observed, I commonly heard suggestions for actions that bypassed any actual event, heading straight for the at-home audience through "photo opportunities," mixed in with suggestions for actions that almost no one will see. Much of this confusion is exacerbated by an openness of exchange and decentralized decision making born of ACT UP's democratic structure (in San Francisco, decisions are made consensually). The loose organizational structure acts against focused planning and action.

A second point of confusion is that while ACT UP professes to be inclusive, and ideas are often brought up that target nongay aspects of AIDS (issues of concern to injection drug users, for example, or access to health care for those who cannot afford it), there are few signs that ACT UP in fact succeeds at including or actively pursues nongay members. This does not mean that the membership is exclusively gay men; in fact, a good portion of the activists are women.[24] The formation of coalitions is sometimes brought up as a good idea—"we need to join with others in solidarity around common suffering and common enemies," said the keynote speaker at the ACT NOW conference in October 1988—but generally not effected. Cooperative actions with other groups generate less excitement in San Francisco meetings. Actions are aimed mainly at targets with particular relevance to lesbians and gays; there are few black or Hispanic members, gay or straight. Despite the goal of inclusiveness, ACT UP continues to draw from and recreate the white middle-class gay and lesbian community.

A third and related problem is perhaps even more fundamental: AIDS politics and gay politics stand in tension, simultaneously associated and dissociated. ACT UP is an AIDS activist organization built and run by gay people. Historically, this is neither surprising nor problematic; among the populations first hit hardest by AIDS, gay people were alone in having an already established tradition and network of political and self-help organizations. Still, it has meant, as Dennis Altman writes, that "AIDS groups have found it very difficult to establish themselves as nongay, even where they have deliberately presented themselves as such."[25] AIDS activists find themselves simultaneously attempting to dispel the notion that AIDS is a "gay disease" (which it is not) while, through their activity and leadership, treating AIDS as a gay problem (which, among other things, it is).

While this dilemma is in part due to the course the disease itself took, how it plays itself out in ACT UP is instructive. For some—particularly those members who are not newly politicized—ACT UP *is* gay politics, pure and simple, a movement continuous with earlier activism. They emphasize the need for "sex positive" safe-sex education, for example, linking AIDS politics to the sexual liberation of earlier gay politics. The main organizer of a November 1988 election-night rally in the Castro district, for the gay community to "Stand Out and Shout" about results, envisioned it as a return to the "good old days" of gay celebration. In planning the rally, he and others quickly generated a long list of possible speakers—from the gay political community. Here, AIDS issues often get buried.

For other members, it is important to maintain some separation, albeit a blurry one, between the two sets of issues. In New York, for example, when a newspaper calls ACT UP a "gay organization," ACT UP's media committee sends out a "standard letter" correcting the error.[26] The ACT UP agenda, when the balance is toward distinctively AIDS politics, often focuses more narrowly on prevention and treatment issues—as in, for example, a San Francisco proposal for an "AIDS treatment advocacy project," which argues that "whether it is an entire family with AIDS in Harlem or an HIV+ gay man in San Francisco, treatment is ultimately the issue they are most concerned with."[27] More commonly, though, ACT UP actions don't fall on one side or the other, but combine an active acceptance of the gay-AIDS connection with an active resistance to that connection.

VISIBLE AND INVISIBLE ENEMIES

Why do these particular confusions occur? They eventually come to make sense as the particularities of ACT UP's actions are examined. These three confusions within ACT UP, which seem to give its action a somewhat unfocused character, in fact prove to be core elements of the group's being. Explaining ACT UP's confusions, and those of social movements like it, hinges on the answer to a pivotal question: *Who is the enemy?* Asking this question of ACT UP, one often finds that the enemies against which their anger and action are directed are clear, familiar, and visible: the state and corporations. At other times, though, the enemy is invisible, abstract, disembodied, ubiquitous: it is the very process of "normalization" through labeling in which everyone except one's own "community" of the denormalized (and its supporters) is involved. At still other times, intermediate enemies appear, the visible institutors of the less visible process: the media and medical science.

The second enemy forms the basis of my core theoretical claim: that ACT UP is responding to a gradual historical shift toward a form of domination in which power is maintained through a "normalizing" process in which, as Michel Foucault describes it, "the whole indefinite domain of the nonconforming is punishable."[28] Through labeling, or socially organized stigmatization, behaviors and groups are marked as abnormal; in the last two centuries, the norm has largely replaced the threat of violence as a technique of power. As Foucault argues, individuals are differentiated "in terms of the following overall rule":

> that the rule be made to function as a minimum threshold, as an average to be respected or as an optimum towards which one must move. It . . . hierarchizes in terms of values the abilities, the level, the "nature" of individuals. It introduces, through this "value-giving" measure, the constraint of a conformity that must be achieved. Lastly, it traces the limit that will define difference in relation to all other differences, the external frontier of the abnormal.[29]

In this process, the dominator becomes increasingly abstracted and invisible, while the dominated, embodied and visible (and, importantly, "marked" through stigmatization), becomes the focus of attention. In effect, people dominate themselves; rather than being confronted with a punishment (physical, material) as a mechanism of control, they confront themselves with the threat of being devalued as abnormal.

These ideas are not incompatible with those put forward by the sociology of deviance and discussions of stigmatization, which of course call attention to the process of labeling and its impact on the "deviant." However, the various forms of labeling theory have also been challenged by collective action since the 1960s. Those theories, by studying how one "becomes deviant," and the defensive reaction of "deviants" to an identity defined for them—the "management of spoiled identities," in Erving Goffman's terms, and "secondary deviation" as a "means of defense" against the "problems created by the societal reaction to primary deviation," in the words of Edwin Lemert[30]—are ill equipped to explain the organization of the stigmatized into social movements. As John Kitsuse argues, the accommodative reactions analyzed by deviance sociology (retreat into a subculture, nervously covering up or denying aberrations) do not "account for, nor do they provide for an understanding of, the phenomenal number of self-proclaimed deviant groups that have visibly and vocally entered the politics" of recent decades.[31] Earlier theories are hard pressed to account for historical change and for the assertive building of collective movements based on self-definitions that reject the dominant definitions. Foucault, on the other hand, treats pressure for conformity not as a given problem for the "deviant," but as a technique of power with a variable history.

Identity strategies are particularly salient and problematic within this domination form. When power is effected through categorization, identity is often built on the very categories it resists. ACT UP's expressive actions, in this light, are part of a continuing process of actively forging a gay identity while challenging the process through which it is formed *for* gay people—at a time when the stigma of disease has been linked with the stigma of deviant sexuality. ACT UP members continue to organize around the "deviant" label, attempting to separate label from stigma. Identity-oriented actions accept the labels, and symbolic actions disrupt and resignify them.

Identity actions and representational strategies thus stand in awkward relationship: they are increasingly linked in the attack on the normalization process itself. In a simpler identity politics—the celebration of gay liberation, for example—labels are important tools for self-understanding. That sort of politics involves what Kitsuse calls "tertiary deviation," the "confrontation, assessment, and rejection of the negative identity . . . and the transformation of that identity into a positive or viable self-conception."[32] ACT UP members, however, push past this "new deviance" to use stigmas and identity markers as tools against the normalization process. The representation of oneself as abnormal now becomes a tool for disrupting the categorization process; the labels on which group identity is built are used, in a sense, against themselves.

Why, though, is this response to "normalizing power" coming into its own now? Stigmatization is certainly not new. Foucault, in *Discipline and Punish*, traces a shift in the eighteenth and nineteenth centuries, a shift that takes place primarily in technologies of control—the rise of surveillance techniques and the constitution of the subject by "experts" and scientific discourse. This shift has arguably solidified in this century in Western societies. Yet, while state institutions and actors in the twentieth century certainly have still been involved in the normalization process (as well as in direct repression), they have evidently been *less* involved in the latter half of this century (or, stated less strongly, less visibly involved). One sees this in the history of civil rights: racism continues while state-sponsored racism and racist policies become less acceptable.[33] Similarly, state definitions of women's "roles" have been liberalized, as the state has withdrawn somewhat from prescribing "normal" female behavior. One sees this as well in the response to AIDS: the federal government, while conservative or split in its policies, has over time become somewhat more liberal in terms of labeling. Public health officials advertise AIDS as an "equal opportunity destroyer," the Surgeon General warns against treating AIDS as a gay disease and argues in favor of protections against discrimination; the Presidential Commission calls for "the reaffirmation of compassion, justice, and dignity" and indicts, among other things, "a lack of uniform and strong antidiscrimination laws."[34] State institutions increasingly refuse to "discriminate," that is, to set policies based on social labels. As the state becomes less directly involved in normalization, the process itself necessarily becomes more an independent point of attack by the denormalized—and is resisted as a process. It is within this overall historical shift in methods of domination, I propose, that ACT UP's social movement activity makes sense.

ACT UP AND NORMALIZATION

How does this resistance play itself out? What is the link between enemies and actions? Let's begin with the old forms of domination, which are very much still at work. The state is certainly involved in the domination of people with AIDS, as it is in the repression of sexual minorities. The federal Food and Drug Administration has been sluggish in approving AIDS-related drugs; it is perceived as allowing bureaucracy to get in the way of saving or prolonging lives. In October 1988 ACT NOW organized a conference, teach-in, rally, and day of civil disobedience in Washington, D.C., to "seize control of the FDA."[35] The Reagan and Bush administrations have been notoriously inattentive to the AIDS epidemic. Reagan first mentioned AIDS publicly at a time when over 36,000 people had already been diagnosed and over 20,000 had died from the disease. While subsequently calling AIDS "America's number one health problem," the administration has consistently avoided initiating a coordinated, adequately financed attack on that problem.[36] Reagan and Bush have become common targets of ACT UP "AIDSgate" signs and t-shirts, of "zaps," of posters charging that "the government has blood on its hands," of disruption and protest during campaign speeches. In this case, specific state institutions and actors are targeted, mostly through conventional protest actions and media-geared actions. In these cases, it is quite clear who is responsible for needless death and who is controlling resources, and ACT UP functions as a pressure group to protest and affect policy decisions. Here, AIDS politics and gay politics are quite separable and separated.

Similarly, pharmaceutical companies are manifest enemies; they control the price of treatment drugs and make decisions about whether or not to pursue drug development. That drug company decisions are guided by considerations of profit is a direct and visible instance of oppression and represents an embodied obstacle to the physical survival of people with AIDS. For example, AZT (azidothymidine, the only drug approved at this writing for treatment of AIDS illnesses) cost $13,000 a year in 1987. Again, ACT UP attacks these targets with pressure tactics: boycotting AZT manufacturer Burroughs-Wellcome, zapping that company and others with civil-disobedience actions, publicizing government–drug company relations.[37] In this example, again, the focus is specifically on issues of relevance to all people with AIDS.

Yet AIDS has also been from the outset a stigma, an illness constructed as a marker of homosexuality, drug abuse, moral deficiencies—stigmas added to those of sexual transmission, terminal disease and, for many, skin color.[38] AIDS has

> come to assume all the features of a traditional morality play: images of cancer and death, of blood and semen, of sex and drugs, of morality and retribution. A whole gallery of folk devils have been introduced—the sex-crazed gay, the dirty drug abuser, the filthy whore, the blood drinking voodoo-driven black—side by side with a gallery of "innocents"—the hemophiliacs, the blood transfusion "victim," the newborn child, even the "heterosexual."[39]

Bolstered most commonly by the image of the male homosexual or bisexual AIDS "victim" or "carrier," vaguely responsible through deviant behavior for his own demise, AIDS has been appropriated to medicalize moral stances: promiscuity is medically unsafe while monogamy is safe; being a member of certain social groups is dangerous to one's health, being a member of the "general population" is dangerous only when the un-general contaminate it. As Simon Watney notes, in AIDS "the categories of health and sickness . . . meet with those of sex, and the image of homosexuality is reinscribed with connotations of contagion and disease, a subject for medical attention and medical authority."[40]

The construction and reconstruction of boundaries has been an essential aspect of the story of AIDS. The innocent victim is bounded off from the guilty one, pure blood from contaminated, the general population from the AIDS populations, risk groups from those not at risk. Those who span the boundaries arguably become the most threatening: the promiscuous bisexual, the only one who can "account for and absolve the heterosexual majority of any taint of unlawful desire," and the prostitute, with her longstanding position as a vessel of disease.[41]

Who achieves this demarcation of boundaries? Who has made AIDS mean what it does? Who is the enemy? Two manifest producers of stigmas appear (in addition to certain public figures who disseminate them): the mass media, on whose television screens and newspaper pages the stigmatized are actually visible, and medical science, which translates the labels into risk-group categories. ACT UP thus challenges the medical establishment, largely by undermining the expertise claimed by them: activists keep up to date on and publicize underground and foreign treatments, sell illegal treatment drugs publicly, yell the names of known AIDS-illness drugs in front of the FDA ("Show them we know!" the organizer calls). They wear lab coats, and prepare a "guerrilla slide show" in which they plan to slip slides saying "He's lying" and "This is voodoo epidemiology" into an audio-visual presentation by a health commissioner.

ACT UP also sets up challenges to the media. An ongoing San Francisco battle had ACT UP shutting down production and members negotiating with producers over the script of an NBC drama, "Midnight Caller." In the script a bisexual man with AIDS purposely infects others and is shot and killed in the end by one of his female partners. It was objected to by ACT UP members as playing on "the great fear of the 'killer queer' "[42] and implying that, as an ACT UP representative put it, "basically it's justifiable to kill a person with AIDS."[43] A similar response has been discussed for the San Francisco filming of Randy Shilts's *And the Band Played On*, a controversial history of the American AIDS epidemic. The media are usually treated by ACT UP as allies in the public-relations operation of garnering coverage. As one New Yorker put it in October 1988, "the media aren't the enemy, the media are manipulated by the enemy, and we can manipulate them too." When actively involved in the labeling of people with AIDS as murderers, however, the media become the enemies to be fought. This ambivalence makes sense: the media, as the institutional mechanism through which normalization is most effectively disseminated, are both a visible enemy and a necessary link to a more abstract form of domination.[44]

The question of who is behind the generation and acceptance of stigmas, though, for the most part doesn't get asked as activists plan and argue, perhaps because the answer is experienced daily: everyone and no one. No one actually does it and everyone participates in it—your family and your neighbors as well as the blatant bigots farther way. It's a process that appears usually as natural, as not-a-process.

PLAYING WITH LABELS, CROSSING THE BOUNDARIES

Fighting this largely hidden process calls for different kinds of strategies, mostly in the realm of symbols. Examining the symbolic maneuverings of ACT UP, we can begin to see how fighting the process calls for particular strategies. ACT UP's general strategy is to take a symbol used to oppress and invert it. For example, ACT UP makes explicit challenges, guided by other AIDS activists and particularly by PWAs, on the kind of language used to discuss AIDS. In place of the "AIDS victims," they speak of "people with AIDS" (or "people living with AIDS"); in place of "risk groups," they insert the category of "risk practices." They talk about blood and semen rather than "bodily fluids" and challenge the exclusionary use of "general population."[45]

The strategy runs much deeper than speech, however. The visual symbol most widely publicized by American AIDS activists—"SILENCE = DEATH" written in bold white-on-black letters beneath a pink triangle, the Nazi mark for homosexuals later coopted by the gay movement—provides a snapshot look at this process. Here, ACT UP takes a symbol used to mark people for death and reclaims it. They reclaim, in fact, control over defining a cause of death; the banner connects gay action to gay survival, on the one hand, and homophobia to death from AIDS, on the other. ACT UP's common death spectacles repeat the inversion. In AIDS commentary death is used in a number of ways: it is either a punishment (the image of the withered, guilty victim), an individual tragedy (the image of the lonely, abandoned dying), or a weapon (the image of the irresponsible "killer queer").[46] A "die-in," in which activists draw police-style chalk outlines around each other's "dead" bodies, gives death another meaning by shifting the responsibility: these are deaths likened to murders, victims not of their own "deviance," but shot down by the people controlling the definition and enforcement of "normality." You have told us what our deaths mean, their actions say; now we, who are actually dying, will show you what they mean.

A similar shift of responsibility takes place around the symbol of blood. In popular discussions of AIDS, blood typically takes its place in discussions of "purity" and a benevolent medical establishment working to keep "bad blood" out of the nation's blood supply. In many ACT UP activities, "blood" is splattered on t-shirts or doctor's uniforms. Members want to shoot it out of squirt guns, blood-balloon it onto buildings, write "test this" with it on walls. Here, on one level, they use the established discourse of purity against its users as an angry weapon: "infected" blood is everywhere. On another level, though, the frame is shifted from purity (in which the blood supply is "victimized") to crime (in which PWAs are victimized). The blood becomes evidence not of infection, but of murder. The activists are blood-splattered victims, as was made explicit in posters originally directed at Mayor Koch in New York and later translated into an indictment of the federal government. "The government has blood on its hands," the sign says, "One AIDS death every half hour." Between the two phrases is the print of a large, bloody hand. In a San Francisco rally against Rep. William Dannemeyer's Proposition 102, which would have required by law that doctors report those infected and those "suspected" of infection, require testing at the request of doctors, employers, or insurers, and eliminate confidential testing, ACT UP carried a "Dannemeyer Vampire" puppet. The vampire, a big ugly head on a stick, with a black cape and with blood pouring from its fangs, was stabbed with a stake later in the action. Here, ACT UP activates another popular code in which blood has meaning—the gore of horror movies—and reframes blood testing as blood sucking. It's not the blood itself that's monstrous, but the vampire who would take it. By changing the meaning of blood, ACT UP activists dispute the "ownership" of blood; more importantly, they call attention to the consequences of the labels of "bad" blood and "purity" and implicate those accepting the labels in the continuation of the AIDS epidemic.

Boundary-crossing, although tactically similar, goes on the offensive while inversions are essentially reactive. The spectacle of infiltration and revelation runs through real and fantasized ACT UP actions. Members speak of putting subversive messages in food or in the pockets of suit jackets, of writing messages on lawns with weed killer, of covering the Washington Monument with a giant condom, of replacing (heterosexual) bar ashtrays with condom-shaped ashtrays. They place stickers saying "Touched by a Person with AIDS" in phone booths and stage a mock Inauguration through the San Francisco streets during rush hour. The idea, as one activist puts it, is to "occupy a space that's not supposed to be yours," to "usurp public spaces." San Francisco's underground graffiti group, specializing in "redecorating" targeted spaces, sums up the principle in its humorous acronym, TANTRUM: Take Action Now To Really Upset the Masses.

The ideas that charge brainstorming sessions and the eventual choices for visual and theatrical activity at actions are not arbitrary. The selections are revealing. Spaces and objects are chosen that are especially American (that is, middle American—lawns, cocktail parties, baseball games, patriotic symbols, suits) and presumably "safe" from the twin "threats" of homosexuality and disease. ACT UP here seizes control of symbols that traditionally exclude gay people or render them invisible, and take them over, endowing them with messages about AIDS; they reclaim them, as they do the pink triangle, and *make them mean* differently. In so doing, they attempt to expose the system of domination from which they reclaim meanings and implicate the entire system in the spread of AIDS.

It is important to notice that ACT UP's identity-oriented actions often revolve around boundary-crossing and label-disruption. These are strategies for which these mostly white, middle-class gay people are particularly equipped, largely because their "stigma" is often invisible (unlike, for example, the stigmatized person of color). They can draw on a knowledge of mainstream culture born of participation rather than exclusion and thus a knowledge of how to disrupt it using its own vocabulary. Here the particular cultural resources of ACT UP's membership become important; they are resources that other movements (and gay people from other races or classes) may not have to the same degree or may not be able to use without considerable risk.

Gay campiness, raunchy safe-sex songs in front of the Department of Health and Human Services, straight-looking men in skirts wearing "Fuck Me Safe" t-shirts, lesbians and gay men staging "kiss-ins," a general outrageousness that "keeps the edge"—these actions simultaneously accept the gay label, build a positive gay identity, challenge the conventional "deviant" label, connect stigmatization to AIDS deaths, *and* challenge the very process of categorization. This is the power of the pink triangle and "Silence = Death": the building of an identity is linked with the resistance of a stigma as the key to stopping the AIDS epidemic. "We are everywhere," says a sign at an ACT NOW rally, a sign common at gay political demonstrations, and the noisy expressions of collective anger and identity add up to the same claim. Here, the gay "we" and the AIDS "we" are melded; the destabilizing effect of the suddenly revealed homosexual is joined with the fear that suddenly no space is safe from AIDS. A chant at several San Francisco protests captures the link between asserting an identity and challenging the labels: "We're fags and dykes," the activists chant, "and we're here to stay." Meaning: we are what you say we are, and we're not what you say we are. "We're here," they chant, "we're queer, and we're not going shopping."

What exactly is being challenged in these symbolic inversions? Certainly, in symbols like the Dannemeyer vampire and the bloody hand attributed to the government, the old and consistent enemy, the state, is mixed in; but it isn't exclusive. ACT UP disrupts symbolic representation, heeding the call to "campaign and organize in order to enter the amphitheater of AIDS commentary effectively and unapologetically on our own terms."[47] It does so, moreover, often through symbols that are not tied to the state but to "mainstream" American culture. In the case of inversions, AIDS and gay labels are not necessarily linked: any oppressive marker is taken over. In the case of boundary-disruption, AIDS and gay labels are connected: the fear of gay people and the fear of AIDS, now linked in the normalization process, are used to call attention to themselves. In both cases, the *process* of stigmatization, by which symbols become markers of abnormality and the basis for decisions about "correcting" the abnormal, is contested.

STRATEGIES AND OBSTACLES REVISITED

The mix of strategies can be seen in terms of the visibility of enemies.[48] More familiar, instrumental pressure-group strategies attempt to change the distribution of resources by attacking those visibly controlling distribution. Identity-forming strategies are particularly crucial and problematic when the struggle is in part against a society rather than a visible oppressor. Label disruption—contained in identity-forming strategies, and the core of symbolic strategies—is a particular operation on the cultural field. It is made necessary by a form of domination that operates through abstractions, through symbols that mark off the normal. (I am not suggesting, of course, that these are discrete types in concrete actions; actions are always mixed exactly because the forms of domination are simultaneous.)

We can also make sense of ACT UP's internal obstacles through this lens. It is not surprising that the question of audience becomes a difficult one to address. First of all, the audience often *is* the group itself when identity formation becomes a key part of the struggle. Yet at the same time, we have seen that identity struggles involve pushing at the very labels on which they are based, and here the audience is the entire society. Actions are thus often founded on a confusion of audiences. More commonly, the question of audience is simply lost as the underlying target of action is the normalization process. While it might be more "rational" for ACT UP activists to try to spell out the particular audience each time they design an action, the struggle in which they are involved makes the particularity of an audience difficult to see. When stigmatization is being protested, the audience is the undifferentiated "society"—that is, audience and enemy are lumped together, and neither is concretely graspable.

Understanding that ACT UP is attacking this particular form of domination, we can also see why ACT UP is caught between association and dissociation of AIDS politics from gay politics. Clearly, PWAs and gay people are both subject to the stigmatization process; this process, as it informs and supports responses to AIDS, has become literally lethal for PWAs, gay and nongay, and dangerous for those labeled as "risk group" members, gay men (and often by an odd extension lesbians), drug users, prostitutes, blacks, and Hispanics. Socially organized labels that, before AIDS, were used to oppress are now joined with the label of "AIDS victim." This form of domination is *experienced* by ACT UP members as a continuous one. AIDS is a gay disease because AIDS has been made to attribute viral disease to sexual deviance. Separating AIDS politics from gay politics would be to give up the fight against normalization.

Yet joining the two politics poses the risk of losing the fight in that it confirms the very connection it attempts to dispel. This is a familiar dilemma, as Steven Epstein points out, and one that is not at all limited to the gay movement: "How do you protest a socially imposed categorization, except by organizing around the category?"[49] Organizing around a resisted label, in that it involves an initial acceptance of the label (and, in identity-oriented movements, a celebration of it), can tend to reify the label. Identity politics thus contain a danger played out here: "If there is perceived to be such a thing as a 'homosexual person,' then it is only a small step to the conclusion that there is such a thing as a 'homosexual disease,' itself the peculiar consequence of the 'homosexual lifestyle.' "[50] The familiarity of the dilemma, though, should not obscure its significance. This is a dilemma attributable neither simply to the random course of AIDS nor to mistakes on the part of activists, but to the form of domination to which social movements respond.

In this light, it is not surprising that ACT UP has difficulty including nongays and forming coalitions. In some ways, ACT UP is driven toward inclusiveness because AIDS is affecting other populations and because the fight includes more broad-based struggles over resources. But, as we have seen, resistance to labeling involves accepting the label but redefining it, taking it over. Group identity actions are bound up with this resistance. This drives ACT UP strongly away from inclusiveness. The difficulty in walking these lines—between confirming and rejecting the connection between gay people and AIDS, between including and excluding non-gays—is built into the struggle against normalization in which ACT UP is involved.

BODIES AND THEORIES

I have argued that ACT UP responds to the script of the AIDS plague by undermining that script, resisting the labeling through which contemporary domination is often effectively achieved. This seems to be missed by most observers of AIDS, who interpret the politics of AIDS on the model of conventional politics. Randy Shilts's 1988 bestseller, for example, ignores the development of grassroots AIDS activism even in its updating epilogue. AIDS serves as a particularly vivid case of disputed scripts in American politics, in that the epidemic of disease, as others have noted, has occurred simultaneously with what Paula Treichler calls an "epidemic of signification"; AIDS exists "at a point where many entrenched narratives intersect, each with its own problematic and context in which AIDS acquires meaning."[51] ACT UP illustrates this, treating the struggle over the narratives opened and exposed by AIDS as potentially life-saving.

ACT UP also illustrates major effects of this historical shift. If, as I propose in drawing on Foucault, domination has gradually come to operate less in the form of state and institutional oppression and more in the form of disembodied and ubiquitous processes, it is hardly surprising that diseased bodies become a focal point of both oppression and resistance. As the enemy becomes increasingly disembodied, the body of the dominated—in this case, primarily the diseased, gay male body—becomes increasingly central. The AIDS epidemic itself fits this process so well as to make it seem almost inevitable: the terror of the disease is that it is an enemy you cannot see, and, like the labels put to use in normalizing power, it is spread invisibly. AIDS activism in part struggles against this disembodied type of power by giving that body— its death, its blood, its sexuality—new, resistant meanings. The plague script meets here with the script of new social movements.

But what does this tell us about theorizing new social movements? First, it calls into question the value of "newness" as a reified category of analysis. In suggesting that the history of "enemies" and types of domination is central to understanding ACT UP, this study points to a gradual shift rather than a radical break in movement activity; "newness" militates toward a focus on a moment (the sixties) rather than a history that reaches back into, for example, the eighteenth and nineteenth centuries (as in the historical transformation that Foucault describes). It obscures what may be instructive continuities across time.

Second, this study points toward ways of distinguishing among contemporary movements. To assert that ACT UP exemplifies contemporary movements would clearly be to overstate the case; rather, this analysis demonstrates the insufficiency of analyzing different movements as like phenomena simply because of a shared cultural and identity focus. Operating on the "cultural field" means something more specific than focusing on problems that "deal directly with private life"[52] or even targeting and using narrative and artistic representation. ACT UP's cultural strategies reclaim and resignify oppressive markers. Orienting actions toward identity formation means something more specific than "defend[ing] spaces for the creation of new identities and solidarities."[53] Identity assertions in ACT UP point up boundaries, using the fear of the abnormal against the fearful. These are specific operations that may be shared by other contemporary social movements—those subject to stigmatization, for example, and which are also in a position to "shock"—and not by others. Stigmatization, moreover, may take different forms and give rise to different types of movement activity. Whether in Shea Stadium or at the FDA, discerning the types of enemies to whom movements are responding is a task for analysts of social movements as well as for activists within them.

AFTERWORD: THE PROBLEM OF PROBLEMLESSNESS

At the end of my first week in the field, having been to one ACT UP meeting, I had lunch with a fellow graduate student, whose expertise in the sociology of AIDS I wanted to tap. As I described the meeting I'd attended, he detected a certain irritation. He recommended that I pay close attention to that irritation—some of which was simply discomfort with being in a new situation and with being in an explicitly gay situation—and not let it get in the way. Good advice.

The substantive target of my irritation, though, was that ACT UP couldn't seem to successfully distinguish between gay politics and AIDS politics. That was something, my colleague said, that was simply taken for granted—perhaps a problem for the actors but not central to discussions of the politics surrounding AIDS. So I dropped the issue. It wasn't until two months later that I returned to this as a central problem, a central dilemma to be explained. This is odd: a problem that no one has been able to resolve, that I was able to dismiss as simply part of a description of the field. Why couldn't I see it?

Observing myself in retrospect, I see that I stumbled on some major obstacles built into the method of participant observation. Basically, I suffered chronically from the *problem of problemlessness.* The block was not just my stupidity, although my stubborn insistence that each new perception of mine was "obvious," and my stubborn drive to disdain the obvious, certainly exacerbated the problem. The first major barricade was what I would call the problem of obviousness. The roots of this problem, I think, were a too-closeness, an overlap between my background and experience and the people I was observing, and an immersion in the field.

I had worked in political organizations before; I had made consensus decisions with sixty people before; I had sat through discussions pulling in different directions before; I had even been in anti–Vietnam War demonstrations, albeit in a baby carriage. These people were around my age, with the same sort of socioeconomic backgrounds; I had gone to college and graduate school with people very much like this, people who looked like this, dressed like this, talked like this, joked like this. In fact, I was very much like this. Although gay culture, with which I was not especially familiar at the time, played an important part, ACT UP members didn't seem much different from the primarily straight social and political settings to which I'd been accustomed. I may not have been comfortable in ACT UP at first, but it certainly felt like a familiar scene. Thus, in my first set of field notes, I complain of feeling, "Oh, this again": "The same shoestring radical organization shtick, trying to do everything, pulls in a million different directions. The same questions for me of how effective things really are. The same liberal-radical tensions, the same lofty ideals vs. realistic goals tensions."

I wasn't feeling that I knew it all, that I had it pegged, but that I needed to find the "unfamiliar elements." The more I became immersed in the research, the more used to ACT UP modes and ACT UP meetings, the more obvious everything seemed. Because I was so much the same as the people I was studying, and because I became so easily involved in what they were doing, every new problem or observation made me think, "Of course"—of course AIDS politics and gay politics are meshed, everybody knows that, now let's get on with it. What was going on seemed too obvious because it was too like my experience; I longed for a project on old people, fascists, primitive tribes.

The sense of obviousness became a constant frustration and source of anxiety: Am I really seeing anything distinctive or new? Am I really saying anything distinctive or new? Where's the problem? This dynamic itself now seems to me, of course, obvious. The deeper problem, though, was not anxiety, but a genuine sense of being stuck. I was registering what would later become core problems, but registering them descriptively: symbolic politics, blood-throwing and kiss-ins, identity politics, all got detailed play in my field notes, but without a sense of strangeness.

How, then, to get on with it? Apparently, I needed a distance from my "subjects" that I wasn't likely to find or able to create in the field. At Michael Burawoy's suggestion, I turned to the literature on new social movements as a way of pulling back from the field site. It did provide distance, but also led me to what I would call the problem of theory worship. Riding my bicycle to campus after a day of reading, I pulled over suddenly to scribble a theoretical framework that would bridge the theory and the interest I had started with: I could ask how the balance between strategic and identity-oriented actions (which the new social movements were reputed to involve) affects the production and power of representations that challenge the dominant discourse (my original interest). From here, I went into a period of wild abstractions; the problem for me—and I was still in search of something that felt like a genuine problem to be worked through—was how to use the theory to shed light on ACT UP. More accurately, I was trying to squish my data into a somewhat prefabricated theoretical framework, to make them fit.

This meant that I wasn't attentive to exactly what's interesting in a setting: the things that don't fit. Having found at first that the way ACT UP worked was obvious, and obvious things weren't problematic, I had run to theory; there, from the great distance provided by theory, I approached ACT UP as data to be taken as instances of already developed theory, again militating against seeing problems as problems. The question of why particular characteristics were found in my setting was already answered by the theory. So, still, no problem.

Interestingly, I think it is a move toward arrogance, a principled chutzpah, that allowed me to see, at least hazily, the problems in front of me as problems. Rather than allow the theory to tell me what ought to be going on in ACT UP, I would use ACT UP to show what was wrong with, or incomplete about, the theory. This approach directed me toward those distinctive components that the literature didn't anticipate or couldn't make sense of—the weird symbol plays, the AIDS-gay inseparability—as well as alerting me to vagueness and slippage in the literature. It directed me, that is, to see the most obvious characteristics and dilemmas of ACT UP as crucial ones rather than dismissible ones; these were the data that the theories should be able to make sense of, and these were the data that would challenge the theories and force revisions in theorizing.

The arrogance, though, however useful in direction, led me to a final obstacle, in presentation: the problem of overstatement. I had tried not only to trip up the theories I was addressing, to point to weaknesses and directions for reconstruction, but to make a positive claim about what was "really new" in new social movements. In fact, my data were not in a position to make such a broad claim. In writing, I could feel myself slipping into rhetorical devices that would assert this bigger claim despite my knowledge that it wasn't justified; it wasn't conscious, though, until a friend pointed it out. Attempting to allow the data to challenge the theory, I wound up distorting, and in some sense betraying, what I knew to be the situation in the field: for example, asserting before revisions that the disputes were over "cultural resources rather than material ones" (when in fact much crucial action is over material resources), or implying that the state is not overly involved in the oppression of PWAs and gays (when in fact it is still very involved). This was to bolster the argument that I was on to something distinctive and new—an overcompensation, perhaps, for the discovery of a problem after months of problemlessness.

FOUR

"Fight the Power":
Two Groups Mobilize for Peace

Josepha Schiffman

It's a rainy San Francisco night, and an affinity group of Bay Area Peace Test (BAPT) is meeting to plan an upcoming act of civil disobedience at the Nevada Test Site. One woman volunteers to facilitate, and the group collectively constructs an agenda. First they deliberate alternative actions, making sure that everyone has a chance to express an opinion. They also discuss how they're going to maintain a sense of community in the Nevada desert, how they will support each other through the various hardships they're likely to encounter: radioactive dust, dehydration, possible police brutality. The meeting ends with an evaluation of the group's process, and finally, holding hands, they sing a freedom song.

At the tranquil conference facilities of Beyond War, another meeting is taking place. About eighty people from all over the country have been discussing the future direction of the organization. Paintings of religious symbols and aphorisms hang next to a large photograph of the Earth and lend an air of solemnity to the gathering. They have spent the weekend reporting on various team projects: seminars on environmentalism, study groups on myth and cosmology, cross-cultural exchanges. At this closing meeting, hosted by the president of Beyond War, people are invited to stand up and individually affirm their commitment to the new heterodox direction the organization is taking.

Bay Area Peace Test (BAPT) and Beyond War are both peace groups. BAPT, a local affiliate of the national American Peace Test, is a coalition that organizes civil disobedience campaigns against nuclear testing and arms production. Beyond War is a national organization dedicated to changing the way people think about war. It sponsors a variety of educational programs and cultural activities. Broadly, both groups share similar goals: eliminating the necessity for war, reducing military arsenals, ending the ecological damage wrought by arms production and testing, and redirecting national resources from military to social programs.

Both groups are also guided by a similar orientation, one they share with other "new social movements" (NSMs). Wary of institutional politics, they neither lobby nor try to secure power for themselves. Instead, both groups focus their activities in the civil arena. They appeal directly to people, encouraging citizen initiatives, networks, and assemblies. Grass-roots organizing is a self-conscious strategy for both, as the process of building community and an alternative sense of identity is in itself considered a countervailing force to militarism.

Yet despite these similarities, there are some striking differences between the two groups, as the opening descriptions clearly underscore. BAPT believes in confrontation, Beyond War in harmony. BAPT engages in direct action, specifically acts of nonviolent civil disobedience. Beyond War purveys ideas, focusing on education, dialogue, and spiritual reflection. BAPT hopes to transform social relationships by creating prefigurative communities. Beyond War works to transform individual consciousness, believing that this will ultimately lead to a new thinking in the society as a whole. Even to hear them talk about one another, one might imagine they belong to entirely different movements. Each group sees the other as misguided. BAPT disdains Beyond War's tactics as elitist and naive; Beyond War thinks BAPT unnecessarily contentious and inflammatory. Neither thinks the other is addressing the root cause of the problem.

The differences between these two groups can best be understood by examining their respective assumptions about power. For BAPT power implies domination or control. In its most overt form, power involves the use of force—the force, for example, that police use to arrest protesters. (And of course even the threat of force can be coercive.) BAPT also identifies a second, more diffuse form of power: domination, which is inherent in the "system." The logic of the "system" and its bureaucratic apparatus, whether state or corporate, intrudes into all aspects of people's lives to control them. They are ruled by everything from test scores to draft status, social security numbers to credit ratings. Finally, BAPT goes even further to argue that domination is latent in all human interactions. Power is exercised in a variety of ways, through social roles, introjects, and norms, through language and semiotic convention. Even custom and procedures can be arenas of power.

Beyond War's conception of power differs sharply. For this group, power is neutral. Like energy, there is nothing inherently abusive about it. The power of the sun, for example, or a magnetic force can be used either constructively or destructively. Certainly power can be abused to dominate others. When people have an atomized sense of themselves, they may marshal this energy to serve their own interests. They may attempt to exercise power *over* others. If, however, people understand that all life is interconnected, that their interests are inextricably linked with the good of the whole, power can lead to cooperation. It becomes simply a life-giving source of creativity. This is expressed as "the power *to*." Power is perceived variously as domination or affiliation depending on one's sense of self and place in the world.

These different notions of power lead to important distinctions between the two groups. Curiously, the literature on "new social movements" undertheorizes the whole dimension of power and so is unable to make useful distinctions between groups within the same movement. "The self-defense of 'society' against the state (and the market economy)," an abandonment of "revolutionary dreams in favor of . . . self-limiting radicalism," and a focus on "forms of communication and collective identity"[1] are seen by theorists as the defining characteristics of NSMs. Nothing is said about new representations of power.

In this chapter I challenge the prevailing understanding of NSMs. By fleshing out two distinct notions of power in BAPT and Beyond War, I show how each leads to entirely different approaches to politics and social change. I trace how different strategies, tactics, and internal organizational structures emerge from each group's assumptions. And finally, assuming these notions of power to be representative of two modal tendencies, I look at the implications this holds generally for theories of NSMs.

ASSUMPTIONS ABOUT POWER IN BAPT AND BEYOND WAR

"BAPT doesn't really exist," I was told by one activist. "It's just a cluster of affinity groups." And indeed BAPT is not an organization in the conventional sense, with an office, letterhead stationery, and dues-paying members. It is a coalition of peace groups, anarchist collectives, and independent activists, loosely affiliated with the national American Peace Test (APT). BAPT participates in direct-action campaigns around the Bay Area, at weapons labs, and at the sites of defense contractors. For the last few years BAPT has also organized the Bay Area's participation in civil resistance at the Nevada Test Site. BAPT handles local publicity for the actions, including outreach to schools, churches, and community groups, and raises funds to subsidize those who want to travel to the test site but can't afford to go. BAPT also coordinates transportation from the Bay Area to Nevada and conducts training in nonviolent resistance as well in the legal and political ramifications of civil disobedience.

The group is almost exclusively white. The "hard core," those who do most of the organizing, have rejected their predominantly middle-class backgrounds for the life of full-time activists. They support themselves by taking on a variety of part-time, often menial jobs. Those who participate in the actions are mostly of the new middle class, with professional or paraprofessional jobs (medical technicians, union organizers, writers, students). There is a fairly equal mix of men and women.

At BAPT, *power* has extremely negative connotations. In the words of one activist, "I'm scared of power—all the ways people use power over you. It's power that's gotten us into the trouble we're in." It matters little which particular class or system of authority is pulling the levers. Power in itself is something to be feared because it implies a relationship of domination. BAPT recognizes three different forms of power. Firstly, power is coercion, whether force is actually used or, as is more often the case, there is an implied threat of force. Secondly, power is reflected in the state and the market's often invisible encroachment into civil society. And finally, power manifests itself in the myriad "micro" contexts of everyday life.

The most straightforward form of power, BAPT believes, is the power the state wields over its citizens, which despite the appearance of democratic restraints in this country goes increasingly unchecked. The state has unprecedented coercive force at its disposal, though it is rarely marshaled against the civilian population directly. Yet when individuals or groups challenge the state's authority, even in something as benign as a church sanctuary program, they experience the brunt of that force. The state puts them under surveillance and arrests and prosecutes them.

BAPT points to a second form of power: the encroachment of the state and marketplace into all aspects of life. The more the logic of the marketplace and state bureaucracy inserts itself into all arenas of society, the more we see the breakdown of important civil institutions. When all human interactions are mediated by bureaucratic regulations, people lose the ability to deal directly with one another. Thus bureaucratic mediation undermines the ability of communities to regulate their own affairs and forces them into an ever-greater dependence on the state. If a weapons plant jeopardizes the health of the community, for example, local residents, rather than organize to shut down the plant, are just as likely to rely on another state agency to mediate, either state government, or the Environmental Protection Agency, or perhaps even the Occupational Safety and Health Administration. This estrangement of people from one another and from their ability to determine the conditions of their own lives represents a more insidious and possibly more dangerous exercise of power than coercion, BAPT contends.

BAPT argues, however, that our government is not necessarily more malign or our corporate managers more pernicious than elsewhere. Large bureaucratic structures simply invite the abuse of power because of their centralized character. But even if we could do away with these institutions of authority, domination would not disappear, for they are only the most explicit manifestation of power. Power relations and domination exist also in the myriad interactions of everyday life. They creep into all relationships, even the most seemingly benign: between parents and children, between lovers, or between members of the same peace group. Power is exercised when we are forced to conform to particular roles. It is woven into our work routines, into our values, even into our language. In some ways, BAPT feels, we must be even more vigilant about power relations in these "micro" contexts because they are much less explicit and therefore easier to miss. But they are just as dangerous.

Beyond War is a distinctly different organization. Formed in 1982, it emerged out of Creative Initiative, a nonprofit foundation offering workshops in personal growth and communications skills. A group of people affiliated with the organization were so awed by the magnitude of the nuclear threat that they pledged to dedicate themselves to the eradication of war. Beyond War has grown considerably since that time; it is difficult to estimate the number of people associated with the group, because it is not a membership organization. Circulation figures for their newsletter, however, suggest that approximately 10,000 people may be currently involved.

Like BAPT, Beyond War is also predominantly white. Many couples are involved in the organization, with one partner working (usually at a professional job) and the other volunteering on a full-time basis at Beyond War. The full-time volunteers (both men and women) have often given up lucrative professional careers to devote themselves exclusively to Beyond War organizing.

The group undertakes a variety of consciousness-changing projects. It develops educational television and radio programs, conducts seminars, and disseminates literature. It also sponsors a host of cross-cultural events, including art exhibits and musical performances, international satellite conferences, and individual acts of citizen diplomacy.

Now that the nuclear threat no longer seems to generate the same sense of urgency it once did, Beyond War is reassessing its mission. Many at Beyond War find themselves concerned about other social problems, including homelessness, drug abuse, and the degradation of the environment. It is possible that a new organization will emerge with this new set of priorities, but the national office seems unperturbed. Beyond War considers itself a social movement rather than an organization, and if the movement should take on a new form, so be it.

Unlike BAPT, people at Beyond War are not at all wary of power. They feel that power is a neutral force and can assume different forms. "Power over" describes a posture of domination and control, but "power to" is a relationship of wholeness, of connection with all life. This power emanates from the life force, from the creative energy that is latent in everyone and everything. The challenge is to move from the first system of power to the second, from domination to affiliation.

The notion that *power* necessarily implies power over another, its association with institutions of authority and even with force, is misguided, according to Beyond War. It is only possible to have power over others when you deny any affinity with them, when you turn them into something wholly other. "This," in the words of a Beyond War volunteer, "describes the Hobbesian universe which we have inhabited," in which life is a struggle of each against all. Individuals pit themselves against the alien outsider, zealots against the infidel, righteous nation against an evil empire. To the extent that we identify ourselves in these limited ways, we also define our interests in correspondingly limited terms and find enemies all around—people we need to subdue or prevent from trying to subdue us.

But Beyond War members are confident that if people develop a sense of identity that reaches beyond the members of their immediate group—clan, religion, race, geographic region—and includes all life, then the notion of power over others will simply melt away, and all people will be able to enjoy the power to. As we come to recognize the unity of all life (that "we are one") we understand that the well-being of each person or group is inextricably linked to the welfare of everyone else. We come to redefine our interests in terms of what benefits the whole. The image of an organism is an apt metaphor for social relationships. We see that all life on the planet is interwoven, that we are all part of an integrated living system: a single breathing organism in which each diverse part has its own unique function.

When we recognize ourselves as part of this undifferentiated whole, Beyond War members believe, we realize that relationships of domination are unadaptive, even absurd. This spiritual insight makes political power virtually irrelevant. We need look no further than the relationship between mother and child to find a poignant example of the power to. As one Beyond War volunteer pointed out, "a mother would never use her power to dominate her child. She is profoundly connected to him. She uses her power to nurture him." This kind of connectedness becomes the prototype for all relationships in the human family.

Whether we constitute power relations as power over or power to depends on how broadly we define ourselves and our interests, according to Beyond War. There is nothing about power itself, nor anything in us as humans—greed, irrationality, or simply the will to dominate— that is inherently corrupting. Our perceptions are at the root of power dynamics, and we can shift from one system of power to the other with a gestalt switch.

STRATEGIES AND TACTICS

At one of the BAPT outreach meetings, a young man asked what the protesters hoped to accomplish in Nevada. A woman who was returning to the test site for the second time replied, "It helps make their power visible." This oblique reference to the state highlights an important objective of the test site actions: to make the exercise of state power explicit. When ordinary citizens protest government policies, albeit nonviolently, they come up against the full power of the state. Even during a training session in which arrests were simulated, one of the participants confessed that she felt devastated: "There was something really frightening about this kind of confrontation with the police." And another responded, "I grew up in the suburbs. We'd say, 'There goes Joe, our friendly neighborhood policeman.' Now when I see a policeman, I don't trust him, or anything he represents. I'm not sure what I trust." When people are arrested, imprisoned, sometimes even brutalized, the inherently adversarial nature of our relationship to the state and the coercive nature of state power become palpable, BAPT argues. The state tries to position itself as social guardian, defending us from enemies abroad and "anarchy" at home. But being arrested for expressing political dissent forces one to look at whose interests the state actually serves.

BAPT encourages people to confront this power nonviolently by refusing to acknowledge the state's legitimacy when it behaves coercively. The means of confrontation include passively resisting arrest and refusing to be processed through the penal system (not giving one's name, refusing to post bail, not cooperating in jail). The way to confront the coercive power of the state is to simply "withhold our cooperation from those who abuse power."

The thought of fighting state power on its own terms may seem sisyphean, inexorably frustrating and compromised. After all, the apparatus is so gargantuan, the control it exercises often so mediated, where does one begin? But in the Nevada desert—stark, barren, sixty miles from civilization—the conflict is put into sharp relief. The struggle is over land. Who controls it? Who, if anyone, owns it? In the geography of contemporary protest, the test site has become a fault line between the state and society.

The protests in Nevada are an effort to "reclaim the land" from state control. This land was granted to the Western Shoshone Nation as early as 1863, but after a century of federal maneuvering, various state agencies now control it without having renegotiated the original agreement. The Department of Energy exercises jurisdiction over the test site itself, a piece of land about the size of Rhode Island. The Bureau of Land Management administers the surrounding land.

The protesters deny the state's jurisdiction over this land. As one BAPT member stated, "the line there is a line they have drawn." It is an imaginary line, and "it's important to cross it." The peace camp is pitched on one side of this arbitrary line, and representatives of the state are poised on the other side, ready to defend the boundary.

The state stakes out the land quite clearly, with barbed-wire fences, cattle guards, and holding pens for protesters, but activists find many different ways of crossing the boundary. During the April 1989 actions, over 1,500 people "trespassed" onto DOE land (and were arrested). Most who crossed onto the test site brought visitor permits from the Shoshone, underscoring the latter's continuing claim to the land. Activists staged blockades of the road leading to the test site. They tied masks or wove patterns into the fence. And over a hundred people risked both exposure to radiation and long prison terms by launching incursions several miles into the test site. One woman hiked fifty miles to the control point with two others, put up a banner that read "Food Not Bombs," and chained herself to the complex.

Pushing back against overt state power is only one target of the Nevada actions, however. BAPT talks about the struggle against a more covert and insidious form of power: the intrusion of the "system" into all domains of life. Just as the capitalist economy attempts to put a consumer product between every itch and scratch, bureaucratic logic inserts a regulation into every human interaction. Nothing is more harmful to a sense of community. People become insulated from one another. They grow used to having all their relationships mediated, by licenses and contracts, laws and procedures. They even come to believe that state mediation is the only way their interests will be served. People are out for themselves, following this logic, but the state is there to protect us.

The antidote to this alienation from one another is community. Indeed, according to BAPT, the test site actions are "as much to show we are a community as to fight nuclear testing." It is a way to rebuild bonds between people in a system that is designed to make the individual feel weak and alone. While the government conducts its nuclear tests in Nevada, BAPT is conducting its own tests—peace tests—which are experiments in self-organizing and self-determining community.

At the peace camp, participation in all work—the provision of food and water, cleanup and recycling, medical care, and transportation—is voluntary. People are asked simply to contribute whatever they can. In the words of one activist, "You take what you need, give what you can. . . . What happens: strangers become friends, friends become family, family becomes community! . . . That's a movement."

Through both work and play the spirit of community is rekindled. The camp reverberates with music and singing. People dance into the night. They stage solemn processions, comic theater, and impromptu ceremonies. They construct giant weavings, create sculptures and masks, or paint murals. It may seem vaguely quixotic to deploy balloons and banners against the might of nuclear weapons, but peace campers believe that one can confront the massively destructive power of these weapons only by undermining the system that produces them. They affirm community in the face of alienation, life in the face of death, dignity in the face of barbarism.

In contrast, Beyond War tends to ignore the realm of politics altogether and focuses instead on changing the way people think. For members, consciousness is the basis of social change. Peace is only possible, for example, when there is a consensus about certain values, chief among them the unity of life. But the strategy is not strictly educational, even though the group refers to itself as an educational foundation, because abstract knowledge is not enough. Social change also involves a decision to live one's life differently. It requires a profound personal transformation that verges on the spiritual. Thus it is not surprising that there is a decidedly gnostic cast to the organization's beliefs and practices.[2] And it also makes sense that its strategy follows a basically religious model, a tripartite process of conversion, living testament, and proselytizing.

First comes the conversion process. Because the roots of war are embedded in a particular world view, change can occur only with a "paradigm shift" to a new perceptual framework. Thus Beyond War works to bring about a transformation of consciousness by exposing people to a new way of thinking. It offers a series of workshops, beginning with the "interest evening." Here speakers introduce the Beyond War principles, the most important of which is the "perennial principle: I am one. We are one. All is one".[3] Not merely an ontological statement, this principle is a revelation, a "mystical memory of the garden of harmony, the primal unity of all life." Of course spiritual insight alone is insufficient. Knowledge must be accompanied by decision, a decision to live one's life differently. This is a profound commitment, and therefore should not be entered into lightly.[4]

But knowledge and decision must ultimately be converted into action if they are to lead to social change. People's lives must become a testament to the Beyond War principles and, like any spiritual discipline, the practice of making one's actions congruent with beliefs becomes a consuming project. Beyond War helps people in this process by offering "implications seminars." Members are given the opportunity to reflect on the personal ramifications of the Beyond War principles. What does it mean, for example, to resolve conflict without using violence? How can people learn to live without enemies, without casting adversaries in the role of the other? How can people work together with others to build a world beyond war? And most important, how can individuals translate the principle "we are one" into daily practice?[5]

If the organization is to usher in a world without war, this shift in consciousness must occur on a broad scale. Therefore, individuals must work together to proselytize, to spread the truth that "we are one." They must work to build "agreement" about the new mode of thinking. As one Beyond War member put it, "we are committed to something great, and then spreading it." Volunteers are extremely dedicated and resourceful in doing this. In 1984, for example, seventeen families pulled up roots in the Bay Area and moved to strategically selected states around the country, much in the same way missionaries might do, to spread the word. Small house meetings, seminars, convocations, and various journalistic media are all used to get the word out. The goal is not to aggrandize the organization, but rather to build consensus about the Beyond War principles. A member from the Pacific Northwest stated succinctly, "We're not trying to build an organization, but to purvey an idea. After all, organizations come and go, but ideas live forever."

The importance of ideas in this movement is patently clear. Peace is directly related to consciousness. Beyond War works to develop a critical mass of people who embrace the new mode of thinking because, it believes, this is the surest way to eliminate war. Drawing on marketing research, it has concluded that 50 percent of the population must be exposed to the Beyond War principles for them to be accepted by 5 percent. But with a mere 5 percent, the new mode of thinking will be "embedded" in the culture, and with 20 percent it will have become "unstoppable." Thus, the dissemination of these ideas is the most important thing people can do to end war. And with Gorbachev's "new thinking" the foundation of so many of the changes in the world, Beyond War believes it is right on track.

INTERNAL ORGANIZATION

For BAPT, concern about power is a major influence on how it organizes internally. Personal empowerment is not just a movement shib-
boleth, not simply an effective strategy for organizing: "Reclaiming a
sense of personal power is a major goal of the actions." It is an essential
feature of BAPT's politics, integral to the elimination of nuclear weapons. In contemporary society, BAPT contends, "we see masses of people kept and keeping themselves uninformed and powerless." A def-
erence for authority is evident throughout our culture—in hospitals, in
schools, in the workplace, and especially in the defense establishment.
BAPT believes that the direct opposition to nuclear weapons is only
part of the struggle. It is equally important, it argues, to oppose the
kind of authority relations that make nuclearism possible. Wherever
experts, elites, hierarchies, or classes emerge, they must be fought. Not
surprisingly, then, BAPT tries to be scrupulous about decentralizing
power within the organization.

The lack of formal structure within BAPT is designed to encourage
the direct participation of all members. The basic organizational unit is
the affinity group. These groups emerge out of neighborhood, workplace, or political affiliations. Comprising anywhere between five and
twenty people, they are a decentralized base of operations for planning
and carrying out acts of civil disobedience, and are also intended to be
a source of community and support for activists. Sometimes affinity
groups must select an individual to represent them, but whenever possible, direct democratic participation is preferred.

Affinity groups are based on the principle of sharing power equally
among all members. Usually, a consensus process is used at meetings
and is seen as a way to elicit contributions from all group members so
that "everyone has power over what happens and the group is able to
come to an agreement that everyone can live with." It is considered by
many at BAPT the principal means of empowering individuals. (Personal empowerment does not necessarily imply harmony, however;
conflict often arises not only over substantive issues but, ironically, over
the best process for empowering the group.)

There are no formal leaders at BAPT, "no mimicking of the establishment hierarchy." Each group has several roles, which rotate: usually
a facilitator, a note taker, a timekeeper, and a "vibes watcher"—
someone who monitors the emotional state of the group. The facilitator
guides the group, and so potentially has more power than the others.
But facilitation is supposed to be nondirective, and everyone is encouraged to take responsibility for monitoring the group's process. Facili-

tators are frequently interrupted with process suggestions and reminders.

Like any other organization, BAPT needs writers, public speakers, and people who can conduct training or act as media liaisons. While some of these areas demand particular skills or experience, the group tries to be sensitive to the need for transferring skills as quickly as possible, so that power doesn't begin to congeal in the hands of a few dedicated activists. Every effort is made to enable all group members to perform different functions, and because roles are rotated, members seem to have little ego investment in their positions. This was demonstrated rather forcefully on the eve of a mass action in Nevada, during a particularly tense planning meeting. A BAPT activist thought that they were getting bogged down and suggested that the facilitator allow someone to take his place. He stood aside gracefully, and a woman stepped in. If his pride was bruised by this encounter, he did not show it.

Of course this self-reflexivity about power can reach the point of infinite regress. The group can become so meticulous that it creates a new "process elite" and can virtually paralyze itself when concern about the process of mobilization takes on a greater significance than the action itself.[6]

Beyond War, on the other hand, is relatively unreflexive about power relations within the organization. Members believe that abuses of power are a result of perceptual distortions, a failure to recognize that we are all one. They assume that once people experience the unity of all life, a profound sense of connectedness replaces any impulse toward domination, and the notion of power over becomes essentially irrelevant. Ironically, the emphasis on unity tends to obscure power dynamics within the organization and leaves Beyond War quite vulnerable to internal forms of domination and control.

Ostensibly Beyond War promotes a decentralization of power. It argues, for example, that "the individual is determinative," that each person must take the initiative to make peace happen. And of course, the notion that "we are one" implies we are all equal. But, in fact, the internal dynamics at Beyond War seem to engender conformity rather than personal empowerment. Conformity is generated in two ways. Firstly, all the activities of the organization are tightly managed, but it is unclear by whom because the hierarchy is invisible and thus difficult to challenge.

For example, who is chosen as a delegate to the USSR, who will speak at a particular convocation, who is invited to the Beyond War award ceremony—it is unclear exactly how these and many other decisions are made. It seems to be Beyond War strategy to recruit well-educated, successful, and financially secure individuals—those who can influence "opinion leaders." How was that strategy arrived at, and can it be challenged? There is a policy of incrementally dispensing information about the new mode of thinking. Who determines what knowledge is a prerequisite for the more intense weekend seminars? These decisions are not made consensually or through an open forum, but seem to be made behind the scenes and then handed down to the organization.

Even the workshops and meetings are highly controlled. Only approved Beyond War materials are used. Agendas are tightly structured.[7] New facilitators are paired with veteran members, who oversee the proceedings and generally ensure that things are on the right track. And the conference facilities are governed by a rigid set of rules. Even informal gatherings are subject to tacit codes of behavior. For example, when a participant brought a jug of wine to an evening pot-luck meeting, she was ushered into the kitchen and informed, with some embarrassment, that "we don't drink at Beyond War," even though individually most of the people in the room had no such prohibition against alcohol.

A second way the internal dynamics generate conformity is the "new mode of thinking." It takes on the character of a credo, which people adopt somewhat unquestioningly, and there is little tolerance for dissent.

The new mode of thinking requires a leap of faith, a kind of surrender. The decision to adopt this arcane knowledge comes first, with a promise that deeper understanding will come later. Individuals cannot embrace this new world view until they have cut completely with the past. Old identities, ideas and beliefs, ties to family, ethnicity, or religion are all entrapments, things that bind them to the "old mode of thinking" and prevent them from identifying with the "Truth." They must first shed the past and make a total commitment to a new identity based on unity and the good of the "whole." They can then work out the subtleties of this new world view in workshops and seminars.

But the "new mode of thinking" tends to reduce complex social phenomena like war or slavery to simple formulas, and there is little room for alternative explanations. For example, when someone in a workshop came up with a materialist interpretation of war, the facilitator responded with, "That's an interesting concept. Perhaps you could hold that thought. We're going to get to it later," but the topic was never mentioned again. It is apparent that members are not supposed to challenge Beyond War tenets, that they are to have only positive thoughts about the group, its leaders, and its ideas.

Former Beyond War volunteers report that when they felt skeptical about something, it seemed like heresy. They assumed that the problem lay with them. Perhaps they had failed to grasp some essential principle or were insufficiently committed to the movement. If they actually expressed their doubts to others, they usually encountered overt resistance. Challenges tend to be met with rationalizations: "Yes, when I found out that the Beyond War award went to Reagan and Gorbachev, I was shocked too. But. . . ." If the challenge poses a threat to internal authority, it is often met with a Beyond War slogan, such as "You've got to trust the process" or "You seem to be preoccupying yourself with an enemy here." Doubters sometimes even experience stony hostility. One man wouldn't talk to me or even make eye contact after I challenged something he said.

But perhaps harder than explicit resistance is the internalized sense of guilt dissenters feel. If one accepts the premise that individual well-being is linked to the good of the whole, it seems unconscionable to block the progress of the group, particularly a group with such a lofty goal as world peace. Disagreement seems like an act of hubris, a demonstration of individualistic "old thinking." And so Beyond War volunteers suspend their own judgments in favor of the Beyond War principles, they trust the process, and subject their own power to the power of the group.

Nowhere has this been more clearly evinced than with the recent shifts in the organization's focus. The United States hasn't dismantled a single warhead since Beyond War was founded, and yet the board issued a statement in December 1988 declaring that its goals had largely been met. Eighty Beyond War volunteers from around the country concurred unflinchingly that the move away from the nuclear issue was appropriate, that the "discovery" process to arrive at new organizational objectives was healthy, and that the organization was "right where we need to be." Beyond War's very reason for being was being questioned by the leadership, and yet there was not one dissenting voice.[8]

POWER AND THE PEACE MOVEMENT

How is it that theories of new social movements (NSMs) cannot account for these important differences between BAPT and Beyond War? I believe it is because they ignore the key concept for making sense of these differences: orientations to power. Instead, they tend to distinguish between groups on the basis of their "modern" or "antimodern" tendencies. This framework leads them to conflate groups as diverse as BAPT and Beyond War (both would be considered "antimodern"), and it also prompts them to disapprove of groups that they perceive have an "antimodern" or "fundamentalist" strain.

Fundamentalist groups reject modernity, these theorists believe, and instead want to recreate some kind of bygone halcyon era; thus they are open to charges of romanticism and regressive utopianism. In their tacit dialogue with Marxism, NSM theorists want to defend movements against such charges and so focus most of their attention on "modern" groups.

Many NSMs take modernity as given, the theory suggests. These groups do not want to turn back the clock but to preserve and advance those aspects of the enlightenment tradition that are positive, while challenging those that are not. Andrew Arato and Jean Cohen argue, for example, that for many groups, "it is not cultural modernity, per se, but its selective institutionalization and resulting cultural impoverishment that is problematic."[9] Jürgen Habermas also cautions that the increasing complexity of modern life is not *inherently* pathological, only those features that contribute to the rationalization of the lifeworld.[10] Movements must be able to distinguish between the two.

Although most civic institutions—schools, the media, unions, political parties—have become seriously compromised, they still contain an emancipatory potential.[11] The effective "modern" NSMs are able to recognize the dual capacities of these civic forums and to protect and even extend them. Even further, these groups take an offensive role, attempting to reform economic and political systems from within civil society. Cohen argues that it is important for NSMs to counter the fundamentalist tendency to completely disengage from the political process.[12]

From the perspective of these theorists, a peace group like SANE/Freeze would be the prototypical NSM. This group organizes in civil society. Canvassers go door-to-door attempting to engage people in peace issues. They use journalistic media to educate and mobilize. They encourage citizens to become involved in the debate around defense by organizing large assemblies and conferences. But they also attempt to reform political institutions through the initiative process and extensive lobbying. In fact, they are primarily a political pressure group.

On the one hand, this "modern"-"antimodern" distinction makes sense in light of the problems the U.S. peace movement faces. After all, what is the best way to confront the threat of global annihilation and ecocide, problems of such stunning magnitude? It is reasonable to have some tangible goals—to try to redirect U.S. defense policy and to nudge the economy toward civilian production. The impetus may come from within civil society, through citizen initiatives, mass rallies, and referendums, and for these to be successful, the movement may have to reinvigorate some foundering civic institutions. But if the peace movement is to be successful it must place pressure on the institutions that perpetuate militarism, something "antimodern" groups are unwilling to do.

It is important to recognize, however, that many supposedly "antimodern" groups like BAPT and Beyond War view "nuclearism" as an outcome and not really the crux of what they struggle against. They believe that a system of power is at the heart of the problem, a particularly modern or even postmodern system of power that makes "nuclearism" possible. Consequently, they do not simply fight militarism in its various manifestations. In the words of the popular rap song, they "fight the power."

To be sure, this concern with power is not solely the province of the peace movement or even of political actors, for that matter. Intellectual and artistic currents have converged with the political on the central significance of power. Virtually every intellectual enterprise has been touched by this reconceptualization of power, and while Foucault is the avatar, the theme has been taken up by many others. The project is very much embedded in the historical moment.

Part of this project involves identifying the locus of power and how it works, which is difficult to pin down. There is something irreducible about power. It is not only vested in institutions, in the state apparatus and the marketplace; it is much more ubiquitous. It exerts itself in internalized values and beliefs; it is woven into language; it is manifest in rules and customs and procedures.

At first glance it may seem that the peace movement is operating within a more monolithic framework of power. It may seem that a leader with a finger on the button represents the apotheosis of premodern sovereign authority. But in fact it is not experienced that way. People have a diffused sense of this power. They tend to remove "a human hand from the trigger" and instead think of "the bomb" as an all-powerful force unto itself. It is not a particular individual or party that is responsible, but a labyrinthine system in which human actors are caught up. The power becomes internalized as a vague sense of hopelessness and fatalism in the face of an arbitrary holocaust.[13]

Power is structured into the discourse on defense. Who is permitted to speak and what are they permitted to speak about? (The logic of deterrence is never questioned, for example.) Even the timbre is preestablished. "Rational" value-free language sets the tenor, which serves to sanitize the violence being considered and to purge, in the words of a consultant to the Department of Defense, the "influence of 'guilty'

scientists and 'religious, political-theoretical, and frankly emotional premises.' "[14] In other words, it removes any moral reasoning from a discussion of defense.

Power is also manifest in the social values that sanction violence,
which fetishize technology and a mastery of nature. In short, the postmodern system of power is not something that can be understood in
reified terms. It is not found only in structures and institutions. It is not
even always strictly coercive. Rather, it is ubiquitous, multiplex, and
circuitous. It is something that seeps into every corner of people's lives.

With this in mind, BAPT and Beyond War's strategies seem less like
a fundamentalist or "antimodern" search for a lost Arcadia, and more
like a postmodern concern with the multiple layers of power. Interestingly, despite its centrality within other theoretical frameworks, the
complexities of power are largely ignored in the NSM literature.

Arato and Cohen, for example, in their recapitulation of Habermas's
theory of communicative action, argue implicitly for a unidimensional
conception of power: the power of the "system." The "system colonizes
the lifeworld" through the media of political power and money. (The
very metaphor of colonization smacks of traditional sovereign notions
of power.) Even if civic life has become partially corrupted by the incursion of system power, it nevertheless still contains an immanent
emancipatory potential, which can be approached through the revital-
ization of institutions in civil society. Presumably then there are inter-
stices, arenas of civil society, that are exempt from considerations of
power.[15]

Touraine understands the character of modern or "postmodern"
power better than the other NSM theorists. He argues, for example,
that "individuals, and groups [are] being confined in thicker and
thicker networks of signals, rules, and interdictions" that are virtually
inescapable, and yet he too sees the dual nature of these forms, and the
possibility that people can free themselves "from the constraints of order, or, most often, of using them to [their] own advantage."[16]

The "modern"-"antimodern" framework of these theorists obscures
an essential feature of the NSM project—a concern with power—and
also obscures important distinctions between groups within the same
movement.

CONCLUSION

BAPT and Beyond War both attempt to confront the system of power
that underlies "nuclearism," and both challenge traditional understandings of what that system entails, but, as we have seen, they do so in
fundamentally different ways. They have divergent assumptions about

the specific nature of this power and are therefore drawn to different forms of mobilization.

For BAPT, power is negative. It always implies domination. It may involve outright coercion or it may be an unintended consequence of bureaucratic control. Most significantly, it can insert itself into any relationship—no interaction is exempt. Like a spider's web in which we are all trapped, there is something ineluctable and pervasive about it. The best we can do is be constantly vigilant to guard against any emerging encrustations.

Beyond War, on the other hand, sees nothing inherently malign about power. In fact, members believe that it has a constructive potential. But the prerequisite for the nonexploitive exercise of power is a moral consensus about human interdependence. People must share a sense that we do not exist each against all, but rather each for all.

Does this antinomy of power have any relevance for other NSMs? I believe it does. It is probably most fruitful to think of it, not in terms of rigid categories, but as ideal types. Then we can begin to trace the same modal tendencies in other contemporary U.S. movements.

Consider, for example, the environmental movement. We find, on the one hand, the militant environmental group Earth First! Like BAPT, its members are suspicious of power, and specifically the modern industrial system of power. They also engage in civil disobedience, including what they call ecotage or monkeywrenching. And like BAPT, they are careful not to reproduce the same power relations they are attempting to subvert.

Contrast this with the Northern California Green Alliance. For this group, like Beyond War, the root cause of contemporary enviromental problems is a particular perceptual framework. Fritjof Capra, author of a book on Green politics and active in the Bay Area Green movement, argues that a "self-assertive value system" is the basis for the world's major problems. For the Green Alliance, politics begins with the recognition that every aspect of life is interconnected. Understandably then, the Greens focus much of their activity on public education, on changing the way people think about the world and their place in it. They sponsor lectures and discussion groups on spirituality and Green theory; they plan Earth Day events and solstice rituals.

The same polarity is evident in the women's movement. Take, for example, a group like BACOR (Bay Area Coalition against Operation Rescue). It is one of the many groups around the country that have sprung up in defense of abortion rights. Like BAPT they regard power as domination or control, and they see it as similarly ubiquitous. The patriarchal system of power is exercised through political, legal, and religious institutions. (It is, of course, the Supreme Court that handed down the *Webster* decision.) But BACOR believes patriarchal power also manifests itself in less overt ways, in the "right to life" discourse, even in the fact that men presume jurisdiction over women's bodies. Because patriarchy is so pervasive, BACOR has little faith in the political process as a way to ensure that women maintain control over their lives. It relies on direct action. It organizes demonstrations, protest rallies, and boycotts. It faces confrontation and arrest to keep abortion clinics open and defend clients from harassment. And though members don't follow strict consensus process, like BAPT, they tend to be reflexive about the internal politics of the organization.

The profusion of women's spirituality groups stands in sharp contrast to more militant organizations like BACOR. Small and informal, they are reminiscent of the consciousness-raising groups of the 1970s. Like Beyond War, they conceive of power as a neutral energy, a *power within* or *power to*. By learning to channel this energy, these women believe, they "transform inner foes into allies." They begin to heal themselves and their relationships with others, and from that point they can begin to heal some of the world's ills. Like Beyond War, they believe that personal transformation is the basis for social change. They teach a female-centered spirituality, one based on harmony with nature, wholeness, and integration. They study women's history ("herstory"), learn to practice women's arts like herbology, midwifery, and healing, and they study myth and ritual.

Beyond War probably has more in common with these women's spirituality groups or with the Northern California Green Alliance than it does with BAPT. And correspondingly, when BAPT talks about "the movement," it is often referring to organizations like BACOR or militant environmental groups rather than other peace groups like Beyond War. Movements are defined as much by their assumptions about power as by an issue like peace or feminism. Power is probably the central category for understanding NSMs. It enables us to distinguish NSMs from movements, like labor, that have more traditional understandings of power relations. It is therefore crucial in determining what is distinctively new about "new" social movements. It also permits a more nuanced articulation of the differences within those social movements that have been classified as "new" and have been previously viewed as homogeneous.

AFTERWORD: THERE'S MADNESS IN OUR METHOD

My introduction to participant observation was Alison Lurie's novel *Imaginary Friends*. The book tells the story of two sociologists from upstate New York who undertake the study of a rather bizarre cult. One of them winds up falling in love with the high priestess of the group, and the other gets so carried away with the role he is playing that he eventually comes to believe he is Ro of the planet Varna, and descends into madness. With this vivid image of how *not* to do research implanted in my brain, I thought I'd be somewhat fortified against the vagaries of doing field research. This was naive.

In the course of doing participant observation, I slid into my own insanity. I came to feel like Eve—the one with the three faces. I was doing research at three different field sites and I developed a separate identity at each one. I was simultaneously trying to keep a grip on my identity as a researcher. And I even hoped that there would be some small piece of me left over to maintain a private self. I quickly abandoned the latter as hopelessly delusional and concentrated instead on juggling the alter egos.

Initially I had one site and one role: I worked at SANE/Freeze and I defined myself primarily as a researcher. Life was easy in those days. I simply observed everything. Even when nothing was happening, I'd do things like draw floor plans, document the different kinds of herbal teas, or note the health of office plants.

But my data prompted me to redefine my project, and I went from working in one field site to three. (SANE/Freeze had formed a coalition with BAPT, and for purposes of comparison I felt it necessary to add Beyond War to my study.) This made things more complicated, but I still defined myself primarily as a researcher at that time, so my main tasks, as I saw it, were to observe and to "belong."

I did my best to install myself in the three organizations. I worked at two of them doing things like organizing information evenings and fundraisers. At all three, I attended countless meetings, briefings, seminars. I also hung out, went for walks, drank coffee, and even drank beer for the sake of my research. At first, I was a conscious dissembler. I molded myself to fit in, and usually I played the role of being a group member rather convincingly, but part of me was always vigilant for juicy material, something that would look good in my field notes.

As I spent more time at each field site, however, by degrees I actually became the roles I was playing. They took on a life of their own. I was caught up in the web of relationships, in the everyday dramas of each group. I felt like I had a stake in what happened at each organization. I found it difficult, if not impossible, to work next to people without forming attachments, without beginning to care about them as individuals and without having them make some personal demands on me. And oddly, even though I spent less time in all three organizations than I would have spent at an ordinary 9-to-5 job, I became obsessed. I lived, breathed, even dreamt about my field sites.

Moving between different groups engendered a kind of dislocated personality. My identity kept shifting, and I found myself seeing things differently depending on which organizational perspective I brought to the experience. To compound the disorientation, my eyes as a researcher saw things differently than as a group member. I experienced a gestalt switch every two minutes.

It happened gradually and imperceptibly, but one day I realized that I had begun to feel more distant from one group, and at the same time I had become completely enmeshed in the other two. Beyond War proved to be a difficult field site for me. They seemed to want not only my time and commitment but my soul. It was an organization of believers and consequently a bit clubby. It was frequently painful to be there. I felt like an infidel, an outsider.

Both SANE/Freeze and BAPT, on the other hand, were open organizations, eager for people's participation. I slipped comfortably into the role of insider. The SANE/Freeze staff invited me to become a board member. People at BAPT expressed confidence that I could hold down the fort in San Francisco while most of them went to Nevada to begin the action. And not only did these groups trust me, but I had become incrementally committed to them. Little things gave it away, like the fantasies I had of abandoning academia and running away to join the ranks of the peace army, or the responsibility I felt for SANE/Freeze's financial solvency.

I was both gratified and terrified by my status in these groups. I felt I was in danger of becoming so firmly ensconced in these organizations that I would lose touch with my identity as a researcher. I was being pulled in too many directions. But at least there was one advantage to this identity crisis: it helped my research. The role I assumed in each organization, how people responded to me, the kinds of personal relationships and loyalties I formed, how I was integrated into the group—all this gave me invaluable information about these organizations.

Fortunately, I was able to get a bit of distance at the Nevada Test Site. It wasn't deliberate; it just seemed to happen. Most BAPTers were ecstatic at the beauty of the desert. I, on the other hand, was none too fond of the radioactive dust and the cactus thorns that pierced my shoes. Moreover, the prospect of being handcuffed and held in a pen under a sweltering 100-degree sun for eight hours, without water or latrine, seemed like undue physical hardship. I reproached myself with the memory of all those researchers who troop off to face unknown dangers in hostile field sites. But as I was throwing up in a cheap Las Vegas motel (accommodations my fellow protesters disdained as far too cushy) from drinking contaminated water, I resolved that my next participant observation project would be studying the leisure habits of the very wealthy. Perhaps, despite all these multiple identities, there was an essential self after all, someone with a predilection for comfort. I knew then that I had reached a turning point.

My disenchantment with the rigors of being a peace activist coincided with an impending deadline to complete my research. I now had more than enough data. I knew I should begin to pull back from the field and devote more attention to writing. But how? How could I extricate myself gracefully? I was committed to these organizations; I had become part of them and I didn't want to abandon the cause. It was, after all, my interest in the peace movement that had led me to study these groups in the first place. I felt torn, like a rider in one of those westerns, straddling two galloping horses, hoping desperately that I wouldn't fall and break my neck.

As it happens, I hurt my back instead, and this furnished me with an immediate reason to leave the field—not the graceful exit I had hoped for, but it did give me time to focus on writing. I still had multiple perspectives, however, which I struggled to integrate into a coherent picture. These competing visions still haunted me even once I had left the field. What, for example, was the most reasonable way to mobilize for peace? Did it make sense to lobby, to resist, or to educate? Could the three different approaches be reconciled? During moments of clarity, I could hold all three groups in my mind simultaneously and see them in a larger framework, but often the picture would dissolve again into competing perspectives.

Of all the difficult things that occurred in the course of my field work—abandoning my original project, having to entirely reconceive what I was doing, expanding from one to three field sites—nothing was more disconcerting than moving continually from one identity to another. It's difficult enough with one field site to shift back and forth from the researcher role to participant. Multiple field sites can drive you crazy. It was a wrenching experience, and one for which I was totally unprepared. I had always thought of research as an active process. I never anticipated how much I would be affected personally by the experience of doing participant observation.

PART TWO

Reorganizing the Workplace

Introduction to Part 2

The following two chapters analyze workplaces at opposite ends of the organizational spectrum—a state bureaucracy and a collective bakery. In the Mandana County Welfare Department, regulations and job classifications order the workplace, while at Wholly Grains Bakery there are a minimal division of labor and ever-changing guidelines. In different ways and with varying success, workers in both organizations seek to maintain or expand their control over the work environment.

In the Mandana County Welfare Department there are two types of workers: professional social workers (MSWs), who provide social services to clients, and eligibility workers (EWs), who determine clients' needs for economic aid. They are organized into a common union, which develops strategies to resist the erosion of workplace autonomy. At Wholly Grains, collective members have rejected conventional work arrangements and constructed their own work organization. They struggle to maintain a flexible division of labor against pressures toward deskilling, rigid hierarchies, and specialization.

Within the Welfare Department MSWs and EWs oppose the bureaucratic regulation in different ways. MSWs are protective of the one portion of their work that cannot be easily quantified or regulated: client counseling and recommendations. Their grievances cite the incompatibility of standardized tasks and their professional responsibilities to clients. Heavily surveilled and lacking discretion in any of their duties, EWs simply refuse to meet the steep production quotas through slowdowns. The duties EWs deem most onerous, providing highly standardized services to welfare clients, are publically rejected by them as unnecessary. Working within a heavily supervised and regulated workplace, welfare workers nonetheless attempt to fight and, in some cases, subvert the administrative control over their work.

In the late 1960s public sector unions formed effective coalitions with clients to oppose the regulations and budget cutbacks that distressed both clients and workers. Today welfare department workers no longer forge alliances with clients, and they have sacrificed broader political goals. However, they do continue to use clients as a resource: client work, often taking place outside of the view of supervisors, becomes the social workers' rationale to avoid further routinization of their work. EWs, who lack any discretion in their dealings with clients, nonetheless deploy their own critical definitions of clients in the media and with politicians. Welfare workers who are given a measure of authority to define clients' needs use their welfare clients to negotiate a compromised workplace control.

Founded in 1975, the Wholly Grains bakery collective was one of thousands of experiments in building alternative social and economic institutions that grew out of the countercultural movement of that period. Most were short-lived, but a few like Wholly Grains proved more durable and continue to be vital orgainzations. But this survival has not been easy. Organized around principles of worker ownership and control and a minimal division of labor, collective members must be constantly vigilant against pressures to normalize their structure and workplace relations.

Maintaining a flexible nonhierarchical division of labor was particularly difficult for the collective. The delicate tension between the need for coordination and the rejection of managerial domination has resulted in crisis and the need for reorganization. Ann Ferguson focuses on the pressures toward evolution into a conventional business enterprise and on the resources that the collective draws on to mitigate against such degeneration.

Both Ann Ferguson and Alice Burton found that workers and collective members draw on resources outside of the workplace in their struggle for control over their labor. These lateral linkages, neglected by contemporary theorists of work organization, are crucial factors in shaping struggles. Collective members draw on a rich community network of institutions and cooperatives for moral and material support as well as for potential members. They also take advantage of an expanding market for what they produce: craft-made, healthful, whole-grain bread. Contemporary welfare workers, now without political alliances with clients, use them instrumentally in bargaining for workplace control. Workers who are able to make alliances with others with similar interests can still stem the tide of bureaucratic rationalization.

Alice Burton
Ann Arnett Ferguson

FIVE

Dividing Up the Struggle: The Consequences of "Split" Welfare Work for Union Activism

Alice Burton

We've got a divided house in Jackson County [a pseudonym]. Last year when negotiations stalled, there was a strike that left everyone mad. The eligibility workers had a strike vote and won. I thought the contract was going to go through and the next day I was putting up picket lines. . . . They got the votes together by promising the social workers that they wouldn't get mad if they [the social workers] crossed the picket line. The social workers crossed the lines. Then the EWs got mad. It lasted three weeks—right before Christmas. It was a real disaster. Their wage gain was minuscule and it severely damaged relations between the EWs and social workers. (Union Field Representative for Jackson County, Local 222)

This short-lived, divisive strike in Jackson County in 1987 is emblematic of deep rifts in the California local of the welfare workers' union. The eligibility workers (EWs), who screen and process welfare applications, are unionized together with professional social workers (MSWs) who provide social services to children and families,[1] and the EWs and MSWs are often at odds with one another. The strike vote was taken when contract negotiations with the county broke down over the EWs' demands for a limit on the number of cases assigned to them. Routinely assigned 150 to 500 clients at a time, EWs view reduced and standardized caseloads as one of their primary goals. Although enough of the social workers were sympathetic to support the strike vote, most of them did not share the intensity of the EWs' grievances. Serving fewer clients and exercising more discretion than the EWs, social workers in Jackson County are concerned more with preserving their "professional" autonomy. The social workers were further alienated from the EWs' strike because it seemed to them too abrupt, aggressive, and nonstrategic.

The Jackson County strike demonstrates a second, less obvious split between state service workers and their historical ally, welfare clients. In the 1960s and early 1970s, employees of California county welfare departments joined with clients' groups (such as the locally organized welfare rights organizations) to protest punitive welfare and workplace policies. But the Jackson County EWs' clients, whose applications were delayed for three weeks by the 1987 strike, were not assisted or organized by the union, were not included in any strike activities. This omission of clients reflects more than careless organizing: EWs' grievances consistently exclude clients' agendas for increased and improved services. Neglecting clients as potential allies and failing to secure support from the social workers, the EWs' strike was, as their field representative said, "disastrous."

ELIGIBILITY WORKERS AND SOCIAL WORKERS: THE NEW PROLETARIAT?

The fissures between the state welfare workers and their clients evident in the Jackson County strike have not been anticipated by scholars of public-sector labor movements. In fact, analyses of state service work have predicted that it will become increasingly proletarianized and lead to workers' alliances with clients.[2] James O'Connor, the most notable proponent of this view, suggests that in the current constrained fiscal environment, welfare workers and clients experience similar hardships and thus will join together. Cutbacks in services threaten both clients and the workers who administer the programs. Increasing bureaucratic surveillance and sanctions against clients and service workers will propel them into a struggle against punitive state welfare regulations. O'Connor argues that a movement of public-sector workers and their clients could transcend special-interest union politics to make joint demands for a broader constituency of state workers and dependents.[3]

O'Connor's predictions are rooted in solid ground. The decline of the Great Society funding in the early 1970s evoked a wave of protest from grass-roots coalitions of social welfare unions and hundreds of locally organized welfare rights organizations. The passage of Governor Ronald Reagan's 1971 welfare reform bill in California mandated a new emphasis on fraud prevention, restricted access to welfare, and standardized services to cut costs.[4] Anticipating reductions in aid and layoffs, workers and clients protested the results of welfare reform in work actions and demonstrations in 1970. The Local 222 newsletter of March 1970 described joint client-worker actions that had occurred in a two-month period:

On Friday, the 13th, Social Workers in Los Angeles demonstrated at the
. . . Sheriff's Station over the police killing of a client at the 76th Street
welfare office. The demonstration followed a protest work-stoppage at
the 76th Street office on March 11, when workers negotiated improvements in security, staffing, and cash aid for GR [General Relief] clients to
forestall such incidents in the future. Another Los Angeles work-action
over deplorable working conditions loomed after a client fell down a
poorly lighted, long flight of stairs at the Ramparts office on March
12. . . . In other counties members of Local 222 are acting against the
abuses imposed on workers and clients through cut-backs, staffing limitations, and short-sighted county policy. On February 16 over 300 clients
and workers staged a noon demonstration in Sacramento County over
budget cut-backs in AFDC [Aid to Families with Dependent Children],
Licensing, and General Assistance. The demonstration was followed by
union . . . meetings with county management and much of the program
cuts were restored.

The contrast between Local 222's joint client-worker defense of welfare programs in 1970 and the disunity between groups of workers and
clients in the Jackson County strike in 1987 raises questions. Fiscal strin-
gency has continued to dictate high caseloads and low wages for welfare
workers, while clients receive reduced services and benefits that keep
them below the poverty line. None of the conditions O'Connor emphasizes in his explanation of worker-client activism have changed. Given
the plausible argument that state workers' and clients' shared material
interests and opposition to welfare regulations would be heightened
during a fiscal crisis, we would expect to see continuing labor solidarity
and struggles with clients. The departure point for this study then is a
question: Why are workers and clients who have apparently allied interests divided?

The answer lies in the changes in welfare work organization. One of
the welfare reforms implemented during the fiscal crisis of the early
1970s was the division of casework into "eligibility" and "services." Caseworkers, who had provided income maintenance and social services to
clients, were replaced by EWs and MSWs, who are each responsible for
a portion of these duties. Eligibility for aid is now determined by EWs,
and professional social workers provide noneconomic counseling and
referrals. O'Connor, who ignored the specific effects of the fiscal crisis
on work organization and workers' consciousness, could not anticipate
that the reorganization of welfare work in the early 1970s would transform state workers' and clients' movements.

Although social work and eligibility work are both more standardized and more closely monitored than was casework before the fiscal
crisis, the administrative control of work has been enacted differently
among MSWs and EWs. Caseworkers all carried out similar tasks and

were subject to standardized rules and working conditions. In contrast, MSWs and EWs occupy different workplaces with distinct duties, regulations, and working conditions. Consequently, social workers and EWs have distinct experiences of client work that lead to different and sometimes conflicting grievances. While both MSWs and EWs have suffered from cutbacks in the welfare system, this deprivation has been meted out in different degrees and ways.

Separated in different offices and work sites, providing different services, and reporting to different supervisors, EWs and social workers have only one opportunity to make workplace policy together: union meetings. For four months I attended lunch-hour membership meetings, informal grievance sessions, executive board meetings, and negotiations with management. Directly assisting the field representative of the union's Mandana County chapters [a pseudonym], I had the opportunity to get to know most of the chapter's union activists as well as other field representatives. After this period of participant observation research, I conducted informal interviews with three social workers and three EWs. The following three sections examine how the specific workplace experiences of caseworkers, social workers, and eligibility workers have generated three distinct forms of public-sector unionism.

CASEWORK AND CLIENT-WORKER ACTIVISM

Beginning in the early 1960s, Local 222 spearheaded organizing drives among caseworkers in California county welfare departments.[5] Previously represented by public employee associations narrowly concerned with wage gains, caseworkers were organized by a union of political activists. The union first gained formal recognition in 1966 by the Los Angeles County Board of Supervisors after a highly visible twenty-two-day strike in which caseworkers and clients shut down local welfare offices. Welfare reform, designed largely to "stabilize" the rapid growth in the California welfare rolls in the 1960s, was the focus of union protest as early as 1969. Local 222 caseworkers and welfare clients responded to the reforms with a defense of welfare benefits, assaults on proposed fraud detection programs, and lobbying efforts aimed at local politicians.[6]

Such militant client-worker activism would appear to support an explanation of state service workers' movements linked to fiscal crisis: workers and clients become aware of their shared material interests and bureaucratic regulation when threatened with budget cutbacks. However, when we consider caseworkers' specific exposure to clients' needs at the dawn of the fiscal crisis, it becomes apparent that the structure of caseworkers' formal duties provides a more compelling explanation of the alliance. Caseworkers were given discretion both in providing services and in granting benefits to clients. Serving the "whole client," caseworkers formed personal ties with their clients, which paved the way for activist alliances between the union and welfare rights organizations.

Caseworkers became client advocates because using the welfare system to meet their clients' economic needs was part of their legitimate agency job description. Welfare managers, prompted by city officials anxious to assuage the growing number of militant welfare rights organizations, gave caseworkers discretion in granting aid.[7] Because caseworkers determined eligibility for welfare benefits by complex and in some cases nonstandard criteria, they were able to interpret regulations broadly and liberally. For example, caseworkers could supplement clients' monthly checks with special grants for items, such as winter coats or new appliances, not covered in the client's monthly budget.[8] Administering liberal welfare regulations, caseworkers had the tools with which to help clients.[9]

Welfare work, combining a set of economic remedies with a continuous personal relationship, led to caseworkers' structural understanding of clients' problems and advocacy. The following report, written by a caseworker and published in the union newsletter in 1969, shows how the worker's direct contact with her client's impoverishment leads to her economic definition of the problem:

> Client X, mother of 3 married children and 2 dependent boys (9, 11), calls to ask me to come out and discuss her problems. House in upset condition due to recent moving in. Problems: rent too high but had to get out of other house; mistake in grant causing shortage; shortage of food; PG&E [gas and electricity] to be turned off; no money to get furniture from storage; alimony not coming in; trouble with mail and husband's own bills coming to her; real nervous and unable to think straight. Sister, daughter and daughter-in-law relate (1) she had slight breakdown a few wks ago due to these pressures (2) she's talking of committing suicide (3) she's talking of giving up two boys. References made in orderly manner to help her plan how to counteract various problems—visiting post office and PG&E, calling lawyer. Talk to calm her and try to make her feel less tense. . . . Talk with Supervisor re: mistake in grant and special need for storage money. Transmittals made out. Called church for extra food . . .[10]

Though Client X is clearly experiencing severe emotional problems, her caseworker understands the problem to be based in unmet material needs (rather than clinical dysfunction) and is able to address them. A service worker who did not have an intimate knowledge of this client's financial problems might not have recognized their primacy in this case.

Caseworkers, whose daily work involved the manipulation of the state welfare system to serve their clients' needs, formed a union that tied good working conditions to adequate services for clients. Although there were caseworkers who came to state service work with a political agenda that included organizing the underclass, most welfare employees did not share this vision. For the majority of workers, the experience of their daily work life most significantly informed their activism. Because the discretionary aspect of casework lay in serving clients' economic needs, caseworkers were able to identify their own interests with those of clients. Welfare rights organizations that wanted to make services and aid more accessible to clients were natural allies for the advocate caseworkers.

Begun as a caseworkers' craft union with an overt political agenda, Local 222 added EWs to its chapters in the early 1970s. Recruited by the counties in large numbers almost exclusively from the ranks of former welfare clerks, EWs were and are largely Black and female.[11] Welfare clerks, who had authorized and disbursed checks to clients, were given the caseworkers' task of determining clients' eligibility for aid when they became EWs. Income maintenance, however, was stripped of its special grants and complex formulas that allowed caseworkers discretion in distributing welfare. The number of MSWs added to the county welfare system declined sharply from the total number of caseworkers previously employed.[12] Union activists resisted the reorganization of casework because they believed it would cause layoffs, hamper communication between workers, and erode already strained services. Despite Local 222's spirited opposition to the plan, by 1972 the politically popular separation was in effect in California as well as most other states.

SOCIAL WORK AND PROFESSIONAL GRIEVANCES

The grievances contemporary social workers bring against their state employer present a stark contrast to the earlier joint caseworker-client activism. While MSWs represent their clients' need for professional services in grievances and actions, they do not solicit their participation in organizing. And although social workers are willing to demonstrate or strike over what one social worker called "life-and-death issues" such as health insurance cutbacks or the elimination of flextime, they negotiate most of their grievances quietly through the formal process.[13]

Casework, which generated welfare workers' political advocacy through their economic duties for clients, has been replaced by state social work, which in contrast gives MSWs discretion only over their provision of noneconomic social services. MSWs, while coming into contact with clients' material deprivation, do not have the intimate knowledge of their finances that caseworkers had. From the social workers' vantage point, clients' domestic problems, substance abuse, or poor school performance are unconnected to their impoverishment. Furthermore, social workers are rewarded with workplace privileges for instrumentally defining clients' interests as a need for MSWs' protective services, rather than material support.

Consequently, client activism has become largely outmoded, both in the MSWs' appraisals that it has become impractical and in union practice. Social workers, invested in a defense of their workplace control based on client needs that are legitimated by managers, find confrontational union activism to be irrelevant or even contrary to their goals. Dismissing joint organizing with clients and any direct confrontation of bureaucratic authorities, MSWs have narrowly bounded their union struggles to their own interests.

Mandana County MSWs, represented by Local 222, are nonsupervisory employees who provide direct services, such as counseling and referrals, to clients. Social workers generally have small, stable caseloads of clients whom they know by name. The vast majority of their clients are children and families who receive AFDC benefits such as food stamps, Medi-Cal, and a monthly stipend. In contrast to the caseworkers, however, the social workers' formal responsibilities to their clients no longer involve advocating for economic aid. When confronted with a client in need of benefits, social workers make routine referrals to EWs in other offices. The MSWs' discretion lies in providing noneconomic services to clients.

Social workers now investigate and counsel clients in programs that emphasize clinical or institutional solutions to clients' problems with drug abuse, child abuse, truancy, foster care, and adoption cases, among others. A social worker succinctly describes herself and her work as "part attorney, part cop, and a little casework." A social worker will influence, for example, the court's decision on whether or not to take a child away from her parent, or place an adolescent in a juvenile detention facility or psychiatric institution. Spending about half their time in direct contact with clients, social workers' other major responsibility involves writing reports and filling out standardized forms necessitated by state and federal funding agencies. Though the form of the social workers' recommendations and reports is largely standardized, the decisions MSWs make in these cases are based, in their terms, on their professional judgment.

Acting as liaisons between the welfare agency, clients, and state institutions, MSWs work with their clients not only in the welfare office but in clients' homes, courtrooms, and schools. Unlike most nonsupervisory bureaucratic employees, social workers can make their own schedules, choosing to come in an hour late one day and stay an extra hour on another. Social workers, moving in and out of the office and often on irregular schedules, are frequently outside their supervisors' view. Even when under the scrutiny of a supervisor, social workers are allowed to bypass some of the agency rules. A social worker commented that an EW might be docked for coming in three minutes late, but a supervisor wouldn't "dream of even mentioning the time to a social worker." Managers generally "leave MSWs alone" according to another social worker, because they "don't want to mess with their productivity." The measure of autonomy enjoyed by MSWs in their work is widely understood by county management to be necessary if social workers are to fulfill their diverse responsibilities to clients and state institutions.

Many social workers consider themselves to be client advocates. One long-time union activist, who refers to his adoption caseload as "my kids," voiced the prevalent view of client advocacy when he said, "In my job it means getting involved with clients, providing services . . . wanting to help." Agency bulletin boards advertise garage sales, ethnic dances, and food fairs sponsored by social workers to benefit child welfare clients. MSWs periodically hold bake sales in the agency lobby to buy new furnishings and toys for client waiting rooms. Other social workers mentioned that they have gone to clients' baptisms, graduations, and weddings over the years. Though she will always be considered "that white lady from the agency," one social worker said that she has developed a bond with some of her clients. Counseling small caseloads of families and children, social workers have developed a client advocacy that is expressed in personal relationships or a set of voluntary services.

Social workers are at once genuinely concerned about clients' needs and strategic in their use of clients to maintain and expand their autonomy from bureaucratic supervision. Their grievances typically call for a reduction of workplace regulations so that clients can better benefit from social workers' professional services. For example, social workers in a child abuse emergency response unit protested the rigorous enforcement of a county policy that demanded written or telephone authorization for all overtime. Although most of the social workers indicated that they found making a check-in call demeaning when at a hospital, they focused their complaint on their inability to provide quality services to the children. One social worker said: "We can't go running off to the phone in the middle of the child's examination . . . it gets in the way of the job we're paid to do." Because the MSWs' direct client services have been defined by the county administration as necessarily discretionary, social workers have a legitimate basis for an argument that they need further flexibility in their schedules.

MSWs commonly speak for their clients in their grievances. One of their long-standing complaints against the increasing paperwork assigned to each case is based on their argument that they cannot provide crucial direct services to clients when bureaucratic records multiply. Similarly, clients' needs for quick, dependable, private services provide a rationale for the MSWs' requests for privacy in their offices, a well-maintained motor pool, and more flexible schedules. Although clients may be incidentally better served by such workplace reforms, MSWs—unlike the caseworkers—do not consult clients and their representatives to determine what clients define as their most pressing need. The same MSW, who considers himself a client advocate, explained, in an unusually frank statement, clients' irrelevance to the union: "Providing better services to clients is not the point of the union. The protection of membership is the point. . . . We may use clients to make a point, but we aren't storming the barricades to say that we've got to get services to clients. . . . We are protesting onerous work." Unlike the caseworkers' advocacy, the MSWs' personal commitment to clients is completely distinct from their grievances in the workplace. Their struggle against the bureaucratic regulation implicit in a strict overtime policy or mounting paperwork only symbolically involves and serves clients.

The MSW's assertion that clients' movements are irrelevant to union grievances is reflected in the absence of political organization between the union and clients.[14] Client organizing, when suggested by the Mandana County field representative during executive board meetings, receives at best a lukewarm reception from social workers. MSWs, while supportive of voter registration drives and legislative lobbying with clients' representatives, view direct political participation with clients as a "thing of the past." Clients, according to social workers, are now more likely to be "chemically dependent," "uneducated," and "dysfunctional" in a group environment than they were in the 1960s. One MSW interested in making broader coalitions between mental health workers and community groups noted that his schizophrenic patients "cycle" and are heavily reliant on drug therapy. While acknowledging the importance of direct alliances with clients, this MSW sees organizing with these clients as almost impossible because "they have no sense of rights."

Social workers' pessimism toward organizing with clients is, in part, a product of the constraints their work places on their advocacy. Charged with treating the problems of the poor with only clinical or institutional remedies, MSWs are equipped to serve only a portion of clients' needs. They can offer little or no help other than referrals to welfare eligibility services or legal aid if a client is losing utilities or being evicted. Social workers, unlike caseworkers, have no obvious way in their formal duties to help clients meet their material needs. Caught in a frustrating position, many social workers understand advocacy as no more than a personal relationship with their clients or an offering of funds collected from an agency bake sale. Direct political action with welfare clients or striving to empower the schizophrenic who is unaware of his or her rights appears irrelevant to the MSWs' role of providing "protective" services to clients.

Reinforcing this disaffection with client organizing are the workplace privileges social workers have acquired by instrumentally defining clients' needs. MSWs continue to have flexible schedules, are treated with relative benign neglect by supervisors, and are allowed to provide services outside of the office because they have convinced the county administration that this discretion is necessary if clients and other state institutions are to be served. MSWs, who are savvy in using clients' needs as a rationale for their own interests in grievances, would have to give up the control they exercise in these complaints if they were to participate with clients. Furthermore, if county managers were to be confronted with grievances that linked welfare rights organization agendas with those of the MSWs, they would be likely to amend some of the social workers' privilege. MSWs who make claims for professional privilege, but do not question the administrative design of client services, have negotiated a compromise with state managers who are willing to give them limited discretion.

MSWs claim a need for workplace control, expressed in flextime and discretionary duties, because their work with clients demands it. Using this argument they have successfully maintained their autonomy from close supervision when providing direct client services, both in and out of the office. However, they have not managed to maintain their freedom from regulations in the standardized recordkeeping and reporting that makes up a major portion of their work. "Court work," such as petitions, reports, applications for foster care payments, and legal notices that must be completed according to a strict time schedule, leaves the MSW little room for discretion. However, MSWs' grievances concerning this work do not demand more autonomy from bureaucratic regulations; rather, they attempt to quietly minimize or sidestep these duties.

An MSW, in a social work subcommittee meeting, proposed a reorganization of social workers' duties that would not draw attention to the change. Reading aloud from a list of "improvements" she had drawn up for the foster care division, she said:

It's ridiculous that when we do W.O.D.[15] we end up answering the phone ... $35,000-a-year employees making copies and answering the phone! We need another clerical worker in the unit. It isn't professional to hook the phones up to an answering machine. . . . Also we waste a lot of time filling out court reports. Some of the response categories are standard and don't need to be written in sentence form.

MSWs attempt to deemphasize the more regulated portion of their work by trying to standardize it further, or preferably by reallocating it to another worker. Hoping to appeal to managers' interests in cutting costs, the social workers in the subcommittee meeting consciously framed their grievance so that it would be noncritical of the forms.

Social workers, who argue that paperwork takes away time from their "real" job, client services, subjectively define their work to include only discretionary client duties. The MSWs' division of duties into tedious, nonprofessional tasks and autonomous client contact, however, ignores the fact that all of the MSWs' contact with clients is expressed in standardized reports. Social workers' tangible product, the court report, for example, has been formulated for the sake of regulating clients' lives according to welfare policies that are determined by state administrators. Ultimately, then, the discretion social workers exercise over clients is based only in MSWs' experience of flexible schedules and personal freedom from close supervision, and not in the product of their work. If social workers were to argue for discretion over the form of court reports, they would be forced to confront the authority of managers. As it is, MSWs chose to maintain narrow professional privilege through the orderly grievance procedure. By attempting to side-step rather than fight against their duties, which are highly regulated, social workers ultimately reallocate the struggle to other workers who cannot use a high salary to justify its inappropriateness.

MSWs' grievances, which ask for more workplace control because it is necessary if the county wants their "professional" services, exclude both clients and nonprofessional workers, such as the EWs. State social work that locates the MSWs' discretion in direct services, but gives them no economic resources to provide to clients, personalizes and depoliticizes welfare advocacy. Given the authority by managers to define client need, social workers use clients in their grievances as leverage to avoid close supervision. Having based their argument for workplace control on a rationale of professionalism that management legitimates, MSWs cannot openly fight regulated work without jeopardizing their privileges.[16] Social workers, who produce documents that legitimate the regulation of welfare clients, ultimately have little discretion over their own work that extends beyond their personal experience. Rejecting political organization with clients and any confrontation with authority, MSWs are engaged in a defense of a constrained and narrow workplace control.

ELIGIBILITY WORK AND WORKERS' STRUGGLES

Like social workers, EWs place clients at the center of their grievances and activism. EWs' complaints about poorly run client services and their unwieldy caseloads, however, are expressed not only to managers, but also through public activism aimed at taxpayers, politicians, and state agencies. This public activism, in contrast to the agitation of caseworkers, is in opposition to clients that they claim are lazy, addicts using welfare to support their habit, or simply crazy. EWs use clients negatively to oppose workplace programs and policies that are most punitive to workers. Further separating themselves from the MSWs, EWs are willing to disturb the workplace order and their already tenuous relationships with managers. Engaging in illegal collective slowdowns, flamboyant work actions, and, in the past, strikes, EWs show little respect for the order of their workplace. Viewed as undisciplined and erratic by social workers, EWs pursue their own brand of unionism with little support from the MSWs.

EWs' periodic attacks on clients are generated and fueled by their daily interaction in welfare agencies. Responsible for reviewing and checking the welfare applications of hundreds of nameless clients, EWs have little opportunity to form personal relationships with clients, usually described by them as their "caseload." The rushed and standardized interaction of EWs with clients builds resentment among EWs that becomes focused on welfare clients in general. EWs' dislike of providing these unpleasant services is invested in their public attacks on specific programs that add additional client services to their already overwhelming workloads. Lacking the compact social workers have with administrators, which guarantees MSWs a measure of freedom from close supervision, EWs have resorted to grievances that extend beyond the formal process and into the public arena.

EWs do the paperwork and brief interviews to determine clients' eligibility for aid primarily in the agency office. Carrying anywhere from 120 to 500 shifting clients in their caseloads, EWs do not have the opportunity MSWs do to form personal relationships with their clients. The contact EWs do have with clients, rather than building bonds between worker and client, is likely to contribute to disaffection. Unlike the MSWs' small, attractive waiting and interview rooms, the EWs' clients wait in a large area posted with security guards and decorated only with signs that prohibit eating and drinking. By the time the interview begins the EW's client may have waited up to an hour in lines that stretch out the agency door. Both the EW and client are likely to be irritated and hurried at the start of the interview.

EWs, who determine whether a client's application for aid fits standard eligibility criteria such as income and number of children, lack the broad discretion caseworkers had to adjust formulas or authorize special grants. Most of the EW's time is spent checking clients' applications and records for consistency and authenticity. For example, each month welfare clients submit a statement of their income and assets, and EWs must ensure that the documentation is comprehensive. Any incomplete or potentially fraudulent forms are returned by the EW in the mail to the client, who has a month's time to correct the problem or be dropped from the welfare rolls. EWs also perform annual renewals, which consist of a face-to-face interview and a further audit of the client's income to ensure, according to an EW, "that she isn't driving a Cadillac." Augmenting contemporary eligibility work's emphasis on monitoring rather than serving welfare clients is the fragmentation of aid categories. Assigned to separate aid programs, such as AFDC, food stamps, Medi-Cal, or General Assistance, EWs are able to provide only one source of funding to a client who may receive several.

The services EWs provide to clients in face-to-face interaction are highly regulated, leaving EWs little opportunity to sympathize with the clients' needs. Even in the few stopgap programs that would seem to emphasize client service, such as Emergency Food Stamps, EWs are chiefly responsible for apprehending defrauders. An EW who works in the program commented:

> The strongest point about my job is that you have to recognize certain techniques that people use. For some reason each month we get a different story. They say, like my boyfriend's beating me up. . . . Most of the time with that eye-to-eye contact you look at a person, and there's a way to ask questions. I might ask the question five times. And if I keep getting different answers I'll compare them with the application. The main thing we look for is consistency. There are about three different places on the application that we have the same questions. If you can't provide proof then the application will be denied. . . . We tell you that you have to go through the regular process that can take anywhere from thirty-five to forty days.

EWs are instructed to respond to a client who does not meet the Emergency Food Stamp criteria by going through an agency list of referrals to places such as the Salvation Army. If the applicant responds that she has exhausted all of these resources, the EW will hand out canned food from her agency food bank. Any other response, such as making phone calls to other state agencies, is prohibited. Though the EW comes into direct contact with the victims of welfare cutbacks, the agency covers every contingency of the interaction with a routinized procedure. An EW, even if sympathetic to the client's distress, finds her advocacy restricted by workplace regulations.

Walking into the administrative portion of the EWs' offices past the security check, one sees rows of desks piled high with baskets of welfare applications and a few computer terminals. One office may serve as many as sixty workers. Unlike Mandana County social workers, who often have dividers between their desks, EWs have no privacy in the office. Nor are EWs allowed the privilege of leaving the office, except for occasional home visits for the more senior workers. Because most of the EWs' responsibilities are highly standardized and easily quantifiable, EWs are monitored and held to a standard of productivity by their supervisors. An EW who is a shop steward commented on how his supervisors' surveillance of him stepped up after he became active in the union:

> I was recruited to the position basically because no one else wanted it . . . because as a shop steward you become a target. They have a tendency to start looking for little things like are you late, are you abusing lunch period. They look for little things to harass you. As a shop steward, you shouldn't have any medical problems. . . . You can't leave yourself exposed.

Managers' treatment of the EWs is characterized by EWs, MSWs, and union representatives as consistently punitive.

EWs are most likely to react harshly to clients in work situations in which they lack resources to provide to clients in need.[17] Clients, frustrated by the limitations of the welfare system, react angrily, and EWs, also conscious of the chinks in the system, are furious that clients blame them for the late check. An EW who expressed sympathy for hungry, homeless clients explained that she found the limitations of her concern when she worked with an AFDC caseload:

> When someone comes in and says they need this money, and, as workers, we make a genuine effort to get them this money and a document bounces, that doesn't mean that we did it intentionally. That doesn't mean that we should be called out of our name because an accident happened, but they do that. . . . Sometimes it's our fault that it happens, sometimes it's a supervisor's, sometimes it's an accident and couldn't be prevented.

I'm not going to baby a client. I'm not going to cry just because a person cries that they're broke.

EWs who answer phone calls from distraught clients desperate for money have developed a similar lack of sympathy that translates into disbelief that the clients are really in need. When confronted with a call from a woman who said that her children had been without food for a day, one EW said, "I don't always believe them. We have to be polite to them, just provide the list of referrals." Providing clients with checks that are inevitably late and insufficient, EWs experience clients' anger and desperation daily. Not being in a position to aid clients, EWs decide that clients' demands for aid are unreasonable or simply unbelievable.

EWs' jokes and comments about client services in union meetings suggest that they too are cumbersome and of no value. The instances of EWs' harshest condemnations of clients and welfare services, however, are saved for the public arena. In the newly instituted state Homeless Program, EWs interview clients and grant emergency funds and hotel vouchers to people who can document their identity. Most of the applicants do not have any identification, so the EWs have been assigned an impossible task. A group of EWs, furious at an added client service that they see as absurd, threatened to call the press and report that the homeless were using the new grant program only to buy drugs. They reluctantly agreed to withhold their press release only when their union representative convinced them that it would cause problems. Although EWs sincerely dislike the homeless clients, their press release was also a strategic attempt to use the public's concern about drugs to sabotage a program that placed unrealistic demands on them.

Some EWs who are experienced union activists realize that client advocate groups can make good allies, but they are unwilling or unable to publicly support clients' agendas. For example, EWs' desire that a caseload maximum be set clashes with the concerns of client advocacy groups who want to extend welfare coverage. Advocacy groups are concerned that if the caseload standards are adopted without concern for clients' needs, the county may not hire enough EWs to provide services. An EW who is a union officer expressed ambivalence about working with these advocacy groups:

I think organizing with clients' rights groups is a good idea. . . . I refuse to work with a clients group who wants to keep people on welfare. . . . I won't try to defend the amount of time a person can receive welfare benefits because that's my own personal belief. I don't believe welfare's set up so people can receive welfare for the rest of their lives. People should use the system fairly.

This EW sees value in organizing with clients but cannot support the advocates' central goal, extending welfare services and benefits to cover more people for a longer time. EWs' work experience, which makes providing services to clients so loathesome, ensures that linking a movement to extend client services with the EWs' struggle for a caseload standard will be highly problematic. Even as a savvy union activist, this EW finds the alliance personally unappealing.

EWs' negative use of clients to fight their highly regulated duties is a genuine expression of hostility and a strategic attack against onerous work. EWs' potential client advocacy, like that of the social workers, has been constrained by the structure of their work, which regulates all contact. Unlike the MSWs, the EWs have client duties that offer them no discretion from supervision; indeed, their client duties are the most obviously regulated portion of their work. Receiving no workplace benefits from extending economic services to clients, EWs reject even the instrumental grievances of the social workers to extend client services. EWs hope that by discrediting clients' needs for services in the public arena, taxpayers, politicians, or even their managers will listen to them and reduce their overwhelming caseloads. Union representatives discourage EWs from taking these complaints beyond the work site, and most criticisms of clients do not become public. However, EWs' struggles against their working conditions are aggressively deployed against county managers and not limited to the workplace.

Most of the EWs' grievances, both formal and informal, are a defense against unreasonable caseloads and overtly racist harassment from supervisors. Predominantly people of color, probationary EWs in the first six months of work routinely receive a harsh initiation from supervisors, predominantly white, who deliver racial slurs.[18] EWs see the grievance procedure as "too slow" and supportive of the "status quo" when attempting to resolve complaints about both caseloads and racial intimidation. Without the MSWs' legitimated argument for discretion, based on the county's need of "professional" services, EWs take their grievances to managers in work actions and into the state arena. EWs, who rely on a broad combination of the formal grievance procedure, work actions, and state worker activism, alienate social workers who don't want to damage their "working relations with managers."

Closely monitored in their work, EWs may also be openly harassed by supervisors. EWs who are active in the union or who display any insubordination to a supervisor quickly become targets for poor evaluations and dismissal. First-level supervisors, who have close contact with EWs and prepare evaluations, typically express this pointed harassment through racist comments. One EW and union activist who

endured a year of racial slurs from her supervisor described the abuse
and her reaction:

> My supervisor was making racist comments to me . . . every dirty thing
> she could think to say to me. She would walk over and say it to me . . .
> in open groups of people. She would make statements about Black cul-
> ture. . . . It hit me one day. I was mad. . . . I looked at her, "Are you sure
> you're saying what you're saying?" This woman told me that I made her
> sick and that she could just throw up all over me. I went off 51-50 and
> told her, "You better call the sheriff's department first and then you
> better call the ambulance because if you don't retract what you just said,
> I'm going to pick up this stapler and knock the hell out of you."

In response to racial harassment in the workplace, many EWs have
turned to the Civil Service Commission, the Equal Opportunity Commission, or directly to county politicians, such as the board of supervisors. An activist EW has implemented letter-writing campaigns to local and federal politicians protesting racial discrimination in the
workplace.

MSWs and EWs, serving together with managers on county committees concerning workplace issues, demonstrate their clashing style. During a report on a health and safety committee meeting, the MSW representative admitted that he felt unable to confront the management
"experts" on the committee. He said,

> It was difficult for us [the workers] to ask appropriate questions to the
> county officials about work environment because none of the workers are
> experts. . . . There are big black chunks of insulation coming through the
> [air conditioning] vents. They said that they were too big to be a respi-
> ratory problem, it's not a health issue. . . . No one is trained on the com-
> mittee; we need more information.

Demonstrating respect for the managers' expertise and indicating little
understanding of the managers' and workers' different interests, this
MSW touched off a torrent of advice from an EW listening to the
report:

> *Big black chunks?* You should put the officials on the defensive. Ask for
> documentation for everything. . . . How do you know this clown is an
> expert? Even if you don't know, ask questions. If you don't, they will lead
> you. Get OSHA [Occupational Safety and Health Administration] in-
> volved . . . have them write a nice little letter.

EWs combine aggressive tactics against managers, whom they consistently identify as their enemy, with state sector resources such as
OSHA.

Although EWs' and MSWs' union activism often remain separate in different work sites and with different managers, these groups of workers have ample opportunity to conflict when dealing with top county managers or voting on joint actions. EWs see the MSWs as inactive and often willing to let a few union activists fight their battles for them. Citing the vacancies in the social workers' seats on the union's executive board as an example, EWs believe that the MSWs are currently in decline in the union. Social workers, angered by the EWs' confrontational style, claim that EWs are "too emotional" and "too angry." One long-time social worker commented about EWs, "You can't tell your adversary [manager] that he's full of shit and expect to work with him." Although there is currently no sign of a formal split, several years ago some MSWs attempted to break off from the Mandana chapter and start their own representative body exclusively for social workers.

EWs' union activism, which extends from formal grievances against caseloads to utilizing state watchdog agencies, takes place without the solidarity of MSWs and any alliances with clients or their advocates. Eligibility work, by eliminating all of the EWs' discretion and leaving them to cope with needy, angry clients, effectively undermines all of EWs' potential advocacy. Lacking any interest in even maintaining existing client services, EWs cannot even establish working relationships with client advocate groups, much less participatory unionism with clients. Providing no services that require discretion under the existing structure of eligibility work, EWs have no argument management considers legitimate to stave off repressive caseloads and close supervision. EWs consequently take their complaints, against demanding client services and racist supervisors alike, to the public arena. Taking a confrontational stance against welfare administrators, EWs alienate MSWs who are heavily invested in a defense of their workplace privilege. Because EWs are unable to make coalitions with clients and fellow state workers in their use of state resources, their public-sector unionism does not realize its promise.

CONCLUSION

The argument, made by O'Connor and others, that as public-sector work becomes more rationalized and less discretionary state workers will become activists unified with their clients, is challenged by the case of Local 222. Although both social work and eligibility work are generally less discretionary than casework, and thus objectively proletarianized, workers do not experience solidarity with one another or their underclass clients. The fragmentation of welfare workers' duties, working conditions, and rules has undermined these workers' recognition of their common interests. Social workers' and EWs' daily experience of work in the welfare agency reminds them of the disparities in the privileges they receive, their different relationships with supervisors, and their contrasting responsibilities to clients. Furthermore, this divided work constructs two distinct views of welfare clients held by MSWs and EWs, both of which exclude clients' full participation in union grievances and actions. Rather than leading toward a convergence in identity and a solidarity movement, state service work after the fiscal crisis has created a myriad of divisive experiences for workers.

This chapter has emphasized the alienating effect of work organization on state employees, but for clients the reorganization of state services has had perhaps even more profound consequences. Clients, rather than working with a single caseworker, are shunted between unresponsive, impersonal eligibility services and the MSWs. Even within eligibility services, clients must negotiate various aid programs, all administered by different EWs. The client who is unable to decode the required regulations to apply for and maintain her welfare may have difficulty determining even who will be able to help her. Similarly, within the MSWs' social services, client "dysfunctions," such as substance abuse, truancy, or schizophrenia, are separately categorized and made the responsibility of a series of different personnel. Welfare clients, whose political organization has always been tenuous, find themselves individually sliced up between various welfare programs.

The argument that clients and workers, as state dependents, both have a common material base and paradoxically are controlled by state services holds true here. However, for state clients (as we have seen for workers), oppression is experienced as coming not from a unitary "state" or even a single welfare program, but from a multiplicity of services administered by transitory employees. Solidarity struggles, even among clients, are unlikely considering the wide variety of regulations, aid programs, and county institutions. It would be virtually impossible for clients to unite in opposition to punitive welfare regulations such as "man in the house rules," as they did in the 1960s, because few rules apply to all clients. Client advocacy groups are active in Mandana County, but not surprisingly, clients' direct participation has diminished greatly since the preeminence of welfare rights organizations in the early 1970s. Any struggle to expand state welfare services or to make services more responsive to a class of state dependents is seriously constrained by the fragmentation of clients' experiences.

Given the pervasive divisions between state service workers and among clients, public-sector unionism will have to chart a course outside the organizing and activism that drew on workers' and clients' shared experience in the 1960s and 1970s. Though there have been calls both inside the labor movement and from analysts of public-sector unionism for unions to recognize their bonds with clients that are based on inclusive criteria such as race, state citizenship, and gender, unions have been slow to respond. The barriers to workers' and clients' alliances appear from this analysis too great to be overcome with consciousness-raising around gender or racial politics. However, it is clear that an alternative to traditional organizing must be found if workers or clients are to wage effective opposition to state domination.

AFTERWORD: LETTING THE FIELD SPEAK TO YOU

"Letting the field speak to you" is a phrase that was thrown around a lot in the early days of our research as we struggled to orient ourselves to unfamiliar settings and faces. This was a reminder that we needed to be sensitive and responsive to the things people told and showed us in the field. Later we advised each other, somewhat more ironically, to "let the field speak to you," when trying to formulate sociological questions relevant to our site. The irony came out of our sense that this phrase misleadingly makes field work sound obvious and comfortable. It suggests that the participant observer is in some symbiotic relationship with informants and setting that will neatly translate into cogent, compelling analysis. Nothing is further from the truth. And in fact, the more we abandoned our preconceptions about the field and set theoretical or political agendas, the messier it became.

In the beginning everyone you speak with, every meeting you attend, and each interaction you observe in the field is potentially fascinating. I joined a group of union activists (about fifteen people) as quietly and unobtrusively as I could. I introduced myself to the unionists in vague terms, as a graduate student "interested in learning about unions." Asking a few orienting questions and listening a lot of the time, I kept a low profile during my first weeks in the field. In this beginning stage I was listening to the field uncritically and unselectively. I was euphoric about each new discovery, thrilled to be let in on budget meetings and chitchat in the elevator. I spent several hours sitting in a snack bar, in one of the office buildings where I did my field work, listening to random conversations, watching what people ate, breathing in the buttery fumes of microwave popcorn. I was convinced that this immersion in office culture would yield results.

This hope that all interactions in the field will be grist for one's analysis is, in part, a result of the fact that many of us asked very broad, undefined questions when we started researching: "What are women doing in the Cambodian community?" "How democratic is this union in its recognition of women?" I was ready to abandon my questions about union democracy if something more interesting came up. This suspension of my expectations, to be open to discovery, surprise, or exciting twists, was helpful, if not absolutely necessary at the beginning of my research process. Though I never considered looking at union activism as anything other than political action, most of my other assumptions were put aside at various points, in some cases to be reintroduced later.

Pursuing my original questions about women's political voice in their union, for example, initially would have forced me to ferret out information from people who didn't know or trust me. Because women's interests were not being explicitly discussed by unionists and there were no active local committees organized to address women's concerns, I found myself initiating conversations about gender that were foreign to male and female unionists' everyday experience. Part of my decision to redirect my question away from gender came from the time pressure we were all under to formulate questions and propositions about our field site. Submerged gender politics seemed too elusive given the time I had to study the union. I decided after the first few awkward conversations about women's workplace concerns, in which I was told patiently or indignantly that all unionists have to stick together, that I needed to sit back and learn what the unionists themselves considered important. Stubbornly probing for hidden struggles between men and women in the union would have made my interactions with informants intrusive and uncomfortable at this early stage.[19]

My early focus began to shift from gender not only because of its inaccessibility, but, more positively, because I found myself increasingly caught up in the principal drama in the union: the interaction between two strikingly different groups of activists who also happened to do different types of work. Eligibility workers and social workers alternated between looking faintly bored by one another in group discussions to being openly antagonistic in conflicts. Camaraderie and engagement tended to flow among EWs or among MSWs but not between them. For the most part both groups made visible efforts to tolerate each other, but occasionally, when this veneer collapsed, they burst out into angry, stubborn tirades. The emotional tenor of these interactions turned my attention away from the more pallid dynamics of women and men toward the unmistakable estrangement between EWs and MSWs. I sought new questions about union activism that would address my daily findings of this rupture between the unionists.

My first stage of research, which had resembled a wide-lens photography session, had to come to an end. Remaining in the field without a conscious, articulated set of expectations (even if they were revamped constantly) and questions, while exciting, at this point would have led to analytical stagnation. I couldn't have made progress in interpreting my observations without committing myself to a more specific focus. Practically, also, it was necessary for me to adjust my perspective on the field if I was to sustain an interest in the project. While highly sympathetic to the aims of the union activists, my engagement with the study was maintained through a series of "discoveries" (many of which would be blatantly obvious to an insider) I made about the field site. Thus as the union and management became increasingly familiar to me and new observations declined, it was essential for me to balance my unqualified enthusiasm for participation with an outsider's perspective.

The explanations that I began to entertain more seriously came, in part, from outside my site. I read about the history of this union and others like it, theoretical perspectives on public-sector and service workers' union activism, and had discussions with others in my class who knew little about the union. Discussions with persons outside the field or engaging a different perspective pushed all of us to explain what was truly compelling about the welfare workers, Cambodian women leaders, or AIDS activists.

Faced with presenting my second set of field notes to my classmates (who by this time were impatient with the miscellany of the field), I began to more clearly define "what was going on in the union" between these two groups of workers. I attended to the subject matter of their heated disputes, as well as what bored them the most. I focused on the encouraging actions as well as the less successful fragmented strategies of MSWs and EWs. Discovering that clients, professionalism, and militant activism continued to emerge as important themes, I formulated my questions even more specifically: "Why are clients the focus of disputes between workers?" and "Why do EWs pursue more militant actions than do MSWs, who reject them in favor of arguments for professional privilege?"

The way that I interacted with people in the union or watched members in meetings also changed when I began to narrow down my research questions. No longer did I linger in the coffee shop; now I more systematically sought out representatives from these two groups of workers and asked them about different kinds of clients, about MSW training and licensing. In meetings I continued to listen to everyone's comments about everything from union bylaws to child-care provisions, but with an ear to filling in missing pieces of a puzzle. My awareness of the field and intention in listening to it became more selective and ultimately more fruitful for my analysis.

In retrospect, the dynamic between what I observed in the field and the explanations I formulated was that of a push-pull. However, the movements back and forth between participant observation and analysis were delayed and awkward. Rather than neatly going back and forth between these two modes in the beginning, I pursued one strategy of uncritical acceptance until chaos threatened. Even when I came to see the site in terms of a single set of questions, I still harbored a secret fear that I might discover an inconvenient fact that would destroy my carefully constructed argument. Ultimately we all made moves toward more or less rational, neat explanations for the richness of what we observed, but the process of getting there was anything but neat.

SIX

Managing Without Managers: Crisis and Resolution in a Collective Bakery

Ann Arnett Ferguson

The members of Wholly Grains bakery collective are, as is often the case, discussing a change in the organization.[1] For the past month they have been delivering bread to two stores in the Safeway supermarket chain, and now that decision is being carefully evaluated because it marks a big departure from their traditional outlets. The bakery has been forced to add the Safeways as an emergency measure because of the recent closure of People's Co-ops, a local chain of consumer co-ops, which were among their best outlets. Now they are deliberating. Should they continue to supply these two stores? Should they consider expanding to even more branch stores in the chain? Or should they halt supply entirely because it compromises their principles?

I have recently begun field work at the collective and am sitting in on the Steering Committee meeting at which the discussion is taking place. One member who works on delivery expresses his doubts. "I don't like it. There's no room for negotiation, for one thing. They tell us what we can deliver and they set the markup. We don't deal with individual stores but with someone in the central office. The whole psychology is different than at our other stores."

"Whatever Safeway wants, Safeway gets," chimes in someone else.

Another member points out that sales at the Safeway stores have been good and have replaced some of the business lost when People's Co-ops closed down. Someone offers reasons why they should supply Safeway stores: they will finally have a chance to reach masses of people who don't shop at alternative or specialty food stores. One of the coördinators mentions that two more Safeways are willing to carry their bread and are just waiting to hear from them. The delivery shift representative on the committee expresses concern about drivers' workload if additional routes are added. By now the discussion has run well over the allotted time, so the topic is closed (for the time being anyway) with the decision that the delivery shift, because of routing and scheduling constraints, will make the final decision about additional stores. However, the decision to continue to supply the two Safeways on a regular basis is approved.

I dutifully recorded this exchange in my field notes, little realizing at the time that it provided important clues to solving the puzzle at the heart of my study: since it is widely assumed that collectives are ephemeral, fragile organizations, here today and gone tomorrow, how has Wholly Grains managed to stay in business for over fourteen years? What is the secret of its survival as a collective?[2]

Collectives such as Wholly Grains are outgrowths of the social movements of the 1960s and 1970s.[3] This is consistent with the pattern observed over the past two hundred years in the United States of worker cooperatives emerging from the wake of social upheavals.[4] While few were in operation in 1970, by 1975 about 5,000 existed, providing services that ranged from illegal abortions to whole-grain bread.[5]

Many of these experiments were short-lived. Some flourished for a while, then either went out of business or were reorganized along conventional capitalist lines.[6] However, a few, like Wholly Grains collective bakery, in which I did field work for six months, first as a participant observer, then as a worker, neither folded nor became regular businesses but persisted as vital, productive organizations based on principles of worker control and participatory democracy.

Founded in 1975, Wholly Grains is a remnant of a relatively large network of cooperative wholesale and retail stores and warehouses in the Bay Area whose aim was to wrest the monopoly of food production and distribution away from giant corporations. The guiding philosophy of the larger, now defunct network, "food for people, not for profit," still remains the ideal that informs the decisions made by the collective about new products, pricing, and distribution.

In spite of the turnover of members over the years, the composition of the collective still reflects the student movement from which it sprung: the majority are white, from middle-class families, and highly educated. About half are men and half are women.[7] From the beginning there has been a strong commitment to diversify the class and racial composition of the group to fit the image of the kind of organization it would like to create. But the few people of color who have come into the group have not stayed long. One member told me that he believed the collective works best when it is homogeneous. This homogeneity is continually reinforced by the fact that most new members come through friendship networks, a recruiting practice wide-spread among collectives.[8]

At the same time, Wholly Grains has changed considerably over the years. It has grown from three to twenty members and from a symbolic hourly wage of $1 when it started to the current $7.25 with benefits. Productivity has been increased through the addition of small machines—a loafer, a "state-of-the-art" mixer, and a slicer—a vast im-provement from the first years when mixing was done in an antiquated machine, loafing by hand, and all loaves sent out unsliced. They now produce about twenty different kinds of bread, muffins, and rolls using all whole-grain flour and no refined sugar.

In the early days a few people did all the tasks necessary to get the bread baked and distributed. Now production and distribution is di-vided up among teams, called "shifts." There are four main production shifts: bread, sweets, delivery, and bagging and loading. Trainees are expected to work on at least two shifts in order to be considered for full membership. In principle, this means that everyone is involved in skilled as well as unskilled work.

Members are no longer paid according to the actual length of time each individual takes to do a task. The wage bill is now monitored and controlled by the "efficiency standard," a calculation of the average rate of time required to accomplish a particular task. This change is one which I will argue threatens collective social relations.

The collective has weathered the turnover of members, the instability created by internal reorganization, and financial crises such as the sea-sonal cash flow problems, typical of any small business. In spite of the lack of the institutional support that other small businesses can rely on, such as bank loans through regular financial channels, the collective has grown to what is perhaps an optimal size for its present level of pro-duction. How has Wholly Grains managed to accomplish this?

ARE WORKER COOPERATIVES VIABLE?

Democratic workplaces are short-lived, unstable organizations that must, sooner or later, degenerate into conventional business enterprises run on capitalist lines. Inevitably, democracy is undermined as leaders within the group emerge and take charge. These are assumptions about the durability of organizations such as Wholly Grains that have been "a cornerstone of twentieth century social science."[9]

In the last decade, however, social scientists in the United States have become increasingly interested in "the movement against bureaucracy and toward greater autonomy and participation in the workplace" of which Wholly Grains is a part.[10] Worker cooperatives are now of interest because they have the potential of resolving some of our economic problems "in a way that is in keeping with our most deeply held tradition, our democratic heritage," of saving jobs, reducing the need for supervision, cutting costs, reducing worker dissatisfaction, and being as productive as capitalist firms.[11]

The dominant theme in this recent literature is the difficulty of keeping these anomalous enterprises alive and healthy given the external pressures and internal dilemmas they face. There are many case studies of failed experiments that seek to establish the causes of degeneration; a few tell of successful ventures.[12] All, whether pessimistic or optimistic about the chances of survival, tend to emphasize the primacy of either internal or external factors.[13]

In this chapter I argue that the collective's internal structure and the external environment in which it is located should not be treated as separate entities but should be seen as inextricably interrelated in a dynamic process. There are no inherent paradoxes or tendencies within this alternative form that lead it inexorably down the path toward normalization, nor do systemic pressures always shape outcomes. My contention is that it is an interplay between the internal organization of the collective and specific factors in the surrounding society that have created the terms of the bakery's longevity.

As it makes decisions every day, the collective has indeed been dogged by pressures to make a profit, to be efficient, to rationalize production, and to obtain capital. It has become bogged down in the slow pace of democratic decision making and frustrated by personality conflicts. That in spite of all this Wholly Grains has been able to reproduce collective social relations is, I will demonstrate, a result of the specific conditions in the environment that it can draw on to support collectivity. When the collective can tap these resources, then pressures toward degeneration can be offset.

To illustrate this relationship between the external environment and the continuity of the internal structure of the collective, I will examine three organizational crises of the bakery to show how they were shaped by external conditions. First, however, it is essential to indicate what is indeed different about Wholly Grains—what is "collective" about the collective.

STRUCTURING POWER: THE INTERNAL PROCESS

We are all too familiar with how the conventional capitalist firm works; every individual in the United States will probably work in one at some time or another. Our schools prepare us for entering "the world of

business." But we are unlikely to be familiar with an organization that
is

> worker-controlled; directly democratic (consensus decision making; no
> internal hierarchy); autonomous (not subordinate to any hierarchical or-
> ganization); and nonexploitative (using resources, skills, and surpluses to
> help enrich community life rather than reinforce the commodity relations
> of the dominant system).[14]

Or, as Wholly Grains describes itself:

> [We are] not just another bakery outlet. It's true you can buy freshly
> baked bread there, as well as cookies, baked on the premises, granola, and
> other natural goodies. But you can also find right-on politics, and a col-
> lective, worker-owned organization dedicated to producing food for peo-
> ple, not for profit.[15]

Two organizational principles set Wholly Grains apart from the conventional capitalist firm: worker control and a minimal division of labor. Both are grounded in an ideology of collectivity that not merely
reflects production relations but, more important, is essential for their
reproduction. The following is a brief description of how these ideally
structure the operation of the bakery.

Unlike the typical bureaucratic organization where power and control is concentrated in the hands of a few and exercised by owners or
by the managers who represent them, at Wholly Grains authority resides in the entire collective membership or in subgroups and committees established by the collective whose members are subject to recall.
The collective meeting is therefore the highest decision-making body.
This is the place where decisions are made about all major matters: the
type of bread produced, where it will be sold, how profits will be distributed, the "hiring" and the "firing" of members, and the physical
relocation of the bakery. Most major decisions are made by consensus,
but this is not a hard and fast rule since occasionally votes are taken.

The structure for coordinating the operation and facilitating day-to-
day organizational decisions has changed over time. Presently, two coordinators elected by the members are paid for a certain number of
hours of coordinating duties in addition to their regular work in the
bakery. A steering committee consisting of the two coordinators, a representative from each shift, and representatives of standing committees
is authorized to make certain decisions between collective meetings and
carry out tasks delegated by the group as a whole. Standing committees
such as personnel and finance meet whenever necessary. Finally, each
shift is supposed to meet at least once a month to discuss matters directly related to their own work.

Hardly any written rules and regulations exist as a mechanism for exercising social control: there is no thick manual spelling out the rights, duties, obligations, sanctions, and penalties of each position, just a few sheets of paper with information about hiring, firing, and wage policies. In fact, the only policy identified consistently as a rule was that missing a shift twice in a year without notifying someone of one's absence was grounds for discharge. Even this "hard and fast" policy was not etched in stone. During the time that I worked at the bakery, the Steering Committee discussed the case of a member who had violated the rule more than once to see whether they would in fact rehire that person. Somewhat exasperated by my probing about the firmness of rules after this deviation from policy, one member tried to make me understand: "Look, they're just a set of guidelines. You need them to guide you, otherwise you lose control. But they're not a punishment."

While this ambiguity of expectations and outcomes can be extremely frustrating for the newcomer who must learn piecemeal about the custom and practice of the group, rules function to institutionalize power relationships, so they have to be kept to a minimum and always regarded as provisional. Furthermore, this arrangement leaves room for newcomers to reshape custom almost immediately, as I found soon after I began working on the bagging shift. I was questioning the efficiency standard set for the baggers. I expected some rationalization from longtime members, but the response from the very people who had done the calculation was, "Well, it's probably time to revise the standard. There have been several changes in the work since we calculated it. It needs to be done again." I found myself responsible for coordinating the effort to establish the new rate.

Wholly Grains also rejects prevailing practices and assumptions about the appropriate division of labor in our society. Members are expected to take on routine, manual work such as bagging bread as well as skilled work such as baking and mental tasks such as calculating production figures. Trainees should work on at least two different shifts (in other words, become familiar with at least two different jobs in the bakery) before they can be admitted as members. People hired on as "baggers," the most routinized job in the bakery, expect to begin training before too long to take on other tasks. Thus an effort is made to integrate individuals into several levels of the labor process to prevent the development of an internal hierarchy between mental and manual, skilled and unskilled labor. This prevents an individual or group of individuals from wielding power over others by virtue of their knowledge or their ability. One member that I talked to divides her hours between baking (the most skilled job in the bakery), bagging bread (the least skilled), coordinating the scheduling of shifts, and mediation, and at the same time was coordinating the search for a new location for the bakery when it was being evicted. Longtime members told me that at some time or another they had done every task in the bakery.

The machinery that keeps this system in motion is a never-ending cycle of meetings. All decisions, major and minor, provisional or final, are made at meetings. Special committees, which must also meet, mushroom out of each regular meeting to tackle projects or iron out problems. And just as Robert's Rules of Order play out and reinforce certain social relationships in the world outside the collective, the process at Wholly Grains affirms the ideal that power is distributed equally to all members. While meetings are organized around agendas, with time-keepers and facilitators to ensure smooth flow, there is usually no attempt made to force a decision, no matter how pressing it might seem. Until I became conscious that the most important thing that happened at the meetings was not the actual decision made but the decision-making process itself, I would leave feeling dissatisfied about the lack of closure on topics.[16]

Meetings serve many functions. In addition to being the mechanism by which democratic decisions are made, they are also the site where individuals are reshaped into members of a collective. Here grievances are aired, positions are tested, tongues are held, and acquaintance is made with the foibles and strengths of other members. The meeting is in fact the place where the culture of the collective becomes visible as something removed from what we take for granted as "normal."

Indeed, the "normal" features of our work life are the very elements that the collective must struggle against. Outside of the bakery, for instance, it is taken for granted that it is "normal" to have clearly defined job responsibilities; to receive a wage with a concomitant status meted out according to one's position within a system of ranked jobs; to have or be a supervisor, manager, owner. But at Wholly Grain, there must be a continual struggle *not* to become "normal." The practice of the group must reflect a consciousness of the necessity to remain different, oppositional, and not to become institutionalized. A key defining factor of the collective, therefore, is the ideology of the group, its shared assumptions about worker management and control, a consciousness of its difference.

The culture of the bakery is characterized by an affinity for innovation. Change is not something to be staved off by structure, but celebrated. An illustration of this tendency is the two major structural reorganizations of the group that have taken place since its inception. Even at this writing, another alternative organizational form seems to be emerging out of everyday practice. This is one reason why it is so difficult to transmit the norms of the organization to the researcher or to a new member—there are many, and they change over time.

But the role of the collective is not seen as being one of exercising social control through inculcating members with values in the mechanical way that an ordinary business might indoctrinate a new employee with the company philosophy. "You can't give collective membership. You have to feel like an owner. You can't feel like you're working for someone else" was how it was described at a collective meeting in the evaluation of the performance of a trainee.

Members see themselves as responsible for the production process and capable of doing whatever task is necessary. As one member said about her experience of being a part of the collective, "Now I have more self-direction. I like my co-workers, I like not having a boss. I feel good about what I'm producing, I'm not ripping anybody off." She does a lot of calculations for invoices, something she thought she would never be good at, so now, she says, "I feel like I can learn whatever I want to learn." It is something she is able to do because of the wide dispersal of skills. One of the baggers tells the following story to illustrate this:

> One night, when we were about halfway through the shift, we discovered that 200 loaves of Wheatberry hadn't been baked. X suggested that we bake it ourselves and since Y who is an experienced baker was working that night, we began helping her right then and there to get the dough going. We were up till 4 in the morning waiting for the bread to cool. But we got it done. Honestly, I felt like one of Santa's elves when Santa got sick.

For the individual member, the "spirit," the sense of self-efficacy called empowerment by some members, is crucial to the vitality of the organization. Empowerment is a concept that is hard to pin down neatly. It has a multiplicity of meanings and behaviors attached. It includes responsibility and reliability; self-directed action for the benefit of the community of which you are a part; being autonomous, and at the same time achieving that autonomy only through experiencing oneself as part of a collective venture.

The search for or experience of empowerment is one of the major reasons why people put up with the heavy work, open-ended responsibility, and insecurity of the collective. One woman contrasted her experience at Wholly Grains with that at one of the giant mass-production bakeries: "Hey! I made a wage you can live on and had good benefits. We were unionized so we had to take regular breaks. But all I did was push buttons. The machines did everything. I never even saw the dough; that was mixed on a whole other floor." She sought refuge in the collective from the stultifying boredom of this experience.

A CONTEXT FOR SURVIVAL: MARKET NICHE AND COMMUNITY

Wholly Grains takes advantage of two salient features of the environment to offset pressures to normalize. The first is the market niche the bakery occupies in the Bay Area. The debate over whether to add Safeway outlets to regular delivery routes illustrates one aspect of this market niche: the ability of the bakery to expand into new, mass markets at the same time that some of their original outlets disappeared. The second is a loose network of individuals, institutions, and alternative organizations that sustains Wholly Grains with services, with customers, and with a pool of potential members whose background and education suit them for collective work.

The Market Niche

I became aware of the market niche that the collective occupied when I accompanied one of the drivers on the delivery shift. We delivered bread to three types of stores: countercultural and alternative foodstores, neighborhood and local market chains, and branches of large supermarket chains.[17]

The traditional outlets are represented by the cooperatively run, community-based stores in the area. They range from tiny markets with crammed shelves to a large collective grocery store and deli in the city. Stores such as these retain a sixties activist, countercultural ambience. Flyers announce demonstrations and consumer boycotts, while posters of political figures such as Nelson Mandela are on the walls. Some attempt is made to keep goods as low priced as possible, many products are sold in bulk, and decisions about what goes on the shelves are made on the basis of the politics of food.

The second type includes a wide spectrum of stores from Mom-and-Pop small neighborhood stores to large but locally owned supermarket chains. The neighborhood stores cater to an ethnically diverse clientele and carry a range of foods and convenience items. The fact that these stores now carry a good selection of whole-grain breads demonstrates nicely the growth in the demand for whole-grain breads in the last decade.

This growth is reflected even more vividly in the new chain stores that have burgeoned to feed the demand of an affluent sector of the population preoccupied by their own physical and mental health and racked with anxiety about the adulteration of food.[18] These consumers have the money to pay for specially produced "pure" food as well as gourmet, custom-made items. Stores with names such as Living Foods, Real Foods, and Whole Foods have transformed the image of the small, slightly dingy health food store of the past to places to buy sausages without preservatives, tofu pâté, freshly squeezed tangerine juice, frozen health food dinners, and even obtain (at $3.29 a dozen) Aracana eggs whose pedigree was announced in the sign above them: "great eggs, richer flavor, claimed lower cholesterol, from wild-running hens in Sebastopol of Peruvian descent." These chains also tend to be innovatively managed: there is little centralization; the manager of each store works out relationships with individual organic producers who sell their produce directly to the store. Salaries are dispensed by the managers from profits, an incentive to keep the stores lean and productive.[19]

Finally, bread is delivered to branches of Safeway, one of the giant supermarket chains. Safeway's operation is completely centralized, so unlike the other places that Wholly Grains does business with, negotiations are not conducted at the individual stores but with someone in a central office. This relationship is the only one in which the autonomy of the bakery becomes problematic. However, the very willingness of such a chain to deal with a bakery like Wholly Grains reveals the demand that now exists for this kind of product. Supermarket chains are beginning to pay attention to this demand and capitalize on it.

The Community
The Bay Area attracts a large number of individuals searching for alternative, politically meaningful occupations and lifestyles, likely candidates both as consumers of bakery products and as participants in collective life. In addition, major universities in the area seem to be an important source of potential members. A third of the members are recent graduates of the nearest one, with degrees from departments such as Peace and Conflict Studies, Anthropology, and Political Science. I believe they see the bakery as the site for putting into practice some of the theories that they acquired in the academic setting.

Several other collectives exist nearby and are not only a source of potential members already schooled in the organizational practice but also a place to move on to for people who are having conflicts in their own collective. It is possible that if these options did not exist, people who were committed to collective activity but who were having problems with the group might stay on to struggle around divisive matters, weakening the organization. There are several examples in the group of people coming to Wholly Grains from other collectives or leaving to join others.

Neighboring collectives provide not only a pool of committed new members and an outlet for disaffected old members but also a range of services. For example, Wholly Grains' ability to distribute its products beyond the Bay Area is augmented by a network of alternative organizations. Each week boxes of bread are delivered to a trucking cooperative that distributes Wholly Grains products to stores throughout Northern California and to an organic produce distributor for supplying stores to the south.

Not only is Wholly Grains sustained in many ways by this community, but it also is self-consciously an active part of it. The "talking bread" program nicely exemplifies this aspect. The bread talks to the consumer through inserts in the package noting upcoming political events, cultural programs, and community concerns. Most of these inserts are created by the organizers of the event itself, but the bakery also uses it to communicate with its customers. A recent talking bread advised consumers that the price of their bread would be going up 3 cents because of a rise in the price of flour. It connected this price rise with the "greenhouse effect" and encouraged people to tune into the local listener-sponsored radio station for a day of programming on the global environmental crisis.

The location in which the bakery is situated is therefore highly conducive to its success. There is a population to draw from whose education, life-style, and political leanings make it open to alternative work situations; several other cooperatives and collectives help to compensate for the dearth of institutions built around co-ops; and the consumer demand for whole-grain bread continues to grow. The collective is able to use this environment to offset pressures to degenerate into a more conventionally run business.

CRISIS AND RESOLUTION: THE REPRODUCTION OF THE COLLECTIVE

I have presented Wholly Grains as a collective enterprise, one that is substantively different from the capitalist firm. This version is an idealized one, reflecting the organization as it ought to be, the vision of the members of the group itself. While it suggests the principles and the problems they are likely to encounter, it obscures the actual essence of the collective: its fluid, flexible, changing nature in which a constant effort to reproduce collectivity must be made in the face of pressures from the environment that foster capitalist production relations.

I turn now to examine actual situations in the bakery that have the potential to undermine or transform collective relations: organizational crises that challenge the collective nature of the bakery. These situations are defined as crises because they are crucial points around which struggles are waged, the resolution of which tend to tip the scales either on the side of collectivity or on the side of more conventional organization. These crises are triggered by external pressures that impinge on the group, in some way threatening its survival as a collective and placing in jeopardy some of its fundamental assumptions.

Just as these crises are precipitated from outside, the group's ability to resolve them as a collective depends on its ability to dip into the community in which it is located for support. When the collective is able to reach out and extract resources for its survival, then problems can be resolved in the direction of collectivity. When the environment is not a source of sustenance, then the tendency to make decisions detrimental to the collective can be intensified.

The three crises that I have selected took place during the period that I did my field work. The first, the white flour debate, a crisis of principle, was relatively easily resolved in a manner that reaffirmed the goals of the collective. The other two, the management and the delivery shift crises, typify chronic dilemmas of the organization that are likely to crop up again and again. While the outcome of the struggle over management and coordination was the restoration of collective relations, the delivery shift crisis was still in flux when I left the bakery and had the potential to be a divisive factor in the group.

The White Flour Controversy: A Crisis of Definition

When Wholly Grains' members make a decision about a new product, it is grounded first and foremost in their commitment to using certain ingredients such as whole-grain flour and not using others, refined sugar for instance. Their production goal as a collective is not primarily centered on profit but to further certain objectives basic to the organization.[20] At the same time, they are in competition with other bakeries largely constrained only by considerations of profit and loss. So it is not surprising that there is always pressure to become more competitive, thus more profitable, by watering down the standards of the product "just a little bit" to make it more palatable to a mass audience.

Everyone in the collective has some stake in this growth: more profit translates potentially into higher wages, better benefits, a cushion for emergencies, or relocation to a more comfortable setting. Yet when the white flour crisis came to a head, the resolution seemed to fly in the face of profitability and expansion and uphold the principles of the bakery.

The crisis erupted when one of the bakers began experimenting with a whole-grain loaf that had some organic white flour added to the mix. He baked a few loaves for people to taste, and for a number of weeks there was a great deal of taste-testing going on. While some members scathingly dismissed it as "cotton candy," others seemed quite enthusiastic about it. Whether to add this hybrid to bakery production was put on the agenda of the bread shift meeting where, surprisingly, there was support for the white flour bread. Then one of the oldest members spoke up: "This is a whole-grain bakery," he said. "We're part of the Whole Grain Association. If we start using white flour and it sells, I'm afraid we'll be drawn more and more to white flour. If we decide to add white flour, I'll have to resign." This speech, delivered with a great deal of passion by one of the quieter members, stunned shift members. It was clear now that the addition of white flour bread would be seriously divisive. Word of what happened at the meeting went around the bakery rapidly. I was told that the question of white flour would probably be put on the agenda of the next collective meeting to be discussed by the whole group. But it never was, and the subject was dropped. Within weeks the "white flour" baker left to join another collective bakery in the area, one with less uncompromising nutritional stands that uses white flour and sugar.

The crisis was ostensibly resolved by the decision of the baker who was its chief proponent not to remain in the collective. But the decision to add a little white flour to make one variety more widely appealing than others might not have been so easily shelved if the market for Wholly Grains type of products had not been flourishing. Indeed, that baker and his supporters could very well have won the day. As it is, however, the market for whole-grain breads is expanding as people become increasingly conscious of what they eat and anxious about what has been added to food to make it last longer on the shelves. Right now, Wholly Grains, instead of watering down its principles by making its bread more acceptable to a wider audience, can afford to stick to its standards knowing that there is a growing demand for what it produces. In fact, the market situation is favorable enough at this point that some members were talking of producing an even more "pure" and possibly more expensive bread that contains only organic ingredients.

Structuring Power: The Management Crisis

The present system of coordination in the collective is a new one put in place to undo an arrangement where one member managed the operation and was paid more for doing so. This system deeply undermined the character of the collective. According to one member, for a time "apathy and stagnation were the result."

But the decision to hire a manager was a desperate survival strategy adopted because the bakery was facing a severe financial crisis. One of the founding members proposed to take on the position in return for a higher salary than the rest. "We hired him because we hoped he'd provide leadership, move the collective forward," I was told. "We got through the financial crisis, but he didn't turn us around as a collective."

Resentment of the manager and resistance to the new setup began to surface after only a few months. It crystallized around a new member who led a struggle for the restoration of what she described as "a real collective, what I expected to find when I joined." She was appalled instead to find that "they couldn't call themselves a democratic workplace. There was a manager and he was paid more than the rest of us. He controlled all the information about the operations of the bakery so it was hard for us to make any real decisions at the collective meeting." She found support from some old members who were rejoining the group as well as from others who were disturbed about the inequitable relationship that had evolved. What had seemed to be the only way out of a bleak financial situation had become an intolerable one. They began the task of developing something new, and they found outside help to do so.

The members were able to call on the services of a consulting firm in the area whose "primary purpose is to help develop and improve the effectiveness of democratic organizations."[21] With the firm's help, the present system of coordinators and committees was developed and steps were taken to improve the business operation of the bakery.

It is hard to predict exactly what would have been the outcome of this crisis without the support of outside mediation and expertise and impossible to be sure of the result without the infusion of enthusiasm, ideals, and expectations of personal empowerment brought into the group in the form of new members. It is possible that the struggle to oust the manager would have occurred anyway. On the other hand, it seems likely that the managerial structure would have become more and more entrenched as the "efficiency" of this method of control was demonstrated by an improved financial condition.

While the new system has reinvigorated the collective principle at Wholly Grains by rejecting the conventional division of labor and authority and redistributing power throughout the membership, it is not, as one longtime member of the collective observed, "all that successful." Only months after the changeover, one of the coordinators, a respected person who had led the struggle against the managerial structure, resigned. In her formal resignation at the collective meeting she said: "I don't mind doing the things that a coordinator has to do. But I don't want to be the coordinator. It's not the new structure. That's OK. It's me. I'm a perfectionist and I take on too much of the stress of the job."

Since then, no one has come forward willing to run for the position. The former manager explained this to me: "People understand that the position incurs the resentment of others. They saw [her] going crazy without getting paid anything extra for it. They don't want to take it on."

But it is far more than just the lack of monetary incentive that makes members reluctant to take on the job. The coordinator role in the collective is not simply a neutral figure but the day-to-day locus of collective power. One of the consultants described the position as being "like a lightning rod in that framework. You take every shock on."

Also highly significant is the meaning of the role that members bring from the outside world. Managing others and being managed are relationships which I believe the majority of members of Wholly Grains are consciously rejecting. One member explained to me my first evening working on the bagging shift, "We're not very good at training people—telling them what to do—but you must have figured that out by now. We don't like to do that kind of thing. That's why we're here."

The management crisis was resolved by a thorough restructuring of a relationship that threatened to reshape the bakery along more conventional lines and by reestablishing some process by which power can be shared among the entire membership. The presence of new members with a strong commitment to workplace democracy and yet untested ideals about what a collective should be facilitated this resolution. New members provide a regular injection of enthusiasm and optimism into the group.

Also crucial was the existence of a consulting firm in the area specializing in worker cooperatives. Even though the new system seems to conform only partially to the blueprint worked out with the firm's help, it nonetheless brought about a dispersal of managerial responsibility and knowledge that seems to be shaping the newly emerging structure. A member who has recently been doing some of the calculations essential for production remarked, "I used to be totally mystified by the bake sheet. I have to do it now, and it's really quite simple." She envisions a system of coordination that parcels the duties and tasks out among many people. This seems to be indeed what is evolving.

A Warrior Caste? The Delivery Shift Crisis
More than half of the income of the collective goes to pay members' wages and benefits. The rest goes to buy ingredients, packaging material, and insurance, pay the rent, repair machinery and equipment, and so on. These are all costs which are outside the control of the collective and which they must absorb in some way. What is spent on wages, however, is regulated entirely by the collective as members themselves decide on how much of their intake they will use for that purpose.

During a financial crisis about two years ago brought on largely because of an ever-expanding wage bill, the collective agreed to adopt a
mechanism to control labor costs, "the efficiency standard." Up to that
time, productivity had been recorded but no norm established for how
long tasks should take. At the time of the crisis, the ex-manager told
me, "more people were on the shifts than ever, but we were producing
the same amount as before. We had to do something."

The efficiency standard is based on the average time that it takes to
do a task. Baggers, for example, are supposed to bag seventy-five loaves
an hour, bakers to produce forty-two loaves an hour. Each shift has a
half-hour leeway. Should a shift consistently go overtime, then wages
are docked—they are not paid for the total number of hours worked.
On the other hand, shifts that complete their task under the allotted
time can receive bonuses. People that I talked to seemed ambivalent
about the standard: "[The] efficiency [standard] is useful because rising
labor costs are always a big problem for us. But it has its drawbacks.
The system rewards people for going fast. Bakers may spoil a batch by
forgetting to put some essential ingredient in because they are hurrying
to get the work done."

The standard has a very different impact on the shifts in the bakery.
Certain shifts are more easily monitored than others. A shift such as
bagging, which produces a certain quantity of items per hour and in
which the work takes place in the bakery in sight of other members, is
more easily controlled than one such as delivery, which provides intangible services and operates all over the Bay Area. And in fact, the system is officially in place for all the shifts in the collective but delivery.
At the same time that the bakers had to cut back the number of workers
on a shift to conform with the standard and when baggers had been
warned that they were operating below standard and "efficiency" would
be enforced, delivery workers were relatively free to go about their
routes as speedily or as slowly as they chose.

The drivers, under pressure from the rest of the collective to come
up with shift norms, claim that it is well-nigh impossible to calculate
how much time it takes to do deliveries because there are so many
factors involved in their work over which they have no control, from
traffic conditions to public relations in the stores. Nevertheless, it
should not be impossible for them to come up with some reasonable
average since they know that the other members would accept whatever
they propose. It would seem, therefore, that what they are really doing
is resisting any control (even in principle) over the terms of their job.

How has the delivery shift managed to retain control over their wage
and the conditions of their work while others have not? To address this

question, I will examine the nature of the drivers' work and how that relates to who the drivers are.

The delivery shift had eight members at the time I was doing my field work. While delivery tends to be a male job in the work force outside the collective, half of the bakery's drivers were women.[22] One of the women and one of the men had been members for several years. The delivery shift is responsible for distributing Wholly Grains' products to retail outlets in the area every day except Sundays. On my day accompanying one of the drivers, I found that it could be a long and lonely day with no company but the radio. Drivers leave early in the morning to cover certain routes. Most routes are choked with traffic, and parking is impossible. On arrival at a store, they first check to see how much bread remains on the shelves, make a decision about how many fresh loaves to put out and how many to pull, arrange the loaves on the shelves as attractively as space assigned allows, take care of billing arrangements, then go on to the next store. Back at the bakery, the drivers unload the "returns" and do the necessary paperwork. It is a stressful, arduous day.

On the other hand there are many attractive aspects to delivery. As a driver you are out and about town. No one monitors or supervises your work—you are truly on your own. Since you are on your own, no one depends on you to get your part of a task done, so you have a much greater ability to pace yourself. The delivery shift seems to have a strong sense of identity as a work team. One of the members told me that they are the only shift that meets outside of the bakery and the only one that refused to allow the manager to attend their meetings as he was no longer a driver.

I would like to speculate on some possible reasons why the delivery shift has been able to resist the collective's efforts to standardize their work. First, experienced delivery people who want to join the collective are hard to find. Drivers make good money working for regular businesses. While a job with a regular firm might involve more supervision and less autonomy, it is still inherently a more independent and flexible occupation than most others. So they have less to gain from being a part of a collective. Second, the nature of the job is such that it cannot be monitored like other in-house tasks. Third, as the conduit between the production and sales ends of the operation, the delivery shift has the best overall picture of market conditions. Others have only a partial view. This knowledge is extremely valuable for the bakery in terms of decisions about future products and gives the drivers a lot of say in decisions. Finally, drivers work on their own outside of the bakery, so they are unlikely to experience the full impact of the culture of the collective, and the pressures to conform are more easily avoided.

The delivery shift crisis has created internal distinctions among collective members as one shift becomes differentiated from the others. But other members have become very sensitive to this potential "elite" in their midst. "A warrior caste" is how one person characterized them. And so the collective has begun the process of reining the drivers in. For example, a newly instated requirement of all recently hired drivers is that they work on the bagging shift, which is the least desirable, most routinized work in the bakery. Supposedly, this would involve drivers in on-site cooperative work as well as one part of the production process with which they are most directly concerned, the packaging. Still, this strategy is only partially successful. Some drivers pay lip service to the requirement; others refuse to bag. It appears that when drivers can survive on delivery hours, they quit bagging. Furthermore, the chances of drivers getting all the hours they need are excellent since their wage is still not controlled by the collective but by the drivers themselves.

This crisis was still unresolved as I finished my field work: the delivery shift was continuing to take their time over the calculation of a norm; the other members were grumbling over the number of hours that certain drivers were able to claim. Given this stalemate, the possibility for an entrenchment of inequity between work shifts looms large in the collective. It threatens the collectivity of the group as it contains the seeds of a division of labor where one work shift has greater control over the conditions of work and more access to the fruits of the collective labor than the others.

Yet my time with the group gives me reason to be optimistic about the outcome of this crisis. Once again, time and place seem to be particularly fortuitous for its resolution. First, several members of the delivery shift are also representative of that very infusion of new idealism and enthusiasm for workplace democracy that helped to turn the management crisis around. They have a personal stake in seeing the collective work as a collective.

The growing demand and appreciation of whole-grain products already noted means that while profits remain small, the bakery has been in a position to give some shifts bonuses and to not enforce the efficiency standard on shifts such as bagging that tend to consistently go over the norm. The forecast might be far more dismal if markets were shrinking and declining profits meant that the total wage bill had to be drastically cut.

Finally, the very nature of what it means to be a collective might point us in the direction of why there is likely to be a resolution given the previously listed external conditions: each individual is not only a worker but also an owner. So, paradoxically, while it might seem in each individual's interest to appropriate as much as he or she can as a

worker, because each is also an owner, it is in his or her best interest to
control the wage so that the whole enterprise can grow. The drivers are
able to manipulate the situation so that they maintain control over the
size of their wages, while others act within the bounds established to
ensure the survival of the collective. But it is possible that the combination of self-interest and collective vigilance of other members as well
as the drivers' own sense of membership will induce the drivers either
to conform to the collective will or to force a reconceptualization of how
the wage is distributed among the entire membership.

WHAT ABOUT THE FUTURE?

Worker cooperatives in the United States have indeed found it difficult
to survive. Born out of the turbulence of hard times, they have tended
to degenerate as the economic situation improves. Yet Wholly Grains
bakery collective remains in business after fourteen years in spite of
internal upheaval and financial hardships. Can the terms of success of
this one collective tell us anything about the prospect for worker cooperatives in the future?

There is optimism in the literature about the future viability of
worker cooperatives. Jackall and Levin, for example, suggest three reasons for this optimism. The first is the persistence of the hard economic
times that have historically given birth to cooperatives. Second, they
speculate that the continued deskilling of work might result in large
numbers of people seeking the "greater challenges and involvement"
that work in cooperatives provide. Finally, they predict a recurrence of
a sixties-type revolt by young people whose skills, education, and creativity are not being used by "an increasingly bureaucratized economy"
and who, as in the past, will seek an outlet in cooperative organization.[23]

This forecast, while encouraging, misses what is significant about the
present economic crisis: a fundamental shift in the economy has taken
place. This change is brought into focus by Michael Piore and Charles
Sabel in *The Second Industrial Divide*. They argue that the present economic crisis in the United States is not just a temporary downturn but
the result of the outmoded nature of the mass production model of
industrial development on which capitalism in the United States has
been based. As mass markets stagnate, enterprises have competed for
customers by distinguishing their goods from those of others and re-
educating consumers to "appreciate" this uniqueness. In this process,
firms have developed the technology to cut the cost of customized production, narrowing the gap between the price of mass-produced and

craft-made products. This has made it easier to win customers away from mass-produced goods.[24]

These fundamental changes in the economy require a new model for production, "flexible specialization," which is characterized by its flexibility: a propensity for innovation, for "accommodation to ceaseless change rather than an effort to control it."[25] It is based on skilled workers, working collaboratively, able to respond to frequent changes in the production process. Central to the success of such a model, Piore and Sabel argue, is its embeddedness in a community of similar, related enterprises and supportive educational, political, and cultural institutions.

Worker cooperatives such as Wholly Grains appear to be prototypes of Piore and Sabel's flexible specialization. But, significantly, Piore and Sabel do not consider them. Indeed, they do not consider alternative forms of ownership and control that would meet the requirements of flexible specialization. They take for granted differences in power between owners and employees and gloss over the conflicting interests of capital and labor. Because they don't problematize these dimensions of capitalist production, they don't pay attention either to the despotic character of most forms of "flexible specialization" or to the possible ascendancy of worker cooperatives.

Their analysis of the second industrial divide does point to a widening space within which collectives such as Wholly Grains can exist as viable financial enterprises. No longer just marginal, anomalous creatures of hard times, these organizations are in fact structured along the lines considered most adaptive under the present economic circumstances. At the same time, they continue to offer something unique, an alternative for people who are determined to create and control their own conditions of work.

AFTERWORD: WRAPPING IT UP

I knew I would have to go back to the collective and present my paper sooner or later. But I tried to put it off for as long as I possibly could. On one hand, I strongly believed that I was bound to give the members some accounting of the time we had spent together. They had taken me in, told me their life stories, taken time to show me how bread was baked, loaves bagged, the product delivered, and patiently answered my questions. Now it was my turn. They expected and had a right to have a look at what I had to say about their organization. Several members had told me during my field work that they wanted to see my paper and I had somewhat glibly assured each that she would be the first to have a copy. I knew that their responses to my paper would be some of the most important I would receive. I wanted the group to validate my findings by recognizing themselves in the story I was telling. I hoped that what I had to say would resonate with their own experience. But what if it didn't? What if they did not find my presentation meaningful or could not recognize themselves in it at all? I barely whispered this question to myself, so I had no clear answer as to what I would do, how I would feel given this eventuality.

My commitment to take my paper back to the bakery and my desire for their opinion did not automatically inhere in the process of field work itself. The many aspects of this final act as a researcher were discussed in our seminar; it was something that we each had to consider independently based on the nature of our specific field sites. We counseled each other, felt it was most ethical to do so, but agreed it was a decision we had to make for ourselves. We concluded that going back was not always feasible or wise. While it was possible for most of us to contemplate doing so, we envisioned situations where this would not be the case. We had all selected groups to study with whom we shared certain basic philosophical and political assumptions. None of us had been covert in the field; our identities and purpose were known to all members.

There were other considerations as well. How best to communicate the information? Would sending a copy of the paper to the group be enough? While we had all tried to write clearly, making one's way through a thirty-page sociology paper can be a tiring task even for sociologists. Moreover, one of us had participated in a group of women for whom English was a recent second language, so just handing them a copy of the paper was an empty gesture. We decided that it would not be enough if we wanted real feedback from individuals. If we really wanted their opinions, we had to not only give them a copy of the paper but to make an oral summary presentation to the group.

During the months that I had been around the bakery, I had begun to feel very much a part of the membership. I worried about the imminent move to a new location, a drop in sales, and members who weren't showing up for work. I identified with the collective's goals; I wanted the bakery to thrive. Most important, I believed that the problem central to my paper—how the bakery was able to count on resources in the external environment to offset the many pressures to normalize—would be of interest and useful to them. So I decided to send my paper to the collective and to follow it up with an oral presentation to the membership.

But I was terrified to take the first step. The picture that I had painted was not always flattering and I had singled out one group within the collective—the delivery shift—as being able to remain outside of the collective will. The bakery was a small, tightly knit organization, as one member described it, "like a village: you can't keep any secrets," so it would be clear to everyone who I was talking about or even whom I had heard a story from. I was worried that this familiarity, this transparency would cause ill feelings and be divisive among the members. I was afraid that collective members would charge that my paper did not reflect their experience at all, that I was just wrong. I envisioned anger, resentment, and feelings of betrayal from people I had come to know fairly well and who had accepted me into their midst in an open and trusting way. I had to confront the fact that it was one thing to scribble observations in a private notebook, to share "theories" about what I was seeing with my colleagues in the seminar, to write a paper and make sociology out of the twenty lives and over a decade of experience of this unusual group. But it was quite another thing to stand in front of these twenty people and explain or defend what I had done.

I suppose I expected antagonism and resistance because of what had taken place in our own seminar when Charles Kurzman, who had done his observation of the class, presented his field notes, followed by his sociological analysis of what was really going on. As a group we had vociferously challenged his theories of us, and it was clear that the person he had singled out to make his point felt hurt and angry. We resisted being defined, objectified, classified, and categorized. Charlie may have been right about us, but once he had made his presentation we distanced ourselves from him by continually reminding him of his difference from us in the seminar.

One day I could avoid the collective no longer because it stood blocking my path in the shape of one of the members. This was not just any member, but one of the bakers, someone who was very much concerned with the emotional temperature of the bakery, the member most likely to be called upon to mediate when they were having problems. I felt that she was the right person with whom to share my dilemma. We greeted each other and she asked if I had finished my paper. Yes, I'd been meaning to bring it by, I told her.

Then I confided in her that while I wanted to know what the group thought about it, I was also concerned that it might hurt certain individuals and might force issues out into the open that could be divisive. She agreed to read the paper first and then let me know how she thought it might be best handled. In addition, I offered to come to a meeting of the collective to present my findings. A week later, she called to tell me that she liked the paper and had made copies for the other members to read, and that I was on the agenda of the next collective meeting.

The collective meeting is low-key and, given all my fantasies, anti-climactic. People greet me as I arrive with welcoming smiles and nods. I take my seat. We are meeting in the very same room in which I had met with the Steering Committee on my first visit to the bakery. Again we sit in a circle. The agenda is on butcher paper tacked up on a post. Once again the issues to be taken up at the meeting look likely to involve lengthy discussions: Three new members are being inducted into the group, the move to a new location is to be discussed, and there are problems staffing all shifts. Serious, life-and-death matters for the collective are to be deliberated on. My part seems like a mere diversion. I feel neither a stranger, as I did at first, nor at home, as I did later. Now I am a visitor.

By the time my turn comes, we are already pressed for time and I must be brief. I thank the group for allowing me to work in the bakery and to gather the data for my research, and I outline my argument. As I speak I realize that there are two or three new people in the room who are unaware that I had been a part of the group only a few months before and are probably a bit puzzled as to who I am. The person who had received the most negative attention in the paper avoids my gaze throughout the entire meeting. I conclude by explaining that my paper might be published as a chapter in a book, so I am especially eager to get comments from them.

There are few questions. One is about the book. One of the new members asks if I had discovered anything that would be useful to them in the collective. This question is seriously put, without a trace of irony. I go over my conclusion: there are certain crises endemic to the collective, they have managed to survive these, I believe, because of certain conditions in the environment in which they are located. Some crises are more difficult to overcome and endanger collectivity. I believe that how wages are distributed, as well as the ability of certain groups to stand outside the control of the collective body, is such a crisis and should be discussed. Surely, someone will take me up on this contention. There is silence, however. I get up and make a quick exit so that the rest of the long agenda can be covered.

But to my surprise this was not the end but rather the beginning of an exchange that continues. As I left, one of the delivery shift members, J., one of the most lively, argumentative, and opinionated members, told me that he had some comments on my paper. Later he sent me six single-spaced typewritten pages. We met twice in the next few weeks to discuss them. It was through this discussion and my subsequent meeting with other collective members individually outside the bakery that I learned how people really felt about the paper. I gathered from these conversations that people in the bakery were talking about what I had to say. One member told me that the bread shift liked what I had to say. I also discovered the ire of one of the new delivery people, who felt I had ignored how diligent and committed the delivery team is.

One of the founding members said that my paper just goes to show that no outsider can really capture the reality of the bakery. Perhaps this is true. Yet as I reflect on his comment I realize that my position as outsider made it much easier for me to write the kind of paper I did. While I had stage fright about presenting my paper in case feelings might be hurt, I did not hesitate to take one position finally, discarding a number of other valuable, interesting positions I might have taken. I envisioned what it might have been like to write the paper as a collective effort with the bakery members. It would have been extremely difficult to come to any decision about which issues to emphasize and what perspective to take on those issues. I believe we could have generated a number of position papers and debates, a myriad of whole-grained perspectives. We could have come up with something truly practical and grounded in questions inspired by their most pressing needs. My bias tells me that to force one composite voice out of twenty-one would have produced one bland smooth product, a white-bread version of reality, that we could all feel comfortable with.

I am especially grateful to J. for his pages of comments. He meticulously went over the paper correcting factual errors I had made and providing background information where I had been vague or misleading. "It's of course very flattering," he wrote politely, "for our small organization to have been chosen as a paradigm of progressive producer, full of problems and potential. . . . Clearly I don't agree with all your facts and opinions on each critical issue which you choose to examine in some depth, but I agree with the overall thrust of the paper that the resolution of crisis is one of the more important facing a relatively small and relatively democratic producer/distributor co-op."

But the overwhelming message that I get from the six pages and from my intense discussions with him that followed is that this particular member of the delivery shift was contesting the formulation that I devised. He definitely did not agree with what I said about the role of the delivery shift. He challenged my assumptions and disagreed with my interpretations. These discussions help me to air my perspective with an insider. In this process I became clearer and more confident that what I have seen, though only one of the multiplicity of things to be seen and perspectives to see it from, is in fact there.

J. had questions of his own to raise in response to mine. These questions seem singularly fruitful to pursue. But he had neither the time nor the desire to follow these up on such an abstract level. He is busy with other collective members struggling to keep the old delivery trucks running, delivering the bread, and helping to manage the business. I am left reflecting on the division of labor in which I find myself. Paradoxically, I was drawn to do research in a collective in order to examine their attempt to erase the distinction between mental and manual work and find myself firmly on one side of that divide: a mental worker interpreting the manual work of others.

PART THREE

New Immigrants

Introduction to Part 3

Recent years have seen a new wave of immigration to the United States. After plummeting during and after World War II, the number of incoming immigrants began a dramatic rise in the 1960s. In 1985, the influx reached a million for the first time in nearly half a century. Only two decades earlier, in 1965, immigration was less than one-quarter of that magnitude.[1] These new immigrants can be distinguished from their predecessors not only by their numbers, but by their area of origin. Whereas earlier immigrants were overwhelmingly European, the new immigrants come primarily from Asia and Latin America. Despite the salience of this distinction,[2] both Shiori Ui and Leslie Salzinger emphasize in their essays that culture accounts for few of the ways in which their survival strategies differ from those of groups who preceded them. Instead, both authors insist that the element of new immigrants' experience in this country that most sharply distinguishes it from that of their predecessors is the distinctive structure of constraints and opportunities they encounter upon arrival.

The new wave of immigration can also be distinguished from previous waves by its gender ratio. Whereas men predominated in most earlier immigrations, women tend to predominate in this one.[3] This is attributable in part to the fact that war takes a particularly steep toll on men, so that in many cases only women are left to immigrate with their children. However, it is also attributable to the structure of demand in the contemporary U.S. economy. Sassen emphasizes the fact that jobs in two of the most vital sectors of the economy, the state social services sector and the private service sector, are culturally defined as "women's jobs." Thus, she notes the "feminization" of the job supply, linking the predominantly female gender composition of new immigrant flows to

this new structure of demand. Both Ui and Salzinger analyze developments at this crucial nexus between growing numbers of immigrant
women and the evolving service economy. Both analyses focus on the
evolving structure of constraints and opportunities defined by the state
and the private sector and on the impact of this structure on the occupational strategies of immigrant women.

Both authors identify economic and political developments since the
mid-1960s, when immigration began to climb once again, as providing
the relevant context within which the survival strategies of new immigrants can be understood. During this period, manufacturing jobs
moved from the United States to the Third World in growing numbers,
eroding opportunities in the sectors that traditionally provided immigrants with jobs. At the same time, some of the major North American
cities became centers for new service sector industries, requiring large
numbers of support services. Immigrants, who once flooded North
American factories, are now feeding and cleaning up after multinational managers coordinating manufacturing in the developing world.
Thus, new immigrants face a dramatically different labor market than
did their predecessors, one dominated by service rather than by factory
jobs.

During this same period, the North American state became directly
involved in the provision of ongoing social services for the first time.[4]
The initiation of the War on Poverty signaled a new level of federal
intervention and involvement in the lives of its citizens. Community
Action and Model Cities Programs brought large numbers of federally
funded professionals into the cities to work with, and on, the poor.
Despite the erosion of funding for these programs in recent years,
these developments have fundamentally shifted the relationship of the
state to those in need, creating an apparatus designed and expected to
develop services as well as distribute individual subsidies.

As a result of these developments, new immigrants encounter a fundamentally different state than did their predecessors. Today, American foreign policy determines not only who enters the country,[5] but
their access to welfare and social service programs after arrival. Thus,
the relationship of new immigrant groups to the emerging service economy is fundamentally mediated by their relationship to the state and by
their ability or inability to improve their market situation through the
use of state services. In the following section, Ui focuses on a group that
has been legally defined as a refugee population — Cambodians — whereas Salzinger discusses a group that has not been so defined — Central
Americans. The impact of this designation is dramatically highlighted
in the contrasting survival strategies of the two groups.

Ui looks at the emergence of female leaders in a Cambodian enclave in Northern California and identifies the conditions that allowed for this apparently unprecedented development. Because Cambodian refugee status provides them with access to state services, the structure of these services emerges as a crucial element in her account, explaining both the presence of an ethnic enclave in the first place and women's access to extrafamilial resources within it. Salzinger looks at two internally diverse Latina domestic worker cooperatives. She asks what accounts for the presence of even middle-class women in these jobs and what accounts for the divergent attitudes of women in the two groups toward domestic work. Because Latina women do not have refugee status, they are not shielded from the market by the presence of the state. As a result, in her analysis the growing service economy emerges as the relevant context within which the occupational strategies of immigrant domestic workers can be understood.

Although the two authors emphasize different contexts, both focus on the way in which the community configuration and survival strategies of new immigrants respond to possibilities and limits defined by the state and the economy in the United States today. However, both Ui and Salzinger are ultimately interested in immigrants as agents: in their capacity to use preexisting structures of constraint and opportunity to create lives they can live with. Thus, both authors highlight the way in which new immigrants shape the world around them, molding the limits of possibility in an increasingly familiar world.

Leslie Salzinger
Shiori Ui

SEVEN

A Maid by Any Other Name: The Transformation of "Dirty Work" by Central American Immigrants

Leslie Salzinger

I am teaching an English class at Choices, a cooperative of immigrant Latina domestic workers.[1] We are practicing tenses of the verb "to be." "In El Salvador I was a teacher, here I am a housekeeper." "In Nicaragua I was a businesswoman, here I am a housekeeper." Embarrassed laughter ripples through the group at the end of each sentence. "Oh, how the mighty have fallen," I say, reflecting the discomfort in the room. Another co-op member comes in and a woman in the class explains what's going on, quoting my comments in summary. But then she turns back to the group. "It makes us embarrassed, but it shouldn't. We're trained, we do good work, and they pay us well. We haven't fallen." Everyone nods in agreement.

A few weeks later I am teaching a similar class at Amigos, another local domestic worker cooperative. As we go around the room the sentences falter and trail off into uncertainty. "In El Salvador I was a cashier, here I am. . . ." "In Guatemala I was a laundress, here I am. . . ." I suggest "domestic worker." They agree matter-of-factly, but there is no conviction to their responses. Whether positive or negative, they have not claimed this identity as their own.

I spent the fall of 1988 observing and sometimes participating in the meetings, gossip, English classes, and job-reception work of two immigrant Latina domestic worker cooperatives in the Bay Area. As the months passed, a few questions began to surface with increasing frequency. Many of these women had been in the United States for close to a decade. Why were they doing domestic work after so many years here? Domestic work is a paradigmatic case of immigrant "dirty" work—of work that is irredeemably demeaning.[2] Why did some of these women speak with such pride of their work? And even more puzzling, what accounted for the dramatically different attitudes members of the two groups held toward their work? As my attention was drawn to these anomalies, I realized that many of the explanations were to be found not within the cooperatives that had generated them, but in the market for domestic work. In this chapter I look at the occupational strategies of these women and locate them in the structural context within which they were formed. I argue that the human capital resources they brought—or failed to bring—with them account for little of their work experience in this country. Rather, it is within the context of the constraints and opportunities they encountered here that we can understand their occupational decisions, their attitudes toward their work, and ultimately their divergent abilities to transform the work itself.

WHY DOMESTIC WORK?

Although many immigration theorists emphasize the role of culture or human capital in explaining occupation,[3] such arguments provide us with little help in accounting for the occupational strategies of many of the women in Choices and Amigos. Teachers, cashiers, peasants, laundresses, housewives, recent immigrants, longtime residents, persecuted organizers, jobless mothers, documented recipients of political asylum, undocumented refugees, Nicaraguans, Guatemalans, Colombians, Salvadorans, single women, wives, widows, mothers . . . the most striking thing about the women I encountered was their diversity. No group seemed to lack its representatives. There are some whom we might expect to find: those who did domestic work in their countries of origin, or who come from rural areas, or who never obtained legal documents. However, we find others whose presence is harder to account for: urban, previously professional women who have been here long enough to obtain work permits. Why are they doing domestic work after so many years in this country?

The work of Saskia Sassen-Koob[4] moves away from the characteristics of individual women, or even of individual ethnic groups, to focus directly on the structural context entered by contemporary immigrants to American cities. During the last twenty years, immigrants have entered the United States' "declining" cities in ever-increasing numbers, and contrary to all predictions they continue to find enough work to encourage others to follow them. Sassen-Koob asks how these immigrants can be absorbed by an economy that is rapidly losing its industrial base. Her explanation for this apparent anomaly is that while these cities are losing their place as manufacturing centers, they are simultaneously undergoing a rebirth as "global cities," dedicated to the coordination of scattered factories and to the production of "producer services" such as banking and insurance for an international corporate market. Retaining her focus on the niche filled by immigrant workers in contemporary cities, she emphasizes the direct support services and one-of-a-kind luxury goods financed by this new, export-directed service economy. Thus her analysis points not only to the financial analysts but to the clerical workers who punch in their data, not only to the advertising executives but to the workers who stuff their futons and sew their quilts, not only to the commodity brokers but to the workers who clean their offices, buildings, and apartments. Like early analyses of household labor, her schema makes visible the denied: the work that enables the smooth operation of both the offices and the lives of those who run them.

Sassen-Koob's research points to the way in which a new international division of labor affects the opportunities and constraints directly facing job seekers. She distinguishes between the suburban middle class of 1950–1970, based in a manufacturing economy, and the urban middle class of the 1970s and 1980s, based in the new service economy, and she traces the impact of their divergent life-styles on the market for low-level service work. Her claim is that whereas suburbs were made possible by the construction of roads and cars and household "labor-saving" devices, new professional life-styles depend on the creation of labor itself. She identifies two historically specific systems: the manufacturing-based middle class with life-styles undergirded by a physical infrastructure constructed by past immigrants, and the service-based middle class with life-styles supported by a labor infrastructure made up of recent immigrants.

Such an analysis highlights not only the existence of low-level jobs, but the two-tiered nature of contemporary economies. The bulk of available jobs generated by the growing service sector either require formal training—generally certified by North American credentialing institutions—or presuppose and provide no training at all. Mobility, when it occurs, is achieved through off-the-job training. There is no way to "advance" from clerical worker to executive or from janitor to nurse without formal education. Unless one enters the country with transferable professional credentials, there is no way to cash in on previous status unless one has the resources, either in capital or in family support, to get formal training and credentials here.

Many of the women I met are aware that a lack of locally legitimated training is what is holding them back. An Amigos board member ran a trucking business in which she bought and sold goods throughout Guatemala, Honduras, and El Salvador. In Guatemala, her husband and children did almost all the housework, and she hired someone to come in and do the extensive preparation required for festivals. However, since her arrival in this country ten years ago she has consistently done one form or another of domestic work. "I hope I don't keep doing cleaning," she says. "First of all, because I'm forty-eight years old, and I'm worked out. And to tell you the truth, I don't like cleaning. In two years my daughter will start working and then maybe she can support me and I can study something. Then I could do something else. We'll see."

It is not that the only jobs in this bottom tier are domestic work. Sassen-Koob remarks on the emergence of sweatshops to manufacture the "craft goods" so attractive to the new professional class. And in fact, among these women there are frequent references to the choice to do domestic work over low-paid factory jobs. A man who called Amigos in search of women to work full-time sewing sequins and beads found few takers. At $5 (taxable) an hour, it would have meant a cut in pay. A woman who had worked as a seamstress in Nicaragua commented, "I worked sewing for a while when I first got here, but the boss yelled all the time. The only thing he missed was plugging us in." Another commented, "I've done everything, packing, inventory, stuffing pillows. . . . But I like this work. You don't have to punch in. You can negotiate your own terms." Domestic work, for at least some of these women, is a choice. But it is a choice made within limits.

We can better understand why such a heterogeneous group of Latina immigrants are doing domestic work when we shift our gaze from them to the society they face. The diversity of the human capital they bring to the labor market is matched—and made irrelevant—by the lack of diversity in the opportunities they find there. If we look at these women outside the context of the local economy, their occupational strategies are opaque. It is only when we pay attention to what they are choosing *between* that their strategies become comprehensible. The contours of the job market, rather than the limits of skill, vision, and ambition of those entering it, construct the boundaries of possibility.[5]

TWO DOMESTIC COOPERATIVES

Latina domestic workers in the Bay Area find jobs in a multitude of ways: through friends, churches, agencies, chance street contacts, radio and newspaper advertisements, recommendations, and job-distribution cooperatives. Cooperatives are a recent addition to the list. They have emerged in the 1980s in response to the incoming flood of undocumented Central American refugees unable to turn to the American state.[6] Their presence is a reflection not only of the growing numbers of job seekers, but of the changing nature of domestic work. Today, employers often hire someone to clean once a week or once a month rather than to work full-time. This means that workers need a large number of employers to support themselves. In addition, the rise in professional cleaning agencies has accustomed many employers to finding domestic workers through advertisements, rather than through personal networks. Cooperatives provide workers with an alternative to agencies; the co-ops give them access to a pool of jobs gathered through advertising without having to surrender a large percentage of their salaries to an intermediary.

Amigos was the first Bay Area Latina domestic worker cooperative. It was established in 1983 by a neighborhood social service organization to alleviate the most pressing needs of its clientele. The only requirement for admittance is being a Latin American refugee.[7] There is a great deal of turnover in membership. Currently, the group has about sixty members who pay $15 monthly for the right to take jobs. Twenty to thirty people show up at any given meeting. The group is roughly half Salvadoran, half other Central Americans, with a scattering of Mexicans and South Americans. Most, but not all, come from urban areas. Their class backgrounds are extremely varied, ranging from medical technician to country washerwoman. There is a wide range of ages, but the bulk of members are between twenty and forty. The overwhelming majority have been in the country for less than five years, more than half for under a year. Only about a fifth of the group have long-term work permits, although roughly the same number are involved in a drawn-out asylum process through which they are issued work permits as well. No one in the group speaks English fluently, and most speak too little to communicate at even the most basic level.

The current staff person, Margarita, originally came to the cooperative as a member and did domestic work for several years. She stopped housecleaning as soon as her husband found work, however, and she considers it work of last resort. In response to the application of an Argentine woman who has been in the United States for twenty-six years, she comments: "Look, Leslie, if I'd been here twenty-six years, I'd have learned something else by now. I wouldn't be turning up here looking for cleaning work. . . . I put her on the waiting list." This is the land of opportunity, she asserts frequently, people should not content themselves with cleaning, they should study, better themselves, do something else.

Like Margarita, the co-op's founders saw the group as a stopgap solution, designed to provide as many refugees as possible with a way to survive until they found other work. They assumed there was a trade-off between quality and quantity, and quantity was always their priority. Thus, from the outset their marketing strategy was for members to undercut other workers by entering the market at the bottom. This framework was, and is, reflected in their advertising. Their listing in the local paper, two lines under "Domestic Jobs Wanted" rather than under "Domestic Agencies," reads simply, "HOUSECLEANING Garden. Latin American Refugees," with the phone number. The crookedly photocopied flyers they leave under doors convey the same mix of amateurism and desperation. Their ads proclaim not their expertise, but their need and their vulnerability. The subtext of such publicity is exploitability.

The emphasis on quantity over quality of jobs is also evident in the group's wage scale, which is relatively low for domestic work. Members are paid $6 an hour plus transportation for cleaning jobs, $4.50 an hour for child care, and $4 an hour for child care that takes over twenty hours a week. The group charges a formal minimum of $450 monthly for live-in work, but in fact sometimes accepts jobs that pay less. During one meeting Margarita raises the issue of pay, evidently in response to rumors that some members have been asking employers for higher wages: "You all deserve $10 (an hour), but $6 is the going rate. If we ask for more, we're going to lose jobs."

Pay is the only aspect of the work for which the co-op sets any standards at all. In fact, the few times an employer complained that a worker had attempted to negotiate other aspects of the relationship, Margarita and board members sided decisively with the employer. One woman who had been having problems with a live-in employer attempted to get her to sign a contract in November promising to keep her through January. When the employer called complaining that one of the board members had suggested this course of action, the office was in an uproar. Ana stoutly denied doing any such thing: "God forbid," she said. "If I don't like a job, I just leave. I don't stick around complaining and negotiating!" Incredulous irritation swirled through the office at the incident. "Imagine!" "Can you believe it?" "If she doesn't like it, she should just leave!"

Staff and board member expectations for workers are almost as low as are their expectations for employers. The group does no training of new cooperative members, and since most of the group cannot read the (English) instructions on cleaning products and machinery, there are constant mishaps. Virtually every week there is a new complaint from an employer: someone left the gas on and almost blew up the house; someone used the wrong cleaning product and destroyed an antique wooden table. According to Margarita, they used to have a cleaning workshop "to avoid problems," but it eventually took too much time, money, and energy. In any case its purpose was always to forestall disaster, never to transform members into "skilled" workers. Today new members set off for their first jobs without even this minimal introduction, armed only with a bilingual list of common household tasks.

Weekly job-allocation meetings are simultaneously authoritarian and fractious. Board members, three previous members who volunteer their time, read job descriptions and then go down a list of names until the job is claimed. At any given meeting, about a quarter of those present receive jobs—usually for one four-hour stint every two weeks, although most weeks at least one live-in job is taken as well. Since many employers request some knowledge of English, and since board members often warn people not to assume that "just knowing how to say hello" is enough, jobs are often taken by the same women week after week. There is never any collective discussion during meetings; instead, there is the constant hum of private ("unauthorized") conversation between members who are or have become friends. Favoritism based on ethnicity and the unfairness of job allocation are constant topics of discussion among these cliques. There is a sense that members have gathered to compete with each other for a scarce resource, not that they have gathered either to create a collectivity or to support each other as workers.

Conversations at meetings not concerned with problems within the group generally revolve around survival issues: rent, documents, the scarcity of jobs. Strategies for handling bad employers or filthy houses—even complaints about these occupational problems—are conspicuously absent. It is as if the work they spend their days on is not worthy of comment, purely a means to survive and thus significant only in those terms. This attitude is best summed up by Nora, a young Guatemalan woman who has been in the country for little over a year. When I ask her if she thinks cleaning is good work, she is taken aback: "Any work's fine with me. The thing is to make money." She is not looking for a career, she is looking for a job.

Choices was set up in 1984, inspired by the success of Amigos during the preceding year. The group accepts any Latina woman who is over forty years old. Today, it has about fifty members who pay $3 weekly to participate. Jobs are allocated during twice-weekly meetings. About twenty-five women attend each meeting. Although new members join almost every meeting, at least half of the group at any given time have been members intermittently over several years. They come from all over Latin America, and although there are still many more Central Americans than South Americans, Salvadorans constitute less than half of the group. The membership is overwhelmingly urban. More than half come from middle-class backgrounds, and several come from quite elite families. In their countries of origin, they worked as teachers, secretaries, cashiers, or housewives; some ran small businesses of their own. Almost none were manual laborers or domestic workers before their arrival in this country. Many of the women have been in this country as long as ten years, and almost every member who did not already have a work permit has recently qualified for the federal amnesty that requires proof of continuous presence in the country since 1982.[8] About half of the group's members speak enough English to get around, although very few speak with any fluency.

The group was set up by a feminist organization dedicated to helping older women establish meaningful and self-directed careers. Founders initially attempted to serve Latina women in the same program in which they served their other, primarily Anglo and middle-class constituencies. However, to their frustration, they found that gaps in language and formal credentialing were keeping them from placing anyone. Hearing of the relative success of the Amigos Cooperative, they turned reluctantly to domestic-work placement. Unlike the founders of Amigos, however, they framed this work in the context of a commitment to career development, not survival. Thus, within the constrained context of domestic work, they continued to focus on the development of secure, dignified, and relatively decently paid work for their members and on the right of members to determine the course of their own work lives.

When Choices was founded it charged $5 hourly, taking its cue from its model. However, members soon began to push for higher wages. Unlike Amigos, where such a move was seen as subversive, Choices staff were supportive of the shift. In fact, the push by members for higher wages made it easier for Lisa, the group's first staff person, to come to terms with "just channeling women of all different abilities into domestic work," because it not only increased wages, but also meant that group members were beginning to take control of, and define, the work on their own. Today members charge $10 hourly for the first cleaning and, if it is an ongoing job, $8 hourly thereafter. They charge a minimum of $6 hourly for child care, but they do very little, engaging mostly in cleaning work. They have no formal set of standards for live-in jobs, but the current staff person, Lilian, says that she would tell anyone considering paying under $800 a month that she wouldn't be able to find anyone in the group willing to take the job.

The experience of raising prices and continuing to get work orders gave Choices staff a different view of the demand for domestic work than that held by staff at Amigos. Lisa comments that there are "different markets" and mentions advertising in particular newspapers as a way of targeting "better" employers. The group also runs a display ad in the *Yellow Pages* offering "Quality HOUSECLEANING at affordable rates. [Choices] domestic referral service." At the bottom in fine print it says "A non-profit community service by [Choices' sponsor]." Their advertisements look essentially like those for profit-making cleaning agencies and contain no reference to the Latin background of workers. Leaflets do not figure in the marketing strategy at all.

When employers call in, the intake call continues in this professional tone. Lilian mentions that all the workers are Latina women, but makes it clear that anything the employer needs to communicate can be communicated through her. She also lets them know that all workers are "trained." There is a sense that employers will be taken care of. From the employer's point of view, apart from the fact that the worker is paid directly, the group could easily be any one of a number of for-profit cleaning agencies, run by Anglos, that hire Latina women to do the actual work. This sense of worker connection to a white agency is enhanced by the fact that every worker takes an envelope from the office to each new job. The envelope contains Lilian's card, a bilingual household task sheet, a list of appropriate cleaning products, and an evaluation form to be filled out by the employer and mailed to the office. These evaluations not only function to provide employers with a sense of worker accountability, but are also used by co-op members when employers request a worker with references. This process allows workers, as well as the group as a whole, to develop marketable personas.

The professional context within which the co-op sells itself has led it to develop its own standards for members. Soon after raising its prices, the group instituted a short training for members "in order to earn those two dollars," according to Lisa. The training is currently conducted by a member who is paid by the sponsoring organization. It involves going through cleaning tasks and products and discussing how one solves specific cleaning problems, particularly when the employer does not have the standard cleaning products. Trainings also discuss the use of nontoxic cleaning products, as this is one of the group's specialties. The tone of these sessions is casual and friendly, and training for new members takes place while everyone else sits around gossiping about other matters and occasionally kibitzing about the training. All members are tested on the material (orally or in writing, depending on whether they are literate) and they are retested on those questions they got wrong. The knowledge they are tested on is not extensive, but it is easy to see how not knowing some of these things could lead to disaster. What is most striking about the process are the contrasts: between the informality of the actual training sessions and the formality with which both staff and older members describe them; between the tremendous variation in what is actually involved for different people going through the process and the absolute insistence that everyone go through it. It is not as much how it is done as that it is done at all that appears to be significant for the group.

The group has established clear standards for employers as well as workers. On the phone, Lilian asks for specific information about what the employer wants done. If she feels that the amount of work is un-reasonable given the time paid for, she suggests that the worker may need more time or may need to leave some of the work undone. She makes clear that workers will not work extra time for free. She com-municates this to workers as well. For instance, after listening to mem-bers complaining about unreasonably demanding jobs, she comments, "Don't do them. If you do them, they'll think it's possible for the next one who goes. Tell them it's not possible. You need to learn those phrases in English, to defend yourself. And if they insist, let them go. There are other jobs." Margarita at the Amigos cooperative would never have made such a comment. From Margarita's perspective, the most fundamental purpose of her work was to provide as many mem-bers with work as possible. To Lilian, on the other hand, this comment goes to the heart of what makes this work worthwhile—the develop-ment of dignified work for cooperative members.

Choices meetings are social and members clearly enjoy them. There are even several women who no longer need new jobs who continue to attend. Both the twice-weekly meetings are preceded by an English class, and one is preceded by the cleaning training. During meetings, members sit in a circle, and they have a time set aside for reports on their work, as well as for general "commentaries." Jobs are allocated according to an elaborate point system with which they are constantly tinkering. About a quarter of the group gets a job each week, generally for four hours every week or two. Members who speak little English are encouraged by the group to be brave and take jobs, using the bilingual task sheet to communicate. Responsibility for running the meetings is supposed to be rotated. Although this goal is never completely realized, about half of the group participates by taking or reading minutes or by recording dues payments. In introducing the co-op to new members, the group's collective self-sufficiency is always emphasized. Victoria comments, "We maintain the group ourselves—no one else, not the mayor, not anyone, us."

There are constant complaints that some women come "*just* to get work." This is seen as a serious accusation, despite the fact that dis-tributing work is the organization's reason for existence. Since they charge dues for the right to take jobs, there is no mechanism through which they can exclude those who don't behave like "real" members. As a result, there are repeated debates over what to do about this problem. One woman expressed a sort of tacit consensus when she called out during one of these discussions: "It's a community. It shouldn't be just an agency!"

In fact, the group does operate far more like an occupational community than it does like an agency. Members trade tips constantly, developing and sharing strategies to deal with dirty houses and impossible employers in the same breath. During the English classes they ask the teacher to write out specific dialogues for them to memorize: "The house is big, I need more time." "I can't give you more time." "OK, I'll clean as far as I get in the time I have." Someone comments that she got to a new house and found a filthy oven but no Ajax. What should she have done? Use baking soda, of course. She'd never heard that before. "It's amazing how you just keep on learning." "Yes, there's always more to learn." One member announces that she's giving up a job: "My boss keeps calling Lilian to complain. I told her that I do the work, not Lilian. If she has any problems she should talk to me. But she keeps calling Lilian. I'm not anyone's ward." Her decision to leave an otherwise unobjectionable job because she is being treated in a demeaning manner is supported without question by the group. Meetings serve as a context within which workers collectively set standards for themselves and for employers and in so doing redefine their work as dependent on training and deserving of respect.

This collective image of skilled work is carried onto the job and communicated to employers as part of an ongoing struggle for autonomy. A member comments: "It's good to have training. Sometimes an employer says, 'Don't do it that way, that way won't work,' and then I can say, 'Yes it will. I know because I have training.' 'Oh,' they say. . . . Once I worked for this very rich woman and I told her I had had training, and so she started asking me all these questions and I answered them all, and then she was very impressed and left me alone." Another member goes to the front of the room to tell this story:

> I went to clean a house, but the lady wasn't there. And the man didn't have any of the right products. He gave me Clorox to wash the floor— *hardwood* floors. I told him I couldn't, because it would go against my responsibility and my knowledge of cleaning. ["That's good," someone else responds, "That's why we have training. If you'd done it you'd have ruined the floor and they'd have put you in jail." She nods and continues.] Maybe he didn't like the way I talked to him, because when I was leaving he said, "Next time I'll have a list for you of what you should do," and I said to him, "OK, that's good. Next time I come I'll bring a list of

the supplies I need to do the work." So he said "Oh" and then he drove me home.

Given our earlier discussion of why these women do domestic work, the stark contrast between Choices and Amigos is puzzling. After all, despite their varied life histories, women in both groups have ended up doing this work for essentially the same reason: because it is the best of a limited set of options. Moreover, the literature on immigrants' rising expectations suggests that those who have been here longer would be least satisfied with domestic work. Yet the women in Choices are far more positive about their work than are the women in Amigos. Clearly, the founders of the two groups began with somewhat divergent focuses, but these seem minor in comparison to their shared goals of creating domestic-worker cooperatives for Latina immigrants. How could initial differences in founders' emphases within an otherwise similar set of goals produce such sharp and enduring discrepancies in members' perceptions of their work? The answer lies in the structure of the labor market within which the co-ops are embedded and in the way in which the two sets of organizational priorities position their members in this structure.

A BIFURCATED MARKET

Sassen-Koob points to the contemporary emergence of a two-tiered service economy composed of professionals and those who serve them, both at work and at home. What this analysis overlooks is the two-tiered nature of the domestic services market itself. For not only is there an increasing demand for domestic services from single, elite professionals (the "yuppie" phenomenon), but there is also an increasing demand for such services from the rising number of elderly people living alone on fixed incomes, from two-earner working-class families, and from single mothers who need cheap child care in order to work at all. These groups can afford very different pay scales and thus have different requirements and standards for their employees. Together they constitute a dual labor market within the bottom tier of the larger service economy.

In the Bay Area today, Latin American domestic workers are routinely paid anywhere from $5 to $10 hourly. Live-in salaries range between $300 and $1,000 monthly. In her study of Japanese-American domestic workers, Evelyn Nakano Glenn notes similarly broad discrepancies in pay among her respondents.[9] She attributes this to personalistic aspects of the negotiating process between domestic workers and their employers. However, such an explanation begs the question of how this tremendous range for negotiation came to exist in the first place. The variation is made possible in part by the social isolation of the work and by the lack of organization among both workers and employers. This atomization is compounded by ineffective state regulation; domestic work was not covered by the Fair Labor Standards Act until 1974, and even today it is often done under the table. However, hourly wages that vary routinely by factors of two or three must be produced as well as tolerated. What is the structure of demand for domestic work that has kept some wages so low, while allowing enterprising businesses to consistently raise the ceiling on prices at the other end of the spectrum?

Over the past thirty years, women have entered the paid labor force in ever-increasing numbers. This movement is a response both to the economic shifts mentioned by Sassen-Koob—the decline of (primarily men's) manufacturing jobs paying a "family wage" and the increasing availability of "feminized" service jobs—and to cultural shifts that have made paid work an acceptable choice for women even in the absence of financial need. This has led to the increasing commodification of what was once unpaid household labor, visible in the boom in restaurants and cleaning agencies and in the increasing demand for child care during the last two decades.

Like all large-scale shifts in a stratified society, these developments have had a differential impact on the lives and options of people located at different levels within it. Working-class and lower-middle-class women, having entered low-paid service occupations themselves, generally can afford to pay very little to replace their household labor if they are to gain anything at all from their own salaries. Professional women raising children alone often find themselves in a similar quandary. Women in such situations show up regularly at Amigos. A single mother who works part-time at the post office comes in to interview live-in help. She wants to pay only $400 a month. "I can't afford any more," she says, looking desperate. "All I need is someone strong and trustworthy who can look after the kids while I'm gone." Elderly people living alone on fixed incomes, another growing sector of the population, also need domestic help and have little leeway in what they can pay for it. A manager for a seniors' apartment building calls. "My boss gave me your flyer," he says. "I'm always on the lookout to find cheap cleaning help for them. The most important thing is that people be honest." For these groups, the search for domestic help is less a negotiation process with a single worker than it is a desperate search for anyone willing to accept the inevitably exploitative salary they have to offer.

At the other end of this spectrum are single professionals of both genders, an increasingly significant segment of urban consumers in an era of delayed marriage and childbearing. This group faces very different constraints in their relationships with domestic workers. Regardless of the hourly cost, a weekly housecleaning will absorb only a minuscule portion of any middle-class budget. And even middle-class couples seeking full-time child care can afford to negotiate for particular skills and services. There is considerable plasticity in the amount these employers can pay for domestic work.

Not surprisingly, recent years have seen an explosion of entrepreneurs focused on convincing such people that there is something worth paying more for. Young white middle-class women hang advertising posters in trendy restaurants implying that they are just like employers and so can "make your home feel like a home." Professional advertisements for personalized cleaning agencies abound. "Maid-to-Order" promises an ad in the local *Yellow Pages*: "Your chores are our business. Bonded and Insured." "You've Got It Maid," asserts another: "We'll do the cleaning, run your errands, wash the laundry, drop off and pick up the dry cleaning." In a community accustomed to professionalized personal services of all sorts—therapy, home decorating, personal shoppers—this rhetoric finds fertile ground.

Beneath the seemingly random pattern of wage variations among Bay Area domestic workers there lies a dual labor market constituted by two distinct sets of potential employers: the elderly, working-class parents and single mothers with little money to spare; and professionals already accustomed to paying relatively high wages for work packaged as a personalized and professional service. What is remarkable is that the work done in these homes—vacuuming, dusting, scrubbing— remains similar. Insofar as there is any difference, it lies in the addition of child care to other duties in the *bottom* sector of the market.[10] It is the nature of the employer, rather than of the work, that is most significant in determining wages.

CREATING MEANING

The founders of Choices and Amigos had different goals in creating the two cooperatives. Whereas Choices' founders focused on creating a collective context where women could support each other in the search for decent, long-term work, Amigos' founders focused on the creation of a clearinghouse where women with no other options could find enough work to survive. Thus, Choices emphasized job quality, whereas Amigos emphasized quantity. Ironically, due to the bifurcated market for domestic services, the strategies that emerged to accomplish these divergent priorities did not attract markedly different numbers of jobs, just different types of jobs. Whereas Amigos' marketing strategy ultimately located its workers in the bottom sector of the labor market,

Choices's strategy located its members in the top. Members' differing attitudes toward their work took shape in this context. Within both groups, members' attitudes are revealed as strategies to create viable work-lives within differing structures of opportunity—as struggles at the boundaries of the possible.

The competitive atmosphere and low expectations of Amigos members can best be understood as a set of individual responses to the organization's marketing strategy and workers' consequent location in the bottom tier of the domestic services market. Members have little to gain from sharing work tips in a market in which their skill makes virtually no difference in their ability to get jobs. And in an organization in which resistance to employer exploitation is regarded by leaders as undermining the interests of the collectivity, mutual support is difficult if not impossible. Co-op members' perception that only individual strategies are worth focusing on, and that they share little but need and competition with other members of the group, is an accurate one within this limited framework.

In a similar vein, Amigos members' vision of domestic work as essentially unimportant, as a means rather than as an end in itself, reflects the constraints within which they are hired. There is no reason to struggle over the social construction of work when employers couldn't pay more for it even if they agreed it was worth more. In such an environment, Ana's comment that after ten years of domestic work she is still hoping to get training for other work, rather than attempting to improve the work she is doing, makes sense. In an organization in which collective action is precluded, individualized occupational strategies remain the only option. And located among employers who define workers as cheap labor, the obvious occupational strategy is one that leads out of the occupation entirely.

Choices' market strategy, on the other hand, locates its members in the top tier of the domestic services market. Choices members have taken advantage of the opportunities implicit in this situation by working for individual mobility through upgrading the occupation as a whole. They are collectively redefining domestic work as skilled labor, and on that basis struggling for increased pay and security and for autonomy and control over their work. They are in fact engaged in what in other contexts has been called a "professionalization project."[11]

This struggle takes place simultaneously in interactions with employers and within the group itself. Choices' advertising and intake process uses a white middle-class rhetoric that allows members to enter the top tier of the market. These first contacts introduce employers to a group of skilled workers.[12] Once on the job, workers emphasize their expertise. Comments about their training and their insistence that they be treated as experts who know and are accountable for what they are doing emerge as part of this project. However, it is not only employers who need to be convinced that these women are skilled workers; co-op members also need to be convinced of this. Group meetings become the arena in which members construct and reinforce their professionalized identity, thus the strikingly supportive atmosphere, the constant, repetitive discussions of cleaning techniques, the emphasis on the ritual of training and testing are all revealed as elements in the creation of a collective professional identity. Even the ongoing presence of women who no longer need new jobs makes sense. Members of the group have everything to offer each other, for they affirm their tenuous, shared status as skilled workers.

Understanding Choices as a professionalization project makes problematic my earlier portrayal of skilled workers entering the top tier of a preexisting "bifurcated market," however. It pushes us to reconceptualize the relationship between supply and demand in a more dynamic framework.[13] If the market for skilled workers already existed, a collective effort of this sort would not be necessary; workers could simply get training on an individual basis. Clearly, Choices is not creating this demand on its own. But just as clearly, the market for skilled domestic workers is not an outgrowth of unmediated demographic shifts. Rather, the co-op has joined a host of contemporary entrepreneurs already attempting to create a demand for professionalized personal services among the new middle class. Cooperative members are responding to the market and to the structure of constraints and opportunities they encounter within it; but as a collectivity, they are also part of redefining the market and thus expanding the range of possibilities they face. They are not only individuals lucky enough to have entered a context within which professionalization is possible; they are also members of a group that is part of the collective construction of that new structure of opportunity.

At bottom, the professionalization project is an emergent property of the interactive structure of the group itself—of the existence of an infrastructure that makes the development of a collective occupational strategy possible.[14] This process is made somewhat easier by the life histories of the women in the group. Choices members have generally been in this country longer than their counterparts in Amigos and tend to come from somewhat more middle-class backgrounds. Since they no longer expect to leave domestic work, they have an incentive to improve it. Similarly, their time in this country has given them some security, providing them with more latitude in picking and choosing jobs and consequently encouraging the development of domestic work as a career. In addition, their more middle-class backgrounds may have made them more likely to conceptualize their work—even work for which they initially had little respect—in professional terms. Thus, although neither class nor tenure in this country is completely correlated with membership in the two cooperatives, it is likely that the preponderance of long-term residents with middle-class backgrounds in Choices has been conducive to the development of a professionalization project. However, it is the structure of Choices that has provided a context within which these characteristics could make a difference. Amigos does not provide a space within which workers can develop a collective strategy; as a result, each worker faces the market as an individual. Since domestic work is only partially professionalized, this means that Amigos members enter the market as unskilled, immigrant labor, with all the handicaps that such a label implies. Choices members, on the other hand, participate collectively in the redefinition of this work as skilled, and so realize the potential benefits of their class background and tenure in this country within the context of a more powerful occupational identity.

THE SOCIAL ORGANIZATION OF DOMESTIC WORK

This analysis raises a final set of questions, for while it explains the differential ability of the women in these two cooperatives to professionalize their work, it does not explain why domestic workers have so rarely attempted—and even more rarely sustained—such projects in the past.[15] To understand this shift, we need to look more closely at the evolving social organization of domestic work itself, at the constellation of social relations within which the work is performed.

Until recently, domestic workers in this country were seen by employers, and at times saw themselves, as bound by the web of affective and paternalistic connections that constitute relations in the family. This patriarchal relationship reflected the fact that domestic workers shared both home and workplace with their employers. Not only did the domestic worker live in her employer's home, but her workplace was generally the mistress's workplace as well. These overlapping arenas lodged the worker securely within the family, leaving little room for the development of an independent occupational identity.

The overlap between worker and employer living spaces was the first of these linkages to erode. Live-in work began to decrease in frequency during the 1920s,[16] when the young white women, native and foreign-born, who had previously dominated the occupation began leaving to enter factories. They were replaced by Japanese and Mexican immigrants and by Black women migrating from the South. Unlike their white predecessors, their mobility into other jobs was barred by racism.

Many did domestic work all their lives, instead of as a prelude to other work. As a result, they were generally unwilling to sleep in their employers' homes, and the occupation began to reshape itself to the fact that domestic workers had their own families. This shift to "day-work" was the first significant break in the mistress-servant relationship.[17]

The overlap between worker and mistress workplaces did not begin to erode until much later. Until quite recently, most women who could afford domestic help did not work outside the home. As a result, servants joined the mistress of the house in a realm in which emotions were defined as central and contractual relationships as irrelevant.[18] However, as middle-class women moved out of the home, they blurred the boundaries of this realm and changed the relationship of domestic workers to the household in the process. It is easier to construct a house as a workplace when it contains only workers (or more likely a single worker) than it is when it is shared with those for whom it is "home." Similarly, employers who do paid work are less committed to seeing housework as a "labor of love" than they were when they did it full-time themselves. Thus, the increase in the labor market participation of "mistresses" has meant that paid domestic work is increasingly done in a capitalist wage-labor context, rather than in a feudal master-servant context.

In 1974 domestic work was brought under the aegis of minimum wage laws for the first time. Although wages continued to be paid primarily under the table, many employers responded to this new expectation by paying for fewer hours of cleaning per month (frequently for the same amount of cleaning as before[19]). This speed-up further weakened the personal ties between worker and employer. Seeing workers' time as costly, employers who previously used domestic workers as company and confidantes[20] were less likely to stop their work to socialize. Like other shifts in the social organization of domestic work, the imposition of minimum wage laws made the occupation less personal and affective and more contractually defined.

In recent years, agencies have entered the field in growing numbers. They hire people and send them out to private homes in which they may never see the employer whose home they are cleaning.[21] Although many employers continue to find workers through informal routes, this absolute separation of worker and employer spheres is important both because it is expanding so rapidly and because it embodies a transformation of domestic work from servant to wage labor.

Domestic workers' evolution from the servants of one employer to wage laborers for many has opened up new possibilities both for exploitation and for resistance. Unlike their predecessors, domestic workers today can separate their work from their relationships with particular employers; thus, they can forge a collective identity based on the work itself. And in the current capitalist context, such an ability carries new payoffs. The struggle over domestic work is no longer primarily a struggle to delineate the limits of the employer-employee relationship; instead, it is a struggle over whether the work is to be defined as skilled or unskilled labor. Within the context of a feudal relationship, the redefinition of the servant's work as skilled would not necessarily have resulted in a materially different status. Today, it can make the difference between security and insecurity. Thus, the emergence of grassroots efforts at professionalization today, rather than in earlier periods, can be understood within the context of the changing social organization of domestic work. The shift from servant to wage laborer provided both the opportunity and the incentive for this new form of struggle.

A NEW SORT OF AGENCY?

Although the social organization of domestic work has shifted over time, the migrant origins of the work force have shown remarkable stability. This should come as no surprise. In both academic and more popular contexts, there is a pervasive sense that immigrant labor is a distinct component of the labor force, filling specific low-level functions in developed capitalist economies.[22] Several authors provide analyses that point at immigrants' structured inability to organize as the key both to the ongoing function of immigrant labor within capitalist economies and to the consignment of immigrants to menial, dead-end, low-paid jobs.[23] Domestic work is certainly a paradigmatic example of such a job, as well as of an occupation that has proved resistant to organizing for most of its history.

However, such analyses preclude the possibility of change because they ignore agency. Immigrants cannot organize by definition, thus there is no reason to examine the features of immigrants' daily life that foster or impede the development of collective identity and strategies. However, among human beings, nothing is precluded by definition. The existence of a group like Choices pushes us to reexamine such assumptions and to focus on changes in the social organization of the work immigrants do, as well as on specific collective projects that are initiated within this new work context.

Domestic work has evolved over the last two decades in directions that have weakened the connection between worker and employer and consequently increased the possibility of connection among workers. The creation of an organization such as Choices—one that provides an infrastructure of space, time, and predictability within which the emergence of collective identity is supported—becomes particularly important in this context. It is important because it provides a space within which immigrant workers can begin to organize and so to resist their consignment to "dirty work" within the capitalist economy.

In any particular context, organizing can shift some constraints and not others. Thus, in today's economy, there is no way for a new group to evade the credentialing requirements struggled for by others, and as individuals Choices members still have no access to those credentials. However, they do have access to domestic work, and collectively, they are able to effect change there. Thus we do not see these women moving into more prestigious and powerful occupations. What we see instead is the beginning of a transformation of domestic work itself from unskilled to skilled, from humiliating to respectable, from minimum wage to its double, from employer-controlled to worker-controlled, from "dirty" work to "clean."

AFTERWORD: ETHNOGRAPHY FOR WHAT?

Immersed in another world, watching, analyzing, gossiping, matching hypothesis to reality—moment by moment, participant observation is deeply engaging. But the analysis is another story. In the privacy of head and home I can only sustain research as part of a larger project to understand the world in order to change it. This made choosing a site particularly unnerving. I wanted a guarantee that whatever I chose would illuminate something meaningful.

During those first hectic weeks I scoured the area looking for a site. Inspired by the political success of the Rainbow Coalition, I was eager to explore the creation of inclusive identities at the grass-roots level. To my frustration and surprise, no one in the area was organizing with this as an explicit focus. This situation in itself was food for analysis, but it certainly didn't qualify as participant observation. Eventually, I settled on two Central American domestic-worker cooperatives in the hope that a cross-national "Latino" identity would emerge in such a setting even if it was not an organizational goal.

Then followed weeks of frustration. I went to meeting after meeting. Whenever the problem was an exploitative white employer, the discussion centered around "Latinos." "At last," I thought, "now *this* is oppositional identity." But then a co-op member would complain that someone else had gotten a job unfairly, and national identities would surface once again. As I chatted with people I sometimes tried to slip my questions into conversation, "By the way, do you identify more as a 'Latino' or as a Salvadoran?" It never worked. It sounded absurd, and they looked at me with amused tolerance: "She's a nice girl, if a bit slow." It soon became evident that their identities were—like my own multiple allegiances—flexible, dependent on context. Regardless of how important identity formation might be in the broader political context, my focus on it obscured rather than revealed the particularities of what was going on.

So I kept attending meetings, enjoying the people more and more, but increasingly unsure that anything of importance was taking place. All they talked about in Amigos was unemployment and poverty and each other, and in Choices they talked constantly about cleaning: week in and week out they discussed how to polish silver and clean windows and. . . . Some days I went stir-crazy, coming home and typing out pages and pages of field notes about individual traumas I couldn't fix and heroic feats of cleaning that seemed to celebrate exploitation. A typical excerpt from my field notes in this period reads: "There's no real 'political' work going on here—no discussion of members' social location in terms of race or gender or any power issue at all—so I'm continually thrown back on looking at the organizational dynamics. Everything seems very straightforward—'let's make money'—and I don't know how to get at how people see themselves in this process."

Then somewhere in the second month I began to worry less about where I thought their interests belonged and to listen more to what they were saying. In Amigos they were talking about precarious survival at the edges of an exploitative market, but in Choices something else was happening: they were talking about cleaning as skilled work. I brought my field notes into class, and people kept asking how the women in Choices could possibly speak positively about such dirty work. This was the same question I had struggled with, but hearing it from others it felt wrong. The constant discussions at Choices had changed my vision of housework as necessarily demeaning. I began to question my underlying assumptions about cleaning as work, and about the "legitimate" political bases of identity. Was cleaning more demeaning than plumbing? Why did I assume that identity organizing would necessarily build on race or gender? As I examined my own perspective, I began to take in their world more fully. I realized that whereas Amigos' members were not constructing a collective identity, Choices' members were. It was not the identity I had expected, but nonetheless they were forming a self-respecting vision of themselves as a collectivity, a vision based on their experience of their work.

I began the project determined that my work be useful not only to other researchers, but to activists working within a particular political framework. For a long time, I was so focused on that framework that I was capable of seeing little else. It was only once my expectations had been repeatedly frustrated that I was able to see the autonomous (and political) identities that were actually emerging before me. However, with the analysis behind me, a new set of issues arises. Now that I have come to understand processes that do not fit neatly into a preexisting political agenda, there are no longer obvious groups or institutions who could use the information I have gathered. Thus, finding those who might want this piece of the puzzle becomes a new and ongoing task. As much as it required energy to cull these images, it will take energy to incorporate their analysis into a broader political context of knowledge and action.

EIGHT

"Unlikely Heroes":
The Evolution of Female Leadership in a
Cambodian Ethnic Enclave

Shiori Ui

In January 1989 the community of Stockton, California, was shattered by tragedy when a gunman opened fire on the children of a predominantly Indochinese elementary school. Within minutes anguished residents from the Cambodian neighborhood surrounding the school rushed to the scene. School officials scrambled to find interpreters who could help communicate with distraught parents and family friends. In the ensuing days, after it was learned that four of the five children killed by the gunman were Cambodian, leaders from the neighborhood met with officials of the Stockton Unified School District, urging them to cancel classes for a day of mourning.[1] Commenting on the role played by local Cambodians in serving as interpreters, counselors, and community leaders during and after the crisis, the local newspaper ran an article under the headline "Unlikely Heroes Emerge from School Tragedy."[2] While the story focused on the bravery of these people and their devotion to helping community members, it overlooked what was perhaps the most "unlikely" aspect of the Cambodian leaders—they were women.

"There is no woman leader here." That is what I was told repeatedly in two large cities in the Bay Area where I initially contacted people recognized by Cambodians and Americans as "Cambodian leaders." Again and again I received the same response: Cambodian women are not active in community affairs. Voices of Cambodian women in the United States are rarely heard, despite the fact that many are experiencing rapid changes in their lives.

Some studies imply that Indochinese refugee women face unfavorable conditions or structural constraints which preclude them from assuming leadership roles. Bach and Carroll-Seguin found that such women, especially those who entered the United States after 1980, have a higher degree of incorporation into "an ethnic community in which women are under greater constraints to remain in the home or are less able to make the interpersonal connections."[3] Since an ethnic community functions to preserve traditional customs, norms, and values,[4] one would expect that traditional gender roles would be reinforced and preserved within such a setting.

In Stockton, though, I found a different story.[5] I first visited Stockton at the suggestion of an American woman who had contacts with Indochinese refugee organizations there. Soon after I arrived, I was introduced to women who were very different from the "traditional" refugee women described in much of the literature. Despite their incorporation into a tightly knit ethnic enclave, these women had assumed leadership roles in the Indochinese community as well as within the home. Against all odds, they had emerged as important figures in Stockton's Cambodian neighborhoods and in the city itself.

What these women accomplished was not simply a matter of their exceptional individual characteristics—indeed, they became leaders under conditions that placed great strain on individual psychological resources. Women's leadership emerged, rather, as a result of unique structural conditions in Stockton's ethnic enclaves—conditions that were shaped primarily by the state. Stockton has become a home for secondary migrants, and life in the city's ethnic enclaves has produced new opportunities and constraints that have led to a new division of labor between the sexes. Once the first seeds of female leadership were planted within the community, some women extended their leadership roles from the workplace and family into the community. This expansion of women's domains has been facilitated by social service projects that create formal settings in which women develop and exercise leadership.

SECONDARY MIGRATION AND THE ETHNIC ENCLAVE

A large proportion of Indochinese refugees living in Stockton, as in the rest of the state, are "secondary migrants," people originally placed in other states who subsequently chose to move to California. Secondary migration accounts for 40 percent of the Indochinese refugees in California. In the fiscal year 1986–1987, secondary migration rose by 96 percent, while primary migration increased by only 5 percent.[6]

The practice of hosting Indochinese refugees began in Stockton when a local Catholic bishop arranged for thirty families to resettle there. Since then, the Indochinese refugee population has increased rapidly: from about 3,000 in 1980 to over 30,000—or one-sixth of the city's population—in 1988. (These numbers do not include U.S.-born children of refugee parents.) The greater Stockton area has the highest Indochinese secondary migration rate as well as the highest concentration of Indochinese residents in the state, 6.9 percent.[7] Cambodians now are the single largest ethnic group among Stockton's immigrant population.[8] In 1987 only 700 to 800 new arrivals came directly from refugee camps, whereas about 4,900 came as secondary migrants.[9]

The U.S. federal policy on sponsorship was intended to disperse refugees so as to prevent the development of ethnic enclaves.[10] The aim was to encourage more rapid assimilation by forcing individuals away from other members of the same ethnic group. This policy failed, in part because of differences in the services and benefits offered by different states. California, for example, is known for its generous refugee assistance policy and welfare system.[11]

Secondary migrants move not only to obtain better services, but also to be close to family and friends and to look for employment. Other motives for moving include the desire for a better climate or release from difficulties with initial sponsors and communities. Refugees who used to be unskilled workers, students, or soldiers, and others without marketable skills in the new country are more apt to become secondary migrants.[12] For instance, Boppha's family initially settled in Michigan five years ago. Her parents had some difficulties with their sponsor, who they feared would take their four small children away from them in the name of providing them a "better educational environment." The family moved to Atlanta, Georgia, but there the father could find only a part-time job at a dental clinic. So they moved to Stockton in hopes of obtaining more assistance for the children and better professional training opportunities for the father. Similarly, Rouen remembers her family's sponsor in Texas forcing them to attend Christian church services; in Stockton they are free to retain their Buddhist identity.

Because female-headed families are economically and socially more vulnerable, they are more likely to become secondary migrants.[13] Among the many widowed and divorced mothers in Stockton is Channy, a widow with four sons who moved from Texas two years ago. In Texas she had to start working right away—in a factory, at an airport, and on an electronic assembly line—before she learned to speak English. She also had an obligation to send money regularly to her second husband in Thailand, from whom she was separated. "I had to work, work, work. I had no time to be with my children. My sister was here [Stockton] and told me to move here. . . . I spent lots of money to move over here. But now I don't go out for work, and I am glad that I can take care of my children."

During her second pregnancy, Sophorny's husband was killed before her eyes by soldiers of Pol Pot's regime. She sometimes suffers from posttraumatic stress disorder, which makes it difficult for her to concentrate in her English class.[14] She moved from Tennessee four years ago with her teenage son and younger daughter. Her son is the family's only income-earner. They share a two-room apartment with another family, as do many other female-headed families in the enclave.

In an earlier era the pattern of secondary migration in the United States was from small towns to large cities such as New York, Dallas, New Orleans, San Francisco, and Los Angeles; the metropolises held the promise of physical and emotional support.[15] But at least in California, the new trend is for Cambodians in large cities such as San Francisco, Los Angeles, and San Diego to move to semirural agricultural towns in the Central Valley, such as Stockton, where housing and living costs are lower. "Those who couldn't make it in big cities go to the Valley," observed one refugee resettlement agency worker in San Francisco. Indeed, many of Stockton's secondary migrants are not, in a strict sense, "secondary" migrants: they have moved several times. A large proportion of them came from large cities in other states; many had difficulties even in their second or third residence; many have few transferable skills and little proficiency in English.

Mr. Sam, in his mid-thirties, used to live in Texas with his wife and five small children. He was a farmer in Cambodia, but he had always wanted to return to school and earn a college degree. He and his family moved to Stockton because of the more comprehensive social service support network, and he is now taking courses in a community college as preparation for becoming a social worker.

Sophy and her family arrived in Utah in 1982. After a brief period of English training, her husband started working in the kitchen of a restaurant at a very low wage. Sophy had a health problem, and they were unable to live on her husband's limited income and support from her relatives in the United States. Yet they felt obligated to send money to their relatives in Cambodia. On advice from one of Sophy's sisters who was living in Stockton, they moved there in 1984, looking for educational programs and a better climate. Both Sophy and her husband started English class, and Sophy received a scholarship to continue her education at a community college.

In contrast to Los Angeles, San Francisco, and Oakland, however, Stockton does not offer many employment opportunities. According to a 1987 survey, the area around Stockton has the lowest employment rate in the state among Indochinese refugees, 9.3 percent. In the Los Angeles, San Francisco, and Oakland areas, 39.2 percent, 34.2 percent, and 24.9 percent, respectively, are employed.[16] While large cities need unskilled laborers to fill low-paying jobs in restaurants, hotels, and factories, Stockton is a basically agricultural town in which the agricultural jobs have already been taken by Mexican and Chicano workers, and few employers need more unskilled labor. "In other cities . . . there are more factories and more industrial jobs. But here, a person needs a good education and skills to make it," said a director of a refugee service agency.[17] "Cambodians are difficult to place in jobs, because of their limited resources and [poor] language proficiency," said a county officer. As a result, 70 percent of Indochinese refugees in Stockton are unemployed,[18] and the unemployment rate for Cambodians is estimated to be between 80 and 90 percent.

The majority of the Cambodians in Stockton live in huge, exclusively Cambodian apartment complexes that house from 1,000 to 3,000 people. Some of these complexes used to be occupied by Blacks, Hispanics, and, most recently, Vietnamese. Most of the residents now are secondary migrants searching for a "home" in a foreign land. For them, the ethnic community offers an important source of support: it preserves traditional norms and values, and it provides a sense of security and identity.[19] One woman, whose sentiments were echoed by many others, explained: "I want to live with our people. We miss our country. I felt lonely there [first resettlement place]. When I came here, it is like my village, like our home. We smile to each other. Sometimes I get bored, feel so crowded, but I like to live here with our people."

For women, this feeling of community is particularly important. Closeness to other women of their own ethnicity and background helps to engender security and solidarity. In other communities where the enclave is very small or ethnically mixed, women are especially reluctant to go outside for fear of attack. Some Cambodian women in Oakland and San Francisco told me that in those cities women and children do not leave their small apartment complex alone even in daytime, because they fear that other minorities in the neighborhood may attack them. One woman who has lived in Stockton since 1980 said: "When we came, there was no Cambodian apartment. We were afraid of going outside. My husband was attacked by whites and Blacks. But now, we are many. We are not afraid any more." Once they feel secure in their homes and neighborhoods, women also feel safer journeying outside their homes and neighborhoods.

The feelings of security engendered by the ethnic enclaves are made all the more important by the marginal economic status of most secondary migrants. In the apartment complex enclaves I observed, most of the families are on welfare, even though some family members have part-time jobs. The majority of them receive payments through AFDC (Aid to Families with Dependent Children); those who have been in the country for less than two years receive special refugee assistance. Few Cambodians have full-time jobs, and only a few others are able to go to school to learn English, acquire vocational skills, or earn college degrees. Because unemployment is so widespread, jobless men are less apt to feel isolated or depressed by their inability to serve as their family's primary "rice-winner." But when men who have had no jobs for long periods of time gather at the corners of the enclaves to drink and gamble, the women criticize them as "lazy and playing around." One woman who took a part-time job while her husband was unemployed remarked: "Even if they earned low wages, even if we had to take a cut from welfare assistance, we want to see our husbands working. We don't want our children see their fathers doing nothing." Channy, a single mother, said: "In Texas, everyone works. It's not like here. Men are lazy here."

STRATEGIES OF SURVIVAL

In Stockton the marginal economic status of secondary migrants and the lack of job opportunities for men combine to produce unexpected consequences for traditional gender roles.[20] Women's roles as homemakers and small traders, in particular, have taken on increased economic importance in the Cambodian enclaves. Women's traditional roles of providing food and clothing for family and community members have always been crucial in sustaining ethnic culture. But in Stockton these traditional roles and skills have evolved into informal economic activities that contribute cash to family incomes. Even in the semiurban home setting, many women use their skills to generate extra earnings.[21]

Food is one of the most important aspects of cultural heritage. In daily life and on ceremonial occasions, women play a major role in preserving cultural tradition by preparing food, and in Stockton many Cambodian women have transformed this role into a source of income and power. In one apartment complex, Chanda is known for making noodle soup on weekends, when the residents have weekly Buddhist gatherings. Other residents grow vegetables and spices around their apartments and exchange or sell the products to neighbors. Mora and her daughter buy various fruits and fish in big packages in a weekly open market downtown and bring them home; they then go around the neighborhood to sell the fish and fruit piece by piece. Keo, in her fifties, makes traditional sweets at home and sells them door-to-door, a dollar a package. Coconut jelly is her specialty and the neighbors' favorite. Always a good cook, Keo never sold her food before coming to Stockton. Now she earns up to $50 a day from her sales, while her husband, formerly a farmer, has no job. From the corner of her living room, Rath sells cups of shaved ice, with traditional sweets at the bottom, to children. Poum fries bananas in front of her apartment and sells them to a Cambodian grocery store. On side roads one often sees several parked vans from which various candies and snacks are sold by teenaged women.

Making ethnic dresses brings money as well. Frequent weddings and seasonal religious ceremonies create a demand for special clothing and decorations. Almost every other weekend there is a wedding in the apartment complex. Families and guests dress up, and ceremonies and reception gatherings last the entire day. On most such occasions, women wear traditional costumes, while men commonly wear Western suits.

A large number of orders for dresses keeps Sophy busy on evenings and weekends. She knew basic sewing before moving to Stockton, although she never had any formal training, but only in Stockton did she begin to supplement her family income in this way. She charges $20 a dress (an extremely low price considering the time involved) for her labor. Channy, who received some training in sewing back home, supports her four young sons by making clothes to supplement the welfare checks. She sews the whole day in her family's only room. Sokhon, in her fifties, carries around a big bag of fancy cloth from Kampuchea and Thailand. She imports the cloth through personal connections and sells it in the neighborhood. Women who make dresses often call her to the door to see if good cloth for their next dress is available.

Most of the small economic activities carried on in and around the enclaves are conducted by women and children. One man who used to be a barber in Phnom Penh opened a barber stand outside of an enclave, and several other men specialize in ceremonial music and fortune-telling, but few men start such informal businesses. The women, however, do so when their families do not have enough money or their husbands cannot find jobs. Thus the women's traditional cultural skills have led them to new economic activities that make important contributions to the family.

In addition to opportunities in the informal economy, a growing recognition of the importance of education and training is also changing women's roles within the enclaves of Stockton. Because the Cambodian population is large and concentrated, many services and programs have been created in Stockton to serve men and women facing resettlement difficulties. In those communities where jobs are available, men—the traditional heads of households—become the focus for language and job-training programs. But in Stockton, where traditionally male jobs are scarce, new programs are focusing on the education of refugee women; such efforts are symbolized by the new ESL (English as a Second Language) programs.

Needless to say, English proficiency is related directly to employment opportunities and is also a prerequisite for interacting with the majority population.[22] Refugee adults are placed in ESL classes according to their sponsorship and their level of English proficiency, and they must attend classes to receive welfare and assistance in finding jobs. In most areas of the country, however, women with small children are exempt from this school requirement, and educational and training programs pay little attention to such women. In Stockton, though, one social service agency, backed by a local church, holds ESL classes every morning, as well as a weekly citizenship class, and almost all the staff and volunteers are women. The agency believes that "if we don't reach women, there will not be much chance for the next generation." A child-care room next to the classrooms enables mothers to attend class even though they are not required by the state to do so.

The ESL teachers observed that what motivated many women was a desire to obtain a driver's license. "When we started to talk about the driver's license, those women were so excited. That was what they were waiting for." Public transportation in Stockton is poor, and a driver's license provides women with unprecedented access to outside activities. Sareth, in her mid-forties, obtained her license after she moved to Stockton from Georgia. Her husband is old and sick; she is the only driver in her family. She takes her grandchildren to Cambodian language school, and she also attends the class to learn reading and writing. An ongoing survey in the Cambodian community in Stockton reveals that another motive for enrolling in ESL classes is that parents want to be able to talk with their children's teachers. Kech, for example, voluntarily attends ESL classes so that she can help her daughters in school.

There is even a class especially for women, organized by three cooperating social service agencies. Time and location are arranged at the convenience of women with small children, and some women carry their babies into the classroom. The women are encouraged to study with classmates who are friends from the neighborhood, and the open atmosphere eases young mothers' tensions and their hesitancy to attend ESL classes. A woman neighbor, Sophy, helps in the classroom by keeping attendance records, distributing materials, translating the instructions of an American teacher, and helping the students to ask questions. Such special arrangements are possible only in a community where a large enclave exists.

Social services programs such as these, designed for Cambodians, have created new job opportunities for refugees with professional backgrounds and those who have attained English proficiency and done relevant college-level work in the United States. Some of the Cambodians who are recruited for social service jobs serving their own people work part-time in agencies while continuing their higher education. Initially, the Cambodians employed in these agencies were likely to be men who were in social services or government offices in their homeland. Such jobs provide both prestige and significant income, and these workers usually moved out of the enclaves, but continued to live near them. But because few Cambodians had both experience with social service work and a good command of English, those who acquired English proficiency and attended American community colleges were soon able to be hired as translators or assistant staff members in the growing social service sector.

Now, according to both Americans and Cambodians, women are more in demand in social service work than men, once they attain the same educational and language levels. Because very few women have these qualifications, there is a need for more female refugees with the levels of education and experience required to work with the refugee community. One example of an emerging job opportunity in Stockton is that of bilingual aide within the school system. Federal law requires that ninety minutes of instruction in the children's own language be provided each day, but this minimum is not being met. One school district in Stockton employs 105 Indochinese teacher's aides, most part-time, out of a total of 178; to meet the federal standard the district would need to hire 426 full-time aides.[23]

Secretarial, clerical, and interpreter jobs in social service work are also increasingly available within the ethnic community. Many who take these positions learned how to help others from their accumulated experiences of helping family members and friends. Sophy, a part-time worker of this sort herself, described these jobs as requiring "patience" and "a tolerance for stress": "Men are not patient enough for these jobs." Several agency executives expressed their preference for women over men if they have the same qualifications. One American executive said: "It is common in this kind of work to employ women. There are more women who want to do this kind of work than men. It seems that some ethnic populations relate better to women than men. . . . Another thing is that the pay is so bad." Another director, who is himself a refugee, said: "Women are much easier to work with. They are more sensitive to workers and clients. Their concentration is much better than [that of] men."

Many small-scale American private social service agencies that are run largely by female workers encourage women's participation. One female director emphasized that many refugees need social workers who can go into their communities and help them in their homes. Sophy herself was recruited to work for women's programs with encouragement and assistance from both American and Indochinese social workers. Similarly, when Mrs. Lim applied for her teacher's aide position in public school, she was supported by American female teachers who knew about her background. Dara is a physician's assistant in a public hospital's family clinic and a counselor for Cambodian patients. She is also a medical student in a state university program for which she was recommended and to which she was encouraged to apply by American doctors in the hospital. Other women work as interpreters in clinics and various program offices.

Sophy completed community college in Stockton. She started working while she was still studying. Now she has several part-time jobs in social service agencies as a Cambodian representative. She works for the 4H Club as a Cambodian group leader, for the Agricultural Building and the Women's Center as an interpreter and counselor, for the General Hospital as an interpreter and nurse's aide, and for the ESL class for women in her apartment complex as a teacher's aide. She never worked in Cambodia. She intends to try various jobs and choose one field in which to obtain a professional certificate and work full-time. She is now seeking a full-time position as an eligibility worker in the welfare office, where so far there are only two Cambodian eligibility workers, both male. Her desire to help other Cambodians and the program's needs are a perfect match.

When these women take jobs in the paid labor force, they have to struggle to move beyond the clerical and staff-assistant positions, which are usually part-time, ethnic-specific, and highly susceptible to governmental budget cuts. Sophy feels insecure in her position; budget cuts or a shift in agency priorities could easily cause her to be laid off. She is anxious to get full-time staff status to secure continuing financial support for her family. "Now is a turning point of my life," she said, "what job to choose and how to support my family."

The employment that public sector jobs provide for those women who have acquired skills in English is crucial in a community with limited economic opportunities. Such jobs also have a significant impact on the division of labor within both family and community.

DIVISION OF LABOR IN THE FAMILY

As we have seen, the opportunities and constraints in the ethnic enclaves are transforming women's roles. The first steps toward leadership often occur in the home, where women's informal economic activities contribute to family income and stability. These developments are soon followed by changes outside the home. The feeling of security derived from the presence of a support system in the enclaves contributes to women's confidence in taking on alternative roles. As women obtain access to educational and employment opportunities, job skills, and the freedom offered by a driver's license, they gain power and status in the outside world. Together these changes help to produce a new division of labor in the family.

In the rural, agricultural settings in Cambodia, men and women have roles that complement each other. In the new urban or semiurban immigrant enclaves, however, some roles are strengthened while others are lost. This loss of roles is most pronounced for men.[24] Many of the traditional women's roles endure—taking care of children and managing the housework—and women are both strengthened and transformed by the various informal economic functions they take on. Men, on the other hand, face high unemployment rates, own no land, and have no offices to which they can aspire. Stripped of traditional opportunities for employment, men lose their "place to be" in the new society. While women's roles in the family persist, men are in a prolonged situation of "after harvest, waiting for the next cultivation season."

Thus, in the ethnic enclaves of Stockton, it is often women, not men, who have greater economic opportunities. Whether they work in the informal economy of the Cambodian community or in social service jobs in the paid labor force, women become the primary breadwinners in Cambodian families. And because they have been able to gain skills in English, a sense of security in the enclave, and a driver's license, these women come to serve as mediators between the family and the outside world.

Kiey is a good example. A high school senior, Kiey carries many of the responsibilities in her family; the expectations of her parents and the needs of her eight younger siblings rest on her shoulders. Her family came to Stockton three years ago from a refugee camp. Her parents do not understand English and are unemployed. In her family, she is the only driver and mediator with the outside world. During almost every year of the past decade, her mother has given birth, and Kiey often had to skip classes to take her mother to the hospital or to various welfare offices. She is in charge of transportation, shopping, negotiation with the apartment owner, filling out various forms, and much more. She is expected to provide income as soon as possible, since her family is obliged to send money to relatives remaining in Cambodia. She is torn between her wish to continue her education, the expectations of her family, and her own traditional values concerning her duties as a daughter.

These new roles for women are even more pronounced among couples forced to marry during the Pol Pot regime. Unlike women in more traditional marriages, wives in forced marriages often came to the United States with more marketable skills and higher levels of education than their husbands. Among these couples, many of whom are now in their mid-thirties, women are even more likely to take on the role of primary breadwinner.

Sophy was forced to marry a much older man of rural origin during her labor camp days. Her husband now has physical problems that prevent him from participating in the paid labor force. With her educational background, Sophy had a greater potential to find employment, and she had no choice but to become an income earner. She, her husband, their three sons, and her aged mother live off of Sophy's income from several part-time jobs, weekend dressmaking, a small amount of welfare assistance allotted to her, and the welfare assistance that her mother earns as sole member of a separate household.

Vanny, a woman in her early thirties who was forced to marry, works in a psychiatric hospital as an administrative assistant. She supports her two children and a husband. Her husband has less education and fewer marketable skills than she, and has a part-time job on weekends. She exercises control over many of her family's decisions.

While these women serve as mediators between the outside world and the family, their husbands take on work in the house. In Sophy's family, for example, gender roles were dramatically reversed after she began working. In Cambodia her husband made all the decisions; she was totally dependent on him for survival. Now, her husband always asks her permission to spend money or go out, and she makes decisions ranging from the children's education to how the family spends its vacation.

Changes in consciousness and attitude have occurred among men as well as women. Meah's older brother is supporting his parents and five younger siblings. He said that he doesn't mind if his (future) wife has more education than he and becomes active outside the home, as long as she does not "go around too much." He also does not mind sharing housework. He feels that "it is good if either husband or wife could get well-paid jobs and that whoever gets a job which brings in income should take it, and other members should cooperate."

Mr. Sam's baby son started to cry. He picked up the baby and changed his diaper. He participates more in child care than he used to, he says. "In Cambodia men also help with child care, but not as much as here. Not everyone is like me, 30 percent in Cambodia, 60 percent in America." In Stockton, men spend more time at home due to unemployment and women spend more time outside home and in school.

His wife is illiterate. "My wife is busy with the baby now, but I want her to go to school later, too."

THE EMERGENCE OF WOMEN COMMUNITY LEADERS

Some of the women who have taken active roles in the family extend their leadership roles into the world outside the enclave. As we have seen, both Cambodian and American concepts of gender have facilitated women's involvement in social service work as community liaisons, where women take jobs as mediators, educators, and social workers, jobs that reinforce the development of their leadership roles in both private and public spheres. However, not all women in the enclaves take advantage of these opportunities. So far, those who are visible as outstanding leaders are those who came to the United States with backgrounds and skills applicable to contemporary American society.

The ways in which these women evolve into leaders are diverse. Let us take as examples Mrs. Lim and Sophy. Mrs. Lim was known for her expertise back home before she started to work for the Stockton school district. From the beginning, she was identified as an official delegate of the community, especially in the field of education. She announces herself as the specialist and leader she used to be in Cambodia, and she is primarily interested in working in the Cambodian community. Sophy, on the other hand, became known to her neighbors in the enclave as a helpful woman with a good command of English. "Neighbors just came by for help. Then others heard about me and came." She had no intention of making events take the course they did. "I was very shy, but after getting jobs, I had to talk in front of many people. I don't want to say that I am the leader. I speak 'on behalf of' the people in this apartment complex, because if I don't speak, nobody speaks for us." Eventually her potential was spotted by the American manager of the apartment complex and by social workers who were looking for Cambodian assistants. She first was recruited by a supplementary food program for infants when she was using their services as a client. During the expansion of programs for Cambodian refugee women, she became involved in various projects as a part-time staff member. One result of her public and private activities around the ethnic enclaves is that she is frequently called upon to represent the interests and voices of the residents. She is happy to work on behalf of Cambodians, but plans to extend her frontiers to serve the general population.

To date, though, only a few women have been able to take advantage of the niches in Stockton's enclaves and climb into leadership roles. These tend to be women whose background has facilitated their adaptation to American society and allowed them to enjoy the new opportunities in the United States. Most important, especially during the initial stage of resettlement, is a woman's education, familiarity with urban or semiurban life, knowledge of Western culture, and ability to use available information and mobilize human resources. The earlier immigrants generally came from more well-off families and were better-educated. More used to classroom study, they mastered English faster than later immigrants. Given the same learning opportunities, those who are illiterate in their own language have many more difficulties than those who are literate or have some familiarity with Western languages. Early immigrants also found sponsors more quickly, as they often already had relatives in the United States.[25] And because there was no Cambodian community or enclave, the earlier immigrants also were forced to learn English quickly. Today one finds that an immigrant's knowledge of English depends more on educational and social background than on the length of residency in the United States.

We can see how a woman's educational and social background prepares her to meet the challenges of life in Stockton's Cambodian enclave by returning to Sophy's story. Her father, who was a military officer, was of Chinese ethnic background, and Sophy grew up in an urban area, the city of Swap. Sophy's mother had been a teacher and a nurse, although she stopped working after becoming a mother. Sophy was raised by her grandparents, who always reminded her to behave like a lady. When the evacuation to rural labor camps started, Sophy was a second-year college student in liberal arts and had studied French. In Stockton Sophy's professional interests and motivation were enhanced by her family's financial needs and by the growing need for female leadership within the Cambodian enclave.

For Mrs. Lim, a woman rich in skills and experiences, life in the enclave has served as a stepping stone for her to regain her former position. She was raised in Phnom Penh by her adoptive mother, who was a teacher, and she became a teacher herself, serving for many years in a teachers' college. Later she took an educational administration and planning position, while her husband worked for the royal guard. Both were close to high government officials allied with Prince Sihanouk, and they had close connections with several political leaders. She was also fluent in French. She and her family survived the Pol Pot regime, escaped to a Thai border camp, and in 1980 were sponsored by her son-in-law, who was then working in California as an engineer. A local church also provided support, and Mrs. Lim and her family converted to Christianity soon after arrival in Stockton. There, she mobilized former teachers and administrators in the enclave to start a language school for Cambodian children. She also utilized her extensive political and social network from the homeland, which she reconstructed in the new country.

CONCLUSION

In Stockton, I found the unexpected: female leadership in a community with limited resources and in enclaves where one would expect traditional values to be strong. The extremely limited job opportunities in the Cambodian enclaves have, paradoxically, created conditions highly favorable to the emergence of women's leadership. In particular, new positions in social service programs created by the welfare state are propelling women into leadership roles. In Stockton the rapid growth and concentration of the ethnic enclave has prompted an expansion of service programs for the Cambodian refugee population. Because these positions often entail work similar to women's traditional caretaking role, and because the new programs have expanded opportunities available to women, these new jobs are often disproportionately filled by women.

These government jobs carry prestige, as well as providing an important source of income, and they have enabled Cambodian women in this community to obtain economic and social power. These women are now transforming the nature of their roles both inside and outside of the family; in doing so, they have moved into positions of leadership in the home and in the larger community. Their leadership has emerged as they have struggled to shape their own lives by taking advantage of opportunities present in a new country. After all, the women who were introduced as "unlikely heroes" are not individuals who just happened to become heroes in a moment of community crisis. Rather, their leadership has developed as a consequence of structural changes faced by new immigrants in Stockton's Cambodian community. Despite traditional culture and gender roles, female leadership will develop and emerge when groups are in a situation in which ethnic identity and unity are strong, the employment opportunities for women are greater than those for men, and the intervention of the welfare state is significant.

AFTERWORD: BEHIND THE WALL

I remember my initial apprehension and anxiety about establishing contacts with Cambodian refugee communities. These people had gone through so much; their experiences seemed like a wall before me that

I didn't know how to break through. The first two communities I tried
to contact made me feel entirely out of place. I was afraid I'd be asked,
"What are you—a female Japanese graduate student—doing here?"
Even in Stockton, the idea that I would ever feel at ease seemed far-
fetched. Who would have imagined that the first apartment I visited
would eventually become almost a home for me?

I was brought to Sophy's apartment by the assistant manager of the
predominantly Cambodian housing complex where she lived. During
that first visit I stayed for three hours watching a Cambodian video in
almost complete silence. Discouraged after waiting patiently for so long,
I said it was time for me to catch the bus to go home. Sophy took a
break from sewing and gave me a big fresh apple from a basket in the
kitchen. "Very sweet. Take this and eat on the bus. Come and visit
again." She smiled. Her husband didn't say a word—or even look at
me—during that first visit. I thought he was annoyed with me, a stranger, or that he did not understand English at all. But two visits later he
surprised me with a friendly greeting in English and an invitation to
come into their apartment even though Sophy was not at home.

Every Cambodian family responded to me affectionately. When they
found out that I had come to the United States alone to attend
school—a situation most Americans and I took for granted—they
nearly cried. "Oh, you are alone. Your family is not here. You must be
lonely. Stay with us." "It is such a pity that you have to eat terrible
American dormitory food. Eat with us." Being non-American unexpectedly became an advantage, as we shared concerns about staying in
"a foreign land." Their sympathy for the "lonely foreign student" reflected the hardships they had been through, their separations and
their efforts to reconstruct family and community life. Family concerns
were always the start of our conversations. What I had thought would
be a disadvantage turned out to contribute to establishing positive and
trusting relationships with people. Dismantling the wall was a slow and
frustrating effort for both them and me, but we gained insights and
new perspectives at each stage of our relationship.

As my connection with these people grew stronger, however, I confronted a new dilemma. I was caught in a dual identity: between being
an impartial observer and a friend; between reporting my observations
and being concerned for their privacy. These conflicts were thrown into
relief by two events that forced me to ask myself which role I valued
more. The first was a death in one of the families I had become close
to. One afternoon, when I made my usual visit to Mrs. Lim's school
office, I couldn't find her. Her assistant told me that her husband had
died. I recalled that I had eaten a baked salty fish with him on his porch
some days earlier. I was shocked to lose my "away-from-home" father,

and I wanted to help with the funeral arrangements. Moved as I was to be treated as a special friend by the family, I also felt a conflict—I couldn't seem to separate out my role as an observer. The observer in me was interested: "The family are converted Christians. They are planning Christian and Buddhist funerals for consecutive days. How will they do this? Who is coming? I will be able to see the networks of relationships and power politics in this community." I felt terrible when I realized that I was viewing the funeral as an opportunity for sociological observation. I did in fact observe interesting things at the funeral, and I stored them away in my head as I usually did. But I didn't write field notes about this experience.

The second of these events was even more shocking. A gunman forced his way into the local schoolyard and began firing indiscriminately. Five children were killed and many others were wounded. Families were in turmoil; women I knew and cared about were facing horrifying challenges and were unexpectedly thrust into the limelight. After hearing the news, I wished I had wings and could fly there immediately. I cried over the families' double victimization, first in Cambodia and now here. But still I felt the conflict between my identities as observer and friend. How dare I make a study of my friends' suffering! I didn't want to be another reporter prying into their grief. So in spite of my urge to go right away, I waited for two and a half weeks. The community had changed. People were frightened. I did not ask about the crisis, but I did not need to. People told me their stories, all I had wondered and more. I listened and tried to help. But despite my ambivalence about my role, these conversations also contributed to my study, for the consequences of this crisis strongly supported my still-emerging hypothesis about women's roles in the community.

PART FOUR

From Classroom to Community

Introduction to Part 4

Few contemporary issues have aroused as much controversy as the declining academic performance of American children. In 1983 the National Commission on Excellence in Education reported on America's declining academic competitiveness and urged immediate improvement in the nation's schools. Although the primary focus was on education in general, the commission's report, *A Nation at Risk*, also highlighted the achievement differences between groups of students. According to the report, what is at risk is the promise of a nation to provide all its citizens with an equal opportunity to develop their potential regardless of race or class. What is at risk is the opportunity for children to receive an effective education.

The news is even more disheartening when one considers that the liberal democratic vision of education as the vehicle for individual development and greater social equality is fading. During the last three decades educators and social scientists have offered explanations of and solutions to the problem of educational inequality. When separate and unequal schools were identified as the source of unequal education, busing was implemented. When busing failed to yield the expected outcomes, attention was turned to social attributes of the individual. The recipients of education, their family, environment, background, culture, and values were identified as the source of the problem—certain students were identified as "culturally deprived" or "culturally disadvantaged." Various remedial and compensatory programs were instituted. Some students were helped, but many were not. Other approaches were tried, and sharp debates continued to rage over such related issues as centralized versus decentralized control, priorities in school funding, curriculum, class size, and parents' role in educating their children.

Two themes seemed to have dominated much of the debate and research: the attributes of children and those of the schools. What seemed to be missing was any discussion of the classroom as the primary site of teacher-student interaction. What is the classroom "culture"? What teaching strategies do teachers employ? What is being taught in the classroom? How are academic and social inequality being reproduced in the classroom? How is order established and discipline handled? And finally, what is the relationship between classroom and home? The classroom remained largely a black box outside the reach of social surveys. In the last decade a new ethnography has emerged to examine schooling as a social process, but these researchers have usually focused on the reproduction of class culture.

The two studies that follow work in this ethnographic tradition, but they deal more narrowly with questions of educational effectiveness in terms of the role of teaching and the relationship of school and home. Leslie Hurst volunteered to tutor eighth grade students in Emerald Junior High School and saw teachers, stripped of support from the school and the home, having to negotiate compromises with their students before they could begin teaching. Her study sets the context for Nadine Gartrell's examination of Project Interface, an after-school, community-based program to promote mathematics and science education among African-American children. It sought to reconnect family and education through mandatory contractual agreements among parents, students, and administrators. By all available measures the program was a success inasmuch as it improved levels of educational achievement, but Gartrell asks how generalizable this model can be. Although Project Interface was designed for minority students, only a select group of children enrolled—children whose parents could provide the home conditions, supervision, and participation required by the program. Gartrell concludes that even if such programs were widely adopted, conditions of poverty would exclude the majority of African-American children from them. After-school programs for some children are no substitute for improving public education for all students.

Leslie Hurst
Nadine Gartrell

NINE

Mr. Henry Makes a Deal: Negotiated Teaching in a Junior High School

Leslie Hurst

Roald Dahl's book *Boy* contains stories from his childhood, much of which was spent in schools. First he attended a local school in Llandaff, Wales; then, from age nine to thirteen, a boarding school in England. Dahl's father, who died when Dahl was quite young, had insisted his children be sent to English schools because, he maintained, they were the best in the world. Dahl's mother complied. Dahl describes prep hall and one of the masters this way:

> We called them masters in those days, not teachers, and at St Peter's the one I feared most of all, apart from the Headmaster, was Captain Hardcastle.... The rules of Prep were simple but strict. You were forbidden to look up from your work, and you were forbidden to talk. That was all there was to it, but it left you precious little leeway. In extreme circumstances, and I never knew what these were, you could put your hand up and wait until you were asked to speak but you had better be awfully sure that the circumstances were extreme. Only twice during my four years at St Peter's did I see a boy putting up his hand during Prep.[1]

At St. Peter's the masters had authority over the student's mind, body, and soul. In the classrooms and in the corridors teachers had the right, and were expected, to shape the students into "good" and correct young men. In one passage Dahl describes Captain Hardcastle's proclivity and ability to plague him both night and day, both in class and out:

> For a reason that I could never properly understand, Captain Hardcastle had it in for me from my very first day at St Peter's.... I had only to pass within ten feet of him in the corridor and he would glare at me and shout, "Hold yourself straight, boy! Pull your shoulders back!" or "Take those

hands out of your pockets!" or "What's so funny, may I ask? What are you smirking at?" or most insulting of all, "You, what's-your-name, get on with your work!" I knew, therefore, that it was only a matter of time before the gallant Captain nailed me good and proper.[2]

If the shaping of boys into virtuous men required physical impetus, physical impetus was applied. Headmasters, masters, and senior students had license to use physical force to correct misdemeanors occurring inside and outside of the school. Dahl was once caned by the headmaster because of complaints about his conduct from the town's candy-store proprietor.

In fall 1988 I volunteered as a tutor at Emerald Junior High School, a public school in a lower-middle-class neighborhood in Berkeley.[3] Daily I saw things that Roald Dahl would and could never have seen. I saw Clair (a student) tell Mr. Henry (a teacher) to "quit looking at me like a cow and just answer my question." I was in the room when Ameer refused to pick up his trash, threw a hall pass in the teacher's face, and walked out of the room. I watched Thomas irritatingly and autistically imitate machine-gun fire while Mr. Henry was trying to read a story to the class. What I saw in the classrooms of Emerald Junior High School was worlds apart from Dahl's descriptions.

I had the opportunity to move about and observe other classrooms, but I was officially assigned to assist Jim Henry, an eighth-grade English teacher, in room 112, and I spent most of my time with him. Through Mr. Henry I had access to the lunchroom, other teachers, and English department meetings. Mr. Henry is white, of slight build, bespectacled, and forty-three years old. He came to teaching after studying law and political science, and he came to Emerald Junior High on the third day of the fall semester as a substitute teacher for Betty Fleischacker. When Ms. Fleischacker was unable to return to work Mr. Henry was hired on a one-year contract. Mr. Henry, like all the teachers at Emerald, teaches five forty-five-minute periods a day out of the six attended by the students. Each teacher is given one "prep" period; Mr. Henry takes his during first period.

Mr. Henry's classes vary in size from nineteen to twenty-four students. The students are from age twelve to fourteen. The fourteen-year-olds are generally "held-backs" from last year. Each class has from one to four held-backs and students of widely diverse academic achievement. The school also goes to great lengths to ensure that classes are integrated and gender balanced. Mr. Henry's classes are almost half African-American; the rest are white except for the three or four Asians in each class. The third-period class has an East Indian, Sunny, and fifth period has two Chicanos, Miguel and Rosa.

What I observed and want to explain about the classroom is the student-teacher negotiations. The conditions that make these negotiations possible are most easily delineated by comparison with Dahl's St. Peter's. At Emerald the teachers were to have influence over the students' minds but not over their bodies or souls, for at Emerald there was a division and separation of students' bodies from their minds and souls. This "political-economy of the body" (to borrow Michel Foucault's term) reflects the separation and division of function between the school, the teachers, and the family. At Emerald the body, the student's physical whereabouts and well-being, is the legitimate territory of the school. Once the child arrives at the institution the school takes responsibility for seeing that the student moves from classroom to classroom, eats at the appropriate time in the designated area, and is physically safe from other students, and the school guards the perimeters so outsiders cannot come in.

The student's soul, that is the heart, the will, the personal values, attitudes, and sense of propriety, is the legitimate territory of the family or, most generally, something outside of the school and the classroom.[4] From this outside sphere the student is to obtain values, attitudes, and a sense of decorum. The student comes to school with these already in hand.

The teachers in the classrooms are responsible for the child's mind. The teachers are responsible for teaching. The teachers are to shape and develop the student's intellect.

What I observed is that this separation of body, mind, and soul (school, classroom, and family) works against the teachers and their attempts to teach. Access to a student's mind, the rudimentary condition for teaching, requires some immediate control over the student's body and sense of propriety. But at Emerald teachers are only to "babysit" the body and soul. In these areas the teacher (like a babysitter) must hold the child in charge, but is given no license to shape or punish. The teacher must first negotiate with the students some compromise on how the students will conduct themselves and on what will be considered acceptable classroom decorum.

THE LITERATURE: WHAT OTHER PEOPLE SAW

The most prominent lines of sociological inquiry approach education as it serves social structural needs.[5] According to functionalists, education works to socialize students into the commitments and capacities for future adult roles and to distribute these "human resources" within the adult role structure.[6] Conflict theorists, on the other hand, are primarily interested in the role of schools in the reproduction of class structures.[7] For some, the power of schools is rigid and imposed upon students; the educational system reproduces the hierarchical division of labor through unequal schooling and through class subcultures that provide personality characteristics appropriate to job performance in the parents' occupational role.[8] For others, the power of the school is looser and the power of the students expanded—yet the result, class structure reproduction, is the same.[9] Paul Willis observes how, rather than being stamped with their occupational role, working-class "lads" create their own culture of resistance through which, paradoxically, they disqualify themselves from mobility opportunities, a "self-damnation" experienced as "affirmation".[10]

Despite their differences, both functional and conflict approaches share a tendency to "see a harmonious fit between the educational system and the surrounding society"[11] and, linked to this, a concern with explaining how schools produce and reproduce *future* actions and attitudes. My account differs in that I do not approach schools with a futurist eye. I do not see the school in terms of training, socializing, or slotting people into future hierarchies. To approach schools in this manner is to miss the negotiated, chaotic aspects of the classroom and educational experience. A futurist perspective tends to impose an order and purpose on the school experience, missing its day-to-day reality.

It is this imposition of order that blinds most theories to the constant negotiating that takes place in the classroom and thus, I would argue, to the separation of school, classroom, and family in American society. Bowles and Gintis, for example, posit such "correspondence" between school and society that they need not consider how student-teacher interactions may differ from student-school interactions. Willis, who does see student resistance, interprets it in terms of its parallels to class structure. He does not see the possibility that the lads' resistance is tied to the separation of spheres, the separation of school from classroom from family.

Another major line of sociological inquiry looks at schools as formal organizations.[12] For example, Mary Metz, who also conducted participant-observation research in a Berkeley junior high, depicts classroom relationships in terms of the characteristics, processes, and goals of formal organizations. Metz clearly conceives of the students (in her terms) "negotiating," "adjusting," and "resisting" in the classrooms. However, by approaching schools as formal organizations, Metz places the cause of classroom negotiations at a different juncture than I do and advocates a different "cure."

Placing her observations in the framework of formal organization theory, Metz discovers that the school and the classroom have "contradictory organizational imperatives." The school, with its control goals, requires a "hierarchic, bureaucratic organization." The classroom, with learning goals, requires an organization in which the teacher has "flexibility" and "autonomy" and can use "initiative and intuition."

Having established that the school-classroom relationship is inevitably and "inherently ambivalent," Metz denies it a role in the explanation of classroom bargaining. Instead, Metz traces the important cause (the manipulable cause) of classroom negotiations to the different "definitions of the classroom" between student and teacher. Negotiations are the result of "unshared expectations." Accordingly, the most effective answer to negotiations, "disorder," and "skeptical" students is "for the school either to find links between [students'] studies and their existing values and goals or to take as its first task persuading the students to share the goals the school normally has."[13]

My approach differs from Metz's organizational analysis in two regards. First, I do not see the classroom-school relationship as inherently contradictory. It is contradictory only if one assumes that learning must take place in a "flexible," "autonomous" classroom. I maintain that learning does and can take place in other types of organizations as well. As such, the variable relationship between classroom and school (and family) is one of the key considerations in explaining and influencing classroom negotiations.

Second, I do not locate the cause of classroom negotiations within issues of shared definitions and expectations. Rather, classroom negotiations are best explained by examining the power relations between student and teacher, relations that in turn depend upon the nonimperative relations among school, classroom, and family.

In short, by not working from futurist or reproductionist assumptions I highlight the immediate significance of classroom processes in themselves. But unlike advocates of the organizational approach, I see the significance of classroom negotiations not through the mechanics and imperatives of isolated, formal organizations, but through the relationship of the classroom to wider processes and characteristics, namely, the separation of the school, classroom, and family and the corresponding division of the student into body, mind, and soul.

This chapter follows my own progression of understanding, beginning in the classroom and working outward. First, I show that the classroom is a negotiated order, describe the dynamics of negotiation visible in the classroom, and conceptualize the consequences of negotiation in terms of the teacher's ability to teach as opposed to babysit. Then I widen the scope to consider the separation between school and classroom and its negative effects on teacher-student interactions. Finally, I examine the separation between family, classroom, and school, and analyze its effect on classroom negotiations and teachers' attempts to teach.

THE CLASSROOM

What occurs in the classroom between the teacher and students, both on any particular day and in the long-term relationship, is negotiated. Mr. Henry begins each day and each class with a lesson plan, written on the front blackboard under the title Daily Log. Whether or not the plan is implemented depends on how well Mr. Henry is able to do battle with his resources and how well students decide to utilize theirs.[14]

Negotiations between students and Mr. Henry occur in a number of different areas. Sometimes they bargain over the classroom rules (gum chewing, pencil sharpening, candy eating), sometimes over lesson plans and homework, sometimes over classroom demeanor (arms tucked into shirts, feet on desks), and sometimes over the attention, if any, paid to Mr. Henry's agenda. This is very different from the order described by Dahl. At St. Peter's the teacher had all the power and authority, while the students had little or none. At Emerald, the students have the power both to shape the daily agenda and to subvert Mr. Henry's plans entirely.

The student's shaping power is immediately evident in the pervasive attitude that students are supposed to participate and have a hand in their "learning" and the classroom procedure. "It's your classroom," Mr. Henry tells them as he arranges the tables and storage shelves to best display their work on the walls. While Mr. Henry wants to have control of a sort, it is not the morguelike control of Dahl's prep. At Emerald, too much quiet is suspect. If students are not actively, verbally engaged, they are not learning correctly and the teacher is not teaching correctly. "It is not noise that needs to be explained, it is silence," said Mr. Henry. Correct teaching calls for the teacher to adjust, to listen, and to negotiate with the students. Teachers at Emerald spoke negatively of colleagues who did not approach the students in this accommodating manner. English teacher Betty Fleischacker, for example, was often criticized by other teachers as out of date and old-fashioned, as having "problems with control and authority." She was, in other words, accused of being a Captain Hardcastle.

Students are quick to use and insist upon their right to participate in and criticize the classroom proceedings. Tawanda keeps a notebook in which she records her likes and dislikes, and one day she angrily read to Mr. Fields, a science teacher, her complaints about the injustices of the class. When Mr. Henry confiscated from Katie a history paper that he had mistaken for a note, Lakisha loudly protested. Her response to Mr. Henry's telling her to be quiet was to insist she had a right to say what she felt because it was a class issue and she was part of the class. Bill, refusing to take a pop quiz, justified his refusal with, "It's my prerogative."

Nonetheless, teachers at Emerald not only try to maintain authority but, at times, insist upon it. When Ameer wanted to engage Mr. Henry in a debate over whether or not he should pick up the bits of paper, Mr. Henry refused to respond. Likewise, when Mr. Henry insisted that Craig remove his arms from under his shirt, Craig refused, saying he was cold. Craig tried to negotiate by agreeing to take his arms out when he needed them to write. Mr. Henry gave him detention. These stand-offs happened often, and usually Mr. Henry's response was to tell the students they could discuss the matter after class but for now to do what he said—wipe the desk, sit down, go to the student center, pick it up, or spit it out. Mr. Henry tried to reserve the right to say what was negotiable and what was not, even if it meant denying students a say.

These apparently haphazard claims by teachers at institutionally backed authority ("I am the teacher, so do what I say") struck me as being at odds with the student-centered approach teachers maintained at most times. When I asked Mr. Henry about this apparent conflict, he explained that, yes, teachers want control and authority in the class-room, but that teachers must be "given their authority by the students," teachers must "earn" their authority by displaying to students their ability as teachers and leaders. In this manner a teacher could be the authority in the classroom and still work within a student-centered frame-work. The difficulty is that students are stingy in giving away their power, and occasionally Mr. Henry refused to negotiate for classroom control. At times he did not wait for students to give him authority but tried to demand an institutionally backed, traditionally based, and rationally fortified right to determine students' behavior. If students responded with the antithesis of this claim, an explosion or standoff resulted. Sometimes this dialectical process was initiated by a student's absolutist or nonnegotiable claim for control of the classroom procedures.

These standoffs are evidence of the students' second means of power, the power of refusal. Students can and do shut down the class-room by refusing to cooperate. The substitute teacher's nightmare of chaos, paper storms, and jeers is always an imminent possibility, and it became a reality in room 112 for an unwary substitute one Wednesday. Teachers are aware of this and try to "choose the battle" accordingly. Eighth-grader Jim is notorious for his unmanageability, and one morning in math class I watched him act with particular intransigence. Yet

Ms. Marlow and two assistants, after a few attempts, let him alone as long as he remained seated. You have to choose your battles, they later told me, and today was not a day to confront Jim.

The students can subvert the teacher's plans for order because teachers have little means to stop them. The discipline system is virtually ineffective. Teachers counter their weak position by creating and then invoking personal relationships with the students, trying to influence students' behavior by construing misconduct as a breach of friendship. Mr. Fields, a tall, dignified science teacher in a gleaming white lab coat, is a master of this technique. He told me that once, when Tawanda was on the verge of exploding, he went to her on bended knee, grasped her hand, and implored, "Tawanda, does this mean you don't love me anymore? Does this mean we aren't friends?" He acted out the scene for me, and if Tawanda saw him as I did she could not help but smile and put her anger aside.[15]

Thus students have the means to both shape and subvert the teacher's plans and negotiate accordingly, and teachers try to cement their cracked institutional authority with personal style. The result is a tension in the classroom between a teacher's attempts to promote a situation in which teaching can take place and struggle with a situation in which only babysitting (their term) occurs. Teachers themselves acknowledge the tendency to babysit rather than teach, and they earn high status in the teacher's stratification scheme when they are victorious in the fight to teach.

More specifically, at Emerald teaching is an order in which the students are "focused" on the subject matter and when the subject matter is "official," that is, when the subject matter is that which the teacher is hired to teach. "Focusing," a term I picked up from Mr. Fields, implies more than attention. A focused class is one that is attending to teacher-approved topics. In the best of circumstances the attention in a focused class is controlled and initiated by the teacher. In the worst of circumstances, the attention of the class is merely condoned by the teacher. Focused official activities include spelling tests, lectures, and class discussions.

Pure babysitting, in contrast, is an order in which the students are not focused (what they are attending to is disapproved of by the teacher) and is not oriented to the official class subject. A teacher is babysitting when the students are sitting around doing nothing in particular or talking or playing in small groups, or wandering around the room. This mode is popular with students and occurs often, though any look at the official log sheet denies it.

A third mode of behavior is rare: students are attending to the class subject, but the focus is unapproved. For instance, Maleek is reading from their text, *Johnny Tremain*, while he is supposed to be listening to this week's spelling assignment. Though I observed a few individual instances of such behavior, I never observed an entire class engaged in it.

This leaves open an interesting area in which the students are focused, but the subject is not the official class subject. Examples include a group discussion of why kids fight and how they might avoid fighting, a game of hangman, or drawing on the chalkboard. What is interesting about this last category is that because the teacher maintains a sense of control (as he or she condones the students' behavior), and because subject boundaries are open to interpretation, teachers are able to define these activities as teaching of a sort. One day, when the students were supposed to be reading from *Johnny Tremain*, a group of about five began to use the blackboard for a game of hangman. I recorded it in my notes as a deterioration of Mr. Henry's lesson plan. But in the lunchroom, Mr. Henry talked about it with other teachers as a sign of success. Mr. Henry saw the hangman game as thinking work and as learning. So although the game was not what he had planned, neither did he interpret it as a failure, as pure babysitting.

This fourth category is important because room 112 is often in this mode. The focus is off the subject matter, but there is no active struggle for control. Through compromise, the tension between the teacher and the students' dual attempts to control has decreased, but the gulf between what the teacher is actually doing and his defined role as a "good" teacher has widened. Part of this discrepancy is covered over by the teacher declaring that hangman is an aspect of the official subject, part by handing out bonus points right and left so that grades appear to support the ideal of students succeeding in academic assignments.

Mr. Henry's class, and all classes at Emerald, move back and forth between these different quadrants. Typically, the semester begins in a pure babysitting mode. In the early weeks Mr. Henry was unable to maintain any focus, and when he tried to push his rules and agenda the students would refuse, blow up, and continually test and question them.

By the fourth to sixth weeks Mr. Henry was beginning to "create an environment" in which he could somewhat control and focus the class for part of each period, but rarely on the subject matter. These were the days of hangman, drawing on the board, and high-level socializing, but with few direct confrontations and explosions.

In week nine, Mr. Henry told me he was going to try to spend more class time teaching. And, through negotiations and compromises, he attempted to do so. He loosened rules of gum chewing, candy eating, and pencil sharpening. He no longer tried to control the wildness before the bell rang or when he had finished his lesson plan. He lowered his academic requirements and asked for students' attention far less often than he did at first. In response, the students rarely exploded anymore and gave Mr. Henry their attention and good behavior more often, since they were freer the rest of the time to jump, pound, talk, and even scream in ear-piercing pitches. The classroom is a compromise.[16]

THE SCHOOL

To understand why teachers are unsuccessful in their attempts to teach, we must analyze the conditions for negotiation, that is, the classroom's relation to the school.

The classroom is not the same as the school. The classroom procedures are negotiated; the school's are not. The classroom babysits; the school polices. In the classroom, rules (which are never clear to begin with) can be changed with students' immediate pressure; school rules are followed without question.[17]

School is the procedure of moving through the day in a certain way. School is going from class to class, to lunch, to gym, to a break. Going to school means clearing the halls when the bell rings and getting a hall pass if you need to leave class to go to your locker. At Emerald the procedure is to attend six class periods, with a fifteen-minute break after second period, lunch after fourth, and five minutes in between each forty-five-minute class. The halls are patrolled by Mr. Stern and Mr. Leacher, huge men who thunder the minute the bell rings, "Clear the corridor, clear out. Get to class!"

The school keeps kids off the streets for at least six hours a day. Parents know that if they send their kids to school, for a good part of every weekday they are within school grounds. At any moment it is possible to know what classroom they are in and probably even what desk they are sitting at. Parents know that for forty-five out of every fifty minutes their kids will be in a classroom in the charge of an authorized, certified adult. During class periods, their kids will not be getting into trouble hiding in the bathrooms, since these are locked during classtime.

The goal of the school is to ensure that students come and follow the procedure. When the school fails in this job it is held responsible. Emerald is being sued by the parents of a student who was injured in a fight at the city bus stop. The parents are arguing that the school is responsible for a child while he or she is "at school," even after the child is off school grounds.

Students often try not to be policed and may not always obey rules, but they do not directly struggle to change or negotiate school rules.

Nor do teachers. Teachers must teach the number of students allotted to them, whether they are good students or incorrigible; they must take attendance in each class and they must be on the school grounds a certain number of hours a day; they must also evaluate each student and give a justifiable grade every six-week grading period.

The school regulates the student's body, making sure that the student stays on campus and follows the daily routine of moving from class to class. However, once the student enters the classroom the school's authority largely disappears, for the school abdicates control at the classroom door: There are no school policies on classroom behavior, decorum, or even physical control or positioning. The classroom, borrowing a term from Metz, is "autonomous" from the school. Once the school has delivered the students to the classroom, the teacher is left to establish patterns of classroom behavior; before minds can be shaped teachers must negotiate rules for classroom conduct with the students. On the one hand, this situation leaves teachers free to establish the sort of classroom atmosphere they prefer. But, on the other hand, they have no official resources with which to shape that atmosphere or control students' conduct.

In earlier years, I was told, teachers at Emerald had met among themselves in order to devise schoolwide rules for classroom behavior but could not reach an agreement, so teachers were left to their own standards and devices. Mr. Fields said all the science teachers had reached a consensus on classroom behavior, but it had been largely ineffective because there were no schoolwide standards. Students would come to his class from a class where they had been able to run wild. Each semester, and each day of that semester, each class had to be negotiated to come around to his standard of appropriate classroom conduct.[18]

This separation of school from classroom and the lack of consensus among the teachers explains why a math teacher advised Mr. Henry to first (before even thinking about teaching) "create an environment" in the classroom. She told him to first establish an atmosphere in the classroom that was suitable to his personality and with which the students were comfortable. (In my terms, to negotiate a compromise for physical movements, decorum, and attention.) Even experienced teachers had to renegotiate classroom decorum each semester and with every shift in class composition. The math teacher claimed that in the sixth week of school she was still trying to establish an environment in her second period. She had not yet handed out textbooks or begun systematically to teach math. Just when she thought she and her students had worked out an agreement on classroom behavior, the school had assigned more "compensatory-ed" students (problem kids) to her classes, and she had to begin "creating an environment" all over again. When these new students arrived, she spent the period working (once again) on getting the students to sit in their seats instead of wandering around the classroom.

In sum, the school's exclusive concern with bodies, its silence on the subject of classroom behavior, deprives teachers of institutionalized resources and support for their authority and compels them to negotiate with students what they are to do in the classroom setting. But the relationship between school and classroom and its effects on teacher-student negotiations can be fully explained only if the third sphere, the family, is considered.

THE FAMILY

The family is separate from the classroom and school. It is external, unrepresented, imperceptible, and unknown. Parents are rarely seen on school grounds and stand out as foreigners when they do drop by to collect homework assignments for sick students. Moreover, what occurs in the family sphere cannot be questioned by the school or the teachers. The family is the sole guardian of the child's soul. And the nature of the values, attitudes, and motivations that the family instills, and how it goes about instilling them, is the family's private business. The school has no right to keep an eye on or intrude upon the family sphere unless physical abuse or endangerment is suspected. Similarly, in the classroom the student's soul is inviolable, although a teacher may suggest counseling if a student shows serious distress or suicidal tendencies. But these few exceptions are perhaps best seen within the school's and teachers' legitimate territory, the child's body and mind.

In the classroom this inviolability of the student's soul and family means that teachers are not to criticize or derogate a student's attitudes, beliefs, lifestyle, values, nor the behavior associated with these. A teacher should not condemn what a student holds (or claims to hold) to be the true, the good, or the beautiful. Souls are to remain in the background, unquestioned, taken for granted, sacred. In fact much of the classroom haggling concerns which behaviors are associated with learning and therefore *under* a teacher's control and which behaviors are associated with the soul and the family and therefore *beyond* a teacher's control. The maneuvering to define the teacher's legitimate territory is possible because of the unobservability of minds and souls and their manifestation only through physical behavior. The premise that minds, bodies, and souls are separable promotes freedom of interpretation and allows inventive students to define their behavior as soul-based behavior and therefore none of the teacher's business.

Teachers are thus expected to take a laissez-faire approach to students' values and behaviors, even when they disapprove of them. Randolph can brag to Ms. Smith about his weekend drinking and encounters with the police in the hope of shocking her, while remaining free from teacher retribution or condemnation; she, in fact, said nothing. Jonathan missed excessive amounts of school because of tennis tournaments and practice and, though Mr. Henry thought this "a crime" because Jonathan is smart and should not be missing school, Mr. Henry hands Jonathan the missed homework assignments without comment. Students who said they did not want to read their papers aloud in Ms. Li's class were told she respected their feelings as she moved on to more willing students. The message is that attitudes like cooperation, attentiveness, and interest cannot be demanded of students.

Further evidence of the soul and the separation of the family and its sanctity can be seen in the teachers' resignation to their lack of influence. Mr. Fields said that this is "just the way things are today." The drama teacher, who has taught on three continents, thinks American children are the rudest but, she said, "you get used to it." Mr. Henry told me the story of a colleague's frustration when she met the parents of a girl who had recently committed suicide. The parents came to this teacher to ask why their second daughter did not have more homework. Though the teacher felt like screaming and raving at the parents for their blindness at what they were doing to their daughter, she only said that perhaps the girl already had enough on her mind and did not need more homework, that she was already carrying the required load.

The reaction of Emerald's faculty to John is another case of teachers leaving the family to look after its own affairs in spite of a child's difficulties in the classroom. John is the most angry and hating child I have ever encountered. I vividly remember him declaring he hated the teachers and was going to kill them. The tone in his voice and expression on his face were terrifying. John refused to work, refused to pay attention, refused to do anything except distract his neighbor by insisting the neighbor join him in games of tic-tac-toe. The teachers agreed that John has severe emotional problems and should not be in school. Ms. Marlow said, "I wonder sometimes what his parents are doing to him." But the problems were in a sphere beyond the teachers' control— they dealt with John as best they could. Though among themselves teachers often theorize about a child's family life as a major source of behavioral and learning problems, family life is never addressed in the classroom or while talking with students.

A final example of the inviolability of the value sphere occurred when Mr. Henry crossed the line and tried to directly promote his views on fighting.[19] The discussion occurred after a fight between some Emerald students and a rival school. Mr. Henry stated that fighting was bad and attempted to organize a class discussion about how students could avoid fights. The very attempt surprised me, for by this time I had become accustomed to the teachers' reticence to promote their own values in an open, direct manner. But just as telling was the reaction of the students. Approximately half the class (in each of the five periods) vigorously rejected his claims with a "you don't know what you're talking about." They told him it was stupid to walk away from a fight, that you should fight if someone pushed you around or it would be even worse later. A whole gang might go against you. They thought it was a right to fight back. They thought the suggestion of staying after school for an hour to avoid bus stops during troubled times was ridiculous and impractical. Nor could they imagine their parents suing the parents of other kids who harassed them. They laughed outright at that one. They claimed Mr. Henry did not "see how it is." The students denied his expertise on the merits, value, and necessity of fighting.

To see how this inscrutable separation of the student's values and soul from the classroom is a condition for classroom negotiations, we may turn to Mr. Henry's discipline system. The discipline system in room 112 (and with minor variation in other classes as well) is that the name of a student who misbehaves is written on the board. This is a warning. If the student is delinquent again that day, a check is placed by the name. This signifies a ten-minute detention to be served in room 112 with Mr. Henry after school on Thursdays. A second check means a twenty-minute detention, and a third means the student is put on the school's detention list and is to serve a one-hour detention after school on Friday.

This system proved only loosely effective in controlling students' behavior. Some of Mr. Henry's students simply did not show up for detention, and no more came of it. Just as often, in the rush of classes coming and going the names were erased before Mr. Henry had a chance to copy them down. Furthermore, as with everything else, students could and did negotiate a reduction or dismissal of discipline with promises of future good behavior and improved classwork. Students knew the system was a joke and used ridicule to let Mr. Henry know it. Jason, sharp, quick, and witty, was the first to begin to parody Mr. Henry's habit of writing a name on the board, then pointing his finger and saying, "You're warned." In the fourth week as I walked into class Jason pointed his finger at me and said, "You're warned." I only understood what he was doing as he proceeded to point and warn another student and another. These parody warnings were soon given quite freely by all the students. When a name went on the board during a play reading, the nearby students jeered the unfortunate young man

with "You're warned, you're warned, you're warned." The latest variant
of mockery, a stroke of collective genius, happened when Mr. Henry
refused to dismiss his sixth-period class until everyone was seated.
When he at last released them the class rushed the door with a chorus
of "You're warned." Mr. Henry has a good sense of humor; he laughed.

The school's discipline system works little better, though this does
not curtail its liberal application. Students are assigned a one-hour detention on Friday for classroom misconduct or for breaking school rules
(cutting class, off school grounds, in the hall without a pass, etc.). Every
week Mr. Henry read aloud the detention list in sixth period. One week
I counted sixty-three names—in a school of only six hundred students.
The second list was longer still: the names of seventy-five students who
had missed their detention from an earlier week. If they did not show
up for detention this week they were to be suspended for a day.

According to the multitude of teachers I heard discussing the
matter—discipline is by far the most popular topic among teachers—
detention is ineffective in altering classroom behavior. The physical
education teacher said it best: "Detention is a joke. These kids are
laughing in our faces, and I don't like anyone laughing in my face. . . .
I have watched while the administration walks in the front door and the
kids are running out over the back fence." Teachers feel suspension
gives students a free day to stay home watching television or a free day
on the streets to get into trouble. Suspension means that the students
who most "need" to be in school are missing another day.

The school can and does link the students' grades and promotion to
attendance and behavior. The school can hold a student back from high
school, but only until age sixteen; by law, at age sixteen all students
must be allowed to enter high school, no matter what their grades.
Expulsion is an alternative, but it requires elaborate justification and is
too extreme for most cases.

The repercussions of detention or suspension for a student are,
doubtless, variable. But the separation of the family sphere from the
classroom and school allows students to manipulate their parents' ignorance of school activities. Detentions are easily covered up because
they are of such short duration. Even the school's hourlong detentions
were, so the phys. ed. teacher claimed in disgust, reduced to ten minutes to reward students who bother to show up at all. Suspensions can
also be concealed from parents. Mailed notices are intercepted.

Some teachers did try at times to bridge the gap between the family
and the classroom by phoning parents and visiting them at home. Mr.
Henry relied on this method often in the first part of the term, though
he tapered off in the second part. He told students that he did not
mind dropping by their homes, that he lived in Berkeley and it was no

trouble for him to do so. But such efforts to bridge the gap between family and classroom are impractical and unpredictable, and they have only short-term effects on classroom behavior. For my analysis the unpredictable aspects are the most telling.

The condition that calls for the necessity of a teacher contacting a family is also the condition that makes these contacts unpredictable and of little real value to teachers. Above all, it is difficult for teachers to approach parents on matters of a student's behavior and discipline, on matters of the soul, simply because it is not clear what teachers can ask parents for without overstepping their boundaries. Complaints about a student's misbehavior may sound like complaints about the student's upbringing, which is none of the teacher's business. Concerns about the student's schoolwork can easily sound like complaints about poor study habits, discipline, and the home environment. Some parents are open to suggestions and alliances with teachers, but some are not. Two incidents—though the first may be apocryphal—illustrate the drawbacks of fortifying the discipline system with parental contact.

First, there was Antara. Mr. Henry was having difficulties with her and mentioned to a veteran teacher that he was planning to call Antara's mother. The teacher frantically insisted that he not do so. Antara's mother, so the story went, was a "radical anarchist" who had somehow kept Antara out of school until the fifth grade. If Mr. Henry approached this woman he would be seen as a "dominating white male suppressor," and she would very likely "blow up" in his face. Mr. Henry decided to try other means to elicit Antara's cooperation.

With Katie's parents, Mr. Henry faced a dead end of a different sort. He believed that his phone call had resulted in her parents giving her a beating. He said he would never call her parents again, and fear of similar results made him hesitant to contact other parents as well.

The unpredictability of appeals to the family for support in enforcing the discipline system leaves teachers alone in doing what they can to control the soul and body so they can do their job and teach. The separations of family from classroom and school from classroom are the conditions for teacher-student negotiations. Mr. Henry can warn, but students learn the warning does not foreshadow anything particularly ominous. Students know they can and sometimes do simply shut down the classroom. Teachers are forced to negotiate.

CONCLUSION

English with Mr. Henry is a far cry from Prep with Captain Hardcastle. Captain Hardcastle was teacher, school, and parent in one. And for students, as Dahl so aptly put it, "It left you precious little leeway." The masters too had little leeway. They had the responsibility of mind, body, and soul. Teachers at St. Peter's were always on duty, in the classroom, in the corridors, and in the town. Furthermore, strict school rules and decorum applied to teachers as well as to students, leaving teachers little leeway to create a classroom environment of their choosing.

In contrast, the students at Emerald have leeway. The separation of classroom from family and from school allows them the leeway to participate in shaping the classroom environment in which a large part of their lives is spent. Mr. Henry has leeway also. Being responsible only for the mind allows him (ideally) to concentrate his efforts in this sphere alone. The separation of the school from the classroom allows him the leeway to create his own classroom procedures and environment. The separation of the family sphere allows him room to be friends with students, to relate to them in an other-than-teacher mode, to talk to them of his and their exploits without the necessity of passing judgment. Likewise, in Metz's liberalized school teachers are free to teach in an "autonomous" classroom that is separate from the "rigid hierarchy" of the school—a classroom in which power between student and teacher is not an issue because the goals and expectations of student and teacher are shared. However, Metz's idealistic pictures do not take into account the fragilities I observed at Emerald. Metz does not acknowledge that some form of domination is necessary to teach a roomful of thirteen-year-olds. An autonomous classroom leaves the teacher with few negotiating, let alone coordinating, resources.

By this criticism I do not mean to advocate a return to the days of Hardcastle. Nor am I suggesting that the liberal critique of Hardcastle is misplaced. Along with the academic accomplishments Hardcastle obtained through "discipline" came the danger of rigid tyranny. The liberal critique was right to focus on the absence of leeway for students, teachers, and parents.

However, now the situation has changed. The principal danger is no longer tyranny but the inability of teachers to spend time teaching rather than babysitting and the shocking proportion of students who fail to acquire even basic reading and writing skills. I would not propose addressing these current dangers with a return to the reign of Hardcastle. At St. Peter's the fusion of the spheres, in which a student's mind, body, and soul were under the continuous power of a single institution, gave rise to an intricate microeconomy of power and disciplinary overkill.

Instead of fusion, I propose an *integration* of the spheres. The family and the school must give the classroom teacher the power to achieve the goals of maintaining order and decorum. Teachers must have a minimal authority to discipline the entire child so that they can create an environment conducive to learning. Both the family and school should act to support a classroom teacher's integrated authority, realizing that such authority provides a basis for, not the negation of, liberalized teaching methods. A teacher's authority in the classroom does not preclude an informal student-teacher relationship, nor student involvement in the planning of curriculum and learning exercises, nor the creation of a "student-centered" learning environment. Rather, in a school system of integrated spheres the teachers' classroom authority is the foundation for these methods' success.

Unfortunately, supporting teachers in the classroom so that they can gain access to students' minds is not a cure for all the ills of our education system. Student success will still depend on individual abilities and the quality of teachers. It will still be influenced by institutional racism, the stratification of school resources, and the home environment. However, the integration of spheres must be promoted before all else if the rudimentary conditions for teaching at Emerald, and schools like it, are to be realized.

AFTERWORD: WRITING SOCIAL SCIENCE

Our field work from start to finish, in all of its various stages, had to be translated into written form. At first the form of writing was loosely defined. As long as we were writing, what we wrote and how we wrote were unimportant. Even the work distributed for class discussions could be and was encouraged to be rough, simply photocopies of field notes in raw form. But as it came time to present final papers, and even more so when it came time to present the essays as part of a manuscript for publication, the form of written presentation assumed firm contours. Each essay was to be about twenty-five pages. It was to present one and only one argument. It was to consist of an introduction, literature review, presentation of the argument with supporting field data, and at last, to be wrapped up with a conclusion. (Even the fashion of the titles was merged to a norm.)

This is a standard form of presentation in the social sciences with a standard set of justifications for itself and I was not only willing but eager to comply. I was confident that I could write a tight, clear, concisely argued essay that marshaled field experiences in a way that would not only bring the world of a junior high school to full technicolor, high-definition life, but would also, like lightning flashes, illuminate my analytic claims. Furthermore, my essay would be fun to read. I like to write. I was looking forward to presenting my written work.

I presented a fairly final form of my essay to the seminar during the second semester. I was jarred by my classmates' reactions and by their interpretations of the paper: they seemed to visualize the classroom as a virtual war zone. They also concluded that my conclusions were and must inevitably be radically conservative. They thought I advocated the demise of all liberal teaching methods as well as a return to Hardcastle authority relations.

So I tried to read my paper as they had read it, but then an even more disconcerting twist occurred. For I *could* see how my classmates had read the paper and how they had come to their conclusions. Yet thinking back to what I had seen at Emerald Junior High I did not feel I had distorted, fudged, or misrepresented data. The analysis reflected what I had seen and wanted to say.

After several close rereadings I realized that when I read my paper I was always silently supplying images of students and events that mitigated and contextualized my paper's emphasis on the teacher's weak authority position. Tawanda is the most vibrant example of this process. In the paper I referred to Tawanda's obnoxious behavior in the classroom, her irritating and seemingly constant interruptions. But when I read about these incidents, immediately other images and other aspects of my image of Tawanda came to mind as well. When I read of her interruptions I also recalled her admirable boldness in expressing her opinions. I remembered the times she stood up for herself and refused to accept Mr. Henry's version of events or his punishment if she did not think she was in the wrong. I remembered how she came most appropriately dressed, as she herself proclaimed, as a clown on Halloween. And how, after classroom conflicts with Mr. Henry, when she saw him after school she cheerfully waved and called to him from across the street as if they were always and only amiable friends. And I thought of how these other sides of Tawanda were made possible by the separation of spheres in school life.

Among the manifold consequences of the separation of spheres and the social division of the child, I chose to focus on the consequences for the teacher's authority and capacity to teach because this was to me the most shocking aspect. Still, it is only one facet. And when, to present my argument in essay form, I isolated and emphasized this one aspect, I found it changed. My classmates could not see it as I have seen it. The teacher-authority aspect is only "itself" if seen in the light of and in its relation to the other major facets the division of spheres cuts in classroom conduct: the leeway the division of spheres provides students, the division's support of parents' struggle to retain at least nominal control over childrearing, and the division's relation to the school or state's interest in the control and production of docile bodies.

I would like to have presented my work by examining the teacher's authority in the classroom in strong juxtaposition to the other facets of classroom conduct. These other facets should be examined from their own point of view, in their relation to each other, and in their relation to the separation of spheres as a whole. Bennett Berger beautifully does something of what I have in mind in his analysis of "ideological work" by rural communards in *Survival of a Counterculture*. Also I have in mind Dostoyevsky's approach in *The Brothers Karamazov*, although Steinbeck achieves the same multiperspectival approach with one-eighth the paper and ink in his presentation of Danny and his friends in *Tortilla Flat*.

My essay could not take such an approach. To have done so would have obscured my central concern, which remains the teacher's weak negotiating position. To keep this in the foreground, I had to present the other major facets involved in the social division of the child and the dynamics of classroom negotiation only from the teacher's point of view. To offset the flatness this produced, I tried in the conclusion to flip the Hardcastle-Emerald comparison on its head.

Unfortunately, the essay form that allows me to make my analytical point forcefully also obstructs my making it with richness, roundness, and in its full context. The essay form allowed me to write a solo whereas I would have liked to develop harmonies along with the theme.

So perhaps my point is simply that readers of ethnographic essays must be aware of the possible distortions of the necessarily narrow though forceful arguments that fit into the essay form. And participant-observation researchers should be careful, after going to elaborate, masochistic extremes to understand a social phenomenon in its own time and place, in its richness and complexity, and many colors—in short, in itself—not to lose these advantages in order to serve up "microwavable" fare that, while facilitating consumption and marketability, often has a taste that belies the picture on the box.

TEN

Coming Together:
An Interactive Model of Schooling

Nadine Gartrell

In California the attrition rate for African-American students is twice the rate for white students; African-American students have lower academic achievement scores than their white peers; and in 1986 only 5 percent of African-American high school graduates were eligible for admission to a four-year college or university, compared to 16 percent of white high school graduates.[1] A number of community-based programs have attempted to rectify these discouraging figures. In this chapter I examine one such project: Interface Institute (formerly Project Interface or PI), a community-based after-school math and science college preparatory program for junior high school students. PI is located in the Elmhurst district of Oakland, a predominantly African-American, low-socioeconomic community. PI students attend public and parochial schools all over Oakland, but about half come from four nearby public "home schools."

The philosophy of the program is to ensure an effective educational experience for students by forming a partnership with their parents. Such partnership philosophies are appealing ideologically, but they frequently founder as the "experts" try to make the transition from ideology to practice. Based on six months of participant observation and interviews with staff, students, and parents, I explore the reasons for PI's success in implementing a partnership between education professionals and parents and the importance of such a partnership for educating African-Americans.

BRIDGING HOME AND SCHOOL

Historically, there has been tension and "natural conflict" between the home and school as teachers and parents guard their respective domains.[2] Over the last three decades these two spheres have become increasingly separated, particularly in urban inner-city communities where African-Americans and other racial and ethnic minorities live. There is an absence of a shared culture within schools that have a predominantly African-American student population and a predominantly white faculty. Further, teachers have not been trained to teach the culturally diverse racial and ethnic groups that increasingly populate schools in inner-city areas. As a result, teachers often reject and negate the students' culture and cognitive competencies.

Most African-American parents have the perception that the schools have lower academic standards and lower expectations of African-American children than they have of white children. Consequently, these parents believe the schools are not doing a good job of teaching their children. On the other hand, teachers frequently perceive African-American parents as being uninterested in education, having low educational aspirations, and lacking the skills required to help their children.

Linguistic differences as well as differences in styles of verbal presentation between African-American parents and white teachers also lead to miscommunication. This linguistic divergence frequently amplifies the negative perceptions each has of the other. In other situations African-American parents and white teachers simply avoid each other based on personal histories of racially negative experiences. The result is that teachers and families do not attempt to establish a relationship between the school and home, and African-American children are left to mediate between the two spheres.

Accordingly, in this chapter I make three arguments. First, in the absence of a shared culture, it is imperative to bridge the gap between predominantly white faculties and the predominantly African-American student population. The school system works much better for whites than it does for African-Americans because school and family share a common language, similar educational expectations, and a similar concept of the respective roles of teacher and parent in educating the child. Second, the absence of a partnership relationship between home and school is detrimental to the learning capacity of African-American children and leads to low academic achievement among African-American students. Third, the success of PI derives from its effort to make education a joint project between the student, the program, the family, and the school. PI's interactive pedagogical approach enables students to seek out teaching methods to which they are most receptive, in contrast to the hierarchical, rote accumulation of knowledge that predominates in public schools. Because parent participation in the program is considered key to students' success, parents are required to contribute to the program. PI thus provides a bridge between the home and the school, and also serves to mitigate against the cultural discontinuity between school and home by building on the cultural resources of its African-American community and its families. Moreover, it acts to circumvent the pessimistic and predetermined nature of the dominant theoretical frameworks.

THE PROGRAM

PI is located in one of the four buildings of the Allen Temple Baptist Church complex, a social and political force in Oakland. A barracklike dilapidated structure, which houses many families, abuts the church property. The church faces single- and multiple-family dwellings that are in need of repair. Its sparkling white buildings stand in stark contrast to its surroundings. The neighborhood has a reputation for drug trafficking and related violence.

PI shares space with other church-related programs and activities. As many as eighteen people share the compact, open-design administrative office. Teaching areas are set up daily throughout the building in large assembly rooms and small classrooms. Several classes meet in one room, separated by portable blackboards. Tables and chairs in each area accommodate five students and a tutor. There is also a computer lab that has several outdated computers. The walls are adorned with religious paintings, biblical scriptures, and portraits of past and present famous African-Americans, particularly mathematicians, scientists, engineers, and inventors.

The program was started in 1982 as a collaborative effort between Allen Temple and the Northern California Council of Black Professional Engineers, who were concerned about the underrepresentation of African-Americans in mathematics, science, and engineering. PI's goals have always been:

1. To increase the number of minority students who are capable of entering high school college preparatory classes, eventually pursuing academic and professional careers in math and science.
2. To serve students identified as having promise and potential who are not yet demonstrating the real level at which they can achieve.
3. To expose minority junior high and college students to careers in mathematics, science, and engineering, to the practicality of these disciplines, and to the many possibilities that the study of these disciplines offer.[3]

An initial two-year pilot grant from the federal government supported PI's early efforts. Today the program is funded by private foundations, corporations, and individual grants, contributions, and donations, including parents' monthly tax-deductible contributions.

PI's founders assumed that many African-American students were not being exposed to math and science in the public schools, and that these students were not being prepared academically at the junior high school level to enter college preparatory classes in high school. They also believed that (1) all children can learn and achieve at a college level if they are taught by people who believe they can learn, (2) it is important to develop a program that builds upon African-American culture, and (3) there are college students who are eager to serve and work in minority communities.

There are three components to PI: a tutoring service, a role-model mentor service, and a career-exploration series. Students must participate in all components. The program is designed for students with unrealized "potential," that is, students who are intellectually capable of achieving higher grades at school and who are motivated to pursue college preparatory courses in high school. As a condition of participation, students are required to sign a contract indicating their acceptance of the rules that govern the program. Thus PI does not simply cater to "intellectually gifted" students.[4] Almost all of the students (95 percent) who enter the program are doing C to F work, although their test scores in mathematics are on average higher than those of other students in their schools. PI hopes that some of its students will become mathematicians, scientists, or engineers.

During the 1988–89 academic year, sixty-five students participated in PI's junior high school program—thirty-six males and twenty-nine females, all of whom are African-Americans. Students ranged in age from twelve to sixteen. Classes meet three times a week for two hours; two days are devoted to mathematics and one day to science. Eighteen people staff the program, including three administrators, twelve tutors, and three tutor assistants who had themselves been students at PI. The majority of the staff are African-Americans (thirteen) or other ethnic minorities (two). Eleven employees are males. The tutors are paid college students, most of whom are science, math, or engineering majors.

Students, parents, staff, and school personnel are enthusiastic about PI and convinced that the program works. But, like most community-based organizations, PI is too underfunded and understaffed to pursue systematic data collection and evaluation of the results of its efforts. However, since its inception, PI has analyzed its students' performances on the Comprehensive Test of Basic Skills (CTBS) in mathematics, which is administered to all students in the Oakland Public School District, and used the test results to diagnose students' learning needs. These data cannot substitute for a comprehensive program evaluation, but the CTBS scores for eighth- and ninth-grade PI students in 1988–89 were higher than those of the average student from the home schools.[5] That PI's seventh-graders did not do as well suggests that students may need to be in the program at least two years before academic improvement is manifested. Moreover, it appears that students who remain in the program through the ninth grade not only reap the benefits of the cumulative effects of the program and school, they also consolidate their gains. During 1988–89 fifty PI graduates who were surveyed reported being "on track" in math; thirty-seven students reported that they were taking college preparatory math courses.

INTERACTIVE LEARNING

In her monograph on mathematics and science education for minority students, Diane Beane found that the most effective programs include strategies that develop peer support systems, encourage students to work in teams, provide hands-on laboratory activities, and emphasize the practical applicability of math and science instead of theory.[6] Beane maintains that an interactive approach to teaching is effective in engaging the cognitive and affective abilities of minority students.

The following excerpts are two examples of how the interactive approach works at PI.

It is 9:20 A.M., the beginning of a hot August day. Ms. D. is teaching pre-algebra to five male students seated around a table. The class started at 9:00, and already the students and Ms. D. were hard at work. There were several problems on the blackboard, but at this point students were reviewing their homework. The students took turns working out problems on the blackboard. When a student got stuck, another student helped his classmate. For the next hour, the students and Ms. D. alternated between writing on the blackboard, explaining the mathematical rules that applied to a given problem, working in the full group, and working in smaller groups. Ms. D. alternated between standing at the side of the blackboard and kneeling, on one leg, in her chair. She never sat down. The students did not appear bored, and they did not fool around. They attended to the work at hand.

It is 4:30 P.M. on an October day. Fifteen students are divided between three tutors in the Life Science class, all of whom are sharing the large assembly hall. Today's lesson is "The Scientific Method." Each group of five students is working on a different experiment. The group that I observed tested the effects of adding different chemicals to purple cabbage water. Each student in the group selected a different chemical and each obtained a different result. They bubbled with enthusiasm as they got feedback from the tutor and each other and as they compared their respective results. After each group conducted its respective experiments, it presented its work to the others. Students and tutors asked questions of the presenters. During one presentation, a student asked if paper were live matter. Not only was his question treated with great appreciation, he was invited to perform an experiment to find the answer for himself, which he did. Following the presentations, students were told to develop and conduct their own experiments. The room shook as the noise and excitement escalated.

As is clear from these examples, a variety of teaching techniques were used in each class to engage and to stimulate students: tutors lectured for brief periods; students worked out problems on the blackboard or verbally; students worked in groups, pairs, and trios; and students did peer teaching. Different media were used—visual, audio, and hands-on experiments—to respond to students' different learning styles. Students shared their knowledge informally and formally through study groups or by presenting their work to their peers. This approach enabled students to develop competence, self-confidence, and self-esteem.

PI's philosophy of teaching was best summarized by one of its administrators:

> Yes, we do stress [an] interactive, varied kind of teaching strategy. We are more than a tutoring program. It's a preparatory program, which means mentoring has to be done—role modeling. Tutors serve as role models, which extends beyond the tutor-tutee relationship. It means becoming more involved; to show the kids that there is need to interact even insofar as studying is concerned or when in new learning situations. One of the things that I know that we talk about is black students, as they get older, and when they go on to higher education, tend to separate themselves; they study in isolation. They don't share their knowledge. This is one of the things that we try to encourage here.

Tutors cited the benefits of the interactive approach and the diversity of activities in which they are engaged. In the words of one tutor:

> If you don't want kids to be bored, you have to stimulate them and engage them. These kids come from schools where they are disengaged, and we have a responsibility to engage them in learning. I vary the format of the class, and I watch to see which student responds to what format. I'm strict, but I make learning fun. We want to turn them on to math and science, so we've got to all work hard to make learning interesting.

In PI's interactive approach, the teacher does not have a monopoly over knowledge. Students are also teachers—even the role of teacher and learner is alternated. Students enjoy learning, and the process promotes continued interaction and positive feelings about the learning process.

Another important reason for having students work together is to prepare them for the academically competitive and racially isolated environment they may encounter at some colleges. PI promotes interaction not only between students and tutors, but between students and staff. As the administrators interact with students, they also model the ideology of the program.

STUDENT PERSPECTIVES

To gauge student reactions to the interactive teaching approach, I interviewed thirteen students: six junior high students who had been in the program for at least a year, and seven high school students, five of whom had also participated in the junior high school program.

E. is a freshman in high school; he has been in the program since the seventh grade:

> Before I started here, I was a real disciplinary problem. I didn't respect teachers or anybody. At first, when my mother brought me here, I didn't like it. I didn't want to be here. Mr. J. used to take me aside and talk to me every day. When he left and Mr. Y. came here, he took me aside and talked to me. We had long talks about a lot of different things. I don't know what happened, but I started to like it here and my attitude changed. My grades have improved, and I am getting along a lot better with people. I like the tutors and the atmosphere. People are friendly, and you can come to them when you need help.

S. is a junior in high school; she has been in the program since the eighth grade:

> When I came to the program, I wasn't doing so good in math, and I didn't really like science. I mean, I wasn't serious about studying. . . . Like if you don't understand something real well and you can't get help in your school, you can come here and check yourself and get extra help. . . . You can also get help in preparing for a test. It's fun, you know, coming down here. [Laughs]. I mean, it's like an after-school thing. I mean, I never had that. I [used to] get out of school, go home, and do my homework. You can socialize down here. I come right after school so I can socialize before four o'clock. . . . It [the program] helps you focus on math and get your homework done. It made me look at math and science seriously. It kinda changed my attitude about my studies. I mean, I didn't like biology. But now I love it! Somehow, they changed my mind about it, 'cause I was really having such a hard time in that. It has really helped to improve my grades. I mean, that's what I come here for and that's what the program is all about.

D. is in the ninth grade; she has been attending PI for a year:

I started coming here because I was failing math. My counselor [at school] told my parents about the program and they brought me here. I really didn't want to come here, but now I am glad I did. Last year I was failing pre-algebra. This year I am in pre-algebra and I think I am doing pretty good. Next year, I am going to be ready to take algebra. I like that they [the tutors] do try to help you. They don't want you to fail. If you have a bad test score, you can bring it [the test] in here, and they will go over it with you to see what you don't understand. My tutor will work with me until I do understand. They also help you with your homework and encourage you to do the work, to work real hard. I have changed in my work. I've gotten better test grades. . . . I have been pushing myself to do what I am supposed to do, to do what I have to do. Like, if I am supposed to read, I not only do the reading, but the problems that go with the reading. I am doing more work than I used to do.

These excerpts are representative of the responses of the students who were interviewed. They told a similar story: (1) their grades have improved; (2) their attitude about learning has changed; (3) they like being in the company of "other achievers"; (4) their study skills have improved; (5) some of them reported being "turned on" to math and science; and (6) they all said that they now work harder. Their reports strongly suggest that PI is having a positive effect on its students.

Several themes ran through the interviews. First, the students perceive the tutors as being invested in their success, and they clearly appreciate the almost personal relationship they have with tutors. One student said, "It's like being in a private school." All of the interviewees except one attend public schools, where classes are generally overcrowded and there is limited opportunity for one-to-one attention. "I like the special attention I get from the tutors and the help of other students," said one student. While class size may be a factor in academic achievement, students' comments suggest that the experience of feeling that the tutor is invested in your success and believes that you can achieve is a more critical factor. PI is based on the premise that all students can learn, and staff, tutors, and parents have worked together to develop an educational plan based on that assumption.

The second theme that emerged is that PI students enjoy being surrounded by other achievers. Students are motivated not only by tutors but also by their peers. They experience themselves as being in a circle of achievers, which leads them to identify themselves as achievers and reinforces behaviors that accompany achieving. As one tutor commented, "These students have taken on the trappings of their environment," and define themselves as achievers. Literature on labeling theory supports the view that group interaction can promote and reinforce higher self-esteem and new sets of disciplined behaviors.

The third theme underscores the role parents and other family members play in shaping the educational outcome and aspirations of their children. Ten out of the thirteen student respondents identified a parent or other relative as having the most influence on their post–high school plans.[7] Twelve out of thirteen interviewees were planning to attend college directly after high school, with one student hoping to attend the Air Force Academy. In a state in which almost half of African-American teenagers do not earn a high school diploma, the aspirations of PI students are remarkably high.

INVOLVING PARENTS

In recent years, educators and others have argued that parental involvement in school is a key to educational success.[8] According to James Comer, the basis for academic achievement is an underlying social bonding between the students and their school. This bonding results from an interactive process that fosters positive social relationships between parents and school staff, and thereby promotes the psychological development of students. In this spirit PI attempts to establish close ties with parents, who are expected to participate in PI and to monitor learning at home.

PI staff also seek ways of engaging parents in the education process. Parents were regular visitors at PI. On several occasions, I observed parents at classes and overheard them saying, "I'm just looking around," or "I'm paying a little visit," or "I thought I would just stop in to see how things are going." Parents frequently telephoned PI to speak with their children, to inquire if their children had arrived, or to inform the staff that their children would be late or leaving early. Many parents also picked up their children after class, as PI is in a high-crime area.

During the second of two orientation meetings, the staff solicited and encouraged parents to make suggestions for future program planning. As important as the invitation to participate was the warm atmosphere created by staff, which is captured in the following excerpt from the director's address:

> I won't give a formal welcome. I am among so many friends. As a matter of fact, many of us are like family. [Points to parents in the audience.] This is Ms. W.'s daughter's second year in the program; she's doing beautifully in geometry. Mrs. S.'s son was among our first class of graduates. He is now at Morehouse. We have many success stories, and we know that your children will be our future success stories. *We want to form a triangle around your child, that is, you, your child's school, and our program.* We welcome your children and we welcome you. Mr. C. will tell you more about what we think we can do together.

Throughout the meeting, staff and tutors made frequent reference to the importance of parent involvement in their children's academic endeavors. At one point, on learning that her daughter would be assigned homework from PI, a mother expressed concern that additional homework might put too much pressure on her child. The director began her response by acknowledging how hardworking this woman and her husband were and how supportive they were of their daughter. Then, in a sermonlike fashion, she identified a number of things students need to do in order to complete high school and be eligible for college. Her oratory was received by a round of applause and a chorus of amens from other parents. (I wondered how differently this scene might have evolved had it occurred in a public school, and had the players been a white teacher and an African-American mother.)

In addition to visiting the program and attending meetings, parents serve on standing committees, assist with administrative tasks, act as role models and mentors, and accompany tutors and students on field excursions. There isn't a formal mechanism, such as a parent advisory board, for parents to affect policy and program, but parents articulate their concerns at monthly parent-staff meetings and directly to PI's program administrators. Parents who are also members of the church have access to some members of the program's board of directors and to the pastor of Allen Temple, who is a cofounder of PI. During the application process, parents are asked to identify their areas of knowledge, skill, and interest, as well as to specify their availability.

Cognizant of the discomfort many parents experience in talking with teachers and school administrators, PI hosted a meeting for parents, local school officials, and members of the Oakland School Board. The intent of this meeting was to "demystify" the public school system by providing parents and school personnel with an opportunity to meet on neutral territory and discuss their concerns. Other workshops gave parents information on adolescent psychosocial development.

Just as important as parents' involvement in PI is their monitoring of students at home. PI requires all parents to sign a contract that delineates their educational responsibilities: Parents must agree to provide a quiet environment for students to do their homework, monitor students' progress, attend four out of seven parent-staff conferences, volunteer two hours a month for program-related activities, and attend regularly scheduled meetings with the tutors. By making explicit the respective responsibilities of teachers and parents, the contract mitigates against what Sarah Lightfoot calls "the ambiguous gray areas of authority and responsibility between parents and teachers," which exacerbate distrust between teachers and parents.

PI only accepts children whose parents are prepared to be at least minimally involved in the education process. If parents do not personally return the admission application and attend the orientation meeting, their children will not be accepted into the program. Participants whose parents do not meet their contractual obligations are dropped from the program. During academic year 1988–89, two students were dropped for lack of parental involvement.

WHOSE CHILDREN ARE ENROLLED?

What sorts of parents are willing to be so involved in PI? Of the sixty-five students who participated in the junior high school program in 1988–89, thirty (46 percent) came from two-parent households; twenty-seven (42 percent) came from single-parent households, predominantly female-headed (26.5 percent of Oakland's families are headed by a single parent); six students (9 percent) lived with a grandparent or other relative; and information was unavailable for two students (3 percent).

These parents are employed in a range of occupations. Data from student applications show that 51 percent of the parents are employed in entry-level white-collar positions and blue-collar craft and technical occupations; 29 percent are employed in managerial and teaching occupations (only 12 percent of the wider community is employed in this category); 19 percent of the parents did not list an occupation on the application; and one parent was unemployed.[9]

I conducted six interviews with parents.[10] With one exception all the parents cited "declining grades" or "academic difficulty" as reasons for enrolling their children at PI. Two parents indicated that their sons were not being "challenged" or "stimulated" in public school. In explaining why she enrolled her son at PI, one mother said:

> [Seventh grade] was the transition point for Don. He did OK, but he needed more stimulus, more challenge. He has the potential to do well academically. But I thought I couldn't give him the help he needed. He kept getting low grades in areas that I knew he could do with his eyes closed. It was becoming cyclical—he was getting low grades, being placed in low-motivating classes, and he got caught in a cycle of low expectations from teachers, low motivation to do well. And he started acting out, being disruptive. So I enrolled him here.

One parent was referred to the program by her daughter's math teacher, a member of Allen Temple, as a "preventive" measure or as "another source of support" for a student who had been identified as "intellectually gifted." Although one student attends parochial school, where presumably the class sizes are smaller, her parents thought that she could benefit from being in the small groups at PI.

These parents praised PI for reaching out to involve them. All the parents reported feeling welcome and comfortable at PI. One father said, "the people who are in charge over the teachers ... are greatly concerned [about the kids], and they are not trying to sugarcoat over things because they know their importance—I mean, that day is out! They want parents involved!" While the nature of the interaction be-tween parents and staff appears to be directed by staff, the quality of the interaction appears pleasant and salutary for both parents and staff.

All the parents reported having detected changes in their children as a result of their participation in the program: improved grades, im-proved study habits, improved self-confidence, and improved racial pride. One mother said, "I think that the teachers and the administra-tors are really good. They are on top of things. Like if Shawn's grades slip, they will call me." Another praised

> the way they interact with the kids, I mean they are not intimidated by the kids. They give them room to blow off, but they still hold them account-able for their work as well as the program's rules.... I am so used to [public school] teachers molly-coddling kids, just wanting them to be quiet. Here, the tutors want to bring up their academics. They believe in the kids.

Parents also appreciate the fact that most of the tutors are African-American college students, whom they perceive as role models for their children.

The attitudes and involvement of these working-class parents in their children's school contrast sharply with the way working-class parents are often portrayed in the literature. These parents believe that it is their responsibility to ensure that their kids get a good education, and they seem to have a firm understanding of what PI is attempting to accomplish. While parents reported varying degrees of involvement in program activities, they perceive and experience PI as being supportive of their children and of them.

Overall, these parents appeared to be "take-charge" people who ini-tiated contact with schools on behalf of their children: they sought in-formation to help them make informed choices; they looked for outside resources to support their children's academic and educational aspira-tions; they had some standards for what their children should be learn-ing in school and monitored their progress accordingly; they had ex-pectations that teachers should contact them if their children had problems; and they had a clear sense of their own responsibility. In this regard, PI has not had to teach these parents how to negotiate with their children's schools or serve as advocates for their children's rights.

CONCLUSIONS

In the hierarchial model that predominates in public schools, teachers and parents guard their respective spheres and interact only at structured, infrequent, and brief moments. This model may work well if the culture of the school corresponds to that of the home, and if parents and teachers agree on educational goals and process. But in the absence of such understandings, the separation of spheres undermines the effectiveness of schooling.

In the interactive model employed at PI, the program, parents, and school form a triangle around students to engage them in the learning process and to improve their academic performance. By bringing parents into the educational process, interactive programs like PI attempt to create a shared culture by reconnecting school and home. Students who reported being "turned off" in school or not working up to their academic potential, or who had had no previous interest in math and science, are now "turned on" to education, are working harder, are "on track" in their respective schools, and are improving their grades and quite possibly their life chances.

Yet, despite the glowing reports from students and parents and despite my belief that programs such as PI do offer valuable opportunities to some African-Americans, the program has its limitations. Consider which parents enroll their children in PI. Were these parents already predisposed to participate in the education process? The answer is both yes and no. For the parents who indicated in the interviews that it was their responsibility to see that their children receive an education, the answer is probably yes. Other parents, however, may have felt obligated to participate as a consequence of enrolling their children. Having established the requirement of parent participation, PI created an environment in which parents felt comfortable and consequently became a part of the interactive process. It is unlikely that this group of parents would find mechanisms in place for such a partnership in their respective public schools.

While the purpose of requiring parent participation is understandable (and even laudable), mandatory parent participation necessarily excludes a large number of African-American students: students whose parent or parents are working too hard to leave them time to participate in PI, or who lack the skills to monitor their children's schoolwork, or whose lives are too irregular or unstable to accommodate scheduled meetings and conferences. A more flexible approach to parent participation, one that strongly encourages—but does not require—participation, would enable PI to bring more disenfranchised parents back into the educational equation. PI could serve as one model for reconnecting home and school.

Although PI and other such programs are to be commended for the work they are doing, they do not absolve public schools and society of the responsibility to educate all our children. If public schools are to remain a primary and viable source of mass education, if the literature on the positive effects of parent-school partnership in academic achievement is correct, and if educators really want to form partnerships with parents,[11] then educators will have to find new ways to bridge the gap between school and home. A "collective, concerted resolve" is required on the part of the state, schools, local communities, and families to educate all our children.

It is worth remembering that the daily struggle to survive takes precedence over everything else for African-Americans and poor families. If we as a society are committed to equal opportunity for all our citizens, then we must attend to the myriad of social problems connected with poverty—problems that render PI necessary but also limited in its effects.

AFTERWORD: THE LIMITATIONS OF SPONSORSHIP

Unlike most of my classmates, I had been in the field two months before the participant observation seminar began. While they had to find a field site in order to participate in the seminar, my field site had been handed to me. I entered the field as a paid research assistant under the auspices of the University of California (UC) Task Force on Black Student Eligibility. Whereas my classmates acted on behalf of their own research, I acted on behalf of a research team. This sponsorship had consequences that I could not undo throughout the project.

The study of community-based education programs was part of several research efforts sponsored by the UC task force, which had been charged by University President David Gardner with analyzing the causes of and solutions to the low rates at which African-American students are eligible for admission to the University of California. The goals of our particular research team were to examine the role of grassroots organizations in preparing African-American students for entry into higher education in California and to come up with a set of recommendations regarding what role the university should play in relation to these organizations.

I was one of two graduate student research assistants hired to conduct field work at two sites, one of which was Interface Institute. PI also served as my field site for my seminar paper. As I reflect on the totality of my field experience, I recall the difficulty I had in carving out a piece of research that I could call my own; there was a constant struggle to keep separate the work I was doing for the UC task force and what I was doing for the seminar. Perhaps more important at this point are the nagging, recurring questions about how my identity as a UC researcher may have set the stage for how I was perceived by PI participants and how their perceptions might have shaped the data I collected.

Six months before I was hired, a sociology professor, who was also a member of the UC task force and co-principal investigator of the research project, and a fellow graduate student visited Interface. The purpose of their visit was to explain the university's research interest and to secure Interface's agreement to participate in the study. No additional contact had been made with Interface until I entered the field. The same professor accompanied me on my initial visit to PI. His role was to reestablish contact with PI and to facilitate my entry into the field. The director was forty minutes late for our appointment, and when she finally arrived, she was curt and hostile. I remember the intense dialogue between the director and the professor and the director's often repeated question, "Why should we do this?" which I interpreted as "what's in it for PI?" It was not a good beginning, and I wondered if it were a harbinger of things to come. While no promises were made during that meeting, I am convinced that the appealing possibility of the university, with its rich resources, working in tandem with a financially struggling community organization loomed large on the director's horizon. Moreover, my identity, research purpose, and role in the field had been established during that meeting. I was an "official" researcher for the University of California conducting a "legitimate" study on its behalf.

Both the university's research project and the organization of Interface converged to shape the form of my research—the extent to which I could be a participant or a nonparticipant observer. Tutoring is the core service PI provides. If one conceives of participant observation in a narrow sense, then it would stand to reason that I should have been either a tutor or a student. However, Interface is a highly structured math and science program with paid tutors working three to four days a week, twelve to fifteen hours. The program had a full complement of tutors, the majority of whom were math, science, or engineering majors. Moreover, science and math are not my strengths. What the program lacked was administrative support (receptionist/secretary) and technical assistance (reviewing and writing grants, proposals, program development, etc.), areas in which I have a lot of experience. In addition to the structural constraints and needs of the program, there was also the research mandate of the UC task force to consider. I needed to be able to move freely about the field site, to observe the comings and goings of staff, parents, students, and visitors and to interact with them freely. Being confined to a classroom would have precluded that possibility. Therefore, I literally alternated between being a participant observer—providing technical assistance and administrative support— and a nonparticipant observer, observing the tutor-student interaction in the classroom.

When introducing me to parents, board members, visitors, or anyone who happened to come into the office while I was there, the director said, "This is Ms. Jules [I don't think she ever got my name correct]. She's studying our program for UC." Letters to parents (written on Interface stationery and signed by the program manager) broadly outlined the university's research efforts and requested their participation. In interviews with program participants, I told them that I was also conducting research for a seminar, but this information remained secondary. My "official" university identity was in the foreground, and it was to that identity I believe people responded.

Most of the people I interviewed (staff, parents, and students) questioned me about why the university was interested in PI and what the university planned to do with the information. I had constructed a careful response so as not to say anything that might bias their responses. I explained that throughout California, African-American students have a low rate of admission to UC and other four-year colleges and that the university was looking at a number of after-school programs in African-American communities to see what they were doing to prepare young people for colleges and universities. In this context, students, staff, and parents had motives to be careful about what they revealed to me. They had a vested interest in telling me about the program's successes, amplifying the positive and minimizing the negative. After all, there might be something in this for them: Interface might receive material, academic, or technical assistance; students might conceivably be identified and tracked into UC; parents may have seen this as another opportunity to help their children in some way.

This is not to say that informants painted a totally rosy picture. But staff attributed the program's weaknesses solely to the external factor of inadequate funding. And yet I observed and overheard differences (tensions) related to pedagogy (whether tutors were "tutoring" or "teaching") and classroom decorum. Had I not shared my observations with staff, they would not have identified these as issues. As it was, they acknowledged these differences but downplayed their importance. Even students minimized the weaknesses that they reported. For example, a majority of the students stated that the science module was the weakest academic component. When I probed this point, I discovered that what they meant was that they experienced a disjunction between what they were learning at PI and at school, which they said, when pressed further, meant more work for them. While they didn't want to do "more work" and wished for better coordination between the two spheres, students emphasized that they had fun in science and learned "new things."

Because there were certain questions that I had to ask for the UC task force, the parent and student interviews were somewhat more structured than they would have been if I had been conducting interviews only for my own project. While many parents were pleased to meet an African-American student who was in a doctoral program (and at Berkeley too), and under other circumstances they might have given me more than affirming, positive, appreciative success stories, the fact remained that I was conducting a study on behalf of the university and they had a vested interest in the outcome.

By engaging in this bit of reflection, I do not mean to suggest or imply that the reports of success were untrue or exaggerated, only that when weighing the data, I had to consider the impact of sponsorship. Could it be that my role as a UC research assistant dwarfed my own research project, shaped what I observed, shaped my informants' and my own responses? Did sponsorship invalidate my study?

I can confidently say no to those questions. I was there! It is precisely this aspect of field work, conducted in the time and space of those we study, that saves the researcher from the liabilities of sponsorship. Participant observation affords the researcher opportunities to interact with and to experience the realities of others. Moreover, once in their space, the researcher becomes more self-conscious and attuned to her experiences, which can be used as a barometer of what's happening. I *experienced* something positive occurring at PI. Did I make up the excitement of the science classes? Did I dream up my engagement in the classes—so much so that I sometimes became one of the students and conducted my own experiment? Did I imagine that I wished I had had Ms. D. for algebra and Mr. M. for geometry? I did not! Had I relied solely on questionnaires or interviews, then perhaps I might have been deceived by responses designed to put the best light on the program in order to please the UC investigator. But I did the field work, observed what happened, peeled away the layers, and saw the program as it was.

Moreover, participant observation made me conscious of the liabilities of sponsorship in the first place and allowed me to take them into account in my interactions with students, parents, tutors, and staff.

PART FIVE

Researching the Researchers

Introduction to Part 5

It seems fitting, in a volume so consciously reflexive as this one, to devote a section to researching the researchers themselves. The following two chapters undertake this project in quite different settings: one in an ethnographically based research and service project, the other in a university classroom. Both authors conclude that researchers are no more exempt from interested behavior than are the people they study.

This is not a particularly novel insight. Max Weber made this the basis of his methodological discussions.[1] Alvin Gouldner took the argument a step further and argued that researchers' interests affect not only their choice of focus, but also their theoretical assumptions and conclusions. For example, Gouldner criticized Howard Becker and other sociologists for their self-serving approach to the problem of deviance. Becker's professional interests shape his theoretical approach.[2] Similarly, Gouldner treats Talcott Parsons's structural functionalism as an attempt to justify and serve the growing welfare state.[3]

However, Gouldner's innovative project has not been particularly popular in the social sciences. Nobody likes being subjected to critical analysis, and few have followed in his theoretical footsteps. Even in this postmodern age of academic reflexivity, which has spawned so much methodological navel-gazing, few social scientists have undertaken empirical research on research itself. An exception is the growing school of "sociology of scientific knowledge," based in Britain, which is focusing attention on aspects of natural scientific research—but even here, the social scientists are not studying research in their own fields.[4]

The two case studies that follow attempt to fill this gap. Kathryn Fox examined an AIDS education project directed by professional ethnographers. She worked alongside outreach workers who pounded the

pavement in high-risk neighborhoods, handing out bleach (for steril-
izing syringes), condoms, and streetwise advice on AIDS prevention.
She observed firsthand the limits and constraints facing the project: for
instance, the outreach workers' desire to spend their limited time educating potential AIDS victims conflicted with the directors' research
goals of gathering detailed field notes and statistics. These research
goals were necessary to document the agency's success in reaching high-
risk populations, in order to ensure future funding—a constant subject
of concern throughout the organization. Lipsky describes the tension
between the interests of public service workers and their agencies as
characteristic of "street-level bureaucracies."[5] Time and again the AIDS
Project was forced to compromise its altruistic ideals to fulfill its contractual research obligations to the funding institute. Indeed, the directors even decided not to participate in what they felt was one of the
most effective AIDS-prevention programs, needle exchange, because
their major funding source had threatened to halt their operation if
they did. In this way, the researchers' interests determined the project's
design.

Charles Kurzman studied the graduate sociology class in participant-
observation methods that produced this volume. Approaching classroom discussions from the perspective of the sociology of knowledge,
he observed which statements were accepted by the class and which
were not. He found that statements tended to be evaluated not in terms
of their evidence or their theoretical paradigm, but rather in terms of
deeper values. He identifies two sets of values that are deployed in
different contexts: the opposed values of respecting one's subjects' perspectives or denying them validity, and the opposed values that see
human action as socially determined or outside social determinism. The
availability of contradictory values, Kurzman argues, gives the sociologist's actions a certain flexibility, retaining a certain amount of free will,
which is all too often lost in discussions of interests.

Thus both of the following papers attempt to pursue Gouldner's
insight that social scientific research may be analyzed in the same way
it analyzes others—in terms of interests, relations to the state, normative
orders, or whatever. This project is of course vulnerable to similar analysis itself; the authors are in no position to claim an exemption themselves from the interests that they identify in other researchers' work.
Perhaps this vulnerability explains the paucity of research on research.

But this is really a false vulnerability, because the analysis of social
scientific research does not necessarily make it less valid or worthwhile.
It may be that some analyses denigrate their subjects, taking the form
of exposés and debunking; other analyses, however, may actually enhance the credibility of the research, showing, for instance, the con-

straints and limits within which the research was conducted, or linking the research with the researcher's goals. In any case, such analyses are useful to clear away some of the suspicions and accusations that accumulate in a world where, as Karl Mannheim noted, everybody thinks everyone else is guilty of ideology.[6]

Kathryn Fox
Charles Kurzman

ELEVEN

The Politics of Prevention: Ethnographers Combat AIDS Among Drug Users

Kathryn J. Fox

By 1985 Western City (a pseudonym) recognized its need to address the increasing prevalence of the AIDS virus among injection drug users (IDUs) and their sexual partners. While previously AIDS had been cast as a gay male disease, presently nearly 30 percent of all diagnosed AIDS cases are attributable to injection drug users, their sexual partners, or children born to them.[1] With the onset of this "second wave" of the epidemic, some educational intervention was clearly necessary to prevent the same tragedy from occurring among drug users as occurred in the gay community. However, experts from the Centers for Disease Control and other agencies felt that this would be an unduly difficult task based on their assumptions that drug injectors would be, for the most part, extremely inaccessible and unconcerned about their health. The task itself was undisputed: this population had to be warned about its potential for the rapid spread of AIDS. The issue became just how the mission should be carried out and who could best do the job.

In an era of "zero tolerance" for even casual drug use in the United States, only the threat of AIDS mandated some humane concern for drug injectors, particularly given the risk to their sexual partners and unborn children. However, the federal government's approach to AIDS intervention in this population had to be consistent with its present hardline policy on drug use. Any intervention plan would have to operate within the confines of the present administration's "war on drugs"; such a contradictory set of conditions could potentially disable efforts from the start. Consequently, one federal solution was to couch AIDS prevention services in "demonstration" research projects in selected major cities.[2] Such a political sleight-of-hand enabled the federal response to circumvent criticism from liberals and conservatives alike.

The funding made available by the federal research institute called for research projects to incorporate services and an evaluation of their impact in order to demonstrate how recalcitrant needle users could be reached. Suddenly, experts on drugs, AIDS, and needle-using practices appeared all over, each claiming that their model for intervention would work better than the others.

In this chapter I will outline the arguments and assumptions of two competing approaches to AIDS prevention among drug users. The first part examines the theoretical and subsequent methodological differences between a more traditional public health model for intervention and an innovative outreach strategy based on the principles of ethnographic research. The bulk of the chapter focuses on the "ethnographic" outreach approach to AIDS intervention, using data obtained through a participant-observation study of one such demonstration project. Thus, the analysis begins with the character and frustrations of outreach work itself. I then discuss how the continuation of outreach services depends on the scientific component, on documenting the success of outreach. This mutual interdependence leads to escalating tensions that are often played out in conflicts within the project between the goals of outreach workers and administrators. In the final part I trace these conflicts back to the state-imposed conditions on funding and the way the law inhibits the effectiveness of outreach. I conclude with a discussion of the implications of these limitations for social service work, and applied ethnography more generally.

COMPETITION BETWEEN INTERVENTION MODELS

In Western City a heated political struggle ensued between proponents of the drug treatment community and a group of social scientists who specialize in drug research. Although more complex than suggested here, the debate centered around who could most appropriately claim the educational funds allotted to reach the injection drug using population. The struggle encapsulated a distinct ideological and practical split concerning who had the greatest access to, as well as understanding of, the drug-injecting population. Both camps envisioned themselves as having a better grasp on drug users' best interests.

The two approaches differ theoretically insofar as the treatment community's stance resembles a traditional medical model whereas the ethnographic model incorporates a "social problems" orientation. From the treatment community's perspective, drug addiction is an individual pathology, which requires medical treatment as does any physical sickness. In contrast, the ethnographic model conceives of drug addiction as a socially situated phenomenon. The ethnographers' guiding framework resembles Howard Becker's "labeling theory," in that they view addicts as victims of ignominious drug policies and subsequent stigmatization.[3]

The two polarized strategies for intervention are informed by these perspectives. For example, the drug treatment model would expect drug users to come into their agencies and obey the standards and rules that the organization imposes in order to receive services. The ethnographic model proposed bringing the agency to the streets and addressing the issues that drug users encounter in their own social context and according to their own understandings.

Furthermore, the two approaches espouse different goals. According to the treatment model, AIDS would provide the perfect incentive for convincing people to "stay clean." From their perspective, treatment *is* prevention. Many reason that promoting sterile needle use to reduce the risk of infection is not enough, particularly in light of the connection between needle use and AIDS. In fact, from this perspective, the notion of "safe" needle use is an oxymoron. Many treatment advocates, as well as laypeople, have argued that the promotion of such a concept would be likely to encourage needle use.[4] Treatment programs and their proponents have always had an interest in getting people off of drugs, but now their appeal was to safety rather than morality. The goals of the treatment community were far-reaching. They saw AIDS as an opportunity to further their original agenda. Some cynical observers suggest that treatment agencies saw AIDS as merely an opportunity to shore up their resource base.

The ethnographers, on the other hand, argued that the treatment model was unrealistic. First of all, the means available to treatment centers to reach people were limited at the outset. The treatment community could certainly reach and educate the portion of the IDU population that is in treatment programs, but what about the other 75 or 80 percent? Most injection drug users do not seek treatment.[5] Therefore, the ethnographers argued, the idea that drug injectors will suddenly stop using drugs is naive. Besides, the hope that treatment does offer is too risky to count on in the context of AIDS; treatment of any kind does not ensure permanent abstinence.

In addition, many treatment programs, such as methadone programs, are designed to treat heroin addiction alone. However, as Watters et al. have pointed out, between one-third and one-half of drug injectors prefer stimulants, such as cocaine and methamphetamines, yet "[t]he treatment portfolio . . . is heavily dominated by programs that are specifically geared to the opiate addict."[6] The treatment model fails to address the fact that the connection between injection drug use and AIDS transmission arises from the needle sharing practices associated

with the drug subculture. In addition, treatment schemes are not designed to deal with omnifarious needle use, such as the injection of
hormones and steroids. Of course, advocates of the treatment model
understand that transmission occurs through needles, but they do not
address the importance of firsthand knowledge of the social context
and associated practices of needle use in getting a clear picture of the
spread of HIV. Ethnographers themselves might not have grasped the
complex meanings and necessary practices associated with drug injection had they not regularly observed the process. For example, the
project ethnographers observed that needle users who reported cleaning their "works" before sharing actually only rinsed them out in stag-
nant, dirty water to keep the syringe from getting clogged.

The very fact that the ethnographers had been allowed to witness the
illicit activities of IDUs testifies to the level of rapport and trust they
achieved in this population. The essence of ethnographic research into
"deviant" populations rests in its ability to develop relationships of trust
with people who generally shun contact with official agencies. Finally,
the very avoidance of agencies on the part of illegal drug users makes
traditional treatment clinics inappropriate mechanisms for a far-
reaching AIDS education plan.

Drug researchers have stated that "the enforcement of repressive
and prohibitionist policies in the drug field has resulted in forcing all
activities associated with injecting drugs . . . to be done in a clandestine
way."[7] The ethnographers criticized policies, such as punitive treatment
models, that further distance injection drug users and their practices
from social services that could help them reduce the spread of HIV.
Quite controversially, they attacked policies that use the epidemic as an
opportunity to exercise control over already scapegoated and unpopular minorities. The ethnographic model advocates access to IDUs on
their own terms and delivers the message about risk behavior within
their own community.

Ordinarily, the ethnographers studied drug-using scenes with an eye
toward understanding, rather than necessarily intervening. They became committed to the means of intervention in the first place because
of the gravity of the AIDS epidemic. However, their goals in this vein
were limited to the reduction of risk for transmission among IDUs.
Their nonjudgmental attitude toward these populations would allow
them a level of penetration that the treatment providers could never
achieve. They argued that IDUs would only be receptive to the warning
of their risk for AIDS if it were delivered in an unobtrusive and
nonthreatening manner that would not disrupt the natural subcultural
setting. Whereas the treatment model presumed AIDS to be the perfect
vehicle for an antidrug message, the ethnographers countered that,

realistically, injection drug users would not respond to a message like that. AIDS would be seen as yet another moralistic scare tactic. Besides, envisioning treatment as a mechanism for avoiding HIV infection assumes that effective treatment is readily available to everyone and neglects the interplay of environment, unemployment, and other social factors in individuals' inability to remain drug-free. Rather, if the truly urgent mission is to prevent the spread of AIDS, the concept of "safe" needle usage should be promoted.

Perhaps in a less life-threatening situation, such a proposal would not have flown. However, the ethnographers persuaded the federal funding source, as well as others, that they could indeed reach the drug-using population, voluntarily and beneficially. Thus, in 1986, the AIDS Project received a portion of the monies allotted to promote health information among the IDU population.[8] By 1988, studies commissioned by the Project showed that its strategy for education had been effective: IDUs were concerned about their risk for the virus, they were open to suggestions to combat their risk, and they were beginning to follow advice.

However, even when IDUs knew about their risk, their knowledge of proper needle sterilization was still limited. Because the distribution of sterile needles was infeasible in this city, for a variety of political reasons, the alternative was to encourage cleaning needles that are shared. American drug policy and paraphernalia laws, such as the illegality of syringe possession for the purpose of shooting drugs, has made needle sharing an inevitable aspect of the drug-injecting life-style.[9] The strength of the addiction itself and the relative unavailability of hypodermic needles for nondiabetics encourage people to share needles, regardless of their knowledge of the risk. It is a standard component of the social organization of drug scenes.[10] Clearly, the more realistic option was to urge the sterilization of needles.

In 1986, the AIDS Project introduced the distribution of free one-ounce bottles of household bleach to clean needles, as well as free latex condoms to prevent sexual transmission. By December 1989 the outreach workers had distributed over 230,000 bottles of bleach and nearly half a million condoms. At the inception of this strategy, only 3 percent of IDUs interviewed were aware of bleach as a needle sterilization technique. Fifteen months later, 82 percent mentioned bleach as the way to clean needles. Clearly, the ethnographic project had demonstrated some degree of effectiveness.[11] By 1988 the Project was able to persuade the federal funding agents, as well as the state and city health department, to dramatically expand its efforts.

Federal funding was intended for research and evaluation while it was hoped that state and local governments would see the desirability of funding such outreach services. The federal government could thereby extricate itself from service and avoid accusations of promoting or condoning drug use.[12] An ethnographic research model enabled the government to fund quasi-service projects without violating official policy.

The ethnographic strategy, therefore, comprises two complementary parts. The *outreach* component is designed to deliver services to the communities at risk for AIDS, in the form of information, referrals, prevention materials, and basic assistance. Outreach workers also collect information on their target communities' drug use, AIDS knowledge, and high-risk behaviors. The *research* component is intended to document the activities of the workers within these communities, as well as the inner workings of drug-using scenes. Interview data record needle-sharing and sex practices, AIDS risk knowledge, and information on the client population. The data are used to understand the epidemiology of AIDS in drug-using populations as well as to determine the effectiveness of outreach as a method for intervention. Furthermore, the understanding of drug-using populations garnered from the data is meant to inform the Project's overall strategy and individual workers' strategies for education.

OUTREACH: THE FRONT LINE

The outreach component involves dispatching workers into communities that are known to have high concentrations of IDUs.[13] The workers are hired on the basis of, among other things, a demonstrated non-judgmental attitude toward needle users, prostitutes, homeless people, and those with various sexual orientations. In addition, the workers must have an assumed ability to infiltrate their target communities and establish relationships within them.

Further, it is especially appropriate for outreach workers to have some "street smarts" as they often work in the city's higher crime areas and need to be acquainted with the rules of the streets. Thus, the AIDS Project hires many outreach workers who have previous histories in drugs, crime, or the sex industry. The assumption, too, is that these workers will be more easily accepted in the communities that they target.[14] Because they are often engaged in illegal activities, the populations that workers serve tend to be suspicious of outsiders.

Outreach occurs primarily on the street, in the form of one-to-one interaction with IDUs and their sexual partners.[15] Outreach workers give informal education about risk reduction, along with free bleach and condoms, and explanations about their use and necessity. On a daily basis, outreach workers comb the streets of their target area, identify IDUs, and strike up conversations with street users, their sexual partners, and prostitutes.

The workers are equipped with recognizable bags of free bleach and condoms, which they continually distribute. These tools serve as entry into the community: they give workers a legitimate reason to be there, state their nonthreatening purpose visually, and give them opportunity to engage potential "clients." Although the bleach and condoms are effective AIDS prevention equipment, their primary function for outreach workers is as a means for contact with IDUs. Therefore, the supplies have two functions. The widespread distribution of bleach and condoms may actually slow the epidemic by placing the tools for protection directly into the hands of those who need them. In addition, the AIDS prevention materials identify the workers' purposes in the community, creating a reason for continued acquaintance. Thus, the many interactions that take place daily enable the outreach workers to assess the risk behaviors and the degree of knowledge about risk, and to engage drug users in a dialogue about their lifestyles and needs. Questions about AIDS risk, antibody testing, social services, and related issues arise in these interactions. Finally, the thousands of materials that are readily accepted serve as testimony to the level of penetration the workers have achieved in the communities.

The premise behind the ethnographic strategy is to gain access to the subculture of the participants, and then to deal with them on those terms. As such, outreach workers spend a great deal of time interacting with "opinion leaders" in the area: drug dealers, old-time "righteous dope fiends," hotel managers, and bartenders. Outreach workers are supposed to "know what time it is": to observe trends, police activity, and drug and crime patterns in the area. This delicate information is meant to inform their personal strategy in the neighborhood.

Once rapport has been established and outreach workers are known and trusted in the community, they continually provide assistance. The services provided further enhance one's credibility on the street. Outreach workers give referrals for free food, counseling, clothing, shelter, employment opportunities, AIDS antibody testing, and drug detoxification treatment upon request. Their main value to clients rests in their ability to feed them into services with as little bureaucratic difficulty as possible. Outreach workers provide straightforward, realistic, "value-free" help to anyone who wants it.

The distinction between street-based outreach and other traditional social services is the nonjudgmental, nonpunitive manner in which outreach workers deal with clients. The very idea of bringing the agency to the streets, contrasted to the stringent eligibility procedures and relative power associated with traditional settings, suggests a certain respect for clients on the part of the Project. As many outreach workers have said, "You only have as much authority as you are allowed on the street." By taking the agency to the streets, the Project has voluntarily relinquished the automatic social control other agencies have over their clients.

Outreach work in these populations is inherently difficult. Workers encounter poverty, sickness, volatile clients, and sometimes genuine danger. The tenuous position of workers on the street makes their jobs unduly taxing. Outreach workers must continually negotiate their roles within their target areas. Many of the communities they serve are fairly transient, therefore they have to establish reputations with an ever-changing population.

Often drug users and dealers are somewhat suspicious. As one well-entrenched worker said: "It's just as important to stay away from dealers as it is from the police." Having the trust of key people in the area is essential. The police are sometimes skeptical about the role of outreach workers; they interact too comfortably with drug users on the streets. In fact, the workers have no official sanction from the police, and occasionally are harassed by them. In sum, the police suspect they might be drug dealers and dealers think they might be undercover narcotics agents. The precarious state of being on neither side of the law can be a perpetual source of tension for workers.

An outreach worker's credibility on the streets is extremely important. Consequently, a certain level of identification with clients is necessary to be accepted by the community members. However, outreach workers must strike a difficult balance between being an "insider" and an "outsider."[16] The emotional labor involved in incessantly teetering on this razor's edge proves untenable for some. It is particularly difficult because many of the outreach workers have been on the "inside" themselves. As an insightful supervisor put it:

> Our problem is that we are *so* native . . . that we have every problem you could imagine on the streets within our very agency . . . so in some sense the things that made our project special and *the* model project are what are causing us all this trouble. . . . The people from the communities or with habits or records or whatever, they have the best street contacts, they know everybody, exactly what's going down, so they deal our message, but they sometimes can't separate themselves from the homeboys.

Although there are valid reasons for hiring mostly "insiders" or indigenous members to do outreach work, it can contribute to identity problems for workers embroiled in all-too-familiar street scenes day after day.

In terms of actual service delivery, perhaps the most frustrating feature of outreach work is the relative dearth of services that workers can provide. Outreach workers express a sense of helplessness in light of the lack of alternatives at their disposal. One example that typifies these perpetual obstacles is the system of detoxification in Western City. For a short time, outreach workers were able to give clients coupons for free methadone to treat heroin addiction as part of another study. However, the coupon only entitled the client to twenty-one days of methadone doses, at the end of which the client was "cut loose." After this period of detoxification, the client was generally thrust again into his or her familiar social world, with six weeks or more to wait for an available maintenance program. Most often, the client resumed drug use. Although outreach workers were able to facilitate clients' entrance into detoxification, they were unable to help with long-term treatment programs. In other instances, outreach workers realized that their clients, who may be homeless or unemployed, have immediate needs that require attention before their risk for AIDS would become meaningful. As one worker said: "What's the difference between dying from AIDS or dying from a bullet or dying from not having a job?"

Even though both outreach workers and clients were frustrated by the inadequacy of detoxification and other programs, nevertheless the detoxification tickets enabled outreach workers to develop relationships with street needle users. The word spread quickly on the streets that outreach workers could get them into a drug program or facilitate their introduction to other services. As one veteran worker recounted:

> This guy told me that he had heard I could get him housing, so I get out my list and start writing down all my best referrals. And he said, "Man, this is the same old stuff I get from the Salvation Army or the Red Cross or whatever," and I thought, he's right! We're out there giving out bleach and condoms, referrals, whatever, but these people need housing *now*!

For outreach workers who view their jobs as providing services rather than being researchers, the act of simply handing out supplies can seem absurd. Outreach workers understand that AIDS is only one of the many problems facing their clients and they would like to address the totality of their concerns. Structurally, though, the Project's goals are circumscribed. As Lipsky describes as characteristic of "street-level bureaucracies," the ideals of the workers conflicted with the bureaucratic requirements of the administration and funding source.[17] In managing the conflicting values, outreach workers' zeal becomes tempered. As one outreach worker said of another disenchanted worker:

> He came in with high expectations about changing things and so he was disappointed. But you have to have this built-in mechanism to convince yourself you're really helping. But you're not really changing anything. You can *feel* you're helping one individual and another, you know, a few; but in reality you're not. You have to know that.

The outreach workers with the greatest longevity in the field seem to be those whose expectations about change are or become relatively low. Crusaders are more likely to leave the Project because they see their accomplishments as too few and too shallow. One dissident outreach worker, who left after a brief stint, said:

> I want to help the Chicano community but there is nothing in the framework of these institutions that can really help them, that can really address what the problem is. I just couldn't handle it any more. There was something kinda weird about going up to old dope fiends saying "Hey man, want some bleach?" when it's like "Well, you won't die from AIDS, but man, you might O.D. in two weeks." . . . We didn't even address that.

This same disaffected outreach worker went on to refer to government-supported agencies as "poverty pimps," implying that it is in the best interest of a social service to foster a dependence, rather than to try to eliminate the need for its presence. As Lipsky has pointed out: "Advocacy is incompatible with organizational perspectives."[18]

Offering what one worker termed "bandages" to treat the wounds of the community, rather than addressing the source of social problems, can be demoralizing. The daily grind of facing impediments necessarily moves outreach workers into more routinized and professionalized orientations, if they are to survive in the Project. As Lipsky explains:

> Some street-level bureaucrats drop out or burn out relatively early in their careers. Those who stay on, to be sure, often grow in the jobs and perfect techniques, but not without adjusting their work habits and attitudes to reflect lower expectations for themselves, their clients, and the potential of public policy.[19]

As Liza, a supervisor, said to a despondent outreach worker:

> If you look at the whole picture, at all the things that are wrong, at all the things that need to be fixed, then you'll just go mad with frustration because you can't do everything. You can only tackle one thing at a time.

Most outreach workers envision themselves as social service providers rather than researchers or ethnographers. Their discontent stems not from the clients themselves but from how little they can do to help. As one worker put it: "These people are called 'system-failures'; it's not that they've failed, but the system has failed them."

SCIENCE VERSUS SERVICE: A CASE OF ANTAGONISTIC INTERDEPENDENCE

The task that outreach workers see for themselves is further compromised by the research component of the Project. The outreach workers must write detailed field notes daily. These contain summary descriptions of their observations in the area, as well as specific reports of their activities. The purpose of these notes is twofold: to serve as an account for their whereabouts and to provide documentation of the Project's ability to reach IDUs. Ostensibly, too, the federal government uses the scientific information about drug users' life-styles to develop ways of helping them.

Most outreach workers express anywhere from disdain to indifference regarding the field notes: "I just hurry at the end of the week and just fill up the page. Who cares about the field notes? I write less and less all the time: 'Went to the park, passed out supplies, went home.' " Some workers complain that the field notes take time away from serving clients. Others are concerned about the possibility of their field notes being used for surveillance purposes by the federal government. The in-house researchers attempt to persuade outreach workers to write field notes more conscientiously and punctually. Clearly, the Project has two separate agendas operating simultaneously, yet insofar as street work is a requisite for providing data for analysis, outreach work takes precedence over scientific research.

The demonstration projects are also required to participate in interviewing drug injectors, gathering information on their knowledge of risk behaviors, their needle hygiene, and things of that nature. Outreach workers are responsible for recruiting subjects for interviews, screening them for eligibility, and scheduling the interviews. Although each target area hosts interview rounds only periodically, outreach workers spend a significant portion of their time involving clients in research. However, clients are paid a small amount for participation, so outreach workers are popular during those times and are able to meet new clients. Nonetheless, between the activity of signing up clients for interviews and clients clamoring to get involved, the message about AIDS is often lost. For the Project directors and in-house researchers, on the other hand, the field notes and interviews are vital. As a supervisor said in a training session: "Maybe most of what we do is just get to understand the neighborhoods. The ethnography is the main part."

The field notes, as well as the research interviews, illustrate the different emphases at the two levels of the organization. As Frances Fox Piven found with the Mobilization for Youth program in the 1960s, the research requirements "were in continual tension with the imperatives of providing services."[20] For the outreach workers, who are concerned with service delivery, the field notes are a waste of time and the interview schedules are seen as a necessary evil for pleasing the funding source, as well as for ensuring their survival.

The opposition of the research and service components is exemplified by the different meaning attached to AIDS prevention materials by outreach workers on the one hand and managers of the Project on the

other. One supervisor explained: "After you make contacts, get known
on the streets, we try to lessen the number of condoms put out on the
streets. . . . That's your card until you get known." On the one hand,
the Project is motivated to document a strong need for and acceptance
of condoms and bleach from outreach workers. The researchers affiliated with the Project illustrate the vital role of the workers on the
streets partially by recording the vast numbers of supplies accepted.
Yet, according to one supervisor, the Project must paint itself as "more
than a bleach and condom distribution service. But for some [outreach
workers], that's what we are. Instead of the avenue, the supplies become the end."

The supplies are intended to enable outreach workers to get their
foot in the door to establish relationships, develop an understanding of
clients' situations, and provide support and referrals for services. Yet
many clients come to see them as "the condom lady" or the "bleach
man." Many interactions with clients on the streets are cursory exchanges. Outreach workers report feeling naked without the tools of
their trade. An outreach worker can always feel useful if people on the
street are taking, and presumably using, the condoms and bleach. In
fact, outreach workers routinely supply huge handfuls of condoms to
prostitutes who work the street corners. Doing outreach within this
particular prostitute population is somewhat like preaching to the converted, as the workers are duplicating another organization's services.
Perhaps one of the reasons that outreach workers continue to supply
the prostitutes is to justify the usefulness of outreach and the compli-
ance they have been able to elicit from these populations.

Furthermore, the Project alleges that noncompliance tends to be situational. In other words, clients generally use supplies if they are
handy. Therefore, outreach seems to be influential when the prevention tools are readily available. Yet the directors are being forced by
some staff members to address the concern about "weaning" clients
from the constant supply of prevention materials. The goal is to "train"
clients to get supplies for themselves eventually; to get clients to incorporate the risk message beyond situational convenience. But as far as
many outreach workers are concerned the distribution of supplies is
their raison d'être: "My job is to give out bleach and condoms and AIDS
education. Everything else is extra. . . . If these [IDUs] start buying
their own bleach, then we're out of a job."

POLARIZATION WITHIN THE PROJECT

The lack of commitment on the part of workers to their field notes and
the mission of research is at the core of many small struggles that ex-

emplify the polarized interests of the workers and administration. The directors try to impress upon the outreach workers the fact that their jobs literally depend upon their cooperation in the research effort. However, the outreach workers define the purpose of their work as client advocacy, thus they tend to write perfunctory field notes. Tensions accumulate due to the competing demands of legitimation and funding. Justification of the ethnographic model depends on outreach workers dedicating themselves to client contact as their first priority, while funding depends upon their willingness to establish need and to document their influence on the street.

The separation between the directors and the workers is exacerbated by the dramatic expansion of the Project over the last two years.[21] The directors have become less involved in the daily management of the Project and therefore more removed from the concerns of the workers. The administration concerns itself with writing proposals, training outreach workers statewide, and participating in national conferences. Consequently, the directors, who are professional ethnographers, spend no appreciable time on the streets interacting with drug users or observing how outreach is functioning. Further, the front-line work on the street operates almost independently of the administration. Except for the small extent to which outreach workers must cooperate with research, there is little meaningful interaction between the components. One worker, in expressing his distrust of the research component, said: "I don't know what the politics of this agency are, except for the politics of getting more funding for AIDS [prevention]."

The directors also spend a great deal of time devising political strategies to garner support for their project from public officials and other powerful local agencies. Consequently, staff meetings now focus more on media attention-getting devices and other ways to expand the Project's reputation and influence. In the past meetings focused more on the ethnographic component, that is, an exchange of ideas, problems, and information on trends and strategies in the streets.

The Project has also been generous with its expertise in helping other cities implement similar programs. Consequently, as one director said, "We have essentially created our own competition." Presently, there are numerous projects around the country utilizing their model and competing for the same limited funds. The AIDS Project has previously concerned itself more with service provision and helping to implement their strategy elsewhere. As a result, the research aspect has suffered, and some of their grant proposals are not faring as well as those of some of their competitors.

Operating on "soft money" means that the Project directors are continually searching for renewed and alternative funding. As such, the original mission of the Project is partially thwarted. As a supervisor explained:

> We've lost our objectivity and sometimes our purpose because we are now in the business of keeping people employed, ourselves included . . . so the evaluation component ends up being a justification for our existence. . . . Take, for example, the homeless: if your agency specializes in that social problem, it makes more sense for them to provide specific services than to eliminate the problem, else they write themselves right out of existence.

The somewhat instrumental stance that the directors are required to adopt tends to chip away at the morale of outreach workers. The Project's calculated emphasis on self-promotion and perpetuation alienates workers who envision their jobs as more altruistic. Most outreach workers come to accept that there are two competing levels at which the Project operates and respond by focusing their own energy on the street-based efforts. As one worker commented: "At the outreach level, it's about the epidemic; above that, it's personalities and politics."

UP AGAINST THE LAW

Competing interests within the Project between outreach workers, staff, and directors manifest themselves in conflicts over the role of prevention supplies, the definition of the purpose of outreach, attitudes toward taking field notes, and the importance of research. But these tensions can themselves be traced to the role of various government institutions connected to the Project's funding contracts. As one researcher stated in a meeting:

> We, as an agency, are limited by the biases of our own funding source. . . . For example, when we say 'we'd like to *do* something to slow the epidemic in this population,' and they come back with 'No, but we'd like you to *research* the slowing of the epidemic,' these things filter down to the way we feel about the work we do.

The Project is funded by sources at each level of the government. Each of the contracts imposes different restrictions on the Project's goals. The federal demonstration project grant insists that projects coordinate their efforts with other local social service agencies and law enforcement officials.[22] This provision is at odds with the Project's self-conscious opposition to traditional services. In fact, one of the Project's selling points was precisely the different way it treated drug users. Implicit in its attempt to "take the agency to the streets" is a critique of agencies that do not.

Working together in direct complicity with police and other law enforcement officials would jeopardize the outreach workers' reputations on the streets. The fulcrum of an ethnographic strategy is the ability to elicit trust from otherwise suspicious populations and to be allowed to witness "business as usual." Consequently, the police and the outreach workers do not generally interact. The Project has negotiated a "memorandum of understanding" with the police chief, which provides assurance that bleach will not be confiscated as evidence of drug use and, therefore, justify a search. A similar negotiation assures that possession of large numbers of condoms will not be used as evidence of prostitution. Beyond these negotiations (which are occasionally violated), the Project does not work with the police. In fact, many outreach workers have said that they do not distribute bleach while police officers are present because they do not want to help narcotics agents identify drug users.

In principle, the Project defines itself as being on the side of the drug users. They do not regard drug and needle use as immoral or pathological. Similar to Becker's "labeling theory," they in fact blame American drug policy and other agents of social control for many of the ill consequences of drug use.[23] The motivating ideology behind outreach in drug-using communities is that drug users are "just like everyone else," that the cultural stigma against them is misplaced, and that their lifestyle and factors leading to addiction are generally misunderstood.

In keeping with this orientation, the Project directors have advocated a controlled needle exchange program (in conjunction with other educational efforts) for several years. However, the illegality of such a plan prevents them from being able to participate in one without government sanction. In fact, as the director stated: "The bleach protocol is a scaled-down strategy of intervention to stay within the framework of policy. . . . It's not about the epidemic; it's how do you deal with the political climate *and* appear to be part of the liberal action?"[24] The federal contract prohibits the Project from being directly involved in any vanguard needle exchange plans. A letter was sent from the federal institute to all similar demonstration projects that contained a threat to pull funding from any project directly involved in needle exchange programs.[25]

As a consequence of the federal government's disallowance of their involvement, the Project may not be a part of the sanctioned needle program when it is initiated. Although the Project is well entrenched within the intended communities and is therefore a suitable candidate, one director said: "Now it's not whether or not we should have one, but what it will look like and who's going to do it. . . . Because of the mean and dirty in-fighting that [this city] is known for . . . some favorite drug treatment program will be selected to do an exchange. Treatment will be a condition for getting syringes." Again, the Project directors' design, and their own marketing, which required a critique of treatment models, necessarily alienated them from the other, treatment-oriented providers. The fate of the Project is unclear partly because of the imposed limitations on their services.

In fall 1989 Congress considered legislation that would prohibit the distribution of bleach by federally funded AIDS projects, claiming that household bleach was drug paraphernalia. A couple of amendments made no distinction between giving drug users needles and giving them bleach. Both were considered condoning illicit drug use and promoting the "myth of safe needle use." The language about bleach was eventually removed from the legislation. Nonetheless, the official attitude toward drugs and drug users is incompatible with preventing the spread of HIV in drug-using populations. A similar problem exists in trying to do AIDS education in prisons. In most states, sexual contact between inmates is a felony offense. Outreach workers implicated in condom distribution could face felony charges of aiding and abetting the commission of a crime.[26]

The California state contract, too, imposes limitations. The state funds a few outreach positions and a statewide outreach training facility. Although this funding continues to increase, the Project has been criticized at the state level for not being a community-based agency. The ethnographer-directors are not from any of the minority communities that are targeted for intervention. The fear is that the minority communities are not able to voice their own needs and be served by their own people.

Other state officials object to hiring "indigenous" workers who have some affinity with those on the street. They express concern that workers are chosen on the basis of illicit skills rather than ethnic or community affinities. Doubtful of the need for an outreach training center, one official referred to outreach workers as "just derelicts" who are hired to work the streets. Statements such as this reflect a lack of understanding about the purpose of outreach, as well as a prejudice against drug users and street-educated people, and are examples of the ideological opposition of state officials.

The Project is also trapped between the interests of the state of California in some form of community service and the federal government's interest in research. Thus, the ability to acquire research funds depends on the involvement of credentialed researchers, most of whom are white, while funders of community-based programs targeting minority drug-using populations look for agencies run by people of color.

CONCLUSION

On an everyday basis the Project and its outreach workers experience frustrations caused by restrictions forced upon them by powerful funding sources, and by their own disparate interests pushing them in different directions. External constraints subvert and distort their ideals. Human service provision, in general, is often limited by funding shortages. There is never as much available aid as service providers require to make significant changes in clients' lives.

The peculiar configuration of contracts and grants that supports the AIDS Project places unwieldy demands on their operation. The dual purpose of the Project forces circumspect interventions in communities while functioning inadequately as an independent research agency. The directors recognize that their own constant search for funding has caused them to neglect the scientific community that they also need to impress. Most of their writing efforts find their way into grant proposals rather than scholarly journals. Further, they are expected to research the outreach effort while at the same time being involved in it. Such an arrangement presumes their ability to approach the research objectively, without regard for their own interests.

As is often the case in organizations, the AIDS Project encounters problems with the opposing interests of the management and the workers. Even though management finds itself in the field of human service delivery, the Project is contracted to do ethnographic research. On the other hand, workers who come to this job do so for a variety of reasons, but ethnography is not one of them. The majority of outreach workers are primarily interested in social service work. Even though outreach workers find the Project's unorthodox mode of service delivery appealing, some are unaware that the Project is primarily a research program. The purposes of the federal government's involvement have not been adequately communicated to the workers. The entire outreach project operates at varying levels of understanding and commitment, from the federal level down to the front-line work on the street.

The outreach workers' ability to affect communities is impeded by the external constraints upon them. The amount of funding and services aimed at "hidden populations" such as drug users, their sexual partners, and prostitutes has been, not surprisingly, low. In addition, because of the conservative confines within which outreach workers must work, some of the resources potentially at their disposal are not available to them. For example, workers express disappointment when clients approach them hoping for free sterile syringes rather than bleach. One worker said, "They won't even talk to you if you don't have outfits for them!" Outreach workers, by necessity, become referral sources for other services. Rather than being able to make a more active impact on their clients' lives and offer concrete, immediate alternatives, the workers find themselves shunting clients from one agency to the next.

Consequently, the Project operates at a somewhat typical client-management level. The service that the workers provide, which is trust-worthy, nonjudgmental support and resource information, winds up being more superficial than the Project directors intended. In the final analysis, the Project "manages" the clients at a caretaking level rather than offering empowering alternatives. Moreover, it is not surprising that Project personnel launch their critique at other caretakers, service providers, and middle-level bureaucrats rather than the source of their frustration—the federal and state agencies—so as not to bite the hand that feeds them.[27]

The propitious feature of the Project is not necessarily an ability to offer more profound options for drug-using clients. The fact that the Project is wedded to the federal government through its funding re-lationship clearly locates it within the liberal welfare state. Therefore, that the Project is limited to the purview of traditional social services is neither surprising nor avoidable. The design was intended to strike a balance, or compromise, between more "vanguard" ideals and the countervailing need for funding. If money were no object, the Project would have drawn the battle lines differently.

Rather, the promise that the Project holds for drug users on the streets lies in the manner in which the limited alternatives are pre-sented. The AIDS Project, by virtue of the controversial work it does, encounters more obstacles than most social service agencies. And its obligation to quasi-research, quasi-social work presents problems that academic ethnographers would not confront. Yet, in its efforts it has "normalized" drug users to an extent, and perhaps lessened the stigma against them, by illustrating that they can and will change some behav-iors in order to protect their health.

The Project attempts to view and treat street needle users within their own subcultural context and to accept their definitions of their own situations. The potential that the method of ethnographically de-rived street outreach offers to both social service work and academia is provocative and worthy of consideration. The very idea of bringing the agency to the streets and dealing with "hidden populations" on their own terms is a more humane method than usually informs social service providers, not to mention a more justifiable way of studying exploited populations.

AFTERWORD: FLOATING BETWEEN TWO WORLDS

When I think back to the beginning of my field work in the outreach project, I am astonished by my naiveté. I assumed that my role in the outreach workers' world would be unproblematic. When I was introduced to the entire group at a staff meeting, I assured the workers that anything they might reveal to me would be strictly confidential. I hinted that I respected them already, and that their trust was essential to me. They hinted that they were weary already of white academics coming in to study their communities.

It probably wasn't as inauspicious an entrance as I remember. But I assumed I would have more in common with the outreach workers; after all, I was in sociology and they were quasi-social workers! But what I didn't realize then was that the outreach protocol in this particular project was designed in part in response to straight, white, middle-class "experts," who claim to know more about their subject communities than the members themselves. Consequently, outreach workers privileged "street smarts" over book-learned theories and made hierarchical distinctions within the Project based on experience. In that regard, I didn't fare so well, and many outreach workers were reluctant to cooperate with me. Although I was allowed to accompany them virtually everywhere, I was often reminded that I was an outsider. Some outreach workers made it clear that my training in ethnography could not possibly prepare me to see what they saw, or to interpret what I saw correctly.

I had come into the Project with total zeal about the virtuous work they were doing. Shortly after my entrance to the field, I was influenced by a dissatisfied worker who criticized the work as being "bandages" for the wounds of communities, rather than real cures for social problems. He emphasized that true insiders could never feel comfortable with the kind of work the Project did. I became fascinated by the distinctions outreach workers made between insiders and outsiders. In fact, the first puzzle I tried to work out analytically had to do with whether or not one's status as an insider engendered a disenchanted response to the "bandage" work the agency does. My interest in the insider/outsider debate reflected, I think, my rising ambivalence about academic ethnographers' attempts to understand communities with which they have no natural affinity. I began to adopt the outreach workers' epistemological framework and valued their kind of expertise over my own.

Perhaps more important, I began to see their work in the streets as morally superior to academic undertakings. Every day I would accompany outreach workers as they talked to homeless clients about safe sex, tried to expedite clients' entrance into drug treatment, or visited clients who were dying from AIDS. We would sit in small, horrible hotel rooms with sick clients who had nothing to eat. I felt totally useless. Outreach workers were at least trying to help: they comforted people, and they had chosen this for their job. I was just collecting data.

I wanted to have more in common with outreach workers than academics. I had always been critical of the "body-of-knowledge-building" that goes on in universities at the expense of practical application to social problems. The fact that the AIDS Project's directors were ethnographers who actually *applied* ethnography exposed me to the possibility of really useful research. My involvement with their approach reinforced my disenchantment with academic sociology.

I remember distinctly one time being at a graduate student party. I walked around the room, overhearing conversations about classes, impending paper deadlines, and oral examinations. It was the strangest thing: I hoped no one would ask me anything about my work because I had nothing to say that would make sense to them. Certainly nothing they were saying was making much sense to me! Although I wasn't guilty of "going native" inasmuch as I would never be allowed to identify completely with the outreach workers, I had come to feel an undeniable dissonance between the two worlds I was straddling. I was forced to float between two polarized cultures, speak two languages, attend to two divergent sets of concerns. The gravity of the problems I witnessed on the streets seemed more worthy of attention than the luxury of academic considerations. In the face of working with people blighted by poverty, coping with AIDS, and strangled by addiction, quite frankly the "hell" of upcoming exams seemed trivial.

Moving in and out of my field site every day was excruciating. My problem was exacerbated by the fact that I had already spent a great deal of time in the field and had started my project several months before the rest of my classmates. Furthermore, I spent more time in the field than my colleagues throughout the semester and into the next two because it was also my employment. The movement back and forth between the rather seedy, heavy scenes on the streets and the insulated, abstract world in Berkeley was virtually unmanageable. The clothes I wore, the language I spoke, and the person I thought I wanted to be were vastly altered each time I entered and left the field. As is the case with many field workers who are involved in their setting for a long time, I almost forgot which was my observation site. It is no exaggeration to say that the juxtaposition of both social worlds and my roles in them came to feel completely absurd.

The metaphor of floating between two worlds is really quite appropriate. I always felt that I didn't belong in either place. Self-consciousness plagued me as I was in the field. What did I have in common with these outreach workers, not to mention their clients? And what could I offer them? And back at the university, self-consciousness plagued me further still. My experience in the field forced me to evaluate what ethnography should be and what its potential is. I was unsure about my own research and why I was doing it. My identity switched every time I left and reentered the field.

I suspect the personality change can be somewhat less severe if the disparity between one's field site and real life is not quite so striking. However, it is a built-in feature any time one assumes the role of ethnographer and migrates back and forth between academic and field settings. In this case, I felt guilty being an ethnographer and ashamed of that identity while I was in the field. Because I spent a lot of time in the field, my role as an ethnographer became my whole life, and somehow that role was awkward in the face of such devastation. I was amazed at how the outreach workers could handle what one worker called the "horrors" of their work environment day after day. I remember wondering if their required field notes served a similar function that mine did for me: somehow writing it up in an analytical way makes the characters appear abstracted; they don't seem quite as real. I suppose I wondered if their roles in the field felt as discordant as mine. I wanted to think that they felt awkward collecting data. As insiders, maybe their roles as outreach workers felt like floating between two worlds, too.

I had done ethnographic studies before. In the past, I did participant observation within a local punk scene. In reflecting upon that time, I realize that I didn't experience the tension of moving back and forth for a number of reasons. First of all, I spent far less time in the field, so my time there was bracketed as my research, not my real life. Also, I had been interested in the punk phenomenon for a long time as a layperson, so the transition seemed simple. I knew what I was getting into. Besides, while my participation was marginal, I had a place there along with the other fringe members in the scene. Further, I experienced the whole punk scene as fun and novel, rather than depressing; therefore I didn't feel traumatized facing the insulated university setting. Finally, and perhaps most important, my research had been conducted, in large part, covertly. I was able to lose myself, in a sense, and feel less conspicuous in the field.

In the outreach project, I *felt* like a researcher most of the time. If I forgot, outreach workers would remind me that my time there was limited and my agenda was different from theirs. My experiences could not be as intense as if the clients were my own. Outreach workers would affectionately tease me about my street education. In fact, I had to give a report in a meeting once about the first time I saw someone shooting dope! I became very close to a few of the workers that I accompanied regularly, but I never forgot the distance between who they were and who I was. I was the naive, yet educated, researcher; they were the world-worn experts.

Eventually my romantic image of their work, especially vis-à-vis my own, faded. My puzzle about insider versus outsider status didn't work out; I had assumed that insiders were more committed to their communities, therefore more disillusioned with the work the Project did. But I saw varying levels of commitment, and omnifarious reasons for taking and keeping the job. I started listening to the language the administration used and noticing how different it was from the concerns of the outreach workers. I realized that the entire outreach enterprise had its own set of problems as well. Time with the project showed me that it was filled with people who acted in their own interest, just like sociologists do. The Project had to sustain its funding, and the workers had to participate in instrumental tasks to further the career of the Project. I suppose it's no coincidence that my next puzzle was trying to figure out how those interests undermined the work, and what the constraints were that determined those particular sets of interests. I wanted to rescue the Project from responsibility for those interests. Because I saw the Project's brand of ethnography as more noble than my own, I wanted to save it from the sin of self-interest. Given that, it's also not surprising that I finally felt comfortable looking at the way the state constrains the honorable intentions of the Project. It's clear that my own emotional investment shaped my interpretation of what was sociologically important. Gouldner was right again.

The end of my "honeymoon" with the Project enabled me to feel more comfortable with my role as an academic ethnographer. The tension I felt became less pronounced. I never actually doubted whether or not I wanted to be an ethnographer after my field work in the outreach project. I knew that I did. What I did begin to question is the morality of the enterprise if our work is not at least intended to inform some policy decisions or provide concrete assistance back to our subjects. I had changed substantially since the time when I had no qualms about doing covert research!

Leaving the field has enabled me to look less at the horrors or at the curious features of the scene I studied. As Gouldner astutely reminded me, I didn't want to be guilty of showing off my subjects as a zookeeper would, exploiting them for my own professional gain. Being out of the field and forced to write up what all this "means" in a sociological way has allowed me the necessary distance to reflect on how the experience has changed me. I still believe in the viability of ethnography as a method. I remain hopeful that academic ethnography can learn from the applied approach of the AIDS Project. Leaving the field has allowed me to envision my future, not as a virtuous outreach worker but as an academic ethnographer who has learned and incorporated the value of extending research toward change.

TWELVE

Convincing Sociologists: Values and Interests in the Sociology of Knowledge

Charles Kurzman

It is not particularly novel to note that knowledge is swayed by the interests of the knowers. This is one of the foundations of the sociology of knowledge, as first formulated by Karl Mannheim.[1] Even scientific analyses are vulnerable to the scientist's interests and values, as Max Weber argued in his methodological essays.[2] The recent "sociology of scientific knowledge" has generated a number of case studies in this vein.[3] However, these studies fail to recognize that the values held by scientists are diverse and often mutually contradictory. Moreover, as I shall argue, scientists invoke different values according to their interests in specific contexts of the production of knowledge.

This chapter explores the relationship between values and interests in the production of sociological knowledge. The site is the graduate sociology class on participation-observation (P-O) methodology that produced the essays in this volume. The subjects are the dozen students and one professor who met twice each week for a semester. The knowledge in question consists of the statements and analyses made during class meetings, and tentatively accepted by the others present as accurate.

The conclusion is that we in the class did not evaluate hypotheses in terms of the evidence presented or in regard to the theoretical tradition proposed—the two reigning perspectives on the production of scientific knowledge. The first perspective views scientists as straightforward arbiters of evidence, calmly investigating hypotheses and judging them to be meritorious or unworthy.[4] The second perspective views scientists as members of theoretical communities, willing to endorse or disregard hypotheses on the basis of their compatibility with the community's paradigm.[5] Yet I found little reference to evidence, and no consistent paradigms, in classroom discussions.

Instead, we in the class evaluated hypotheses in keeping with certain metatheoretical values. These values concerned basic attitudes toward the social scientific project, that is, basic approaches to the understanding of human subjects. What was odd about these values is that they were contradictory and mutually exclusive, and that we frequently shifted back and forth on these seemingly immutable fundamentals.

I identified two pairs of values governing the class's treatment of hypotheses. The first pair consisted of:

"respect for the subjects," that is, listening to and respecting the subjects' own analysis of their situation; and

"social silencing," whereby social forces systematically prevented the subjects from properly understanding their situation.

The second pair of values consisted of:

"social determinism," whereby subjects' behavior was held to be caused by broad social forces; and

"voluntarism," namely, the ability of subjects to transcend determining social forces.

Both of these dichotomies operated on a continuum of social distance from our subjects: when we felt closer to them, we were more likely to respect their analyses and to grant them free will. When we felt distanced, we saw their analyses as systematically deluded and their behavior as socially determined.

These sentiments of social distance, I argue, reflected our interests as P-O sociologists. The first pair of values served to define our role in the field setting, allowing us to pursue political goals and to gather information. The second pair served to carve out a niche in the academic setting and defend it against encroachments by individualist analyses on the one hand and dehumanizing analyses on the other.

Thus by maneuvering within the two dichotomies, we defined our relation not just to our subjects, but also to other social scientists. The contrast between these two arenas, the field and academia, is particularly sharp for P-O sociologists, sometimes even painful.[6] However, all social scientists face a similar contrast, and thus the basics of the analysis presented here—conflicting values and interests governing the evaluation of academic hypotheses—might be applicable more widely.

IDENTIFYING KNOWLEDGE: METHODOLOGICAL HURDLES

There are two methodological problems in the study of how knowledge comes to be accepted as such. The first is the ontological problem of identifying proposed instances of knowledge: distinguishing hypotheses about reality from other statements whose goal is not primarily analytical. The second is the epistemological problem of identifying acceptance: distinguishing true agreement with a hypothesis from partial or insincere agreement.

I was dismayed to find during the semester that it was difficult to identify classroom statements as analytical hypotheses. There were questions, suggestions, and ruminations aplenty, but few bold conjectures and analytic arguments. This theme was also taken up by the rest of the class. Carol noted that classroom conversation should be construed as "in process," not finalized or definitive.[7] Sepha made the point that much of the class's discussion was simply not intended to be "factual." In particular, Leslie S. added, students' comments on their classmates' projects should not be construed as hypotheses. With each of these objections to my project came the admonition that I had simply picked the wrong class to study the sociology of knowledge; other classes debated hypotheses, I was told, but not this one.

These objections were to a certain extent on the mark. Classroom discussion was more tentative than in other graduate sociology courses I had participated in; there was less debate of social theories or substantive sociological explanations; and there was much more of an emphasis on helping our classmates work on their projects. However, these objections did not rule out the existence of hypotheses or knowledge production in this class. Specifically, tentativeness did not mean that these statements were not proposals about how the world should be viewed. It does no violence to the intent of the speaker, I think, to study the fate of such tentative statements, and to examine the reasons why some of them were accepted while others were not.

Identifying acceptance was even more difficult. To begin with, the limits I placed on my study—paying attention only to in-class interactions, and only for one semester—restricted my study to short-term phenomena; over the long term people may come to feel they "know" things that they initially resisted. But even in the short term, it was difficult to tell whether people agreed with an analysis or not. The biggest obstacle was that not everyone spoke up on every issue, and a few members of the class spoke quite infrequently. Even those who spoke more often might have been putting forward ideas just to play devil's advocate, or to be polite, or as a gesture of kindness and support, none of which should necessarily be taken as agreement. Sometimes people would nod their heads at some statement, but this too, as several class members told me in discussions of my project, might signify something other than agreement.

Indeed, there are difficulties with the idea of agreement itself. I took part of one class session to ask my classmates whether they had agreed or not with certain of the hypotheses I discuss here. Several students became quite upset that I asked them to write "agree" or "disagree," survey-style, even though I was also asking for longer comments as well. Sepha accused me of trying to "pigeonhole" opinions that were not binary but multidimensional. She was quite right; agreement is not an either-or matter, and it involves a number of subissues: for instance, I might agree with someone's conclusion but not with the reasoning behind it, as Josh pointed out.

Several partial solutions were available to me. I asked everyone straight out if they agreed with items I felt they had agreed with. I asked everyone to write brief statements on what they had learned in the class. I checked my impressions with my classmates informally outside of class. I made outrageous statements in class and watched how people reacted. But none of these efforts were systematic. In the end, I had to rely on my status as a relative "insider" to distinguish actual agreement from unspoken disagreement, and I have tried to stay sensitive to the variations and shades that acceptance may take. In this spirit, I have chosen examples from class that I felt were subject to fairly widespread consensus.

ALICE ON GENDER: THE VALUE OF RESPECT FOR SUBJECTS

Alice was working in and studying a public employees' union. When she first presented her research to the class, she noted that almost all of the public employees in the union were women, while almost all of the union representatives were men. Furthermore, she told us, her subjects divided their clients into two gendered groups: "bad homeless clients," who were mostly men; and "AFDC mothers," who were, in the subjects' eyes, "redeemable."[8] The site seemed to be perfectly matched with Alice's interest in gender issues. This is how she introduced her first presentation to the class:

> *Alice:* Initially . . . I went in very interested in women workers. Social work is a feminized profession, and I really wanted to see how that feminine ideology was being played out in the workplace. And what I discovered is that, at least from what I've seen so far, it's not that important to the workers.
>
> *Michael:* What's not important?
>
> *Alice:* Gender.

Michael: But what do you mean by that?

Alice: Well, there are policy issues like pay equity and comparable worth and child care. That's there, and that's really important. But in terms of the relations in the workplace and the relations between the [union] organizers and the workers, gender is not really very important.

Her justification for the relative unimportance of gender was that she saw few signs of gender consciousness, and she heard few of her subjects complain about sex discrimination. They complained, instead, about racial issues: "Right now I'm really attending to what people are talking about, so I think that was sort of why I was emphasizing [race, as against gender], sort of what's consciously out on the table as an issue."

This reasoning holds that the subjects themselves are capable of identifying the important issues confronting them. This is not an empirical argument: Alice presented no evidence to show the unimportance of gender—indeed she admitted that it did appear to be important. Nor is this a theoretical argument: she presented no alternative theory to explain the workings of her field site, at least not at this early point in the semester. Instead, she appealed to the class to respect the indigenous analysis of her subjects. This "respect for the subjects" argument was frequently adopted during the course of the semester; several other students abandoned or shifted their scholarly perspective because their subjects did not find the scholarly issues to be important. The professor had urged us in emphatic terms in the beginning of the semester to "let the field speak to you" and to "be surprised"; being surprised by one's findings in the field became a running joke throughout the term.

However, Alice's argument, and the others like it, face a constant rebuttal, which I will call the "silencing" argument: namely, that the subjects are systematically silenced by social forces preventing them from recognizing or discussing their true situation. The classic silencing argument is Antonio Gramsci's theory of ideological hegemony.[9] Leslie S. suggested something similar when she objected to Alice's first presentation: "That this is a female workforce where women are doing traditionally female things seems to still be true whether or not people see themselves that way." By implication, the lack of gender consciousness among Alice's subjects did not necessarily signify the unimportance of gender. Indeed, feminist social science has frequently applied a gender analysis over the objections of its subjects, with the intention of thereby creating gender consciousness where it is lacking. Alice's response was to repeat the justification for shifting her focus away from gender:

I was probably being kind of flip when I said [gender] was not important. I guess what I mean is that I'm struck by the fact that in terms of discrimination, that's not what's out on the table. In fact, it's often a white female supervisor supervising a Black female and there's a lot of tension on the basis of race, and there's just not . . . all this solidarity around gender.[10]

This debate between the "silencing" and "respect" arguments was not one to be decided by the application of evidence or the adjudication of competing theories, traditionally held to be social science's primary methods of settling analytical disputes. Instead, both arguments appeared to be on the order of shared values, not open to empirical proof or disproof, guiding the class's treatment of Alice's nongender analysis.

Alice's argument overcame the "silencing" objection—at least, the objection was not raised again. Toward the end of the semester, I asked the class whether my impression had been correct and whether they now agreed with Alice's nongender analysis of her field site. The most vocal members of the class protested vehemently. They had not "agreed" with Alice's argument, they said; rather, they had assented to it, feeling it was not their place to tell her what to study. But in other cases, the class had felt it was its place to use the silencing objection to change a classmate's focus of study. Ann R.'s initial class presentation was one such case.

ANN R. ON AGE: THE VALUE OF SOCIAL "SILENCING"

Ann R. studied a senior citizens' center. Her second set of field notes appealed to the value of respect for subjects:

> 1. The original question I went into the field with, i.e., to listen for body images and metaphors old women use to talk about their aging as a way to get at if, and how, the old internalize a negative stereotype of aging as decline and loss, no longer seems relevant in light of the data I am gathering in the field.
> 2. In the first place *age itself does not appear to matter very much* in the interactions I have had or have observed; in fact age has never been referred to as a limiting factor and most people proudly tell me their age; when Gertrude expressed an interest in tap-dancing, her reason for not taking it up was that she had a bad knee, not that she was too old. [Emphasis in original]

Josh responded by picking up on Sepha's point that there might be a tacit contract at the seniors' center not to talk about negative things:

> *Josh:* You say here that "age itself does not appear to matter very much," and one possible explanation is that there's this tacit contract not to

allow it to matter. There's a big difference between that agreement
and it not mattering.

Ann R.: Maybe that was a clumsy way to say it. I'm not meaning to imply
that age doesn't matter. . . . [It's just that] they don't ascribe anything
about who they are to their age.

Josh: But the thing that I'm saying is how do you know that's not because
there's an agreement in this context, there's a set of rules operating in
this context—I'm not saying that they're consciously repressing these
words, but it may be that in another context they may be—

Ann R.: —more conscious of that. Well, I think some of that has to do—
and some of the literature indicates that too—with the fact that it's an
age-peer setting. Other than me, they're all old.

Michael: It could be construed as a reaction formation: "We are not going
to accept that." Aging *does* matter. People are responding to it and
trying to deny it. The very fact that people are trying to deny it says
that it's part of their self-understanding.

Ann R.: Yes. Yes.

In this episode, Ann R. was talked out of her field-notes position,
which resembled Alice's in that it justified the downplaying of a particular theoretical issue by noting that the subjects did not identify it as
important. But in this case the justification was defeated by a "silencing"
argument. Social forces, namely the norms operating within the community of old people at this seniors' center, kept people from talking
about something that was important to them all, namely age.

I asked the class at our next session whether they agreed with this
silencing argument. Six of thirteen specifically said they agreed. One
said she didn't know. The others gave no indication one way or another. But I sensed that approval was fairly widespread. Indeed, the
discussion of Ann R.'s presentation took such a long turn away from
respect for subjects that by the end of the session we were cracking, and
laughing heartily at, old-folks jokes. Sepha did a wicked, though brief,
impression of a doddering Katherine Hepburn. Ann R. later commented that this treatment was just the sort of age discrimination that
she wanted her work to combat.

Here, again, both the "respect" and the "silencing" arguments were
appealed to not as empirical propositions with evidence in their support, nor as theoretical contributions, but rather as classroom values.
Ann R. argued, just as Alice had, that the subjects had the right to say
what was important in their lives. Just as Leslie S. had observed with
Alice's first presentation, Sepha and Josh pointed out that we cannot
rule out the possibility that "silencing" mechanisms are at work.

SOCIAL DISTANCING AND P-O SOCIOLOGISTS' INTERESTS

Alice's appeal to the norm of respect for subjects succeeded, while Ann R.'s did not, because of social distancing. Class members felt themselves to be different from, and socially superior to, Ann R.'s subjects, while they tried hard to erase the social distance between themselves and Alice's subjects. Alice and Ann R. had—unwittingly, in the latter case—encouraged the different attitudes. Alice had treated her subjects, despite all her disagreements with them and her puzzlement at their actions, as "strategic actors," a formulation in which social distance is minimized. In addition, she clearly declared herself to be on her subjects' side: as poor, overworked, underpaid, Black working women, Alice's subjects had the class's sympathy.

Ann R.'s elderly subjects had the class's sympathy as well, but it was a sympathy tinged with a patronizing aspect that would have raised hackles immediately in the context of Alice's project. Ann R. inadvertently encouraged this attitude by describing a scene in a senior citizens' seminar she had participated in. At one point, the seminar leader had paid tribute to an extremely old woman in the seminar, kneeling before her for no apparent reason and proclaiming, "There *is* radiance coming from you." The episode, as Ann R. described it, seemed ridiculous and baffling, and all of us in the class made thorough fun of it. Only as an afterthought did Ann R. give us the reason for the seminar leader's action: this elderly woman, despite her own infirmities, was doing volunteer work for people with Alzheimer's disease.[11] Having distanced ourselves from Ann R.'s subjects—Sepha, for instance, wondered whether those of us raised in the era of consciousness-raising sessions and support groups will age differently—we were much more willing to discount what the subjects actually said and to impute greater importance to the social forces that kept them from talking about reality.

Social distance, in turn, reflected the class's interests as sociologists. The most direct interest was political: the class, composed of political progressives, was eager to ally itself with workers and workers' movements, while the elderly were not as high on our political agenda. In addition, we as sociologists had a research interest in maximizing information retrieval. Individually, within our field sites, we each manipulated our social distance so as to get the information we felt we needed, sometimes posing as authority figures, sometimes acting chummy and conspiratorial. Collectively, in classroom discussion, we often discussed and suggested roles that students might try to play in their sites so as to get the necessary information.

These two interests in politics and information defined our relation to our subjects, a relation that is especially important and problematic in P-O sociology. Unlike other sociological methods, which require only

short-term interactions with their subjects—an interview, perhaps, or
even a series of interviews—participant observation requires researchers to become more intimately involved with their subjects. The "participant" portion of the P-O moniker describes just this aspect of the
method, and raises the serious question of how the researchers fit in to
a more-or-less alien social situation. Since most field sites have no
ready-made role for participant-observers to play, the researchers have
a particularly uncertain and anxious status, but one that is quite open
to maneuvering.

Maneuvering is necessary because the two interests, politics and information, may sometimes be contradictory. Cozying up to authority
figures in order to get information from subordinates may go against
political values; conversely, a strong political identification with one's
subjects may make the researcher hesitant to pry information out of
them for academic scrutiny. Compromises may result: for instance, P-O
researchers may supplement their regular, collegial, low-social-distance
relations with their subjects with occasional formal interviews, whose
researcher-subject roles involve greater social distance. In this way, P-O
researchers can move back and forth along the continuum of social
distance, in the service of their political and research interests, appealing at any moment either to the value of respect or the value of silencing to justify hypotheses they might make.

This is not the only case where competing values may serve competing interests.

THERAPISTS AND POVERTY PIMPS: THE VALUE OF
SOCIAL DETERMINISM

A recurrent theme in the course was criticism of and disgust toward
people who are trying to help the poor and the troubled. This was due
to no stinginess of spirit, but rather, I think, to the individualistic approach of many of those doing the helping. In the first substantive class
session, Paul, an advanced graduate student who pursued P-O research
several years before and had had his term paper published—which lent
him considerable prestige—described his study of an organization that
counseled wife-batterers. The predominant group of volunteers at this
organization consisted of therapists who had just gotten their professional degrees. He described one of them, whom he called "typical":

> *Paul:* He talked about working [at this organization] in the way you
> would talk about choosing a clientele. If you're a newly minted psy-
> chologist, do you want to work with drug addicts, do you want to work
> with men who beat their wives, or do you want to work with someone
> else? And he thought, this is a good choice to make.

Ann R.: A newly emerging field, not too many people in it. I mean, that's
a very cynical view, but. . . .
Paul: I don't think that's necessarily cynical, and I think it makes sense.

Imputing such careerist motives to therapists had a pejorative tinge to
it, and the class seemed somewhat depressed to hear that the organization was increasingly run by therapists.

The next week, Kathy presented her field work studying an ethnographic project that used ethnographic field work to distribute bleach
and condoms to slow the transmission of AIDS among injection drug
users, prostitutes, and other high-risk populations, while at the same
time studying these groups. Kathy and the rest of the class repeatedly
referred to the project staff—the professional ethnographers running
the project and the outreach workers they had trained—as "poverty
pimps." Ann R. made the analogy to "the people who are hanging
around the elderly, trying to make professional careers out of it." Kathy
responded by quoting one of the ethnographers, a professional social
service worker, who had told her, "Well, I was really smart. I saw this
thing coming way in advance. [The class laughed.] I knew that AIDS
and homelessness were going to be the big issues in [this city] in the late
eighties, so I switched early on and started learning about both issues."

Nadine then spoke about the social service workers in New York who
had hopped onto the methadone-maintenance "bandwagon" as "a way
to make fast money." Kathy's remark that her organization was tilting
toward hiring more professional social service workers and fewer "indigenous" outreach workers—her word for people from the communities being served, such as former drug users and prostitutes—
occasioned a disgusted shaking of heads.

This pattern of insulting those who cared, not always effectively of
course, in social-service professions, was entirely consistent throughout
the term and entirely acceptable. No one spoke up in defense of these
people; surely, given the vitriol of some of the insults, someone who felt
at all sympathetic to social-service workers would have spoken up to say
that they were not being treated fairly.

Why, then, did the class hurl or consent to the hurling of such nas-
tiness? There was no neoconservative sentiment that spending money
to help the poor was in itself a misguided project. Instead, the disgust
toward social service workers had to do with their individualistic approach to what the class saw as fundamentally social problems. Paul said
of his therapeutic organization's approach: "That's how he understood
what he was doing as a way of dealing with the [wife-]battery issue, that
you deal with individuals as individuals, and all these social categories
are not what's real. What's real is individuals being able to be free and
love each other." In her field notes, Kathy quoted a disgruntled subject

who blamed the anti-AIDS project for focusing only on helping individuals: "By focusing on one problem—THE EPIDEMIC, right?—people, agencies can look away from the real issues, like health issues or the conditions around these people which makes them perfect targets for the epidemic to spread." Kathy and several other class members said they agreed with this analysis.

This antipathy toward individualistic solutions was based on no evidence and no theory. Nobody in the class argued that individualistic social services were unhelpful or wrong or a waste of taxpayers' money. It was simply agreed in a series of cases that AIDS, wife-beating, and other issues were social problems: they were examples of human behavior that is determined by social forces. Individualistic analyses of such problems simply miss the point, and in so doing also keep the victims of these problems from seeing the point too.

SPECIAL PEOPLE: THE VALUE OF VOLUNTARISM

Despite the value of social determinism, the class sometimes allowed exceptions to be made. Some subjects were called "special," and their behavior was to be explained in individual terms, not by recourse to social forces.

The first "special" subject, though the class had not yet coined the term, was Kathy's disgruntled outreach worker, M., whom she quoted at length in the first field notes that she distributed to the class. M.'s analysis of the ethnographic project he worked for was quite radical, and wholly social-determinist. Kathy followed her extended quotation of this source with this analysis: "It is clear that there are some real problems with the way that these outreach workers identify themselves. Since the agency's policy is to try to hire indigenous members and former members [of groups affected by AIDS], they encounter a great deal of *role conflict*." (Emphasis in original.) Leslie S. commented on this analysis in class: "After reading all the description of what this guy said, I assumed that you agreed with him, actually. And then I was surprised to read that you were . . . putting it in a framework of role strain, because it seemed like he was the deviant within the kind of [social situation] you were looking at." In other words, Leslie continued, one shouldn't analyze subjects who have "true" perceptions (meaning, I suppose, perceptions we sociologists would agree with) in terms of role strain; rather, one should look at why the other subjects have *not* been able to come up with such accurate perceptions. Only two people in the class (Alice and Michael) later said that they did not agree with this critique entirely; Kathy, Leslie S., and I said we felt that there had been a good deal of consensus on the point.

In another instance, Ui also called her main subject, a dynamic immigrant-community leader, "special." She described her subject as a rare woman who had been able to transcend the traditions in the immigrant community limiting women's opportunities and keeping women from leadership roles. Ui was not interested in how the subject had been able to break the grip of social determinisms and did not pursue the implications of her observation that the subject was the only one in the community with a royal background. Classroom discussion also skirted this issue and focused on the effects of this leader's behavior, the role she played in the immigrant community, and so on. The rest of the community, though, was subjected to deterministic analyses.

Why should certain subjects have been exempted from social determinism? My feeling is that another value was being applied: namely, that social determinism is dehumanizing. It strips away the subjects' free will and treats them as objects, not as fully human beings. This is particularly a problem for P-O sociologists, who get to know their subjects better than interviewers or archival researchers can. This intimacy may cause P-O researchers not to wish to see their subjects reduced to impersonal social causes, and it may lead P-O researchers to become so aware of their subjects' idiosyncrasies and personalities that no social determinism would fit.

DISTANCE AND INTERESTS

As with the previous pair of values, "respect" and "silencing," social distance seemed to determine whether social determinism or the opposite value was applicable. Many students in the class chose field sites hoping to find something progressive occurring in this neoconservative era, and virtually everybody was disappointed to find their subjects not so progressive as anticipated, not so much *like us*. The class seemed to have no problem attributing social causes to such people's behavior; indeed, to have done otherwise would in some cases have been to engage in "blaming the victim." The few subjects the class really felt in agreement with, however, were granted the sociologists' self-exemption from social determinism. Leslie S.'s distinction between "deviants," whose behavior is socially caused, and "true" perceivers, whose behavior is not socially caused, might be translated into the terms "negative deviants" (not like us; behavior socially determined) and "positive deviants" (like us; behavior exempted from social determination).

Where the respect and silencing values served to define P-O sociologists' relations with their subjects, social determinism and voluntarism seemed to define P-O sociologists' relations with their academic competitors. These competitors took two forms: psychologists and welfare-state analysts, on the one hand, and mainstream sociologists on the other.

In the first case, social determinism serves to defend sociology's home turf, namely, the analysis of social forces. This is the only phenomenon over which sociology can claim a monopoly, and it is what distinguishes sociologists—and all who take a "sociological" approach—from other social scientists. This battle between the disciplines is as old as the disciplines themselves. At the turn of the century, for instance, Emile Durkheim argued that sociology and its "social facts" ought to be given priority over psychology and its individual "psychical facts":

> It is therefore in the nature of society itself that we must seek the explanation of social life. We can conceive that, since it transcends infinitely the individual both in time and space, it is capable of imposing upon him the ways of acting and thinking that it has consecrated by its authority. . . . [E]very time a social phenomenon is directly explained by a psychological phenomenon, we may rest assured that the explanation is false.[12]

Of more recent vintage is sociology's battle with the welfare state for control of social analysis. In the two decades after World War II, as the American welfare state grew in size and in popularity, sociologists shifted their focus accordingly: for instance, Alvin Gouldner, cited approvingly by Kathy and others in class, has described how grand theorists and hip deviance specialists alike adapted to the welfare state, its academic agenda, and its social service programs.[13] The welfare state declared society's problems to be social but went about solving them by helping individuals, by treating the symptoms instead of the disease: if there is poverty in society, then give the poor people a little money; if there is drug abuse, then help addicts deal with their addiction. Social problems were thus translated into personal problems. Social scientists willing to shift with the times received full federal funding and produced studies deemed socially useful.

In the 1980s, however, the welfare state became increasingly unpopular: the greatest problem facing the federal government was held to be the budget deficit, and presidents were elected on a no-new-taxes platform. Politically progressive sociologists may find neoconservatism anathema, but they are finding the anti-welfare-state climate surprisingly conducive to the reassertion of their professional domain, indeed to the reclaiming of their subject matter, the analysis of society, from state control.[14] By insulting social service workers and their individualist analyses, we in the P-O class were at the same time reaffirming sociologists' rightful role as the primary analysts of the social world.

While the value of social determinism defines sociologists as against psychologists and welfare-state social analysis, the value of voluntarism defines P-O sociologists as against other sociologists. P-O, it should be noted, is not a mainstream sociological method. It has a fine pedigree, from anthropological ethnography to William Foote Whyte's classic sociological work *Street Corner Society*, but it is not widely taught or practiced, and it is not yet treated on a par with, say, comparative-historical methods, much less with survey methods. In the current era of a fractionated or "multiple paradigm" sociology, minority viewpoints can achieve a certain degree of legitimacy, if only they can organize themselves communally and claim recognition as a new subfield.

Nine of twelve students in this P-O class said they hoped to continue doing P-O work in the future; two students said they didn't know, and one said it would depend on the project. The professor said he was strongly committed to P-O methods, and repeatedly said he considered them the "prototype" for all social science. Thus the value that social determinism is dehumanizing helped create a community of P-O sociologists by setting this group apart from all other sociologists. It was not important whether this actually did set this group apart from other sociologists; for instance, some hermeneuticians who use non-P-O methods also consider determinism dehumanizing; and the P-O class itself was willing to invoke social determinisms quite frequently. What is more important is that class members treated the value as setting them apart, treated one another as fellow community members, and treated their subjects, at least their sympathetic subjects, as deserving of respect.

The best example of this value, and its use as a communal boundary mechanism, came when I presented my first set of written field notes to the class. I managed to violate the value in every way possible, and the class's response was an emotional counterattack. My field notes focused on Carol's first presentation, and my first mistake was to describe Carol's approach as "touchie-feelie," not once but twice. However, nobody mentioned this until I mentioned the term, halfway into the discussion of my project. Even then the class objected politely; Kathy said the term sounded "pretty pejorative" and Josh suggested I use the term "affective" instead. It was only after Carol said she "took offense" at this and other aspects of my description of her that the class started "emoting" (Leslie S.'s word). Ann R. called my field notes "typically masculine"; Kathy said, "the whole way you approached [your subject] was really pejorative"; Michael accused me of feeling there's only one right way of doing sociology. Ann F. drew the broader conclusion: "You objectified us and we're responding in a very emotional way, because I did respond to [your field notes] emotionally. But it made me get very emotional about what I was going to have to do to my own subjects."

In other words, I think, I violated the idea of community by insulting a classmate; I violated the value of voluntarism by objectifying the least socially distanced subjects possible, namely my classmates; and I violated the link between value and community by showing that even P-O work could lead to the objectification and dehumanization of one's subjects. In the spirit of self-reflexiveness that P-O study encourages, I take this as evidence that the class was undergoing a process of community-building, one of the elements of which was the value of voluntarism.

The two interests that define P-O sociologists' relations with their academic competitors are even more clearly contradictory than were the field-site interests of political correctness and information retrieval. On the one hand, the P-O sociologists want to rally with other sociologists in defense of their social determinism. On the other hand, they want to differentiate themselves from other sociologists over the same issue. In sum, then, there are two pairs of conflicting interests and two pairs of conflicting values.

CONCLUSION

I have tried to argue that scientists' values and interests are complex, varied, and even mutually contradictory at times. The source of these contradictions is that scientists operate in several arenas at once. In the academic sphere, they have a variety of competitors with whom they are constantly battling; in the research sphere, they have to determine their relations with their subjects. The balance between these arenas varies from field to field. In the natural sciences, the subjects generally don't talk back (though sometimes their human supporters do). In the "harder" social sciences, such as macroeconomics, the relation between analyst and analysand has become so formalized and abstract that it can almost be ignored.

Participant-observer sociology is at the opposite end of this spectrum. The immediate and relatively intense contact at the P-O field site forces researchers to negotiate relations with their subjects and often creates strong sympathies. The academic arena no longer appears to be the only one, or even necessarily the most important one. Thus the contradictions within and between field-site interests and academic interests are particularly clear in P-O sociology. Moreover, the class I studied, with a progressive and sensitive attitude toward its subjects, and with constant encouragement from the professor, paid close attention to field-site relations. In addition, I focused on the class's verbal interactions, not on the final written products, where conflicts and debates are generally less visible.[15] For these reasons, my case study was especially well suited to the analysis of competing and conflicting interests.

However, the basic analysis may be widely applicable. With respect to their subjects, all scientists have political interests, even if they consist largely in the apolitical support of the status quo; and they also have an information interest in maintaining good relations with their subjects. With respect to their colleagues, all scientists have career interests and hope to carve out a niche for themselves academically; and they all have communal interests that their field, their subfield, and their specialty will all receive funding, achieve prominence, and prosper. It would be interesting to see, in other case studies, whether these interests are linked to when social scientists listen to their subjects, and when they deem their analyses to be deluded; when they grant their subjects free will, and when they deem their behavior to be socially determined.

AFTERWORD: SHARING ONE'S WRITINGS WITH ONE'S SUBJECTS

Sharing one's field notes and final paper with one's subjects recommends itself for at least four reasons:

It allows the subjects to correct any mistakes the researcher might have made.

It can create a sense of cooperation between subjects and researcher in the mutual quest to understand the subjects' social world.

It empowers the subjects by making them active members in their own analysis.

It keeps the writings "clean," that is, it keeps the subjects' possible reactions in the researcher's mind as the writings are being written.

Unfortunately, these are also the very reasons *not* to share written analyses with one's subjects.

Correcting mistakes. There are an infinite number of mistakes to be made in writing about a field site: facts that subjects may feel are taken out of context; imputed thoughts that subjects may deny altogether; generalizations for which subjects can produce counterexamples; and so on. Subjects may help you correct these. But subjects generally do not have the detached eye of a proofreader. Their "native" status that makes them qualified to correct the analysis also makes them interested parties. If they find mistakes, and they are sure to, they may suspect the researcher of being systematically mistaken about the field site. The researcher is already a suspicious character, someone who is studying a particular site for heaven knows what reason, and is going to report back to heaven knows whom. If the subjects feel that the information being collected is off the mark, the researcher's project may take on a sinister aspect in their eyes.

This, I am unhappy to report, is what happened in my case. The graduate sociology class I studied picked up on a few fairly small mistakes—if I say so myself—in my first set of field notes as indicative of a "masculine" and unsympathetic perspective, "masculine" being perhaps the ultimate insult in the Berkeley sociology milieu. They went on to attack me and my project for the better part of an hour, and I was saved from more browbeating only by the ringing of the class bell. More importantly, the class's attitude toward me changed from "wait and see" to "we waited and saw." The damage was not irreparable, largely because I was friends with most of the class, but the class's disapproval lingered throughout the semester and made my project both more difficult and less pleasant.

Perhaps my outlook *was* unsympathetic; for certain, I made a number of insensitive mistakes in my field notes. But the subjects were unable simply to correct mistakes. They were upset by the very existence of mistakes.

Cooperation in analysis. It may come as a surprise to many P-O researchers, but their subjects are rarely interested in theoretical analyses of their lives. At best sociological analysis is generally idle speculation; at worst it is disruptive meddling. This seems to be true even when the sociologist is trying to help the subjects attain some goal. Alain Touraine's interventionist methodology, for instance, had to struggle to overcome the mistrust and resistance of subjects who considered the researcher a threat.[16]

So when subjects read a researcher's writings, they tend to skip quickly over analytic portions and focus on the important things: who gets quoted, and how often; who gets insulted or praised. The researcher's goal of analysis simply is not a high priority in the subjects' lives, even, as I found, if the subjects are sociologists. It was very difficult to get the class I studied to discuss the theoretical issues that were important to my research. In part this was because of the mistakes I had made in my field notes, and in part this was because they did not feel qualified to discuss these issues. However, the subjects went further and denied that my theoretical interests in the sociology of knowledge were even applicable to them. I stubbornly overruled them and continued the study from this perspective, but it was not one that the subjects felt was important to them. I was pleased when a few of the concepts that I had proposed were adopted, usually as jokes, by my subjects, but they were not interested in analytic cooperation.

Empowerment. It is absurd for social scientists to debate the subjects' situation without letting the subjects speak up for themselves. The ideal, then, is to give the subjects a voice in the academic world. By sharing one's writings with them, the researcher can thus show the subjects the debate and incorporate their contributions to the debate. Unfortunately, this attempt at empowering the subjects can also have the opposite effect. Subjects may not feel qualified to participate in academic debates. By inviting them to participate, the researcher may unintentionally rub their noses in their feelings of inadequacy, under-education, or lower social status. This is especially likely when the researcher is young, white, middle-class, and college-educated and the subjects are not. The complex sentences and fancy words in the researcher's writings may remind the subjects of their inability to communicate this way.

Even when the researcher and subjects are on the same social and educational level, as in my case, empowerment may have complications. In the first set of field notes I distributed to my subjects, and in the first draft of my final paper, I tried to lay out the field of the sociology of knowledge for their comments. I succeeded only in confusing everybody. The subjects did not respond by feeling inadequate, as less educated subjects might have; instead, they responded by calling the presentation unclear. Indeed it was, partially because of my own shortcomings, partially because of the difficulties in boiling down a whole sociological subfield to a single short presentation. In any case, the subjects certainly were not empowered by the invitation to participate in their own analysis.

Clean writings. Researchers should not intentionally insult their subjects. They should not refer to them by their physical or behavioral idiosyncrasies. They should not make jokes at their expense. In this sense it is a good idea to keep the subjects' potential reaction in mind when one is writing about one's field site. Beyond these simple matters of good taste, however, the subjects' potential reaction can have a chilling effect on a researcher's writings, both on field notes and in final papers.

In writing field notes, the researcher includes all sorts of details, many of which might seem irrelevant: how somebody dresses, how old someone appears to be, what people eat for lunch, and so on. At the beginning stages when the focus of the project may not yet be settled, it is impossible to know which of these details will later seem very significant, and which might otherwise be lost to the recesses of memory if not written down. Yet these impressions may offend the subjects: if you estimate someone's age as forty and he's only thirty-five, or if you note how deferential someone is toward her boss, and she doesn't feel deferential. Knowing that the subjects are going to read one's field notes can make a sensitive researcher second-guess every detail. It is hard enough to write field notes regularly without the additional pressure of trying to keep them clean.

As for final papers, these suffer both the field notes' problem of offending details and the second problem of objectifying analyses. Every social-scientific analysis objectifies its subjects to a certain extent. Some are quite blatant in the way they obliterate the subjects' individuality, even their free will. Others are more sensitive to their subjects, but still may offend them by taking them as typical, as representative, or as telling. Subjects, by and large, think of themselves as individuals, with more or less special characteristics. To reduce them to a single aspect or a limited bundle of attributes is to ignore a large part of who they are, or who they think they are.

In my case study, for instance, I treated the subjects as hypothesis-makers and hypothesis-judgers, as sociologists, and as P-O sociologists. This is not necessarily how they would have treated themselves, and I knew when I was writing my paper that they would object to this characterization when they read it. It gets quite tricky, then, to find the balance between censoring one's paper to avoid offense and making a social-scientific argument that one feels is justified. I suggest in my paper that sociologists' response to this dilemma hinges on a variety of competing and conflicting interests. In my own case, I felt secure enough in my subjects' friendship, and in my own field-site role as a humorously offensive devil's advocate, to risk offense and objectify my subjects. Other researchers may try to reduce the objectification or refuse to show their papers to their subjects.

In sum, then, the idea of sharing one's writings with one's subjects is fraught with problems. I am not suggesting that researchers refuse to show their writings to their subjects, merely trying to make the issue complex. My view is that field notes should not be shared; they are too raw and too liable to offend. However, I feel that subjects have a right to see and comment on at least one draft of the researcher's final paper.

Conclusion

THIRTEEN

The Extended Case Method

Michael Burawoy

This book treats methodology neither narrowly as the science of technique nor broadly as a branch of theory. Indeed, for us methodology provides the link between technique and theory. It explores ways of utilizing technique to advance theory. If technique is concerned with the instruments and strategies of data collection, then methodology is concerned with the reciprocal relationship between data and theory.

The studies of this book utilize a single methodology, that of the extended case method, for (re)constructing theory out of data collected through participant observation.[1] However, the extended case method is only one methodological response to the two traditional criticisms of participant observation: first, that it is incapable of generalization and therefore not a true science and, second, that it is inherently "micro" and ahistorical and therefore not true sociology. In this chapter I want to clarify the distinctiveness of the extended case method by comparing its response to these criticisms with the responses of other methods, in particular ethnomethodology, the interpretive case method, and grounded theory. Thus, in the first part of this chapter I move from technique to method. In the second part I move from method to theory. There I argue that by focusing on the "macro" determinations of everyday life, the extended case method is also the most appropriate way of using participant observation to (re)construct theories of advanced capitalism.

FROM TECHNIQUE TO METHOD

According to convention, the technique of participant observation suffers from two fundamental problems. The first is the problem of *sig-*

nificance. Single case studies may provide very interesting results, but they provide no measure of their generalizability. Moreover, singularity is compounded by the observer's potential disruption of the situation under examination. The case study is, therefore, so it is said, inherently particular until its results are tested in a sample of cases carefully selected from a population. The second criticism refers to the *level of analysis.* The study of face-to-face interaction, of the social situation, is said to be inherently micro and ahistorical. By its very definition the technique of participant observation is confined to the short term and to limited geographical space. In what follows I try to explicate the extended case method's response to these criticisms by comparing it with three other responses—ethnomethodology, the interpretive case method, and grounded theory.

Ethnomethodologists deny the relevance of the two charges. They argue that social situations of face-to-face interaction must be understood first as a unique product of the competencies, reflexivities, and assumptions of reciprocity among participants. In this perspective the abstractions necessary to make comparisons and thus generalizations across social situations have no "objective" standing. They are themselves constructed from the social situation of the inside participant or the outside observer. Jack Douglas, for example, shows how the official suicide rates that Durkheim used to establish the existence of a "macro" order of external constraining forces cannot be compared, because they take on very different meanings according to the circumstances of their collection.[2] Aaron Cicourel shows how the concept of delinquent is socially constructed by the juvenile justice system: by police officers and probation officers working under organizational and client pressures and with particular theories of delinquency. If the use of general concepts to apply across social situations is sociologically suspect, so too is the postulation of an external level of reality.[3] In the view of ethnomethodology the macro world is not a real world but a construction of participants enabling them to negotiate and uphold face-to-face interaction. There is, therefore, only one sociology and that is the microsociology of the unique social situation, what Knorr-Cetina calls "methodological situationism."[4] The task of ethnomethodology, therefore, is to elaborate the cognitive accomplishments that make social interaction possible. These accomplishments include the social construction of abstractions that constitute both general and macro phenomena.

Like ethnomethodology, the interpretive case method denies the premises of conventional criticisms. Here too macro and micro, general and particular, are collapsed, but in the other direction. The micro is viewed as an expression of the macro, the particular an expression of the general. It is as if the whole lodges itself in each part in the form of a genetic code, which has to be uncovered through a process of hermeneutic interpretation. Clifford Geertz is one of the supreme artists of this interpretive case method. In his celebrated study of the Balinese cockfight, for example, Geertz presents the ritual cockfight as a "paradigmatic event" that displays the social organization of Balinese society and the Balinese sense of self.[5] Through an elaborate system of betting and gaming rules, the warring of cocks brings together and orders villages, kin-groups, lineages, and castes into a status hierarchy. Cocks are the symbolic expression of their owners' masculinity, standing, and prestige, while the cockfight itself simulates the social matrix of Balinese society. The Balinese cockfight holds a key to the wider society in which it is embedded: "Its function, if you want to call it that, is interpretive: it is a Balinese reading of Balinese experience, a story they tell themselves about themselves."[6] Geertz describes his method as follows: "Hopping back and forth between the whole conceived through the parts that actualize it and the parts conceived through the whole that motivates them, we seek to turn them, by a sort of intellectual perpetual motion, into explications of one another."[7] The interpretive case method denies the premises of the conventional criticisms by claiming that, properly understood, the micro and particular are simultaneously macro and general.

TABLE 1   Responses to the Criticisms of Participant Observation

		Significance of Social Situation	
		Particular	General
Orienting Level of Analysis	Micro	Ethnomethodology	Grounded theory
	Macro	Extended case method	Interpretive case method

In table 1 I have summarized the four different responses to the criticisms that participant observation is inherently micro, ahistorical, and particular. By their reductionism, ethnomethodology and the interpretive case method both reject the *terms* of the twin criticisms. Ethnomethodology makes a virtue of necessity and reduces sociology to the micro and particular, whereas the interpretive case method fuses the micro and the macro, the particular and the general, into a single expressive totality. I use them here to shed light on the distinctiveness of grounded theory and the extended case method, both of which accept that micro and macro are discrete and causally related levels of reality and that generalizations can be derived from the comparison of particular social situations.

As we shall see, each of these two preferred methods addresses one of the criticisms at the expense of the other. On the one hand, the extended case method, by explicating the link between micro and macro, constitutes the social situation in terms of the *particular* external forces that shape it. It faces the problem of generalization. On the other hand, grounded theory, by pursuing generalizations across social situations, obscures the specific contextual determinations of the social situation. It faces the problem of the link between micro and macro. Nevertheless, I propose to show that each method can in principle deal with both criticisms: grounded theory can build up the macro from its micro generalizations, and the extended case method can give rise to generalizations through reconstructing theory.

The Rise of Microsociology

Grounded theory works with a particular image of science in which theories are induced from data. Its principles were already laid out in Park and Burgess's classic *Introduction to the Science of Sociology* (1921): "As soon as historians seek to take events out of their historical setting, that is to say, out of their time and space relations, in order to compare them and classify them; as soon as historians begin to emphasize the typical and representative rather than the unique character of events, history ceases to be history and becomes sociology."[8] But Park imposed his naturalistic sociology and the laws of human ecology on the field work of his students. He slotted their studies of the "natural areas" of Chicago into a preordained framework. Only later would field workers be encouraged to construct their own theories from the ground up.

Florian Znaniecki would be the first to theorize the importance of using field work to generate abstract principles or even laws. He called this process analytical induction: "[C]ertain particular objects are determined by intensive study, and the problem is to define the logical classes which they represent. No definition of the class precedes . . . the selection of data to be studied as representatives of this class. The analysis of the data is all done before any general formulations; and if well done, there is nothing more of importance to be learned about the class which these data represent by any subsequent investigation of more data of the same class."[9]

Everett Hughes, one of the most influential teachers of participant observation at Chicago, also advocated this approach. He, for example, compared dissimilar occupations: the physician and the janitor, the real estate agent and the jazz musician, in order to draw conclusions of general validity about the nature of occupations:

> The comparative student of man's work learns about doctors by studying plumbers; and about prostitutes by studying psychiatrists. . . . [W]e seek for common themes in human work. . . . I believe that in the study of work, as in that of other human activities and institutions, progress is apt to be commensurate with our ability to draw a wide range of pertinent cases into view. The wider the range, the more we need a fundamental frame of reference.[10]

Later, Glaser and Strauss codified these methods in their pathbreaking book, *The Discovery of Grounded Theory*, which has become one of the definitive texts for field workers in sociology.[11] They sought to demonstrate that qualitative analysis was neither an anachronism nor doomed as foreplay to the real sociological act. Field work need be no less theoretical than the "grand theory" of structural functionalism and no less scientific than the "abstracted empiricism" of verification.

Glaser and Strauss were at pains to show that theory development was not the prerogative of a few leaders at elite establishments who construct deductive systems of thought based on a priori assumptions and concepts removed from reality. Nor should sociologists be condemned to the slavish task of verifying the theories of the anointed. "[The grand theorists] played 'theoretical capitalist' to the mass of 'proletariat' testers, by training young sociologists to test their teachers' work but *not* to imitate it."[12] Grounded theory is a populist sociology, a way in which all of us can turn our data into the very best scientific theory. By accumulating judicious comparisons constructed from qualitative data, even the participant observer can begin to develop concepts of general applicability to diverse settings.

Grounded theory's claim to science lies in its ardent pursuit of *generalizations*, induced from comparisons across social situations. But in making those comparisons grounded theory represses the specificity of each situation. Thus Glaser and Strauss examine how physicians, families, nurses, and patients deal with terminal illness in different "awareness contexts," related to who knows what and with what certainty.[13] They develop general laws about the way in which the social loss of a dying patient (loss to family and to occupation) affects the behavior and attitudes of nurses and doctors. In moving from this substantive theory to a more formal theory, Glaser and Strauss propose the more general law: the higher the status of a client, the better the care he or she will receive from experts.[14]

Ethnomethodologists, by contrast, prefer to plumb the depths of the single "awareness context" for processes that underlie stable interaction. Typical is Garfinkel's celebrated study of Agnes, whose attempt to pass from boy to girl highlights all the "seen but unnoticed" labors involved in managing sexual identity.[15] More explicitly hostile to the comparative approach of grounded theory is Gilbert and Mulkay's analysis of scientific discourse.[16] Rather than extracting from their interview material some underlying reality, some truth of how science "really" works, they highlight the discrepant discourses of scientists as products of specific social contexts. They show how scientists create two discourses to cope with disagreement: an empiricist discourse in which facts reflect a real world and a contingent discourse in which noncognitive factors account for error. Whereas sociologists have tended to reduce science to the contingent repertoire and philosophers have reduced it to the empiricist repertoire, neither give serious attention to the world of the scientist as a patterning of a *multiplicity* of discourses. In the words of Zimmerman and Pollner, grounded theory uses discourse as a "resource" from which to derive generalization whereas ethnomethodology regards discourse as a "topic" in its own right, something that is produced in specific contexts.[17]

Methodological situationism leads ethnomethodologists in two directions. One tendency is toward extreme relativism, in which there is no real world but only a mulitplicity of situationally specific perspectives. The other tendency seeks invariant properties that make social interaction possible, whether these be linguistic communication, procedures for accomplishing understanding, or the cognitive basis of all meaning production.[18] In contrast to grounded theory, which seeks generalizations across social situations, ethnomethodology, if it makes any claims beyond the particular, seeks *universals* that underlie all social situations. As we shall see, the extended case method also adopts a situational analysis but avoids the pitfalls of relativism and universalism by seeing the situation as shaped from above rather than constructed from below.

The Anthropological Turn to the Macro
Grounded theory defended the scientificity and theoretical relevance of microsociology against the rising hegemony of structural functionalism. Symbolic interaction criticized the ideas of system and structure for missing the creativeness of actors in social situations. "Instead of accounting for the activity of the organization and its parts in terms of organizational principles or system principles, [symbolic interactionism] seeks explanation in the way in which participants define, interpret, and meet the situations at their respective points."[19] Ethnomethodology, on the other hand, turned the problem of order from Parsons's institutionalization and internalization of norms to the prior cognitive accomplishments of everyday life that make normative consensus at all possible.[20] This movement from macrosociology to microsociology was also reflected in actual research. Through their field work, urban and industrial sociologists were busy discovering small-scale communities— the urban village and the informal work group—that were holding back the forces of commodification, atomization, anomie, and alienation

trumpeted by classical sociology as defining the modern condition. Within institutions such as prisons, asylums, the military, hospitals, and so on, microsociology was uncovering an unsuspected world of the inmate.

At the same time that participant observation was being increasingly identified with microsociology in the United States, the opposite move was occurring within anthropology. With the expansion of anticolonial struggles and with industrialization disrupting and connecting the furthest corners of the globe, anthropologists could no longer pretend that their villages were isolated and timeless. The problem became even more acute when they left their villages and ventured into urban areas, where it was impossible to impose boundaries on face-to-face interaction.[21]

One of the first anthropological attempts to come to terms with "macro" forces was Max Gluckman's exploration of the social structure of South Africa in his analysis of a bridge-opening ceremony in Zululand in 1940.[22] In attendance were representatives from both sides of the color bar: on the one side the Chief Native Commissioner, the magistrates, the chief surgeon, missionaries, traders, and recruiting agents for the mines, and on the other side the Zulu king, local chiefs, the men who had built the bridge, clerks, African police, and armed warriors. Analyzing who said and did what, when, where, and to whom, Gluckman was able to represent the ceremony as South African society in microcosm. Based on interrogation of the social situation and on his prior knowledge, he showed how the opening of the bridge contained the key factors with which to construct an understanding of South African society. Presumably had he looked at a bridge opening in the Transkei, or a mine dance in Johannesburg, he would have come to similar conclusions about the nature of South African pluralism. Society was, so to speak, composed of cells each encoded with the same structure, reflecting the essential character of the totality in which they existed. It did not matter which cell one looked at; the purpose was to arrive at features that were generalizable to society as a whole.

This was in effect an application of the interpretive case method. Gluckman was interested in the way the macro was present in the micro situation and less concerned with their mutual determination as two different levels of reality. Subsequently Gluckman and, more particularly, his students developed the extended case method, opening up villages and urban situations to wider political and economic forces associated with colonialism.[23] Whereas in the original study of the bridge opening, Gluckman had regarded the social situation as an *expression of* the wider society, many of his followers viewed the village, the strike, the tribal association as *shaped by* external forces.

Jaap van Velsen elaborated the extended case method in his reflections on his own studies of kinship relations among the Lakeside Tonga of Malawi (then Nyasaland).[24] When he asked the Tonga to describe their kinship system, they told him that they were a matrilineal and matrilocal tribe. A traditional anthropologist would have then diagramed the beautifully symmetrical kinship patterns and called it a day. Van Velsen, however, was not satisfied with just studying norms and began collecting data on actual marriage patterns of the Tonga. He discovered that 40 percent failed to conform to the normative ideal. Whereas a structural anthropologist might have dismissed these as unimportant exceptions, Van Velsen regarded them as the key to understanding the changes taking place in Tonga society. Many of the able-bodied men in the villages were absent for long periods while they worked on the South African mines, and this led to new sources of wealth, changes in the sexual division of labor, and alternative marriage patterns that competed with the ideal. Accordingly, he did not view kinship norms as internalized and then executed, but as an arena of struggle for the realization of competing interests.[25]

In making problematic the exceptional or deviant cases, Van Velsen is driven outside the field situation to the broader economic and political forces impinging on the Tonga. Looked at through the lens of colonialism and industrialization, the social situation becomes a completely different object, one threaded by patterns of power in which kinship norms become the terrain of struggle. The movement outward compels a reconceptualization inward—from self-equilibration and cohesion to domination and resistance.

The differences between the interpretive and extended case methods become clearer on reexamination of Geertz's Balinese cockfight. Whereas Geertz regards it as a "paradigmatic event" that displays the social organization of Balinese society, the extended case method would examine the specificity of the cockfight—how it varies from place to place, how it has changed over time—as a vehicle for comprehending the forces shaping Balinese society. Geertz gives us a few clues. For example, he tells us that most of the fights are organized by petty merchants near to and on the occasion of markets; "trade has followed the cock for centuries in rural Bali, and the sport has been one of the main agencies of the island's monetization."[26] Second, the Javanese government and the Dutch colonial government before it made the cockfight illegal, which Geertz attributes to their modernizing ideology.[27] But from a different point of view the cockfight can be seen as a ritual of resistance to colonial and then Javanese domination. The economic and political forces come together when Geertz explains that the cockfight is the way in which the Balinese raise money for public purposes, in this particular case for a new school that the government had denied them.

We see how the extended case method leads directly to an analysis of domination and resistance, obscured in Geertz's interpretation. We can come to similar conclusions by contrasting the way Van Velsen problematizes exceptions to norms and the way Geertz sweeps them aside. Thus, on the one hand, Geertz says that the cockfight is a *paradigmatic* event that simulates the Balinese status hierarchy, but on the other hand he says it is *exceptional* in excluding women since Bali is a "rather unisex society."[28] Problematizing rather than dismissing this anomaly, one might conclude that the centrality of the cockfight testifies to the importance of male domination despite and indeed perhaps because of appearances to the contrary. It is a fraternal organization that constructs male solidarity and through its association with the cash nexus cements the material, political, and cultural subordination of women. It is a text written by men for men.

Geertz denigrates as reductive and relegates to footnotes what is constitutive of the extended case method, namely the specific historical context that shaped both the cockfight and the domination it produced. In Geertz's own favored metaphor of text he fails to examine who wrote the text and for whom, and how it was received.[29] The metaphor of text is not innocent. One can read and interpret a text without knowing its author or audience. Texts may appear to be autonomous, but nevertheless they have to be created, and they do produce effects.

The extended case method looks for specific macro determination in the micro world, but how does it measure up to the criticism of generalizability? It seeks generalization through reconstructing existing generalizations, that is, the reconstruction of existing theory. In focusing on the deviant marriage patterns among the Tonga, Van Velsen developed a "post-structuralist" theory of kinship that emphasized strategic action in the pursuit of interests rather than the execution of norms.[30] In examining the source of the deviations, Van Velsen rejected the idea that return migration from the towns was due to the strength of primordial ties to a traditional way of life. Instead he showed how oscillating migration was shaped by the policies and institutions of the colonial administration and the South African mining industry. The colonial administration in Nyasaland needed a tax base and the mines needed cheap labor—both objectives were assured by reproducing a system of return migration. For their part the Tonga worked within these political and economic constraints, using entry into wage labor to further their own material interests.[31] By reconstructing existing theories of migration in this way, Van Velsen was able to generalize from his single case study.[32]

The Extended Case Method and Grounded Theory
We have seen how both ethnomethodology and the interpretive case method deny the terms of our two criticisms, by reducing all sociology either to the micro and the particular or to the macro and the general. We are now in a position to directly compare the two methods that *do* problematize the relationship between the particular and the general. Table 2 summarizes the differences between the two strategies, which are discussed below.

TABLE 2   Comparison of the Extended Case Method and Grounded Theory

	Extended Case Method	Grounded Theory
Mode of generalization	Reconstructing existing theory	Discovering new theory
Explanation	Genetic	Generic
Comparison	Similar phenomena with a view to explaining differences	Unlike phenomena with a view to discovering similarities
The meaning of significance	Societal	Statistical
Nature of totality	Uniqueness is located in a context external to itself, which elucidates society	Abstraction from space and time in a setting, which facilitates generalization to population of cases
Object of analysis	Situation	Variables
Causality	Indivisible connectedness of elements	Linear relationship between variables
Micro-macro	Macro foundations of a microsociology	Micro foundations of a macrosociology
Social change	Social movements	Social engineering

As I described in some detail in chapter 2 and above, the extended case method derives generalizations by constituting the social situation as anomalous with regard to some preexisting theory (that is, an existing body of generalizations), which is then reconstructed. Grounded theory, on the other hand, discovers generalizations by abstracting from time and place.

Grounded theory's inductive strategy leads to *generic* explanations, which take the form of invariant laws, such as "all organization tends toward oligarchy." The extended case method constructs *genetic* explanations, that is, explanations of particular outcomes. An example would be Weber's analysis of the historically specific constellation of forces, including the motivational component provided by the Protestant ethic, which gave rise to Western bourgeois capitalism. A generic strategy looks for similarities among disparate cases, whereas the genetic strategy focuses on differences between similar cases. The goal of the first is to seek abstract laws or formal theory, whereas the goal of the second is historically specific causality.[33]

Our two types of explanation work with very different understandings of what we might mean by "significance." In the generic mode we seek out what different social situations have in common, and generalization is based on the likelihood that all similar situations have similar attributes. Here significance refers to *statistical significance*, generalization from a sample to a population. In the genetic mode the significance of a case relates to what it tells us about the world in which it is embedded. What must be true about the social context or historical past for our case to have assumed the character we have observed? Here significance refers to *societal significance*. The importance of the single case lies in what it tells us about society as a whole rather than about the population of similar cases.

In grounded theory society provides "natural" settings for the discovery of recurrent patterns of social behavior. Thus, Robert Park referred to the city as a "laboratory" where, because of rapid change and social diversity, the laws of human nature become readily visible.[34] These laws are not specific to the city but reveal themselves most clearly there. On the other hand, in the extended case method, the city is not an arena where laws are played out but a constellation of institutions located in time and space that shape domination and resistance.

The two approaches also adopt different conceptions of causality. Generalizing across disparate social situations involves not only abstraction from time and space but also the simplification of the social situation itself. Where causal patterns are observed across situations, they tend to be of a simple, linear form such as x causes y, what Herbert Blumer and more recently Charles Ragin call "variable analysis."[35] In constituting a social situation as unique, the extended case method pays attention to its complexity, its depth, its thickness. Causality then becomes multiplex, involving an "individual" (i.e., undividable) connectedness of elements, tieing the social situation to its context of determination.

Glaser and Strauss move from substantive to formal theory, making their generalizations among micro situations ever more abstract. They always remain at the same level of society. Others use microsociology as building blocks for a macrosociology. The simplest way is to argue, as Randall Collins has, that with the exception of space, time, and numbers there are no true "macro-variables."[36] The macro is then the aggregation and repetition of many micro interactions. The purpose of sociology is to arrive at "generalized explanatory principles, organized into models of the underlying processes that generate the social world."[37] Collins thus reduces "macro-phenomena" to the only real experiential reality, the micro situation with its rules of interaction.

Can one derive the properties of the macro world from the micro level laws? Such attempts to establish the micro foundations of a macrosociology ride on both the intended and unintended consequences of the social interaction order. Logically this realm should be the province of symbolic interactionism, which regards social structure as an emergent process. In practice symbolic interactionism, like grounded theory, either ignores or takes social structure as given. Instead the project has been taken over by game theory and economic models, which claim to link the macro to the micro on the basis on methodological individualism. Sensitivity to the social situation, to the symbolically constructed lifeworld, is abandoned in favor of normative assumptions about the rationality of actors.[38] The extended case method takes the opposite approach and seeks to uncover the macro foundations of a microsociology. It takes the social situation as the point of empirical examination and works with given general concepts and laws about states, economies, legal orders, and the like to understand how those micro situations are shaped by wider structures.

Finally, we turn to the vision of social change that emerges from the two methods. Glaser and Strauss self-consciously aim to develop theories that will enhance the control participants exercise over their situations.[39] They distinguish "access variables," which give participants access to "controllable variables," whose manipulation would affect the situation. Grounded theory, for example, should allow nurses to better cope with different levels of awareness of terminal illness just as it gives doctors an idea of the consequences of disclosure.

In advocating social engineering, grounded theory suppresses two related factors. First, it does not consider the dimension of power within the micro context; how, for example, doctors exercise power over nurses and how both exercise power over patients. Second, in focusing on variables that can be manipulated within the immediate situation, it represses the broader macro forces that both limit change and create domination in the micro sphere. Whereas grounded theory might examine the way AIDS patients can be more "effectively" handled in hospitals, the extended case method would examine the way the state has failed to take AIDS seriously, has held back the development of public policy, and has restricted experimentation with new drugs.

Once one highlights systemic forces and the way they create and sustain patterns of domination in the micro situation, the application of social theory turns to building social movements. As Alain Touraine has argued, it is not a matter of applying the knowledge of the expert but of the observer joining the participants in a joint movement of analysis and action.[40]

FROM METHOD TO THEORY

In order to distinguish the extended case method from other methods of using participant observation to advance theory, we had to adopt the general categories of "micro" and "macro." The considerable divergence between the methods requires categories that are so abstract and ahistorical that they are of little use in examining the appropriateness of a given method for studying particular phenomena. We have to respecify the meaning of micro and macro to appreciate the relevance of the extended case method for the study of power and resistance in the modern metropolis.

We may take as our point of departure Alain Touraine's idea of a postindustrial society in which not only the *means* but also the *ends* of production are transformed. Postindustrial society acts on itself and determines its own goals. It is a "programmed" society that rejects the old teleological models of history as evolution and progress in order to embrace "historicity," that is, our ability to create social relations through participation in social movements. "Society used to be in history; now history is within societies, and they have the capacity to choose their organization, their values, and their processes of change without having to legitimate these choices by making them conform to natural or historical laws."[41]

The studies in the volume exemplify the production rather than the consumption of social relations. ACT UP and the antinuclear movement challenge the goals of society: they challenge how society uses its resources, how it legitimates inequality, and how it imposes alien needs. The state fragments and bureaucratizes the administration of social benefits to prevent alliances between worker and client for a more just and rational welfare order. Workers at Wholly Grains oppose the degradation of work with the ideal of self-management in which producers decide how and what they produce. New immigrants show astonishing imagination in articulating alternative visions, as Central American domestic workers create new meaning in their jobs and Cambodian women define the needs of their community. In African-American communities parents band together to counter the denial of public education to their children. Even junior high school students take the classroom into their own hands and challenge the teacher's authority to teach. Social research itself becomes self-conscious about its purposes. An outreach program for drug users employs a sociologist to monitor its activities, and a sociologist uncovers the hidden agendas of his fellow students.

But where does this self-consciousness come from? Where are the new meanings produced and where are they lodged? Jürgen Habermas, drawing on Schutz's concept of the lifeworld, considers their source to be social arenas integrated through mutual understanding and collective will formation such as the workplace, family, community, and school.[42] New meaning arises from communicative labors whose comprehension requires actual or virtual participation. To gain access to the lifeworld, scientists have to enter into dialogue with participants. They have to become real or imaginary participant observers. Like Touraine, Habermas must privilege participant observation as a technique of social research.

But participant observers differ from participants precisely in their status as observers, which gives them insights into the limits of communicative action and the sources of its distortion, that is, how the system world denies freedom and autonomy in the lifeworld. As observers who also stand outside the lifeworlds they study, scientists can gain insight into the properties of the system world, which integrates the intended and unintended consequences of instrumental action into relatively autonomous institutions. Indeed, these can be understood only from the standpoint of the observer.

From this perspective the scientific and hermeneutic dimensions of social research assume an ontological foundation. They correspond to the different types of social action that integrate the system and lifeworld respectively. Thus those who would stress science over hermeneutics—the objective over the subjective—risk stressing the supremacy of system over lifeworld. Such analyses, whether critical or complacent, have a tendency to degenerate into pessimistic overestimations of the power of the welfare state, the capitalist economy, or "the system." Too often, the system is seen as all-determining, so that forms of resistance such as innovation, negotiation, and rebellion are not taken seriously. Max Weber, for instance, waxed pessimistic about the limits of rationality and the bureaucratization of the modern world. His vision of the "iron cage" that imprisoned capitalist society would seem to deny the possibility of autonomous spaces for resistance. In stressing reification, instrumental reason, one-dimensionality, the critical theory of Lukács and the Frankfurt School relegates resistance to an ever-diminishing "rebellion of the marginal."[43]

Habermas is just as critical of those who give primacy to the hermeneutic moment, to intersubjective understanding, such as symbolic
interactionists and ethnomethodologists. In reducing society to the lifeworld, they erroneously assume the autonomy of actors, the independence of culture, and the transparency of communication.[44] They
ignore distortions brought about by the economic and political systems,
particularly through the incursion of the universal media of exchange—money and power.

In Habermas's view the distinctiveness of contemporary society is the
"uncoupling" of the lifeworld from the system world. Whereas the old
Marxian models of society bound class struggle to the unfolding contradictions of capitalism viewed as an economic system, Habermas, like
Touraine, sees a double differentiation, on the one hand between the
economic and political systems and on the other between the lifeworld
and the system world.[45] Once separated, the relationship between system world and lifeworld is one of invasion and resistance.

Although Habermas establishes the theoretical basis for the domination of the lifeworld by the system, he fails to elaborate the sociological basis of their actual interaction.[46] Instead he substitutes a generalized fear that the "system" will overextend itself and "colonize the
lifeworld." Colonization, he argues, not only undermines communicative action but also saps the lifeworld of the motivational and critical
energies necessary for the survival of the system itself. While Habermas
does see new social movements as the reaction of the lifeworld against
the system, his analysis of resistance is no more concrete than the process of colonization itself.

As the studies in this volume show, the interplay between system and
lifeworld, between domination and response, is dynamic and varied.
However, it is difficult to systematize the various forms of interplay.
Forms of resistance are more easily disentangled than are corresponding forms of domination, principally because the system is diffuse in its
operation and less visible in a world that spotlights the subject of domination and hides the deployment of power. Five distinct modalities of
resistance, however, are revealed by the studies in this volume.

Colonization. In some contexts the system so fragments and individ-
ualizes the lifeworld that resistance is impossible or ineffective. This is
the outlying category that gives Habermas's work its critical edge. It is
represented in this volume by Alice Burton's analysis of welfare workers. She shows how the state's reorganization of welfare agencies divides
workers from one another and from their clients. Welfare clients are
atomized into administrable segments so that they, along with the social
workers and eligibility workers, can be more effectively surveilled. Even
in this extreme case workers strike or work to rule, but their rebellion

is ineffective. Kathryn Fox's study of outreach work among injection drug users underlines what we might call "neocolonization of the lifeworld." Here direct surveillance is less important a constraint than financial dependence on the state and laws prohibiting needle exchange. By directly or indirectly destroying the autonomy of these lifeworlds, whether of the welfare client or the drug user, the state systematically erodes the basis of its own legitimacy and effectiveness.

Negotiation within limits. In other contexts the system leaves room for maneuver within institutions while strengthening boundaries between institutions. Leslie Hurst's study shows that such a separation of spheres can in fact facilitate what she calls a negotiated order within spheres. Mr. Henry has legitimate control only over his pupils' minds, while their bodies and souls are outside his control. Students take advantage of this to contest his authority; without support from school or family he has no recourse. Shiori Ui also describes the two-edged character of the operation of state and economy, which limits freedom and autonomy while creating opportunities. Cambodian women are able to exploit their status as political refugees to establish themselves in enclaves and prepare passages into the wider society. In keeping itself at a greater distance and permitting limited terrains of maneuver, the state successfully contains resistance and even turns it to its advantage.

Creating alternatives. Within a fragmented lifeworld people can sometimes go beyond a negotiated order and carve out spheres of self-organization. Although powerless to reshape the boundaries of the system, they can at least defend and reconstitute their lives within those boundaries. Self-organization can occur even within the system as, for example, in the case of Ann Arnett Ferguson's producer cooperative. Although continually threatened by pressures of the marketplace, Wholly Grains manages to survive one crisis after another by drawing on a reservoir of workers' commitment to collective organizations as well as on resources supplied by other collectives. In themselves cooperatives do not challenge the limits within which they operate—they have to compete with other enterprises for both labor and consumers. Yet they do plant the idea that alternatives are possible and thereby question the legitimacy of the boundaries set by the system. Similarly, the tutorial program studied by Nadine Gartrell challenges the pessimism about African-American education. The bringing together of spheres that are normally insulated, particularly family and school, gives students a better chance of realizing their aspirations.

Reshaping limits. Leslie Salzinger shows how workers, organizing in defense of their material interests, can actually reshape the limits of the system. Central American women, faced with slender labor market opportunities, opt for domestic work because it gives them autonomy and flexibility. Individual upward mobility is not feasible, and conditions of employment rule out conventional forms of union organizing. Instead they carve out an occupational community to establish conditions and standards of work and a credentialing system. In so doing they actually construct the demand for their own services, creating a separate tier of domestic workers for richer employers. As they negotiate through the labor market, they also reshape its contours.

Collective protest. For Habermas the "new social movements," with their concerns for issues that transcend class, such as peace, environment, and civil rights, exemplify collective resistance to the encroachment of the lifeworld by the system. Josepha Schiffman's study of dual tendencies in the peace movement and Joshua Gamson's study of gay and AIDS activism can be seen in the same light. Both movements are wary about participation within the system and devote their most original efforts to confronting it or holding it at bay. The peculiarities of their strategies of organization and protest do not derive simply from their antistatist stance but from the difficulties of dealing with a form of domination that is at once ubiquitous and invisible. Before they can begin to think about asserting control over the state and the economy, they have to make what is invisible visible.

The preceding typology of forms of resistance—from capitulation to the creation of alternative organizations, from negotiation within limits to the negotiation of limits, from anarchic outbursts to self-conscious collective protest—demonstrates the varied interplay between system and lifeworld, showing that the lifeworld is not an inert body but a source of continual contestation. But the struggle is an unequal one. We should not overestimate or romanticize the capacity of the lifeworld to fight back. The forms of resistance are constrained and continually challenged by new and more effective forms of domination. Still, resistance there is. We have tried to document its diverse forms, its sources, and its limitations.

Appendix

FOURTEEN

Teaching Participant Observation

Michael Burawoy

As a technique of research, participant observation distinguishes itself by breaking down the barriers between observer and participant, between those who study and those who are studied. It shatters the glass box from which sociologists observe the world and puts them temporarily at the mercy of their subjects. Instead of watching respondents through two-way mirrors, reconstructing them from the traces they leave in archives, analyzing their responses to telephone interviews, or reducing them to demographic data points, the ethnographer confronts participants in their corporeal reality, in their concrete existence, in *their* time and space.

Conventional social science privileges its knowledge by first separating the observer from the participant and then placing the observer above the participant. It divides society into two parts, one of which is superior to the other. The subject becomes an object, a dupe of social forces, whereas the scientist lies beyond social determinism, exercising autonomy and rationality. Ethnographers challenge this bifurcation when they insist that they share a common world with those they study, when they believe that participant and observer are commensurate though not identical entities, and when they recognize that both sides have theories about the other as well as about themselves. Instead of standing above society, contemporary ethnographers veer toward absorption into the society. They are more likely to forsake the authority of science and enter into dialogue with their subjects. Ethnography becomes a collaborative enterprise of participant and observer.

THE POWER OF PEDAGOGY

This view of participant observation as a collaborative enterprise has its counterpart in teaching. Instead of treating students as empty vessels waiting to be filled with knowledge ("here is the truth, swallow it") and instead of students regarding themselves as passive recipients of pedagogic wisdom ("just tell me what I've got to know"), we can try to construct learning as a mutual relationship between educator and the educated. This is a noble goal, but one that is neither easily pursued nor ever completely successful. Mutuality between graduate student and teacher depends on disrupting the structures of micropower. In a doctoral program discipline is exercised all the more ubiquitously and punitively because the authority of knowledge is so flimsy. Impressive syllabuses, impossible reading assignments, grading, interminable examinations, and letters of evaluation as well as the parade of experience and status turn education into a display of power.

How far can one go in disrupting the institutional foundations of a professor's claim to the monopoly of knowledge without undermining teaching altogether? How is it possible to institutionalize pedagogic ignorance, not just proclaim it? To break with an authoritarian order from above, an order, moreover, endowed with legitimacy, one must perhaps create a compulsory autonomy from below. This, at any rate, is how I have designed the structure of my seminars in participant observation. By sending students out into the field to undertake their own projects, I sought to endow them with a minimal independence. I insisted, as a condition of participation, that within one week they had to be in the field, writing field notes. They were now the ones with a monopoly of knowledge, at least on the topic of their own research. After a minimum of reading about ethnography in the first two weeks, we devoted the remainder of the semester to discussing each of the twelve studies in turn. We would learn through active participation and observation both in the seminar and in the field, that is, through doing and confronting the doing of others. Rather than working in isolation, students would participate in and learn from their classmates' projects.

With an independent base, a realm of unquestioned expertise, each student could somewhat confidently launch into a discussion with the others. And because they were all feeling similar tensions and frustrations, they could share those experiences. Precisely because I was not doing field research and did not have any privileged knowledge about their sites, my own participation in the seminars rapidly diminished to the point that I became embarrassed to even summarize the discussions.[1] In teaching, ignorance can be a virtue. Not just my own ignorance but that of eleven classmates compelled each student to translate his or her experiences into a meaningful sociological account. Each student had to convince me and the entire class that something interesting was going on at the field site.

Students were on their own, but they also relied on each other as well as me to help them through the crises that continually erupted both in the field and in their attempts to make sense of the field. If presentations fell apart, and they often did, anxiety beset us all. We were all implicated in each study from the beginning, and we mobilized our energies to recover the broken pieces. As the seminar unfolded and the projects began to take shape, so the students also gained more self-confidence and experience in helping others. The development of each became the condition for the development of all.

But let's not romanticize these dialogues in the field and in the seminar. To be sure there was collaboration, but who set the terms? In the seminar, just as in the field, students had to accept strict ground rules not of their making. I demanded that they be in the field each week and that they submit at least five sets of field notes to me. I expected them to attend every meeting of the seminar, to come prepared to comment on the work of others, and on two occasions to distribute their own field notes and analysis for discussion. I expected a proposal or draft of the final paper halfway through the semester that would situate the study in some literature. There were no incompletes—the final paper had to be delivered by the end of the semester. I was demanding that they do the impossible: complete an ethnography in three months.

These ground rules had repercussions in the field. The intense schedule led students to choose sites with relative ease of access and where they were likely to be comfortable. So they tended to select groups with whom they had some sympathy, the underdogs rather than the overdogs. But the relative ease of entry created unexpected tensions when students found themselves torn between competing loyalties to the seminar and the field. The roles of participant and observer are inherently in conflict, and tension and anxiety are an intrinsic part of field work, I reassured them. Other things being equal, I advised, the greater the tension the better the product.

FIELD WORK AND ITS ANALYSIS

Their anxiety was compounded by their inexperience. Only one student had ever completed a participant observation study before. They didn't know what to expect. Tensions crystallized around field notes: What are they? How much do you write? How often? About what? I tried to counter this fear of the unknown and to demystify field work by distributing some of my own field notes, the first set from the study that became my doctoral dissertation and subsequently the book *Man-ufacturing Consent*. I know sociologists who write wonderful field notes, rich in observation, deep in insight, comprehensive in coverage—but I am not one of them. Students were surprised by my display of vulner-ability in showing them my primitive notes. At the same time they were encouraged because they could see even in these tentative first notes of mine the outline of the book that emerged several years later. This was not going to be so hard after all.

But it *was* hard. I would not accept any field notes without analysis—a commentary on the significance of what they had experi-enced and observed. I wanted them to figure out what was interesting and important about their field observation right from the beginning. Before they could even enroll in the course, I demanded a short "pro-spectus" that described what they expected to find in their field site *before* they entered. Inevitably, what they actually found would violate their expectations, forcing them to ask why they had been so wrong. It is after all so easy to "normalize" the field, to see what is as natural and inevitable. The most difficult part of the ethnographic enterprise is to make the data sound abnormal, sound surprising. One has to make the reader say, "Wow! That's interesting, I wonder why?" How students dragged their feet when it came to analysis![2]

There is probably a trade-off here. Those who find field work most trying often feel more at home analyzing their material than those who manage to cope more effectively with the tensions of the field. The appeal of participant observation usually lies in the integrity it gives to those one studies. Therefore, students resisted violating the authentic-ity of their subjects by locating them within some explanatory frame-work. They preferred to think that the accumulation of data would by itself miraculously turn into sociology, that the final paper would be conceived immaculately during examination week.

Even though we read Howard Becker's *Writing for Social Scientists*, students found it difficult to stomach my insistence that the writing of a major paper begins in the first week, that it is not something hurriedly put together at the end of the semester when all the data are in. Field work and writing proceed together as a process of continual recon-struction of the past in the light of the present with a view to antici-pating the future. From the very beginning the field challenges our preconceptions, forcing us to reconstruct our images, our theories, and even what constitutes our questions. Initially, our understanding of what is going on—what is interesting—may oscillate wildly, but over time the oscillations diminish (if all goes well) as we converge toward a stable interpretation.

Field work becomes a series of self-conscious experiments or interventions in which one first tests out and then reformulates one's hypotheses. It begins with what is often the most dramatic intervention, the initial entry itself. At this point how participants regard the observer reveals more than how the observer regards the participant. When Ann Ferguson introduced herself to the Wholly Grains Bakery, one of the members chuckled, "So you want to observe us, just like Margaret Mead . . . the sexual life of the baking collective." Leslie Salzinger, on the other hand, was an object of suspicion. Was she stealing ideas to give to a competing agency? Subjects' obstacles and resistances to being studied had to be carefully scrutinized, although these were often difficult to interpret before substantial field work had been completed. Similarly, moments of crisis, generated by oneself or others, reveal the true interests of the participants, moving us toward new refutations and conjectures.

OBSERVING THE OBSERVERS

The seminar itself was like any other field site with its own taken-for-granted culture, its own rituals and jokes, and its own crises and interventions. Perhaps it was different from the usual seminar, for it did not establish its content through agendas, sets of questions, or reading lists. It had an uncertain future, mirroring the flux in the field. To remind us that as scientists we were not outside or superior to society, that as observers we were not above being observed, I wanted someone to study the seminar. Charlie Kurzman volunteered. It was a thankless task since, unlike the others, he did not have a monopoly of knowledge. We knew as much about the seminar as he, or so we liked to think. Whether he desired it or not, we would evaluate his paper in the light of how we experienced the seminar. Like the others, he had to distribute his field notes, make a presentation, and give us his final paper. He was in an unusually weak position with respect to his subjects, who were friends and classmates. They were people with whom he spent time outside the seminar and who would (hopefully) be his colleagues for years to come. He could not afford to offend either them or me. But offend us he had to if he was going to say anything interesting, anything sociologically meaningful.

The turning point came when Charlie gave his first presentation. Until then the class had been very supportive of all the projects. That suddenly changed when Charlie revealed how his fellow students identified their subjects as positive and negative deviants, and how those judgments were shaped by professional interests and unexamined political assumptions. Even ethnographers like to think that their judgments have some objectivity. The class flew at Charlie, accusing him of objectification, insensitivity, distortion, and male bias. He had forced us to confront illusions we had about ourselves; he had challenged our political purity and objectivity. We returned in kind but with an unexpected display of passion and resentment. The session turned into a royal Berkeley cockfight that, like its Balinese model, dramatized cleavage and tension in our midst. By pecking away at Charlie's "knowledge claims," we provided grist for his theoretical mill. As sacrificial cock he suffered, but, as so often happens in participant observation, along with suffering came insight.

While some students unleashed pent-up anxieties about being surveilled, others began to worry about their own field work, what they were doing to *their* subjects. Ann Ferguson was so perturbed that she withdrew from the field. She just couldn't face her fellow workers. If they were to see her field notes, surely they would be as resentful as we were toward Charlie. She returned to the bakery only when one of her fellow workers phoned and asked why she hadn't been to visit.

Charlie's intervention had moved the seminar to a new level of consciousness. He opened up a range of questions concerning the possibilities and dangers of the sort of research that we, in principle, endorsed—research that was responsive to the interests of the participants. Students now had second thoughts about handing back their completed papers to the people they analyzed. Certainly this was an ideal way of validating, developing, and reconstructing our theories, but it also had risks that might not be worth taking. Equalizing power relations by allowing participants to contest one's explanations was fine in principle, but in practice it could turn friends into enemies and so compromise what one wanted to say as to make it worthless.

Each project, therefore, went through a life cycle. In order to gain entry students made commitments to those they were studying. But as the semester unfolded they became increasingly committed to one another at the same time that my demands for sociological significance became more insistent. The balance of power was now shifting from participant to observer. As surveillers we do become visible and subject to countersurveillance, but it is not symmetrical. Sooner or later we retreat behind the university walls, whereas our subjects remain to cope with the situation in which we found them. The very possibility of sociology, of partaking in a sociological community whose concern is to explain the particular as a manifestation of the general or the global, resides in this irreducible asymmetry of power. Only Charlie had nowhere to retreat, and so he did not waste much time rejecting his role as observer as soon as the semester was over.[3]

THE EDUCATOR, TOO, MUST BE EDUCATED

In his address to the Eastern Sociological Society in 1969, Everett Hughes took the parallel between teaching and field work in a slightly different direction.[4] He regarded the life experiences of his students as well as their own research projects as material for his own theorizing. Like field work, teaching was a way of interacting with "other" to broaden one's horizons, to move from the particular to the general, to emancipate oneself from parochialism. Hughes had a deep respect for his students—they were not empty vessels but fascinating subjects in their own right. He would question them about their families, their backgrounds, their histories, and how they saw the world. For him field work and teaching were transmission belts of knowledge from participant to observer and from student to teacher. Hughes had no qualms about using his students as informants, just as his students had few doubts about the benefits of ethnographic research. In the pioneering vision of Chicago sociology, knowledge was considered emancipatory.

Today we are more skeptical of the blessings of knowledge and more likely to see knowledge as a vehicle of domination. Counteracting this domination of "expert" over "neophyte" calls for an altered vision of teaching and field work, less as transmission belts of knowledge and more as dialogue. Instead of serving as the instructor's informants, students become participants in a collective process that begins on the first day of class. But that is easier said than done. I remember well how at the first meeting of this seminar, my heart sank as I listened to the vague, incoherent, and tentative proposals. In the seminar I could be a participant much like everyone else, but outside I would play a more directive role: writing comments on people's field notes; incessantly asking "so what?"; cajoling them into formulating a problem or persuading them that they had a problem if only they would recognize it; or directing them to this literature or that. There was mutual irritation, despair, exasperation, and incomprehension.

As the studies took shape, I was being forced to articulate what they were about. I tried again and again to work out the links between the micro and the macro, the particular and the general, and the process of generating anomalies. I was being forced to deepen my own methodological self-consciousness. The group had an extraordinary tenacity. Everyone seemed to be converging on some identifiable theme. Three weeks from the end I could see the dim outline of a possible book. We agreed to continue into the next semester with a view to rewriting our papers while I would contribute chapters on the extended case method and theory construction.[5]

At this point the enterprise changed from being my project and my seminar to our collective project. Undoubtedly, the papers exhibited some sort of unity around the extended case method because of the power I exercised and the pressure I applied, nonverbally in the class and verbally in my office, as well as through the many sets of comments on field notes, literature reviews, and drafts of papers. But in the second semester, the unity having been more or less established and a common project defined, we were now on a more equal footing.

This is not to say that it was easy for graduate students, who are accustomed to moving from course to course and from paper to paper, to now move from draft to draft. Again there was foot dragging. Revisions appeared at the last minute. In the end it was less my influence and more the collective pressure that got things done—pressure that extended as far as Charlie Kurzman in Turkey studying the Iranian Revolution, Shiori Ui laboring in a Cambodian textile factory, and Leslie Hurst observing classrooms in Sri Lanka.

Although I had been doing participant observation research for twenty years and had run seminars on the topic before, I had never written about it. My contributions to the book were at a much more rudimentary stage than theirs, and I thought that if they saw me struggling to make sense of my own ideas, moving from one draft to the next, they would be encouraged to do the same. I was wrong. Rewriting papers and confronting the limitations of one's own work, particularly at the beginning of one's career, is always painful. That I looked forward to rewriting was seen as a mark of eccentricity but more deeply a measure of my security and self-confidence.

However convivial and collaborative we became, we remained professor and graduate students. Just as in participant observation, so in teaching there is always a fundamental asymmetry. There was no escaping the institutional framework of the university and its inscribed hierarchy. In this context too much responsiveness easily leads to anarchy. It works only if the teacher first establishes the terrain of the seminar, its grounds and its broad goals, and then pursues those goals with unflagging determination. The teacher must still teach. The point is not to strip the teacher of all power, but only of disabling power, that is, power that inhibits the development of individual capacities, both of educator and educated. We must aspire to direction without domination, a balance between autonomy and dependence, a shared process of learning.

A MATTER OF GENDER?

How exceptional was this group? I had observed similar dynamics in my other seminars on participant observation, similar engagement and reciprocity. But this one seemed to move that much more smoothly, and I felt less a coercive presence than on previous occasions. There was more mutual engagement, interdependence, and joint endeavor, despite cussedness and obduracy. Unlike previous classes, this group never broke down out of exhaustion, indeed never looked like it was breaking down. I often wondered why. The participants had diverse interests but nevertheless shared a common political culture. There was an inner core that had already established close friendship ties. But all this was not unusual. In terms of career, none of the sociology students had even begun to prepare for their qualifying examinations. That was unusual, but it didn't help me comprehend what was going on. In the end the most plausible explanation is the most obvious one. The earlier seminars had roughly equal numbers of men and women; this one had ten women and two men.

What difference did gender make? Here I can only speculate based on my experiences in other seminars and on well-known theories of gender differences.[6] Certainly it was not a matter of explicitly studying questions raised by feminism, although many of the participants regarded themselves as feminists. Rather I think it was the structure of the seminar, which demanded both autonomy and interdependence, separation and connection. It was sustained from the beginning to the end by students' commitment to their own projects (which involved collaboration with those they were studying) as well as commitment to the success of everyone else's project. It became a genuinely collective enterprise, which raised the level of everyone's contribution. I am obviously not saying that men never excel in this mode or that women always do. I simply think there is a tendency in that direction.

Women are also more accustomed to handling the tensions of moving between spheres, in this case between different field sites and between field and school. This is not to say they find it easier than men. Indeed, they may have more difficulty separating themselves from others with whom they have continuing interaction. It is probably significant, therefore, that in each of the three seminars in which someone has volunteered to study the seminar, it has been a man. On the one hand these volunteers knew they wouldn't have to go into the field and interact with others, while on the other hand, at least initially, they thought they could separate their role as observer from their roles as friend, classmate, and graduate student.[7]

But the structure of the seminar had another feature with which men might have greater difficulty: the presentation of unfinished work, the tentativeness of people's ideas, the tolerance of uncertainty. The seminar was never the arena for students to boast superior erudition and knowledge, to lay claim to some final truth. It was always in flux, in process. It never seemed to end.

NOTES

CHAPTER ONE

I thank Gail Kligman and Erik Wright for their helpful comments on this chapter as well as chapters 2 and 13.

1. See Jürgen Habermas, *The Theory of Communicative Action*, vol. 2, *Lifeworld and System*, particularly chaps. 6 and 8. For Habermas the lifeworld is primarily integrated through intersubjective communicative action, but it is not confined to the micro-world as it includes the "public sphere" where politically negotiated meaning occurs. However, our use of the lifeworld is confined to the distorted communicative action in the micro-contexts of everyday life.

2. See Herbert Blumer, *Symbolic Interactionism*, chap. 1, and Leonard Schatzman and Anselm Strauss, *Field Research*, chap. 1. I don't adopt the distinction between "natural" and "unnatural" sociology because I want to stress what distinguishes the social sciences from the natural sciences, namely the interaction of participant and observer. The idea of studying people in their natural setting connotes the zoologist studying animals or the botanist studying plants rather than people studying people.

3. See, for example, John Lofland and Lyn Lofland, *Analyzing Social Settings*, and Schatzman and Strauss, *Field Research*. For an interesting account of the relative merits of participant observation as compared to survey research and experiential analysis, see Shulamit Reinharz, *On Becoming a Social Scientist*. For a collection of standard readings, see George McCall and J. L. Simmons, eds., *Issues in Participant Observation*.

4. Typically participant observation is described as a method that has been surpassed by advanced scientific techniques of research. Morton Hunt, for example, writes of participant observation as one of a number of techniques that "once formerly dominated the field: today, while still used . . . they account for only a small part of total research effort" (*Profiles of Social Research*, p. 6). According to Hunt the mainstays of sociology are now surveys and experimental techniques.

5. The position presented here owes much to Max Weber, *The Methodology of the Social Sciences*, and even more to Jürgen Habermas, *On the Logic of the Social Sciences*.

6. Paul Ricoeur, cited in Paul Rabinow, *Reflections on Field Work in Morocco*, p. 5.

7. Alain Touraine, *Return of the Actor*, p. 15.

8. Clifford Geertz, *Local Knowledge*, p. 5. Geertz in effect reduces the scientific or "explanatory" dimension to the hermeneutic or "interpretive" dimension by introducing the oxymoron "interpretive explanation" which "trains its attention on what institutions, actions, images, utterances, events, customs, all the usual objects of social-scientific interest, mean to those whose institutions, actions, customs, and so on they are" (p. 22).

9. Anthony Giddens, *New Rules of Sociological Method*, p. 146. Thus one studies "meaning" not only because the attribution of meaning affects how people behave but because without meaning there can be no data.

10. See Jürgen Habermas, *The Theory of Communicative Action*, vol. 1, *Reason and the Rationalization of Society*, pp. 102–42; Harold Garfinkel, *Studies in Ethnomethodology*, chap. 1. K. Knorr-Cetina refers to this move toward situational analysis as "methodological situationism," distinguishing it from "methodological individualism" and "methodological collectivism"; see "The Microsociological Challenge of Macro-sociology."

11. Herbert Gans, "The Participant-Observer as a Human Being." For recent critiques of participant observer as "marginal man," see Moshe Shokeid, "Anthropologists and Their Informants"; and Patricia Adler and Peter Adler, *Membership Roles in Field Research*. It is not an accident that the first anthropologists to have demystified the relationship between participant and observer should have been women. See, for example, Lauren Bohannan, *Return to Laughter*, and Hortense Powdermaker, *Stranger and Friend*. It is interesting to contrast these with Bronislaw Malinowski, *A Diary in the Strict Sense of the Term*, and Paul Rabinow, *Reflections on Field Work in Morocco*. As compared to the women, both men present themselves as more marginal to the societies they study.

12. Geertz, *Local Knowledge*, p. 70. For a critique of the way Geertz uses literary techniques to establish his authority as an ethnographer, see Vincent Crapanzano, "Hermes' Dilemma."

13. Peter Winch, *The Idea of Social Science*, chap. 5.

14. See Talal Asad, ed., *Anthropology and the Colonial Encounter*, and James Clifford and George Marcus, *Writing Culture*.

15. See, for example, Michel Foucault, *Discipline and Punish* and *Power/Knowledge*.

16. I owe this distinction to Erik Wright.

17. C. Wright Mills, *The Sociological Imagination*, chap. 1.

18. Erving Goffman, "The Interaction Order."

CHAPTER TWO

1. See Barney Glaser and Anselm Strauss, *The Discovery of Grounded Theory*. In a slight qualification of the original disparagement of "existing theory," Strauss has argued that there is no reason not to use extant theory from the outset, provided that this is also grounded theory and leads to the same methods of collecting, categorizing, and analyzing of data; see Strauss, *Qualitative Analysis for Social Scientists*, pp. 13–14, 306–11.

2. Glaser and Strauss, *The Discovery of Grounded Theory*, p. 32.

3. There is an obvious tension between the pursuit of formal theory and the idea of grounding theory in empirical reality. It reflects the tension within symbolic interactionism between the urge to generalize across social situations and sensitivity to the particularity of agency and structure as an emergent, open-ended, and indeterminate process. Herbert Blumer, for example, makes clear that symbolic interactionism is at odds with the "variable analysis" of formal theory advocated by Glaser and Strauss; see Blumer, *Symbolic Interactionism*, chap. 7. In an earlier book, *Mirrors and Masks*, Strauss presents an open and fluid perspective on the construction of identity and plays down generalization. The tension between sensitivity to the particular context and the pursuit of generality and abstraction is excellently portrayed in Charles Ragin's *The Comparative Method*. For an incisive account of the methodological and philosophical underpinnings of symbolic interactionism see Dmitri Shalin, "Pragmatism and Social Interactionism."

4. In order to enroll in the seminar, students had to present me with a prospectus describing what they expected to find in their chosen field site and why. In this way, when they spent time there, they were more easily surprised by what they discovered and thus forced to ask why their expectations had been wrong.

5. The adoption of our approach to theory reconstruction does not imply the use of the extended case method. It is quite possible to reconstruct theory on the basis of discovered anomalies *without* extending out, instead confining oneself to the structure and dynamics of the micro situation. On the other hand the extended case method, since it depends on constituting social phenomena in their particularity, relies on existing theory that highlights the situation as anomalous. To put it another way, the extended case method cannot be pursued by applying the principles of grounded theory. Discovering theory through generalization across social situations necessarily abstracts from time and space and brackets the determining macro context. Whereas the extended case method identifies a particular phenomenon as the product of historically specific causes, grounded theory systematically removes particularity.

6. The approach adopted here is similar to what Lazarsfeld called "deviant case analysis," in which deviant cases are used to refine theoretical structures by introducing additional variables or refine the measurement of variables used in locating deviant cases. While deviant case analysis exploits anomalies when they arise, it does not go so far as to advocate the search for theories that constitute

cases as anomalous. See Patricia Kendall and Katherine M. Wolf, "The Two Purposes of Deviant Case Analysis."

7. Popper distinguishes scientific from nonscientific theory on the basis of its falsifiability and not on the basis of its verification. Science does not proceed through the induction of empirical regularities from a number of instances but through the postulation of theories that can be falsified. Whereas induction leads to the search for confirming instances and thus to theories that are highly probable and therefore uninteresting, Popper views science as a succession of bold conjectures and their refutation. He urges us to put interesting, improbable theories to the hardest tests in the hope that they will survive. See particularly his *The Logic of Scientific Discovery* and *Conjectures and Refutations*.

8. Faced with an anomaly we might simply save a theory without reconstruction by a number of stratagems. One is *exception-barring*, in which we claim that the exception is not what we thought it was; that is, we redefine the situation so that it is no longer an exception. So if socialist countries do not realize the promises of Marxist theory we redefine them as exhibiting a form of capitalism ("state capitalism"). Another strategy is to *limit the scope* of the theory, that is, to redefine the theory. Instead of redefining socialist countries as some variant of capitalism, we simply say that Marxist theory doesn't apply to socialist countries. Neither of these "saving" strategies improves the theory itself. The preferred strategy is to rebuild the theory by introducing an auxiliary hypothesis to explain the anomaly. Ideally the auxiliary hypothesis should (1) be consistent with most of the major premises of the theory it is seeking to reconstruct; (2) explain everything the old theory explained as well as the anomaly; (3) lead to new anticipations rather than merely succeed as a patching-up operation. (4) Empirical observation should corroborate at least some of these new anticipations as new facts. These are only criteria for evaluating auxiliary hypotheses; they are very rarely achieved. I am here following Imre Lakatos's reconstruction of the Popperian framework in his *Proofs and Refutations* and *The Methodology of Scientific Research Programmes*.

9. Alvin Gouldner, *Patterns of Industrial Bureaucracy*.

10. Glaser and Strauss, *The Discovery of Grounded Theory*, p. 37.

11. See Ralph Turner, ed., *Robert E. Park on Social Control and Collective Behavior*, and Neil Smelser, *Theory of Collective Behavior*.

12. See Charles Tilly, *From Mobilization to Revolution* and *The Vendée*, and Charles Tilly, Louise Tilly, and Richard Tilly, *The Rebellious Century, 1830–1930*.

13. For an overview see, for example, the excellent collection of articles by Jean Cohen, Charles Tilly, Alain Touraine, Alberto Meliucci, Claus Offe, and Klaus Eder in *Social Research* 52, no. 4 (1985).

14. Everett Hughes, *Men and Their Work*, p. 48.

15. James O'Connor, *The Fiscal Crisis of the State*.

16. Saskia Sassen, *The Mobility of Labor and Capital*.

17. See, for example, Paul Willis, *Learning to Labour*; John Ogbu, *Minority Education and Caste*; Ann Swidler, *Organization Without Authority*; Jay MacLeod, *Ain't No Makin' It*; and Douglas Foley, *Learning Capitalist Culture*.

18. Pierre Bourdieu and Jean Claude Passeron, *Reproduction in Education, Society, and Culture*, and Basil Bernstein, *Class, Codes and Control*.

19. Alvin W. Gouldner, "The Sociologist as Partisan."
20. Alvin W. Gouldner, *The Coming Crisis of Western Sociology*, pp. 54–60, 488–500.

INTRODUCTION TO PART 1

1. Alain Touraine, *Return of the Actor*, p. 65.

CHAPTER THREE

I'm grateful for comments, challenges, and support along the way from Steven Epstein, David Kirp, Kim Voss, Tomas Almaguer, William Gamson, Zelda Gamson, and reviewers from *Social Problems*. Thanks also to the members of ACT UP/San Francisco.

1. *Newsweek*, "Acting Up to Fight AIDS."
2. Susan Sontag, "AIDS and Its Metaphors," p. 89.
3. See, for example, Neil Smelser, *Theory of Collective Behavior*.
4. Ibid., p. 8.
5. Jean L. Cohen, "Strategy or Identity"; Doug McAdam, *Political Process and the Development of Black Insurgency, 1930–1970*.
6. See John McCarthy and Mayer Zald, "Resource Mobilization and Social Movements"; Anthony Oberschall, *Social Conflict and Social Movements*; Charles Tilly, *From Mobilization to Revolution*; and J. Craig Jenkins, "Sociopolitical Movements."
7. See Cohen, "Strategy or Identity"; Herbert Kitschelt, "New Social Movements in West Germany and the United States"; Klaus Eder, "The 'New Social Movements' "; Jürgen Habermas, "New Social Movements"; Claus Offe, "The New Social Movements"; and Alain Touraine, "An Introduction to the Study of Social Movements."
8. See, for example, McAdam, *Political Process and Black Insurgency*.
9. See Eder, "The 'New Social Movements' "; and Hanspeter Kreisi, "New Social Movements and the New Class in the Netherlands."
10. Offe, "The New Social Movements," p. 832.
11. Ibid.
12. Habermas, "New Social Movements," p. 33.
13. Eder, "The 'New Social Movements,' " p. 879.
14. Touraine, "Introduction to the Study of New Social Movements," p. 766.
15. Cohen, "Strategy or Identity," p. 664.
16. Ibid., p. 665.
17. Unless otherwise noted, quotations and descriptions of actions are drawn from my field notes from September 1988 through January 1989 (ACT UP weekly general meetings; Media Committee weekly meetings and activities, and other committee meetings; ACT NOW AIDS Activism Conference, October 8–11, 1988, Washington, D.C.; ACT UP/San Francisco actions).
18. Jesse Green, "Shticks and Stones."
19. ACT UP/San Francisco, "Our Goals and Demands."

20. "ACT UP PISD Caucus."

21. *Newsweek*, "Acting Up to Fight AIDS."

22. Dennis Altman, *AIDS in the Mind of America*, p. 105.

23. Reported in "Workshop on Creative Actions," ACT NOW Conference, Washington, D.C., October 8, 1988.

24. Why so many women are attracted to the AIDS movement is an interesting question to which I've accumulated only brief, speculative answers: some because their friends are dying, some because of a history working in health politics through women's health issues. One woman suggested an answer that seems to run deeper, and along the lines suggested by this study. Oppression through AIDS, she said, is the most severe end of a spectrum of violence to which "all gay people are subject." For her, while silence might not mean literal death, it would mean a symbolic death (not being allowed to live "as me").

25. Altman, *AIDS in the Mind of America*, p. 90.

26. "Media Workshop" at ACT NOW Conference in Washington, D.C., October 8, 1988.

27. "The AIDS Treatment Advocacy Project," proposal drafted for ACT NOW Conference, September 1988, p. 1.

28. Michel Foucault, *Discipline and Punish*, pp. 178–79.

29. Ibid., p. 183.

30. Erving Goffman, *Stigma*; and Edwin Lemert, *Human Deviance, Social Problems, and Social Control*, p. 17.

31. John I. Kitsuse, "Coming Out All Over," p. 5.

32. Ibid., p. 9.

33. See Michael Omi and Howard Winant, *Racial Formation in the United States*, pp. 89ff.

34. Diane Johnson and John F. Murray, "AIDS Without End."

35. For sample reporting on this action, see Susan Okie, "AIDS Coalition Targets FDA for Demonstration"; and Mike Connolly and George Raine, "50 AIDS Activists Arrested at FDA."

36. See Randy Shilts, *And the Band Played On*.

37. Jim Eigo, Mark Harrington, Iris Long, Margaret McCarthy, Stephen Spinella, and Rick Sugden, "FDA Action Handbook" (manuscript prepared for October 11 action at the Food and Drug Administration, 1988).

38. The activist response of Black communities to AIDS has differed greatly from that in gay communities, and this merits careful examination not allowed for here. The lag in Black and Hispanic activism has been attributed by one observer to a combination of lack of material and political resources (minority PWAs are disproportionately lower class or underclass) and "denial" on the part of minority leadership (because of the dangers posed by feeding racism with the stigma of disease, and because of strong antigay sentiments in Black and Hispanic cultures). See Richard Goldstein, "AIDS and Race."

39. Ken Plummer, "Organizing AIDS," p. 45.

40. Simon Watney, *Policing Desire*, p. 126.

41. Jan Zita Grover, "AIDS: Keywords," pp. 21, 25.

42. The figure of the irresponsible killer-victim was popularized by Randy Shilts in the character of Gaetan Dugas, an airline steward Shilts labels "Patient

Zero," charging that he knowingly spread the virus throughout the continent. For a critique of Shilts, see Douglas Crimp, "How to Have Promiscuity in an Epidemic."

43. Dave Ford, " 'Midnight Caller' Script Provokes Gay Activists' Ire."

44. The mass media clearly play a very central and complex role in contemporary activism, an examination of which is unfortunately beyond our scope. See, for example, Todd Gitlin, *The Whole World Is Watching*. It is likely that much of the escalation of symbol play comes from the need by social movements to compete for attention in an increasingly message-dense environment; this does not explain the content of those symbols, though, nor does it explain why the media at times become explicit enemies.

45. See Grover, "AIDS: Keywords."

46. Sander Gilman, "AIDS and Syphilis."

47. Watney, *Policing Desire*, p. 54.

48. One would also expect that the particular balances found in a particular city would be related to the degree of visibility of enemies. New York's ACT UP, for example, is in general more media-oriented and savvy than San Francisco's. Whereas in New York, AIDS policy was "little more than a laundry list of unmet challenges, unheeded pleas, and programs not undertaken" (Shilts, *And the Band Played On*, p. 276), San Francisco's government was more responsive much more quickly: as early as 1982, "nearly 20 percent of the money committed to fighting the AIDS epidemic for the entire United States, including all the science and epidemiology expenditures by the U.S. government . . . was pledged by the city and county of San Francisco" (ibid., p. 188). In this context, it makes sense to find a more highly rationalized and focused orientation in New York and other cities with less liberal responses to the epidemic: The enemies are easier to find and focus on.

49. Steven Epstein, "Gay Politics, Ethnic Identity," p. 19.

50. Ibid., p. 48.

51. Paula A. Treichler, "AIDS, Homophobia, and Biomedical Discourse," pp. 42, 63.

52. Touraine, "Introduction to the Study of Social Movements," p. 779.

53. Cohen, "Strategy or Identity," p. 685.

CHAPTER FOUR

I thank the members of SANE/Freeze, BAPT, and Beyond War for graciously accepting me into their organizations. My appreciation also goes to Hugh Gusterson; I benefited greatly from our discussions. And finally many thanks to William Kornhauser for his comments on this paper.

1. Jean L. Cohen, "Strategy or Identity," pp. 664, 667.

2. As one member put it, "Beyond War is my church." Many in the organization express a hunger for rituals that would reflect the "strong spiritual component to what Beyond War does." One woman even found herself developing a ritual for her Beyond War team. She surrounded a globe with votive candles, and each person lit a candle as they made a wish for the earth. The

children, in particular, seemed to respond to this ritual, since they had grown up "with the image of the globe as an icon of sorts." There is also much discussion of a "new cosmology" and attempts to discover a "mythology for the modern world."

3. The major BW principles: "I will resolve conflict; I will not use violence; I will maintain a spirit of goodwill toward others; I will work with others to build a world beyond war; I will not preoccupy myself with enemies."

4. "The process of building a world beyond war begins with the acknowledgment that war is obsolete and that we are one. Change, then, requires a decision to reject totally the obsolete and to commit totally to build upon the new identification. Decision means "to cut" (-cision) "away from" (de-), to reject forever. . . . Each of us must decide to adopt the new mode of thinking as the basis of his or her life." (From the "Beyond War Handbook for Communicators")

5. Many Beyond War members find that travel or cross-cultural experiences are a way of doing this, that immersion in other cultures gives them "the opportunity to experience oneness with all people and with the earth," if the encounters are entered into in the right spirit. One Beyond War volunteer described a project he had been part of in Jamaica, constructing a community building with local residents. He felt that it was very important to approach the project from the posture of "server/learner," as opposed to the typically Western and somewhat arrogant role of "leader/teacher." This ensured that volunteers did not go down there to help "them," but rather to develop an empathic understanding with them—to recognize their oneness.

6. Debriefings of the test site action, for example, were basically an evaluation of group process rather than the efficacy of the protest.

7. Uncharacteristically, at one weekend meeting I attended, the agenda had not been predetermined by group leaders. Participants had a hard time adapting to the lack of direction and had some difficulty facilitating their own meeting.

8. I must hasten to point out that the unreflexivity about power within the organization does not automatically lead to hierarchical structures and conformity, but it makes the group vulnerable to internal domination and control.

9. Andrew Arato and Jean Cohen, "Civil Society and Social Theory."

10. Jürgen Habermas, *The Theory of Communicative Action*, vol. 2, *Lifeworld and System*, p. 396.

11. Arato and Cohen, "Civil Society and Social Theory"; Jean L. Cohen, *Class and Civil Society*.

12. Cohen, *Class and Civil Society*.

13. R. J. Lifton, "Beyond Psychic Numbing"; John Mack, "Psychosocial Effects of the Nuclear Arms Race"; Michael Newcomb, "Nuclear Attitudes and Reactions."

14. Joel Kovel, *Against the State of Nuclear Terror*, p. 13.

15. Arato and Cohen, "Civil Society and Social Theory."

16. Alain Touraine, *Return of the Actor*, pp. 106–9.

CHAPTER FIVE

I am grateful to the union members and local staff people who allowed me to participate in the daily life of the union and generously shared their thoughtful reflections on welfare work and unionism. Conversations with Elizabeth Armstrong, Jens Hillmer, Anand Swaminathan, and Laura Weide helped me to make sense out of the confusing tangle of data collected in my field notes. Paul Johnston provided highly relevant insights into public-sector unionism and doing field work in unions. Finally, the staff of the University of California, Berkeley Center for Labor Research and Education, all former or current labor organizers, provided a unique education in the past and contemporary tasks of the labor movement.

1. Although all applicants for social work positions must have a Masters in Social Work (MSW), some social workers without professional degrees were grandfathered in under previous guidelines.

2. This argument was first made by James O'Connor, *The Fiscal Crisis of the State*, chap. 9. Following O'Connor, Paul Johnston also suggested that public-sector workers and state clients might potentially join together; see his "The Promise of Public Sector Unionism" and also Dale L. Johnson and Christine O'Donnell, "The Accumulation Crisis and Service Professionals." Johnson extended his analysis of the "proletarianization" of service work in "The Social Unity and Fractionalization of the Middle Class."

3. Although most contemporary public-sector labor unions have come to resemble traditional private-sector unions, O'Connor continues to identify state welfare work as a promising catalyst for allied labor and client movements. In *Accumulation Crisis*, O'Connor asserts that noncommodified state services, necessary to legitimate the capitalist economy, have paradoxically politicized clients' and workers' struggles. Workers' and clients' movements have a common material base in the state sector that supports them, and thus they will be waged together in reference to state bureaucracies.

4. [Wisconsin] Legislative Reference Bureau, "Welfare Reform."

5. Russell K. Schutt, *Organization in a Changing Environment*, p. 41. A rapidly expanding welfare system in the 1960s necessitated an influx of welfare workers. Caseworkers, who needed only an undergraduate degree, filled these positions. Labor shortages led some states to relax the education requirement to a four-year degree in any subject and to hire caseworkers who had no formal training in social work.

6. One of the outcomes of the 1971 California welfare reform—which was federally mandated several years later—was to reduce "inefficiency" in welfare agencies by separating eligibility from services. Most caseworkers protested the division on the grounds that it would reduce services and cut jobs. Initially, however, some unionists voiced qualified support for the division because it offered the prospect of making services voluntary: Welfare clients who didn't want interference from caseworkers wouldn't have to tolerate it. Social workers union newsletter, March 3, 1969.

7. Frances Fox Piven and Richard A. Cloward write: "State and local welfare officials were influenced by the rhetoric on poverty and injustice. . . . Moreover,

relief officials (and the political leaders to whom they reported) were frightened of rioting"; *Poor People's Movements*, p. 274.

8. Schutt, *Organization in a Changing Environment*, pp. 109–10.

9. Piven and Cloward, both active in welfare rights organizing during this period, have argued in *Poor People's Movements* that caseworkers became economic advocates for clients because clients organized their demands. However, also crucial to the widespread practice of caseworker advocacy was its legitimacy in the public agency.

10. This case, which appeared in the union newsletter, was cited to illustrate a "typical" series of caseworkers' duties.

11. The vast majority of caseworkers had been white. Today, roughly half of the professional social workers are white, and the other half are Black, Hispanic, or Asian. There is no overt racial antagonism between EWs and MSWs who are union activists, probably because Blacks, whites, and Hispanics are represented by both EWs and MSWs on the union's executive board. However, the amount of racial prejudice experienced by EWs on the job far outweighs that of MSWs. It is rare for Black, Hispanic, or Asian MSWs to hear, for example, racist slurs from their supervisor.

12. Most of the caseworkers who did not have an MSW were, if they had sufficient seniority, grandfathered in under the new social worker classification requirements. Of course, most of the activist caseworkers had been working for welfare agencies only for a short time, so they lost their social work jobs. Some of them, however, continued to work for the county as EWs.

13. Several of the social workers active in the union now participated in the early union movements with clients, so this new professional view of clients and nonconfrontational negotiation is not simply indicative of individual personalities. It is a reflection, rather, of the change in work organization.

14. Client advocacy groups, which are numerous in Mandana County, actively pursue organizing efforts with the local. In the recent past, a network of homeless advocates, including legal aid attorneys and members of the homeless union, have sought the cooperation of Local 222. Welfare recipients, who have representatives on a county committee on the new workfare program, have also sought the endorsement of Local 222. Though union staff encourage alliances between the workers and these clients, rank-and-file unionists are usually uninterested.

15. "W.O.D." stands for "Worker-of-the-Day," a supervisory duty that rotates among social workers when managers are out of the office. Social workers receive no additional pay for assuming these unwanted duties, and the assignment is highly unpopular.

16. It is evident here that social workers' professional authority, rather than providing any real opposition to bureaucratic control, is given to MSWs by managers. Social workers in the welfare agency do not have what we tend to think of as professional control, such as the right to be supervised and judged only by one's professional colleagues, or the right to privacy for one's client. Instead, social workers have a kind of discretion that does not seriously challenge the managerial prerogative, such as flexible schedules and reduced clerical duties.

17. In *Street-Level Bureaucracy* Michael Lipsky suggests that state service workers who must distribute dwindling and insufficient funds organize their work to restrict or ration services to clients.

18. Racist slurs are a language or mode of harassment commonly deployed by white managers. Many EWs I spoke with had a direct experience with racist treatment. One Black EW, after being moved to a new unit, received a barrage of racist comments from her immediate supervisor. Having been politicized in another work setting in which legal action was taken against her employer, she began keeping a journal of the comments and actions taken against her. When she went public with her complaint and began to bring a lawsuit against the county, many other EWs came forward with stories of racist harassment. Other EWs commented that white supervisors typically don't acknowledge or greet women of color when they see them outside the office. Seating patterns in lounges and cafeterias demonstrate segregation along racial lines.

19. This is not to say that probing for underlying tensions and conflicts in a setting is unimportant. I am confident that had I continued to listen, to learn the language and less accessible intersubjective meanings attached to gender, I could have told a story about gender politics in the union. But I ultimately attended to what was most compelling to me in the field site.

CHAPTER SIX

I thank Ann Swidler, J. Allen Whitt, and collective members for their helpful comments on my paper. I am deeply indebted to the members of the collective bakery who gave me persmission to "study" them, generously shared their precious space and time with me, and introduced me to really good bread.

1. Wholly Grains bakery is the fictitious name I have chosen for the collective bakery in which I did my field work. People's Co-ops is also a fictitious name.

2. *Worker cooperative* is the term used to describe organizations that are governed by two basic principles: the democratic control of the workplace and worker ownership. I use the term *collective* in this chapter to describe worker cooperatives that emerged largely out of the student movement of the 1960s.

3. Jackall and Crain see collectivists as "another cycle in the long history of youthful revolt in this century against the cultural and social consequences of the triumph of industrial capitalism." Robert Jackall and Joyce Crain, "The Shape of the Small Worker Cooperative Movement," p. 95.

4. Frank Lindenfeld and Joyce Rothschild-Whitt, eds. *Workplace Democracy and Social Change.*

5. Data for 1970 from Robert Jackall and Henry Levin, eds., *Worker Cooperatives in America,* p. 88. Data for 1975 from Joyce Rothschild and J. Allen Whitt, *The Cooperative Workplace,* p. 11.

6. There is some evidence that the failure rate of collectives is no greater than that of small businesses in the United States in general. See Jackall and Crain, "The Shape of the Small Worker Cooperative Movement," p. 97.

7. This demographic picture is a configuration consistently observed in other collectives. Jackall and Levin, *Worker Cooperatives in America,* p. 96.

8. Rothschild and Whitt, *The Cooperative Workplace*, p. 55. These researchers see homogeneity as an important mechanism of social control within collectivist organizations where decisions are made by consensus.

9. Rothschild and Whitt, *The Cooperative Workplace*, p. 1.

10. Ibid., p. 56.

11. Jackall and Levin, *Worker Cooperatives in America*, p. 6.

12. For studies of failures see, for example, Raymond Russell, *Sharing Ownership in the Workplace*; Lindenfeld and Rothschild-Whitt, *Workplace Democracy and Social Change*; and Daniel Zwerdling, *Workplace Democracy*. For studies of successes see, for example, Robert Jackall, "Paradoxes of Collective Work" and Rothschild and Whitt, *The Cooperative Workplace*.

13. For example, Jackall's "Paradoxes of Collective Work" emphasizes the internal dynamics of formal and informal mechanisms for mediating conflict among members. Zelda Gamson and Henry Levin, in "Obstacles to the Survival of Democratic Workplaces," focus on the lack of a common culture in the workplace and of experience in democratic decision making. External factors such as economic pressures and capital investment are stressed by Russell in *Sharing Ownership in the Workplace* and by Zwerdling in *Workplace Democracy*.

14. *Bay Area Directory of Collectives*, p. ii.

15. Ibid., p. 21.

16. I thank Ann Robertson, a member of our seminar who had at one time been a member of another collective, for this insight.

17. The alternative food stores are the traditional outlets for producers such as Wholly Grains. Yet on the day that I went out on delivery the fewest stops were at these stores, and most of the deliveries were made to markets that have become customers only within the last few years.

18. *The New York Times* (March 15, 1989), for instance, reported one food shopper as saying, "I'm afraid to eat anything. The cholesterol will kill you, the fish is full of mercury and the chicken has hormones. What next."

19. Alice Z. Cuneo, "A Look at the Man Behind Real Food."

20. They do not of course totally ignore the market, and they do take advantage of certain health food fads. Shortly after oat bran was hailed in the mass media as a miracle food, the bakery came out with oat bran bread and muffins.

21. This statement was taken from a brochure put out by the Alternatives Center, which states that its primary purpose is "to help develop and improve the effectiveness of democratic organizations, including cooperatives, Employee Stock Ownership Plans with significant worker control, and non-profit organizations governed by their membership, including the staff."

22. From my field work I concluded that a pattern of sex segregation into specific occupations identified as male or female within the workplace was not a salient feature of the division of labor in the collective either in the delivery shift or in any other sector of the enterprise.

23. Jackall and Levin, *Worker Cooperatives*, pp. 281, 282.

24. Michael Piore and Charles Sabel, in *The Second Industrial Divide*, define mass production as "the use of special-purpose (product specific) machines and of semi-skilled workers to produce standardized goods" (p. 4).

25. Ibid., p. 17.

INTRODUCTION TO PART 3

1. Saskia Sassen, *The Mobility of Labor and Capital*.
2. James Fallow, "The New Immigrants"; Nathan Glazer, *Ethnic Dilemmas: 1964–1982*.
3. Sassen, *The Mobility of Labor and Capital*.
4. Irene Diamond, ed., *Families, Politics and Public Policy*.
5. Alejandro Portes and Robert Bach, *Latin Journey*.

CHAPTER SEVEN

I thank the members of Choices and Amigos for the warmth, tolerance, and good humor with which they welcomed me into their midst. I also thank John Lie for supporting me in pushing the limits of my analysis, and Mary Romero for insightful comments on the manuscript.

1. The names of the cooperatives and people discussed here are fictional. All conversations quoted in this chapter—except for those with the staff at Choices and the classroom exercises—were conducted in Spanish.

2. Michael Piore, *Birds of Passage*; Judith Rollins, *Between Women*.

3. One of the foremost proponents of this position is Thomas Sowell. For instance, in *Ethnic America*, he attributes the fact that Irish immigrants often worked as domestic servants, whereas Italian immigrants generally did not, to a divergence in cultural attitudes toward gender and family. See Stephen Steinberg, *The Ethnic Myth*, for an alternate explanation of this history based on dramatic differences in the gender composition of the two immigrant flows.

4. Saskia Sassen, *The Mobility of Labor and Capital*; Saskia Sassen-Koob, "New York City: Economic Restructuring and Immigration," "Changing Composition and Labor Market Location of Hispanic Immigrants in New York City, 1960–1980," "Labor Migrations and the New International Division of Labor," and "Immigrant and Minority Workers in the Organization of the Labor Process."

5. In *The Mobility of Labor and Capital* Sassen points out that the distribution of immigrants' occupations in their countries of origin is significantly more "bimodal" than is the distribution of their occupations in the United States. Once here, there is a convergence between those of distinct occupational statuses upon a limited set of jobs. She comments: "The basic factor at work is not so much immigrants' failure or success to carry out their intended occupations, but the characteristics of the occupational structure in the U.S. and the kinds of labor needs it generates" (p. 76).

6. Steven Wallace, "Central American and Mexican Immigrant Characteristics and Economic Incorporation in California."

7. The group officially accepts both men and women. However, it is so difficult to find jobs for men that they are generally put on a waiting list and very few are in the group at any given time. Given the difference in the struc-

ture of the labor market for men and women, I only discuss the women in this paper.

8. The difference in number of years in this country and the class background of members of the two groups is striking. The difference in tenure in this country is primarily a reflection of the fact that Central Americans tend to immigrate during their late twenties. Thus, in selecting for older women, Choices also effectively selects for those who have been here longer. Similarly, earlier immigrants from Central America tended to come from a somewhat higher class background than the compatriots they left behind. (On these demographic issues see Wallace, "Central American and Mexican Immigrant Characteristics.") In recent years, according to groups working with refugees in the Bay Area, these disparities have evaporated. Thus, the difference in class background of the two cooperatives' members reflects shifts in the demographic composition of immigrant flows from Central America over time and is also an artifact of Choices' over-forty membership criterion.

9. Evelyn Nakano Glenn, *Issei, Nissei, War Bride.*

10. Others have noted that an important strategy in transforming domestic work is the elimination of certain tasks. In "Sisterhood and Domestic Service" Mary Romero comments: "Chicana domestics use several methods to define themselves as professional housecleaners. One method involves eliminating personal services, such as babysitting, laundry and ironing" (p. 339).

11. See Magali Sarfatti Larson, *The Rise of Professionalism*, p. 50. I use the term *professionalization project* in Larson's sense to refer to an occupation's ongoing effort to increase its status, rather than to refer to an occupation's already-achieved status. My usage departs from Larson's in that he generally uses the concept to discuss occupations that involve higher education and external credentialing. In this sense, my use of the term in the context of a low-status occupation is unusual. Nonetheless, since the goal of professionalization is to raise the status of an occupation by redefining the work as skilled and getting external support for this definition, to refuse to apply the term to any occupation that has not already gained this external support is to conflate success with "truth." Any sense we have that this strategy cannot be used in currently low-status occupations is a better indication of the overwhelming success of those who have pursued this strategy in the past than it is of the futility of such efforts among those beginning the attempt today.

12. Even the group's relatively high wage scale (for Latina workers) communicates members' professionalism to prospective employers. It not only weeds out those with less money to spare but serves as a marker for those with more discretionary income that there is something worth paying for. In commenting on the impact of raising prices at Choices, the group's first staff person observed: "The lower our prices, the more calls I got saying 'Why should they [co-op members] get $5 when I can get an English-speaking girl who will do it for $4?' It seems to me that if people pay more, they think they're getting something better."

13. For a more general discussion of this relationship see John Lie, "Visualizing the Invisible Hand."

14. In her work on Chicana domestic workers in the Southwest, Mary

Romero also found them "modernizing" and "professionalizing" the occupation; see her "Chicanas Modernize Domestic Service" and "Sisterhood and Domestic Service." What is particularly interesting about Romero's work is that although the women she interviewed were not members of a formal collective, she saw their membership in an "informal network" as a central element in this process. "The controlled environment created by the use of the informal network provides the avenue for Chicanas to establish their self-definition as experts" ("Chicanas Modernize Domestic Service," p. 332).

15. Phyllis Palmer, "Housework and Domestic Labor," p. 87. She notes that eight projects were set up by the National Council of Household Employment in 1964 to create a pool of "certified" domestic workers. Their goal was to simultaneously improve the status of Black domestic workers and increase the amount of help available to (white) working wives and mothers. The projects were never able to break even and eventually folded. In light of the discussion that follows concerning the changing character of domestic work over the last three decades, both the timing and the failure of these projects take on a new significance.

16. Rollins, *Between Women*.

17. Glenn, *Issei, Nissei, War Bride*; Rollins, *Between Women*.

18. Bonnie Thorton Dill, " 'Making Your Job Good Yourself.' "

19. Rollins, *Between Women*, p. 69.

20. Ibid.

21. Palmer, "Housework and Domestic Labor."

22. Mary Jo McConahay, "The Intimate Experiment"; James Fallow, "The New Immigrants"; Manuel Castells, "Immigrant Workers and Class Struggles in Advanced Capitalism"; Sassen, *The Mobility of Labor and Capital*; Piore, *Birds of Passage*.

23. Castells, "Immigrant Workers and Class Struggles"; Sassen, *The Mobility of Labor and Capital*; Piore, *Birds of Passage*.

CHAPTER EIGHT

I thank Eric Crystal for providing continuous encouragement and academic guidance during my time at Berkeley and Jean Longmire at the University of the Pacific in Stockton for supporting me in many ways. Last, but by no means least, I thank all the Cambodian people I met. Their warmth and care gave energy to my work and sustained my commitment to the project.

1. These events occurred at the end of my field work.

2. *Stockton Record*, January 21, 1989.

3. Robert L. Bach and Rita Carroll-Seguin, "Labor Force Participation, Household Composition and Sponsorship Among Southeast Asian Refugees," p. 400.

4. Christine R. Finnan and Rhonda Ann Cooperstein, *Southeast Asian Refugee Resettlement at the Local Level*.

5. I made observations on the life of people in Stockton's Cambodian ethnic enclaves by participating in Cambodian language classes, attending meetings

and conferences, and occasionally helping in the language school office. I stayed with several Cambodian families, both in private homes and in the large apartment blocks. I also participated in community activities such as ESL classes, wedding ceremonies, a funeral, various religious gatherings (Buddhist, Christian, and Mormon), cultural celebrations, and daily family activities. I use pseudonyms throughout this chapter.

6. California Department of Finance, Population Research Unit, *Estimates of Refugees in California Counties and the State: 1987.*

7. Ibid.

8. *Stockton Record,* Feb. 22, 1989.

9. Darrel Montero, *Vietnamese Americans.* Montero characterizes the movement of the Vietnamese, the largest group among the Indochinese refugees, as "spontaneous international migration." Their situation in leaving the homeland was "acute," since they fled in the wake of massive political and military pressure. But their professional background and familiarity with Western culture was more "anticipatory" in character, since many of them were somewhat prepared for the new life before leaving their homeland. Cambodians, on the other hand, can more properly be classified as "acute" refugees according to the categorization found in E. F. Kunz, "The Refugees in Flight." Consequently, they may be expected to face more difficult problems of adjustment in their new country.

10. An ethnic enclave is sometimes interchangeably referred to as an ethnic neighborhood. See Finnan and Cooperstein, *Southeast Asian Refugee Resettlement*; Jose Szapocznik and William Kurtines, "Acculturation, Biculturalism and Adjustment Among Cuban Americans"; and Kenneth L. Wilson and Alejandro Portes, "Immigrant Enclaves." Here I use *ethnic enclave* to mean a concentrated form, especially geographically, of a refugee ethnic community, which Finnan and Cooperstein define as (1) consisting of people of a single ethnic origin who share their country of origin, language, resettlement experience, and cultural background including values and norms; (2) centered in a certain locality, but also including refugees living in other localities in the United States or even other countries; and (3) constituted of members who provide tangible and intangible support to each other—for example, emotional, social, cultural, spiritual, economic, or political support; a sense of identity; and an interpretative framework.

11. David Haines, Dorothy Rutherford, and Patrick Thomas, "Family and Community Among Vietnamese Refugees"; David Haines, "Southeast Asian Refugees in the United States"; Paul J. Strand and Woodrow Jones, Jr., *Indochinese Refugees in America.*

12. Historically, ethnic enclaves have served as an important stepping stone between the old culture and the life in the new country. See Harry H. L. Kitano, *Japanese Americans*; Montero, *Vietnamese Americans*; Gene Levine and Colbert Rhodes, *The Japanese American Community.* The early Asian immigrants to America, such as Japanese and Chinese, moved directly from the homeland to existing ethnic enclaves in the new country. In contrast, the most recent refugee groups had no enclaves waiting for them, and thus had to rapidly form

ethnic enclaves of their own under different conditions. This, in part, accounts for the instability and secondary migration.

13. More than one in five (21.7 percent) Cambodian women are widows, while relatively few (3.1 percent) Vietnamese women are (Asian Community Mental Health Services, *The California Southeast Asian Mental Health Needs Assessment*, 1987). Thus, the percentage of female-headed families is much higher among Cambodians than for any other Indochinese refugee group.

14. Cambodians were massacred in huge numbers during the Pol Pot regime (1975–1979). In California, posttraumatic stress disorder is more prevalent among Cambodians (16.3 percent of the sample) than among other groups such as Lao (11.5 percent) and Hmong (10.3 percent). As a consequence, both physical and mental health services are most needed by the Cambodian population. See Asian Community Mental Health Services, *Mental Health Needs Assessment*.

15. Gail Paradise Kelly, *From Vietnam to America*.

16. Asian Community Mental Health Services, *Mental Health Needs Assessment*.

17. *Stockton Record*, February 19, 1989.

18. *Stockton Record*, February 21, 1989.

19. Finnan and Cooperstein, *Southeast Asian Refugee Resettlement*.

20. For more detailed description of traditional gender roles, see David J. Steinberg, ed., *Cambodia*; May Ebihara, "Khmer Village Women in Cambodia"; Le Xuan Khoa and John Vandeusen, "Southeast Asian Social and Cultural Customs," parts 1 and 2.

21. The development of ethnic businesses in enclaves requires the presence of immigrants with some capital and business skills; see Wilson and Portes, "Immigrant Enclaves"; Indochinese Community Center, *Entrepreneurship Among Southeast Asian Refugees*. Among the recent immigrants, it is reported that such enclave business is much less likely to occur among Cambodians than Vietnamese. See Indochinese Community Center, *Entrepreneurship*; Finnan and Cooperstein, *Southeast Asian Refugee Resettlement*. Businesses are often limited to localities in which a large number of Cambodians are living, since relatively few individual Cambodians have the skills and capital needed for such enterprises. Moreover, later migrants must compete with earlier ethnic groups who have already opened stores.

22. Strand and Jones, *Indochinese Refugees in America*.

23. *Stockton Record*, February 20, 1989.

24. Among Vietnamese the importance of the wife in the family has increased. There has been a drastic downward mobility in employment patterns among men, while upward mobility has occurred for women. A clear increase in labor force participation by Vietnamese women and a trend of changes in gender relationships have also been observed. See Kasumi K. Hirayama, "Effects of the Employment of Vietnamese Refugee Wives on Their Family Roles and Mental Health"; Lani Davison, "Women Refugees"; Ingrid Walter, "One Year After Arrival"; Haines, "Southeast Asian Refugees in the United States."

25. Strand and Jones, *Indochinese Refugees in America*; Bach and Carroll-Seguin, "Labor Force Participation."

CHAPTER NINE

I would like to acknowledge, with sincere thanks and respect, the teachers and students of Emerald Junior High who helped me write this essay.

1. Roald Dahl, *Boy*, pp. 108 and 111.

2. Ibid., pp. 110–11. To underscore the truthfulness of his account, Dahl explains: "An autobiography is a book a person writes about his own life and it is usually full of all sorts of boring details. This is not an autobiography. I would never write a history of myself. On the other hand, throughout my young days at school and just afterwards a number of things happened to me that I have never forgotten. None of these things is important, but each of them made such a tremendous impression on me that I have never been able to get them out of my mind. Each of them, even after a lapse of fifty and sometimes sixty years, has remained seared on my memory. I didn't have to search for any of them. All I had to do was skim them off the top of my consciousness and write them down. Some are funny. Some are painful. Some are unpleasant. I suppose that is why I have always remembered them so vividly. All are true" (p. 7).

3. This and all proper names in the text are pseudonyms.

4. One version of the historical division of the person, the "political-economy of the body," is traced by Michel Foucault in *Discipline and Punish*. In reference to the soul Foucault writes: "It would be wrong to say the soul is an illusion, or an ideological effect. On the contrary, it exists, it has a reality, it is produced around, on, within the body by the functioning power that is exercised on those punished—and, in a more general way, on those one supervises, trains and corrects, over madmen, children at home and at school" (p. 29). According to Foucault, in the eighteenth century a greater economy, a new "micro-physics" of power called forth a different form of punishment and a different view of the body. The objective of punishment shifted away from the body and on to the soul: "If the penalty in its most severe forms no longer addresses itself to the body, on what does it lay hold? The answer of the theoreticians—those who, about 1760, opened up a new period that is not yet at an end—is simple, almost obvious. It seems to be contained in the question itself: since it is no longer the body, it must be the soul. The expiation that once rained down upon the body must be replaced by a punishment that acts in depth on the heart, the thoughts, the will, the inclinations" (p. 16). I use "soul" in much the same manner as Foucault, to mean "the will," "the inclination," the personal values, attitudes, and sense of morality of each student, but I do not include "the thoughts" as Foucault does, the thoughts being closer to the mind. I use the term a step removed from a God-given, essential, immutable "soul-image" (to use Spengler's term) and a step toward the consciously chosen self-sense. Charles Kurzman points out that while Foucault argues the soul-body split served to further the "micro-economy" of power, at Emerald the division of the student and the attempt to treat each part separately is accompanied by the student's ability to resist power. The mind and body are subject to discipline and judgment, but the soul is not.

5. See the review by Jerome Karabel and A. H. Halsey, "Educational Research: A Review and Interpretation."

6. Talcott Parsons, "The School Class as a Social System." For a critical review, see Randall Collins, "Functional and Conflict Theories of Educational Stratification."

7. For a critical review, see Henry A. Giroux, "Theories of Reproduction and Resistance in the New Sociology of Education."

8. Samuel Bowles and Herbert Gintis, *Schooling in Capitalist America*.

9. Paul Willis, *Learning to Labour*; Jay MacLeod, *Ain't No Makin' It*.

10. Willis, *Learning to Labour*, p. 3.

11. Karabel and Halsey, "Educational Research," p. 42.

12. John W. Meyer, "The Effects of Education as an Institution"; Mary Metz, *Classrooms and Corridors*.

13. Metz, *Classrooms and Corridors*, p. 245.

14. To obviate qualifying every sentence I want to make a general qualification here. My interest in classroom bargaining, in power and control struggles, leads me to develop a picture that focuses these aspects, and the ethnography necessarily slants toward the negative. I hope this slanting is not understood as a distortion of the classroom but rather the illumination of one group of behaviors at the expense of others. Second, Mr. Henry is not unique in regard to the issue of negotiation. All teachers worked in the same situation and all negotiated with students. (Metz's work also substantiates this claim.) Differences between teachers could be seen in negotiating skill and in knowledge of tricks of the trade, but not in the necessity of negotiating. I discuss Mr. Henry's class because I spent the most time with Mr. Henry and found it easiest to convert the life of his class into words.

15. Ann Swidler's work on Berkeley's experimental schools, *Organization Without Authority*, highlights another aspect of this process and points out interesting contrasts in different types of classroom control. In Swidler's schools the teachers self-consciously denied the traditional basis for authority and therefore tried to gain control by being "charismatic." In Weber's sense of the term, teachers promoted their possession of extraordinary characteristics or powers (though for teachers charisma was of a secular sort). The source of this charisma originated in teachers' lives outside the school—they were artists or mountain climbers or had some other thrilling hobby or lifestyle—and charisma was to give the teachers the right to command. In sociological theories of authority, the charisma of these activities was the "common moral order" teacher and students referred to for authority earning. The difficulty for teachers was that, as Swidler observed, when a student was more charismatic than the teacher the student, not the teacher, was given authority. Teachers at Emerald were in a far worse position in the sense that they tried to earn authority through teaching abilities. In Weber's typology of domination, this attempt also comes closest to charismatic authority since the principle of legitimation is "extraordinary" and the principle is institutionalized in the "individual." That teachers at Emerald failed to earn authority on the basis of their teaching may mean that students did not share the moral order in which teaching abilities are charismatic, or perhaps, as the work of Metz suggests, teacher and students had

differing ideas of what makes for an extraordinary teacher. Knowing this, perhaps, teachers at Emerald most frequently relied on control through personal relations. I say "control," not authority, because, as the example of Mr. Fields evoking friendship shows, the result of evoking friendship is not a relationship of superordination. Mr. Fields could control some of Tawanda's behavior by referring to a common moral order, to a common sense of friendship, but he could not dominate her and he did not gain authority. Friendship implies reciprocal rights and obligations. The weaknesses of this strategy are twofold: Students may reverse the claims and also demand control over a teacher's behavior on grounds of friendship, or they can entirely refuse to enter into a friendship relation with the teacher.

16. Sometimes negotiations are entirely unsuccessful and the classroom remains in the pure babysitting mode. A history teacher told me that one year she had been assigned to replace, midyear, a favorite veteran teacher. Though a seasoned teacher herself, she never did gain control of the class, and by the end of the year she was still working on getting everyone seated at the same time. Thus teachers cannot assume that their classrooms will naturally settle into a controlled mode as the year progresses. Order must be worked at, and negotiations must begin anew with a change in the participants. Even experienced teachers cannot simply apply a set plan that students will come to accept.

17. It is true in an immediate, but not an absolute, sense that classroom rules and behavior are negotiable while school rules and behavior are not. School procedures are negotiated and questioned, but relatively infrequently and in a different manner. Tawanda, for instance, can legitimately, directly, and immediately voice her complaints to Mr. Fields and push for change. But she cannot enter into immediate one-to-one negotiation with the school's representative, Mr. Leacher. School rules (which are a combination of school policy, district policy, and state policy) can be changed, but only through the proper established channels. Students at Emerald have a student government, and Tawanda could propose to her student representative ideas for how to control Mr. Leacher's bellowings, which in turn could be presented by the student council to the school's representative. It is this difference between the one-to-one immediacy of student-teacher confrontation and the behind-the-scenes mediated representation of student-school relations I am referring to when I claim that classroom procedures are negotiable while school procedures are not.

18. It is difficult to judge when a student is taking advantage of the confusion in a teacher's expectations and flexibilities and when the student truly has a different standard of behavior than the teacher. Ms. Marlow thought the latter was the case in Antara's spontaneous yelling out to her friends as they walked by the open classroom door. Antara had no sense that it might be inappropriate to shout out while the teacher was talking. But my own observations and teachers' conversations lead me to suppose that the majority of instances involve students taking advantage of the lack of consensus among teachers and the school's silence on the subject of classroom conduct.

19. Of course teachers try every means imaginable to *indirectly* and *covertly* affect student behaviors and values. What is unusual about this episode is Mr. Henry's direct, overt approach to the subject.

CHAPTER TEN

This report is an outgrowth of research conducted for the University of California Task Force on Black Student Eligibility. For a detailed report on Interface Institute, formerly Project Interface (PI), see the task force's *Making the Future Different: Models of Community Intervention for Academic Achievement Among African-American Youth in California*, vol. 2. Thanks to Hardy Frye and David Minkus, who read and commented substantially on drafts of this paper. Special thanks to Ella Kelly, who offered advice, encouragement, and critical comments at each stage of the process, and very special thanks to the staff, students, and parents of PI who gave generously of their time.

1. See Katy Haycock and Susana Navarro, *Unfinished Business*, for an in-depth analysis and discussion of the status of minority education in California. See also California Postsecondary Education Commission, *Eligibility of California's 1986 High School Graduates for Admission to Its Public Universities*.

2. For a discussion of the tension between home and school, see Willard Waller, *The Sociology of Teaching*; Gertrude H. McPherson, *Small Town Teacher*; Sarah Lightfoot, *Worlds Apart*.

3. Project Interface, *Annual Report*, 1986–87.

4. Intellectually gifted students are identified by school personnel and subsequently placed in special classes with high academic standards and expectations, and additional resources.

5. The average percentile score for PI eighth-graders in spring 1988 was 55; in spring 1989 this average was 61—a gain of six points compared to losses of three, six, and eleven points at three of the home schools and no change at a fourth. For PI ninth-graders the average percentile score in spring 1988 was 59; in spring 1989, this average rose to 68—a gain of nine points, compared to a gain of two points, a gain of ten points, and a loss of five points at three home schools.

6. Diane Beane, *Mathematics and Science: Critical Filters for the Future of Minority Students*.

7. Reginald Clark (*Family Life and School Achievement*) studied the families of five African-American high and low academic achievers. He found that success in school was enhanced by parents' interactions and ongoing relationship with their children, and by the parents' persistent encouragement to do well in school. He stressed the importance of establishing a relationship between the home and the school since both influence student achievement. Annette Lareau, in *Home Advantages*, argues that the main factor differentiating upper-middle-class and working-class families and students is the role of parents. In middle-class settings parents and teachers are partners in education whereas the working-class view is that teaching is the responsibility of the school.

8. Lightfoot, *Worlds Apart*; Eugenia H. Berger, *Beyond the Classroom*; Donald Seeley, "Home, School and Partnership"; James Comer, "Educating Poor Minority Children."

9. These data are taken from student application forms. According to the staff, the socioeconomic profile of PI students is two-thirds low and working class and one-third middle class. They believe that a number of their students

come from households that receive some kind of public assistance, but they were unable to provide data. Conceivably, some of the parents who did not list their occupations do receive public assistance and were reluctant to write that on the admission application.

10. The parents interviewed ranged in age from their late thirties to their late forties. With one exception, they lived in two-parent households and had two or more children. For most of their married lives, both spouses have worked. All the interviewees were home owners. (Oakland has a 56 percent owner-occupancy rate.) Four parents had taken some college courses, although only one parent had obtained a degree. Of the four working parents, two were employed in clerical positions, one in education, and one in the service sector. One couple's children attended Catholic school.

11. See Lightfoot, *Worlds Apart*, for a cogent and sensitive discussion of teachers' ambivalence regarding teacher-parent partnerships.

INTRODUCTION TO PART FIVE

1. Max Weber, *The Methodology of the Social Sciences*.
2. Alvin W. Gouldner, "The Sociologist as Partisan."
3. Alvin W. Gouldner, *The Coming Crisis of Western Sociology*.
4. H. M. Collins, "The Sociology of Scientific Knowledge."
5. Michael Lipsky, *Street-Level Bureaucracy*.
6. Karl Mannheim, *Ideology and Utopia*.

CHAPTER ELEVEN

This project was supported by a grant from the National Institute on Drug Abuse (RO1 DA05517); Dr. Robert S. Broadhead, Principal Investigator. I thank Bob for his support and generosity, as well as intellectual insight. Also, I would like to thank Peter Adler, Laura Weide, and Todd Rawlings for being continually supportive and providing thoughtful comments on various drafts of this paper. Finally, I appreciate enormously the cooperation, openness, and support of this work on the part of the AIDS Project's administrators and outreach staff. Although I would like to thank particular people publicly, I promised to protect their identities, and all names that appear in this chapter are pseudonyms, including that of the AIDS Project.

1. The U.S. Centers for Disease Control, August 1990.

2. The demonstration research projects were funded by the National Institute on Drug Abuse in 1986 and were implemented in forty-one communities around the country.

3. Howard S. Becker, *Outsiders: Studies in the Sociology of Deviance*.

4. In early 1989 treatment spokespersons publicly endorsed the idea of an experimental needle exchange project. Not everyone affiliated with the drug treatment network supports such a plan. In fact, one health department supervisor charged that needle exchange is tantamount to genocide of the black community. However, it appears that such a project will soon be implemented

as a small-scale experiment. This possibility notwithstanding, the treatment community dragged its heels for a long time and had previously been ideologically opposed to the notion of "safer" needle use. Still, there is no consensus among drug treatment experts on how to handle the issue of needle exchange or how endorsement of such a plan might implicate their programs. The tacit recognition of continued drug injection could be interpreted as an acknowledgment of failure on the part of treatment centers to keep people drug-free.

5. John A. Newmeyer, Patrick Biernacki, John K. Watters, and Harvey W. Feldman, "Preventing AIDS Contagion Among Intravenous Drug Users."

6. John K. Watters, John A. Newmeyer, Patrick Biernacki, and Harvey W. Feldman, "Street-Based AIDS Prevention for Intravenous Drug Users in San Francisco."

7. Harvey W. Feldman and Patrick Biernacki, "The Ethnography of Needle Sharing Among Intravenous Drug Users and Implications for Public Policies and Intervention Strategies."

8. Research projects are also under way within drug treatment settings to establish the effectiveness of treatment-setting counseling and drug cessation as AIDS prevention techniques.

9. Stephen Koester, " 'When Push Comes to Shove.' "

10. Don C. Des Jarlais, Samuel R. Friedman, and David Strug, "AIDS and Needle Sharing Within the IV–Drug Use Subculture."

11. These statistics come from a study commissioned by the AIDS Project, which must remain uncited for the sake of confidentiality. Studies are under way to assess the actual behavior of needle sterilization as opposed to reported knowledge on the subject. However, a fairly recent Gallup Poll reveals a great discrepancy between the knowledge of risk among Californians and their subsequent life-style changes. While 84 percent of the respondents reported knowledge of or experience with AIDS education efforts, only 15 percent reported day-to-day behavior changes resulting from the knowledge; *San Francisco Chronicle*, May 11, 1989.

12. In 1989 the Centers for Disease Control (CDC) became involved in funding IDU outreach service projects, presumably because the number of people infected from needle use is continuing to rise and their sexual partners are at risk as well. While the CDC would have been the logical agency to implement outreach projects in the first place, given its long involvement with venereal disease prevention, projects were instead placed under the aegis of research institutes.

13. For a detailed discussion of this outreach project, see Robert S. Broadhead and Kathryn J. Fox, "Takin' It to the Streets."

14. Patrick H. Hughes, *Behind the Wall of Respect.*

15. Outreach to sexual partners of IDUs involves a somewhat different methodology because most of these partners are noninjecting women who do not necessarily hang out on the street. Outreach to these women involves working within relational contexts with lovers and family to induce behavior change. Here I describe only the methods used to reach street needle users because the intervention model was primarily based on this population. See Mary Romero, "The Use of Women's Culture in AIDS 'Outreach.' "

16. Michael Agar, *The Professional Stranger*; Ruth Horowitz, "Remaining an Outsider"; Robert K. Merton, "The Perspectives of Insiders and Outsiders."

17. Michael Lipsky, *Street-Level Bureaucracy*.

18. Ibid., p. 73.

19. Ibid., p. xii.

20. Frances Fox Piven, "The New Urban Programs," p. 304.

21. The expansion of the Project took place between 1987 and 1989. In the summer of 1990 the Project again faced a major funding crisis, and eliminated over half of the staff. As of this writing, the future funding of the Project is undetermined.

22. This provision was introduced after the federal government's intervention into cities conflicted with local municipalities during the Mobilization for Youth program's implementation; Piven, "The New Urban Programs," pp. 300–301.

23. Becker, *Outsiders*, p. 35.

24. The 1988 Omnibus Drug Act passed by Congress prohibits the federally funded distribution of bleach by state block-grant agencies. However, the Project is only minimally funded by a state block grant. Ostensibly, the bleach money comes from a different fund. Also, the Project is able to skirt the issue somewhat because it is funded as a research agency rather than as a service provider. However, in late 1989 Congress considered measures that would have prohibited federally funded programs from distributing bleach at all, regardless of their research status. The amendments calling for the prohibition did not pass, but the sentiments expressed in the proposed amendments and the debates on them reveal the difficult circumstances under which the Project and others like it operate.

25. In March 1988 this city hosted a needle exchange forum, which heard from experts affiliated with other needle exchange programs in Tacoma, Portland, and other cities. Preliminary data look promising. Also, data from European countries that have legal needle exchange programs indicate a significantly lower HIV seroprevalence rate among injection drug users. Whether or not the relationship between the two is causal is still under investigation. Since late 1988, a large underground needle exchange has been in operation in this city. The Department of Public Health and the mayor's office have endorsed such efforts; however, the illegality of the program prohibits their direct involvement. A few legislators and local government officials are trying to suspend the laws prohibiting needle exchange by declaring a "health emergency." However, few officials are willing to publicly endorse such controversial legislation.

26. In 1989 this city allowed condoms to be distributed in jails, one at a time, for educational purposes. The distribution must be accompanied by a thirty-minute educational session, and a condom cannot be given to any inmate who openly states he will use it for sex.

27. Alvin W. Gouldner, "The Sociologist as Partisan."

CHAPTER TWELVE

This work was supported in part by a Graduate Fellowship from the National Science Foundation.

1. Karl Mannheim, *Ideology and Utopia*.

2. Max Weber, *The Methodology of the Social Sciences*.

3. For an overview, see H. M. Collins, "The Sociology of Scientific Knowledge: Studies of Contemporary Science."

4. See, for instance, Robert K. Merton, "The Normative Structure of Science."

5. See, for instance, Thomas S. Kuhn, *The Structure of Scientific Revolutions*.

6. This contrast and its implications were discussed repeatedly throughout the semester by Michael Burawoy, and are treated in chapter 1.

7. I refer to class members by their first names, with a last initial when necessary. Everyone gave permission to be so identified. Direct quotations are taken from the tape recordings that I was allowed, after some difficulties, to make of class sessions.

8. Quoted from Alice's second field notes. This and other quotes are from the portions of written field notes that students distributed to the class before their seminar presentations.

9. Antonio Gramsci, *Selections from the Prison Notebooks*, p.12.

10. As a footnote to this discussion, Alice later said that she did not particularly believe her own justification for downplaying gender: "I remember Leslie actually questioned it, and said that just because people aren't talking about [gender] . . . maybe we shouldn't just throw it out. It may be very important for the context. And it was funny because later actually I went home and I thought, 'You know, I think that right when I signed up for this course I decided I didn't want to do a paper on gender.' "

11. After reading a draft of my paper, Ann R. pointed out that she was in general quite close to her subjects. I want to limit the analysis to this particular classroom episode.

12. Emile Durkheim, *The Rules of Sociological Method*, pp. 128 and 129.

13. See Alvin W. Gouldner, *The Coming Crisis of Western Sociology* and "The Sociologist as Partisan."

14. Claus Offe also notes the convergence between attacks on the welfare state from the left and the right; see his "The New Social Movements," p. 819. Bourdieu also mentions the competition between social scientists and politicians to control the arena of social analysis; see his "The Specificity of the Scientific Field and the Social Conditions of the Progress of Reason," p. 36.

15. G. Nigel Gilbert and Michael Mulkay, *Opening Pandora's Box*.

16. Alain Touraine, *The Voice and the Eye*, pp. 156 and 188.

CHAPTER THIRTEEN

1. I first learned the extended case method in Zambia from my teacher Jaap van Velsen. That was twenty years ago, and I have been practicing it ever since. As far as I know he was the first to use the term "extended case method." (See

Jaap van Velsen, "The Extended Case Method and Situational Analysis.")
Sadly, Jaap died in 1990 after struggling with multiple sclerosis for a number
of years. So he never saw this "extension" of his ideas.

2. Jack Douglas, *The Social Meanings of Suicide*.

3. Aaron Cicourel, *The Social Organization of Juvenile Justice*.

4. K. Knorr-Cetina, "The Micro-sociological Challenge of Macro-sociology."

5. Clifford Geertz, "Deep Play: Notes on the Balinese Cockfight," pp.
412–53 in *The Interpretation of Cultures*.

6. Ibid., p. 448.

7. Clifford Geertz, *Local Knowledge*, p. 69.

8. Robert E. Park and Ernest W. Burgess, *Introduction to the Science of Sociology*, p. 8.

9. Florian Znaniecki, *The Method of Sociology*, p. 249.

10. Everett Hughes, *Men and Their Work*, pp. 88–89.

11. Barney Glaser and Anselm Strauss, *The Discovery of Grounded Theory*.

12. Ibid., pp. 10–11.

13. Barney Glaser and Anselm Strauss, *Awareness of Dying*.

14. Glaser and Strauss, *The Discovery of Grounded Theory*, p. 42.

15. Harold Garfinkel, *Studies in Ethnomethodology*, pp. 116–85, 285–88.

16. G. Nigel Gilbert and Michael Mulkay, *Opening Pandora's Box*.

17. Don H. Zimmerman and Melvin Pollner, "The Everyday World as a
Phenomenon."

18. This is superbly analyzed by Paul Attewell, "Ethnomethodology Since
Garfinkel."

19. Herbert Blumer, *Symbolic Interactionism*, p. 58.

20. See, for example, Thomas P. Wilson, "Normative and Interpretive Paradigms in Sociology"; John Heritage, *Garfinkel and Ethnomethodology*.

21. Clyde Mitchell, ed., *Social Networks in Urban Situations*; Max Gluckman,
"Anthropological Problems Arising from the African Industrial Revolution";
Max Gluckman, ed., *Closed Systems and Open Minds*.

22. Max Gluckman, *Analysis of a Social Situation in Modern Zululand*.

23. The Manchester School, as it came to be known, was the first systematic
attempt by anthropologists to come to terms with the economic, political, and
class character of colonialism. Among its pioneers were Clyde Mitchell, *The
Kalela Dance*; A. L. Epstein, *Politics in an Urban African Community*; William Watson, *Tribal Cohesion in a Money Economy*; Jaap van Velsen, *The Politics of Kinship*;
and Frederick G. Bailey, *Caste and the Economic Frontier*.

24. Van Velsen, "The Extended Case Method and Situational Analysis."

25. Subsequently, Pierre Bourdieu developed a very similar analysis of kinship. See his *Outline of a Theory of Practice*, particularly chap. 1.

26. Geertz, *The Interpretation of Cultures*, p. 432, fn. 18.

27. Ibid., p. 414.

28. Ibid., p. 417, fn. 4.

29. For a similar critique of Geertz see William Roseberry, "Balinese Cockfights and the Seduction of Anthropology."

30. Van Velsen, *The Politics of Kinship*.

31. Jaap van Velsen, "Labour Migration as a Positive Factor in the Continuity of Tonga Tribal Society."

32. Nowadays, of course, it is not at all unusual for anthropologists to analyze the incursion of international political and economic forces into Third World communities. For example, Aihwa Ong (*Spirits of Resistance and Capitalist Discipline*) studies the resistance of Malay factory women to the all-encompassing surveillance by multinational corporations; Michael Taussig (*The Devil and Commodity Fetishism in South America*) analyzes Colombian plantation workers' fetishization of evil in the form of Satan as a critique of capitalist exchange relations; Maria Patricia Fernandez-Kelly (*For We Are Sold, I and My People*) examines the transformation of family relations brought about by the employment of women in the maquiladores of Mexico's free-trade zone; June Nash (*We Eat the Mines and the Mines Eat Us*) describes how Bolivian tin miners mobilize tradition to launch class-conscious challenges to industrialization; and Laura Enriquez (*Harvesting Change*) studies how agrarian reform in Nicaragua affects cotton and coffee production in the context of a world capitalist economy. Equally, when anthropologists return home they have become adept at revealing the political and economic layers of poverty and resistance in the urban community. See, for example, Ida Susser, *Norman Street*, and Leith Mullings, ed., *Cities of the United States*. Or they start with field work in the factory and work their way out into the community and into the past; see Louise Lamphere, *From Working Daughters to Working Mothers*. It is not an accident that the extended case method should be so commonly used in studies of gender relations as so much of that endeavor is to see how the so-called private sphere is connected to and transgressed by the public sphere, that is, how the macro politicizes and dominates the micro; see, for example, Ann Bookman and Sandra Morgen, eds., *Women and the Politics of Empowerment*.

33. Weber, of course, saw the need for both. The general concepts he developed in *Economy and Society* were necessary to elucidate the distinctive features of Western rationalization.

34. Robert Park, "The City as a Social Laboratory."

35. See Blumer, *Symbolic Interactionism*, pp. 127–39; and Charles Ragin, *The Comparative Method*. Ragin's distinction between the variable and case study approaches parallels a number of our distinctions between grounded theory and the extended case method. But his concern to move beyond qualitative and quantitative strategies leads him to focus on problems of generalization and causality rather than the link between micro and macro and questions of theory (re)construction.

36. See Randall Collins, "On the Micro-Foundations of Macro-Sociology"; "Micro-translation as a Theory Building Strategy"; and "Interaction Ritual Chains, Power and Property."

37. Randall Collins, "Sociology: Pro-Science or Anti-Science?" p. 124.

38. New foundations of social theory may be established, but it still remains to be seen how far rational choice models can illuminate macro phenomena without assuming what has to be explained. One of the most celebrated and extreme forms of methodological individualism was proposed by George

Homans in *Social Behavior: Its Elementary Forms*. James Coleman's *Foundations of Social Theory* is the most ambitious of recent attempts to establish the micro-foundations of a macrosociology. For an overview of the different relations between macro and micro levels in sociological theory that also proposes a new linkage, see Jeffrey Alexander, "From Reduction to Linkage."

39. Glaser and Strauss, *The Discovery of Grounded Theory*, chap. 10.

40. See Alain Touraine, *The Voice and the Eye* and *Return of the Actor*; and Alain Touraine, Francois Dubet, Michael Wieviorka, and Jan Strzelecki, *Solidarity*.

41. Touraine, *Return of the Actor*, p. 40.

42. Habermas's use of "lifeworld" and "system" is not always clear. I understand the distinction to be real and not just analytical. The system world is primarily integrated through instrumental action, although that does not deny the existence of communicative action just as instrumental action can be found in the lifeworld. The boundaries between system and lifeworld do not divide the world into macro and micro but are located such that "the subsystems of the economy and bureaucratic state administration are on the one side, while on the other side we find private spheres of life (connected with family, neighborhood, voluntary associations) as well as public spheres (for both private persons and citizens)" (*Theory of Communicative Action*, vol. 2, p. 310). For an elaboration that links such a conception of system and lifeworld to civil society, see Andrew Arato and Jean Cohen, "Civil Society and Social Theory." One can also think of the divide between system and lifeworld as parallel to the separation of Parsons's adaptive and goal attainment subsystems from his latency and integrative subsystems. Habermas attempts to spell out the nature of the divide further in his "Rejoinders" in *Kommunikatives Handeln*, edited by Axel Honneth and Hans Joas.

43. Habermas, *The Theory of Communicative Action*, vol. 1, chaps. 2 and 4.

44. Habermas, *The Theory of Communicative Action*, vol. 2, pp. 148–52.

45. Ibid., pp. 332–73.

46. In a similar way Douglas Foley (*Learning Capitalist Culture*, particularly Appendix A) has tried to advance Habermas's ideas concretely in his own studies of resistance and accommodation in a school. He redefines Goffman's dramaturgy as "alienated communicative labor," and from there develops a concept of class culture as a speech style adjusted to situationally defined patterns of domination.

CHAPTER FOURTEEN

1. A number of students have objected to the implication that my presence in the seminar was no more important than anyone else's. Even if I was usually silent, I apparently often made up for this with nonverbal communications—frowns, laughter, nods of the head, and so on.

2. Here are the reflections of Annette Lareau on the participant observation seminar of 1982: "[Burawoy] asked me (as well as the other members of the class) to spend a paragraph or two at the end of each set of field notes, ana-

lyzing what was going on in the notes. After each session of observation, we were to write out our notes and then evaluate them in the light of our question. We were expected to assess what we had learned, what new questions had been raised by our observations, and how we planned to proceed. Burawoy's advice was excellent. Today I make my graduate students do the same thing, but, as with much, if not most, good advice (i.e., to lose weight or stop smoking) it was easier to give than to follow. I found the required analyses extremely difficult to do. I hated them. Worse yet, I did them only when I had to—the ten times I was required to give them to Burawoy" (*Home Advantages*, p. 211).

3. At the time I wrote this appendix, everyone, with the exception of Kurzman, had withdrawn from their original field sites, although some had entered new ones.

4. Everett Hughes, "Teaching as Field Work."

5. Unfortunately, the two students who were not from the sociology department decided not to join the book project. They had contributed important and different perspectives to the seminar and their presence was missed.

6. I am thinking of the perspectives that can be found in, for example, Nancy Chodorow, *The Reproduction of Mothering*; Jessica Benjamin, *The Bonds of Love*; Sandra Harding, *The Science Question in Feminism*; Evelyn Fox Keller, *Reflections on Gender and Science*; Carol Gilligan, *In a Different Voice*; Judy Stacey, "Can There Be a Feminist Ethnography"; and Dorothy Smith, "A Sociology for Women."

7. It is also interesting that none of the three men continued to do participant observation research after the seminar. I might add that Charlie has objected vehemently to this interpretation, but since he can't provide a better explanation for why only men volunteered for the position I have chosen to "silence" his protestation.

BIBLIOGRAPHY

ACT UP/San Francisco. "Our Goals and Demands." Informational flyer. 1988.
———. "The AIDS Treatment Advocacy Project." Proposal drafted for ACT NOW Conference. September 1988.
———. "ACT UP PISD Caucus." Informational flyer. 1989.
Adler, Patricia, and Peter Adler. *Membership Roles in Field Research*. Beverly Hills: Sage Publications, 1987.
Agar, Michael. *The Professional Stranger: An Informal Introduction to Ethnography*. New York: Academic Press, 1980.
Alexander, Jeffrey. "From Reduction to Linkage: The Long View of the Micro-Macro Link." In *The Micro-Macro Link*, edited by Jeffrey Alexander, Bernhard Giesen, Richard Münch, and Neil J. Smelser, pp. 1–44. Berkeley: University of California Press, 1987.
Altman, Dennis. *AIDS in the Mind of America*. Garden City, N.Y.: Anchor Press, 1986.
Arato, Andrew, and Jean Cohen. "Civil Society and Social Theory." *Thesis Eleven* 21 (1988): 40–64.
Asad, Talal, ed. *Anthropology and the Colonial Encounter*. London: Ithaca Press, 1973.
Asian Community Mental Health Services. *The California Southeast Asian Mental Health Needs Assessment*. Oakland: Asian Community Mental Health Services, 1987.
Attewell, Paul. "Ethnomethodology Since Garfinkel." *Theory and Society* 1 (1974): 179–210.
Bach, Robert L., and Rita Carroll-Seguin. "Labor Force Participation, Household Composition and Sponsorship Among Southeast Asian Refugees." *International Migration Review* 20, no. 2 (1986): 381–404.
Bailey, Frederick G. *Caste and the Economic Frontier*. Manchester: Manchester University Press, 1957.

Ball, John C., W. Robert Lange, C. Patrick Myers, and Samuel R. Friedman. "Reducing the Risk of AIDS through Methadone Maintenance Treatment." *Journal of Health and Social Behavior* 29 (September 1988): 214–26.

Bay Area Directory of Collectives. Berkeley: Collective Directory Group, 1980.

Beane, Diane. *Mathematics and Science: Critical Filters for the Future of Minority Students.* Washington, D.C.: Mid-Atlantic Center for Race Equity, American University, 1985.

Becker, Howard. *Outsiders: Studies in the Sociology of Deviance.* New York: Free Press, 1963.

————. *Writing for Social Scientists.* Chicago: University of Chicago Press, 1986.

Becker, Howard, Blanche Greer, David Riesman, and Robert Weiss, eds. *Institutions and the Person.* Chicago: Aldine, 1968.

Benjamin, Jessica. *The Bonds of Love.* New York: Pantheon, 1988.

Berger, Eugenia H. *Beyond the Classroom.* St. Louis: C.V. Mosby, 1983.

Bernstein, Basil. *Class, Codes and Control.* London: Routledge and Kegan Paul, 1975.

Blumer, Herbert. *Symbolic Interactionism.* Englewood Cliffs, N.J.: Prentice-Hall, 1968.

Bohannan, Lauren [pseud. Elenore Smith Bowen]. *Return to Laughter.* New York: Harper and Row, 1954.

Bookman, Ann, and Sandra Morgen, eds. *Women and the Politics of Empowerment.* Philadelphia: Temple University Press, 1988.

Bourdieu, Pierre. *Outline of a Theory of Practice.* Cambridge: Cambridge University Press, 1977.

————. "The Specificity of the Scientific Field and the Social Conditions of the Progress of Reason." *Social Science Information* 14, no. 6 (1975): 19–46.

Bourdieu, Pierre, and Jean Claude Passeron. *Reproduction in Education, Society, and Culture.* Beverly Hills: Sage Publications, 1977.

Bowles, Samuel, and Herbert Gintis. *Schooling in Capitalist America.* New York: Basic Books, 1976.

Braverman, Harry. *Labor and Monopoly Capital.* New York: Monthly Review Press, 1974.

Broadhead, Robert S., and Kathryn J. Fox. "Takin' It to the Streets: AIDS Outreach as Ethnography." *Journal of Contemporary Ethnography* 19 (1990): 322–48.

California Department of Finance, Population Research Unit. *Estimates of Refugees in California Counties and the State: 1987.* Report SR 87-1. Sacramento, 1988.

California Postsecondary Education Commission. *Eligibility of California's 1986 High School Graduates for Admission to Its Public Universities.* Report of the 1986 High School Eligibility Study. Sacramento: February 8, 1988 draft.

Castells, Manuel. "Immigrant Workers and Class Struggles in Advanced Capitalism: The Western European Experience." *Politics and Society* 5 (1975): 33–66.

Chodorow, Nancy. *The Reproduction of Mothering.* Berkeley: University of California Press, 1978.

Cicourel, Aaron. *Method and Measurement in Sociology.* New York: Free Press, 1964.

_____. *The Social Organization of Juvenile Justice.* New York: John Wiley, 1968.

_____. "Notes on the Integration of Micro- and Macro-levels of Analysis." In *Advances in Social Theory and Methodology*, edited by K. Knorr-Cetina and A. V. Cicourel, pp. 51–80. London: Routledge and Kegan Paul, 1981.

Clark, Reginald. *Family Life and School Achievement: Why Poor Black Children Succeed or Fail.* Chicago: University of Chicago Press, 1983.

Clegg, Stewart. *Frameworks of Power.* London: Sage Publications, 1989.

Clifford, James, and George Marcus, eds. *Writing Culture.* Berkeley: University of California Press, 1986.

Cohen, Jean L. *Class and Civil Society: The Limits of Marxian Critical Theory.* Berkeley: University of California Press, 1983.

_____. "Strategy or Identity: New Theoretical Paradigms and Contemporary Social Movements." *Social Research* 52 (1985): 663–716.

Coleman, James. *Foundations of Social Theory.* Cambridge: Harvard University Press, 1990.

Collins, H. M. "The Sociology of Scientific Knowledge: Studies of Contemporary Science." *Annual Review of Sociology* 9 (1983): 265–85.

Collins, Randall. "Functional and Conflict Theories of Educational Stratification." In *Power and Ideology in Education*, edited by Jerome Karabel and A. H. Halsey, pp. 118–36. New York: Oxford University Press, 1977.

_____. "On the Micro-Foundations of Macro-Sociology." *American Journal of Sociology* 86 (1981): 984–1014.

_____. "Micro-translation as a Theory Building Strategy." In *Advances in Social Theory and Methodology*, edited by K. Knorr-Cetina and A. V. Cicourel, pp. 81–108. London: Routledge and Kegan Paul, 1981.

_____. "Interaction Ritual Chains, Power and Property: The Micro-Macro Connection as an Empirically Based Theoretical Problem." In *The Micro-Macro Link*, edited by Jeffrey Alexander, Bernhard Giesen, Richard Münch, and Neil Smelser, pp. 193–206. Berkeley: University of California Press, 1987.

_____. "Sociology: Pro-Science or Anti-Science?" *American Sociological Review* 54, no. 1 (1989): 124–39.

Comer, James. "Educating Poor Minority Children." *Scientific American* 259 (1988): 42–48.

Connolly, Mike, and George Raine. "50 AIDS Activists Arrested at FDA." *San Francisco Examiner*, October 11, 1988.

Crapanzano, Vincent. "Hermes' Dilemma: The Masking of Subversion in Ethnographic Description." In *Writing Culture*, edited by James Clifford and George Marcus, pp. 51–76. Berkeley: University of California Press, 1986.

Crimp, Douglas. "How to Have Promiscuity in an Epidemic." In *AIDS: Cultural Analysis/Cultural Criticism*, edited by Douglas Crimp, pp. 237–71. Cambridge: MIT Press, 1987.

Cuneo, Alice Z. "A Look at the Man Behind Real Food." *San Francisco Chronicle*, February 2, 1989.

Dahl, Roald. *Boy*. New York: Viking Penguin, 1986.

Davison, Lani. "Women Refugees: Special Needs and Programs." *Journal of Refugee Resettlement* 1, no. 3 (1981): 16–26.

Des Jarlais, Don C. "Policy Issues Regarding AIDS among Intravenous Drug Users: An Overview." *AIDS and Public Policy Journal* 3, no. 2 (1988).

Des Jarlais, Don C., Samuel R. Friedman, and David Strug. "AIDS and Needle Sharing Within the IV–Drug Use Subculture." In *The Social Dimensions of AIDS: Methods and Theory*, edited by D. Feldman and T. Johnson, pp. 111–25. New York: Praeger, 1986.

Diamond, Irene, ed. *Families, Politics and Public Policy: A Feminist Dialogue on Women and the State*. New York: Longman, 1983.

Dill, Bonnie Thornton. " 'Making Your Job Good Yourself': Domestic Service and the Construction of Personal Dignity." In *Women and the Politics of Empowerment*, edited by A. Bookman and S. Morgan, pp. 33–52. Philadelphia: Temple University Press, 1988.

Douglas, Jack. *The Social Meanings of Suicide*. Princeton, N.J.: Princeton University Press, 1967.

Durkheim, Emile. *The Rules of Sociological Method*. New York: Free Press, 1982.

Ebihara, May. "Khmer Village Women in Cambodia: A Happy Balance." In *Many Sisters*, edited by Carolyn J. Matthiasson, pp. 305–45. New York: Free Press, 1974.

Eder, Klaus. "The 'New Social Movements': Moral Crusades, Political Pressure Groups, or Social Movements?" *Social Research* 52 (1985): 869–90.

Eigo, Jim, Mark Harrington, Iris Long, Margaret McCarthy, Stephen Spinella, and Rick Sugden. "FDA Action Handbook." Manuscript prepared for October 11 action at the Food and Drug Administration, 1988.

Enriquez, Laura. *Harvesting Change*. Chapel Hill: University of North Carolina Press, 1991.

Epstein, A. L. *Politics in an Urban African Community*. Manchester: Manchester University Press, 1958.

Epstein, Steven. "Gay Politics, Ethnic Identity: The Limits of Social Constructionism." *Socialist Review* 17 (1987): 9–54.

Fallow, James. "The New Immigrants: How They're Affecting Us." *The Atlantic*, November 1983.

Feldman, Harvey W., and Patrick Biernacki. "The Ethnography of Needle Sharing Among Intravenous Drug Users and Implications for Public Policies and Intervention Strategies." Presented at the Technical Review Meeting on Needle Sharing Among Intravenous Drug Abusers: National and International Perspectives. Sponsored by the National Institute on Drug Abuse, May 1987.

Fernandez-Kelly, Maria Patricia. *For We Are Sold, I and My People*. Albany: State University of New York Press, 1983.

Feyerabend, Paul. *Against Method*. London: Verso, 1975.

Finnan, Christine R., and Rhonda Ann Cooperstein. *Southeast Asian Refugee Resettlement at the Local Level: The Role of the Ethnic Community and the Nature of Refugee Impact*. Menlo Park, Calif.: SRI International, 1983.

Fisher, Bernice, and Anselm Strauss. "Interactionism." In *History of Sociological Analysis*, edited by Tom Bottomore and Robert Nisbet, pp. 457–98. New York: Basic Books, 1978.

Foley, Douglas. *Learning Capitalist Culture*. Philadelphia: University of Pennsylvania Press, 1990.

Ford, Dave. " 'Midnight Caller' Script Provokes Gay Activists' Ire." *San Francisco Sentinel*, October 21, 1988.

Foucault, Michel. *The Archaeology of Knowledge*. New York: Pantheon Books, 1972.

————. *Discipline and Punish*. New York: Pantheon Books, 1977.

————. *Power/Knowledge*. New York: Pantheon Books, 1980.

Gamson, Zelda, and Henry Levin. "Obstacles to the Survival of Democratic Workplaces." In *Worker Cooperatives in America*, edited by Robert Jackall and Henry Levin, pp. 219–44. Berkeley: University of California Press, 1984.

Gans, Herbert. "The Participant-Observer as a Human Being: Observations on the Personal Aspects of Field Work." In *Institutions and the Person*, edited by Howard Becker, Blanche Greer, David Riesman, and Robert Weiss, pp. 300–317. Chicago: Aldine, 1968.

Garfinkel, Harold. *Studies in Ethnomethodology*. Englewood Cliffs, N.J.: Prentice-Hall, 1967.

Geertz, Clifford. *The Interpretation of Cultures*. New York: Basic Books, 1973.

————. *Local Knowledge*. New York: Basic Books, 1983.

Giddens, Anthony. *New Rules of Sociological Method: A Positive Critique of Interpretive Sociologies*. New York: Basic Books, 1976.

Gilbert, G. Nigel, and Michael Mulkay. *Opening Pandora's Box: A Sociological Analysis of Scientists' Discourse*. Cambridge: Cambridge University Press, 1984.

Gilligan, Carol. *In a Different Voice*. Cambridge: Harvard University Press, 1982.

Gilman, Sander. "AIDS and Syphilis: The Inconography of Disease." In *AIDS: Cultural Analysis/Cultural Criticism*, edited by Douglas Crimp, pp. 87–107. Cambridge: MIT Press, 1987.

Giroux, Henry A. "Theories of Reproduction and Resistance in the New Sociology of Education: A Critical Analysis." *Harvard Educational Review* 53 (August 1983): 257–93.

Gitlin, Todd. *The Whole World Is Watching: Mass Media in the Making of the New Left*. Berkeley: University of California Press, 1980.

Glaser, Barney, and Anselm Strauss. *Awareness of Dying*. Chicago: Aldine, 1965.

————. *The Discovery of Grounded Theory*. Chicago: Aldine, 1967.

Glazer, Nathan. *Ethnic Dilemmas: 1964–1982*. Cambridge: Harvard University Press, 1983.

Glenn, Evelyn Nakano. *Issei, Nissei, War Bride: Three Generations of Japanese American Women in Domestic Service*. Philadelphia: Temple University Press, 1986.

Gluckman, Max. *Analysis of a Social Situation in Modern Zululand*. 1940 and 1942. Rhodes Livingstone Paper 28. Manchester: Manchester University Press for Rhodes-Livingstone Institute, 1958.

————. "Anthropological Problems Arising from the African Industrial Revolution." In *Social Change in Modern Africa*, edited by Aidan Southall, pp. 67–82. London: Oxford University Press, 1961.

Gluckman, Max, ed. *Closed Systems and Open Minds: The Limits of Naivety in Social Anthropology*. Chicago: Aldine, 1964.

Goffman, Erving. *Stigma: Notes on the Management of Spoiled Identity*. Englewood Cliffs, N.J.: Prentice-Hall, 1963.

————. "The Interaction Order." *American Sociological Review* 48, no. 1 (1983): 1–17.

Goldstein, Richard. "AIDS and Race." *Village Voice*, March 10, 1987.

Gouldner, Alvin W. *Patterns of Industrial Bureaucracy*. New York: Free Press, 1954.

————. *The Coming Crisis of Western Sociology*. New York, Avon, 1970.

————. "The Sociologist as Partisan: Sociology and the Welfare State." 1967. In *For Sociology: Renewal and Critique in Sociology Today*, pp. 35–69. New York: Basic Books, 1973.

————. *Against Fragmentation*. New York: Oxford University Press, 1985.

Gramsci, Antonio. *Selections from the Prison Notebooks*. Translated by Quintin Hoare and Geoffrey Nowell Smith. New York: International Publishers, 1971.

Green, Jesse. "Shticks and Stones." *7 Days*, February 8, 1989.

Grover, Jan Zita. "AIDS: Keywords." In *AIDS: Cultural Analysis/Cultural Criticism*, edited by Douglas Crimp, pp. 17–30. Cambridge: MIT Press, 1987.

Habermas, Jürgen. "New Social Movements." *Telos* 49 (1981): 33–37.

————. *On the Logic of the Social Sciences*. 1970. Cambridge: MIT Press, 1988.

————. *The Theory of Communicative Action. Vol. 1, Reason and the Rationalization of Society*. Translated by Thomas McCarthy. Boston: Beacon Press, 1984.

————. *The Theory of Communicative Action. Vol. 2, Lifeworld and System: A Critique of Functionalist Reason*. Boston: Beacon Press, 1987.

Haines, David W. "Southeast Asian Refugees in the United States: The Interaction of Kinship and Public Policy." *Anthropological Quarterly* 55, no. 13 (1982): 170–81.

————. "Vietnamese Refugee Women in the U.S. Labor Force: Continuity or Change?" In *International Migration: The Female Experience*, edited by Rita James Simon and Caroline B. Brettell, pp. 62–75. Totowa, N.J.: Rowman & Allanheld, 1986.

Haines, David, Dorothy Rutherford, and Patrick Thomas. "Family and Community Among Vietnamese Refugees." *International Migration Review* 15, no. 1 (1982): 311–19.

Harding, Sandra. *The Science Question in Feminism*. Ithaca: Cornell University Press, 1986.

Haycock, Katy, and Susana Navarro. *Unfinished Business: Fulfilling Our Children's Promise*. Oakland: Achievement Council, 1988.

Heritage, John. *Garfinkel and Ethnomethodology*. Cambridge: Polity Press, 1984.

Hirayama, Kasumi K. "Effects of the Employment of Vietnamese Refugee Wives on Their Family Roles and Mental Health." University of

Pennsylvania Department of Social Work, Ph.D. dissertation, 1980.

Homans, George. *Social Behavior: Its Elementary Forms.* New York: Harcourt, 1961.

Honneth, Axel, and Hans Joas, eds. *Kommunikatives Handeln* [Communicative Action]. Frankfurt am Main: Suhrkamp, 1986.

Horowitz, Ruth. "Remaining an Outsider: Membership as a Threat to Research Rapport." *Urban Life* 14 (1986): 409–30.

Hughes, Everett. *Men and Their Work.* Glencoe, Ill.: Free Press, 1958.

——. "Teaching as Field Work." In *The Sociological Eye*, pp. 566–76. New Brunswick, N.J.: Transaction Books, 1984.

Hughes, Patrick H. *Behind the Wall of Respect: Community Experiments in Heroin Addiction Control.* Chicago: University of Chicago Press, 1977.

Hunt, Morton. *Profiles of Social Research.* New York: Russell Sage Foundation, 1985.

Indochinese Community Center. *Entrepreneurship Among Southeast Asian Refugees.* Washington D.C., 1983.

Interface Institute. *Annual Report.* 1988–89.

Jackall, Robert. "Paradoxes of Collective Work: Study of the Cheeseboard." In *Worker Cooperatives in America*, edited by Robert Jackall and Henry Levin, pp. 109–35. Berkeley: University of California Press, 1984.

Jackall, Robert, and Joyce Crain. "The Shape of the Small Worker Cooperative Movement." In *Worker Cooperatives in America*, edited by Robert Jackall and Henry Levin, pp. 88–108. Berkeley: University of California Press, 1984.

Jackall, Robert, and Henry Levin, eds. *Worker Cooperatives in America.* Berkeley: University of California Press, 1984.

Jenkins, J. Craig. "Sociopolitical Movements." In *Handbook of Political Behavior*, edited by Samuel Long, pp. 81–153. New York: Plenum Press, 1981.

Johnson, Clarence. "Gays Attack KRON Building." *San Francisco Chronicle*, December 12, 1988.

Johnson, Dale. "The Social Unity and Fractionalization of the Middle Class." In *Class and Social Development*, edited by Dale Johnson, pp. 179–202. Beverly Hills: Sage Publications, 1982.

Johnson, Dale, and Christine O'Donnell, "The Accumulation Crisis and Service Professionals." In *Crisis in the Public Sector*, edited by Kenneth Fox, et al., pp. 34–53. New York: Monthly Review Press, 1981.

Johnson, Diane, and John F. Murray. "AIDS Without End." *New York Review of Books*, August 18, 1988.

Johnston, Paul. "The Promise of Public Sector Unionism." *The Monthly Review* 30, no. 4 (1978): 1–17.

Karabel, Jerome, and A. H. Halsey. "Educational Research: A Review and an Interpretation." In *Power and Ideology in Education*, edited by Jerome Karabel and A. H. Halsey, pp. 1–86. New York: Oxford University Press, 1977.

Keller, Evelyn Fox. *Reflections on Gender and Science.* New Haven: Yale University Press, 1985.

Kelly, Gail Paradise. *From Vietnam to America: A Chronicle of the Vietnamese Immigrants to the United States.* Boulder, Colo.: Westview Press, 1977.

Kendall, Patricia, and Katherine M. Wolf. "The Two Purposes of Deviant Case Analysis." In *The Language of Social Research*, edited by Paul Lazarsfeld and Morris Rosenberg, pp. 167–70. New York: Free Press, 1955.

Khoa, Le Xuan, and John Vandeusen. "Southeast Asian Social and Cultural Customs: Similarities and Differences, Part 1." *Journal of Refugee Resettlement* 1, no. 1 (1980): 20–39.

———. "Southeast Asian Social and Cultural Customs: Similarities and Differences, Part 2." *Journal of Refugee Resettlement* 1, no. 2 (1981): 27–47.

Kitano, Harry H. L. *Japanese Americans: The Evolution of a Subculture*. Englewood Cliffs, N.J.: Prentice-Hall, 1976.

Kitschelt, Herbert. "New Social Movements in West Germany and the United States." *Political Power and Social Theory* 5 (1985): 273–324.

Kitsuse, John I. "Coming Out All Over: Deviants and the Politics of Social Problems." *Social Problems* 28 (1980): 1–13.

Knorr-Cetina, K. "The Micro-sociological Challenge of Macro-sociology." In *Advances in Social Theory and Methodology*, edited by K. Knorr-Cetina and A. V. Cicourel, pp. 1–48. London: Routledge and Kegan Paul, 1981.

Koester, Stephen. " 'When Push Comes to Shove': Poverty, Law Enforcement and High Risk." Presented at the annual meeting of the Society for Applied Anthropology, Santa Fe, New Mexico, 1989.

Kovel, Joel. *Against the State of Nuclear Terror*. Boston: South End Press, 1983.

Kreisi, Hanspeter. "New Social Movements and the New Class in the Netherlands." *American Journal of Sociology* 94 (1989): 1078–116.

Kuhn, Thomas S. *The Structure of Scientific Revolutions*. 2d ed. Chicago: University of Chicago Press, 1970.

Kunz, E. F. "The Refugees in Flight: Kinetic Models and Forms of Displacement." *International Migration Review* 7, no. 2 (1973): 125–46.

Lakatos, Imre. *Proofs and Refutations*. Cambridge: Cambridge University Press, 1976.

———. *The Methodology of Scientific Research Programmes*. Cambridge: Cambridge University Press, 1978.

Lamphere, Louise. *From Working Daughters to Working Mothers*. New York: Columbia University Press, 1987.

Lareau, Annette. *Home Advantages: Social Class and Parental Intervention in Elementary Education*. London and Philadelphia: Falmer Press, 1989.

Larson, Magali Sarfatti. *The Rise of Professionalism: A Sociological Analysis*. Berkeley: University of California Press, 1977.

Lemert, Edwin. *Human Deviance, Social Problems, and Social Control*. Englewood Cliffs, N.J.: Prentice-Hall, 1967.

Levine, Gene, and Colbert Rhodes. *The Japanese American Community*. New York: Praeger, 1981.

Lie, John. "Visualizing the Invisible Hand: From Market to Mode of Exchange." Harvard University, Ph.D. dissertation, 1988.

Lifton, R. J. "Beyond Psychic Numbing: A Call to Awareness." *American Journal of Orthopsychiatry* 52 (1982): 619–29.

Lightfoot, Sarah. *Worlds Apart: Relationship Between Families and Schools.* New York: Basic Books, 1978.

Lindenfeld, Frank, and Joyce Rothschild-Whitt, eds. *Workplace Democracy and Social Change.* Boston: Porter Sargent, 1982.

Linebarger, Charles. "All the Rage: Angry AIDS Activists Pump Up the Volume on Deaf Policy-Makers." *San Francisco Sentinel,* February 23, 1989.

Lipsky, Michael. *Street-Level Bureaucracy: Dilemmas of the Individual in Public Service.* New York: Russell Sage, 1980.

Lofland, John, and Lyn Lofland. *Analyzing Social Settings.* Belmont, Calif.: Wadsworth, 1984.

McAdam, Doug. *Political Process and the Development of Black Insurgency, 1930–1970.* Chicago: University of Chicago Press, 1982.

McCall, George, and J. L. Simmons, eds. *Issues in Participant Observation.* Reading, Mass.: Addison-Wesley, 1969.

McCarthy, John, and Mayer Zald. "Resource Mobilization and Social Movements: A Partial Theory." *American Journal of Sociology* 82 (1977): 1212–40.

McConahay, Mary Jo. "The Intimate Experiment." *Los Angeles Times Magazine,* February 19, 1989.

McInnis, Kathleen. "Secondary Migration Among the Indochinese." *Journal of Refugee Resettlement* 1, no. 5 (1981): 36–42.

Mack, John. "Psychosocial Effects of the Nuclear Arms Race." *Bulletin of the Atomic Scientists,* April 1981, pp. 18–23.

MacLeod, Jay. *Ain't No Makin' It: Leveled Aspirations in a Low-Income Neighborhood.* Boulder, Colo.: Westview Press, 1987.

McPherson, Gertrude H. *Small Town Teacher.* Cambridge: Harvard University Press, 1972.

Malinowski, Bronislaw. *A Diary in the Strict Sense of the Term.* London: Routledge and Kegan Paul, 1967.

Mannheim, Karl. *Ideology and Utopia.* 1936. San Diego: Harvest/HBJ, 1985.

Melucci, Alberto. "The Symbolic Challenge of Contemporary Movements." *Social Research* 52, no. 4 (1985): 789–816.

Merton, Robert K. "The Perspectives of Insiders and Outsiders." In *The Sociology of Science: Theoretical and Empirical Investigations,* pp. 99–136. Chicago: University of Chicago Press, 1973.

––––––. "The Normative Structure of Science." 1942. In *The Sociology of Science: Theoretical and Empirical Investigations,* pp. 267–85. Chicago: University of Chicago Press, 1973.

Metz, Mary. *Classrooms and Corridors.* Berkeley: University of California Press, 1978.

Meyer, John W. "The Effects of Education as an Institution." *American Journal of Sociology* 83 (July 1977): 55–77.

Mills, C. Wright. *The Sociological Imagination.* Oxford: Oxford University Press, 1959.

Mitchell, Clyde. *The Kalela Dance: Aspects of Social Relationships Among Urban Africans in Northern Rhodesia.* Rhodes-Livingstone Paper 27. Manchester:

Manchester University Press for Rhodes-Livingstone Institute, 1956.

————, ed. *Social Networks in Urban Situations*. Manchester: Manchester University Press, 1969.

Montero, Darrel. *Vietnamese Americans: Patterns of Resettlement and Socioeconomic Adaptation in the United States*. Boulder, Colo.: Westview Press, 1979.

Morgan, Thomas. "AIDS Protesters Temper Their Tactics as a Way to Reach the Mainstream." *New York Times*, July 22, 1988.

Mullings, Leith, ed. *Cities of the United States: Studies in Urban Anthropology*. New York: Columbia University Press, 1987.

Nash, June. *We Eat the Mines and the Mines Eat Us*. New York: Columbia University Press, 1979.

Nash, June, and M. P. Fernandez-Kelly, eds. *Women, Men and the International Division of Labor*. Albany: State University of New York Press, 1983.

Newcomb, Michael. "Nuclear Attitudes and Reactions: Associations with Depression, Drug Use, and Quality of Life." *Journal of Personality and Social Psychology* 50 (1986): 906–20.

Newmeyer, John A., Patrick Biernacki, John K. Watters, and Harvey W. Feldman. "Preventing AIDS Contagion Among Intravenous Drug Users." *Medical Anthropology* 10 (1989): 167–75.

Newsweek. "Acting Up to Fight AIDS." June 6, 1988.

————. "The Drug-Approval Dilemma." November 14, 1988.

Oberschall, Anthony. *Social Conflict and Social Movements*. Englewood Cliffs, N.J.: Prentice-Hall, 1973.

O'Connor, James. *Accumulation Crisis*. New York: Basil Blackwell, 1984.

————. *The Fiscal Crisis of the State*. New York: St. Martin's, 1973.

Offe, Claus. "The New Social Movements: Challenging the Boundaries of Institutional Politics." *Social Research* 52, no. 4 (Winter 1985): 817–68.

Ogbu, John. *Minority Education and Caste: The American System in Cross-Cultural Perspective*. New York: Academic Press, 1978.

Okie, Susan. "AIDS Coalition Targets FDA for Demonstration." *Washington Post*, October 11, 1988.

Omi, Michael, and Howard Winant. *Racial Formation in the United States*. New York: Routledge & Kegan Paul, 1986.

Ong, Aihwa. *Spirits of Resistance and Capitalist Discipline*. Albany: State University of New York Press, 1987.

Padilla, Amado M. "Cultural Awareness and Ethnic Loyalty." In *Acculturation: Theory, Models and Some New Findings*, edited by Amado M. Padilla, pp. 47–84. Boulder, Colo.: Westview Press, 1980.

Palmer, Phyllis. "Housework and Domestic Labor: Racial and Technological Change." In *My Troubles Are Going to Have Trouble with Me: Everyday Trials and Triumphs of Women Workers*, edited by Karen B. Sacks and D. Remy, pp. 80–91. New Brunswick, N.J.: Rutgers University Press, 1984.

Park, Robert. "The City as a Social Laboratory." In *Robert E. Park on Social Control and Collective Behavior*, edited by Ralph Turner, pp. 3–18. Chicago: University of Chicago Press, 1967.

Park, Robert, and Ernest W. Burgess. *Introduction to the Science of Sociology.* 1921. Chicago: University of Chicago Press, 1969.

Parsons, Talcott. "The School Class as a Social System: Some of Its Functions in American Society." In *Education, Economy, and Society,* edited by A. H. Halsey, pp. 434–55. New York: Free Press, 1961.

Piore, Michael. *Birds of Passage: Migrant Labor and Industrial Societies.* Cambridge: Cambridge University Press, 1980.

Piore, Michael, and Charles Sabel. *The Second Industrial Divide: Possibilities for Prosperity.* New York: Basic Books, 1984.

Piven, Frances Fox. "The New Urban Programs: The Strategy of Federal Intervention." In *The Politics of Turmoil: Essays on Poverty, Race and the Urban Crisis,* edited by Richard A. Cloward and Frances Fox Piven, pp. 284–313. New York: Pantheon, 1972.

Piven, Frances Fox, and Richard A. Cloward. *Poor People's Movements.* New York: Pantheon, 1977.

Plummer, Ken. "Organizing AIDS." In *Social Aspects of AIDS,* edited by Peter Aggleton and Hilary Homans, pp. 20–51. London: Falmer Press, 1988.

Popper, Karl. *The Logic of Scientific Discovery.* London: Hutchinson, 1959.

————. *Conjectures and Refutations.* London: Routledge and Kegan Paul, 1963.

Portes, Alejandro, and Robert Bach. *Latin Journey: Cuban and Mexican Immigrants in the United States.* Berkeley: University of California Press, 1985.

Powdermaker, Hortense. *Stranger and Friend: The Way of an Anthropologist.* New York: W. W. Norton, 1966.

Project Interface. *Annual Report.* 1986–87.

Rabinow, Paul. *Reflections on Field Work in Morocco.* Berkeley: University of California Press, 1977.

Ragin, Charles. *The Comparative Method: Moving Beyond Qualitative and Quantitative Strategies.* Berkeley: University of California Press, 1987.

Reinharz, Shulamit. *On Becoming a Social Scientist.* New Brunswick, N.J.: Transaction Books, 1988.

Rollins, Judith. *Between Women: Domestics and Their Employers.* Philadelphia: Temple University Press, 1985.

Romero, Mary. "Chicanas Modernize Domestic Service." *Qualitative Sociology* 11 (1988): 319–34.

————. "Sisterhood and Domestic Service: Race, Class and Gender in the Mistress-Maid Relationship." *Humanity and Society* 12 (1988): 318–46.

————. "The Use of Women's Culture in AIDS 'Outreach.'" Paper presented at the Annual Meeting of the Western Social Science Meeting, Albuquerque, New Mexico, 1989.

Roseberry, William. "Balinese Cockfights and the Seduction of Anthropology." *Social Research* 49, no. 4 (1982): 1013–28.

Rosenbaum, Marsha. "A Matter of Style: Variation Among Methadone Clinics in the Control of Clients." *Contemporary Drug Problems* 12 (Fall 1985): 375–99.

Rothschild, Joyce, and J. Allen Whitt. *The Cooperative Workplace: Potentials and Dilemmas of Organizational Democracy and Participation.* Cambridge: Cambridge University Press, 1986.

Russell, Raymond. *Sharing Ownership in the Workplace*. Albany: State University of New York Press, 1985.

Sassen, Saskia. *The Mobility of Labor and Capital*. Cambridge: Cambridge University Press, 1988.

Sassen-Koob, Saskia. "Immigrant and Minority Workers in the Organization of the Labor Process." *Journal of Ethnic Studies* 8 (1983): 1–34.

―――. "Labor Migrations and the New International Division of Labor." In *Women, Men and the International Division of Labor*, edited by J. Nash and M. P. Fernandez-Kelly, pp. 175–204. Albany: State University of New York Press, 1983.

―――. "Changing Composition and Labor Market Location of Hispanic Immigrants in New York City, 1960–1980." In *Hispanics in the U.S. Economy*, edited by G. Borjas and M. Tienda, pp. 299–322. New York: Academic Press, 1985.

―――. "New York City: Economic Restructuring and Immigration." *Development and Change* 17 (1986): 85–119.

Schatzman, Leonard, and Anselm Strauss. *Field Research: Strategies for a Natural Sociology*. Englewood Cliffs, N.J.: Prentice-Hall, 1973.

Schutt, Russell K. *Organization in a Changing Environment: Unionization of Welfare Employees*. Albany: State University of New York Press, 1986.

Seeley, Donald. "Home, School and Partnership." *Phi Delta Kappa* 65 (February 1984): 383–93.

Shalin, Dmitri. "Pragmatism and Social Interactionism." *American Sociological Review* 51 (1986): 9–29.

Shilts, Randy. *And the Band Played On: Politics, People and the AIDS Epidemic*. New York: Penguin, 1988.

Shokeid, Moshe. "Anthropologists and Their Informants: Marginality Reconsidered." *Archives of European Sociology* 29 (1988): 31–47.

Smelser, Neil. *Theory of Collective Behavior*. New York: Free Press, 1963.

Smith, Dorothy. "A Sociology for Women." In *The Prism of Sex: Essays in the Sociology of Knowledge*, edited by J. Sherman and E. T. Beck, pp. 135–87. Madison: University of Wisconsin Press, 1979.

Sontag, Susan. "AIDS and Its Metaphors." *New York Review of Books*, October 27, 1988.

Sowell, Thomas. *Ethnic America: A History*. New York: Basic Books, 1981.

Stacey, Judy. "Can There Be a Feminist Ethnography?" *Women's Studies International Forum* 11 (1988): 21–27.

Steinberg, David J., ed. *Cambodia: Its People, Its Society and Its Culture*. New Haven: HRAF Press, 1959.

Steinberg, Stephen. *The Ethnic Myth: Race, Ethnicity and Class in America*. Boston: Beacon Press, 1981.

Strand, Paul J. "Employment Predictors Among Indochinese Refugees." *International Migration Review* 18, no. 1 (1984): 50–64.

Strand, Paul J., and Woodrow Jones, Jr. *Indochinese Refugees in America*. Durham, N.C.: Duke University Press, 1985.

Strauss, Anselm. *Mirrors and Masks: The Search for Identity.* Glencoe, Ill.: Free Press, 1959.

_____. *Qualitative Analysis for Social Scientists.* New York: Cambridge University Press, 1987.

Susser, Ida. *Norman Street.* New York: Oxford University Press, 1982.

Swidler, Ann. *Organization Without Authority.* Cambridge: Harvard University Press, 1979.

Szapocznik, Jose, and William Kurtines. "Acculturation, Biculturalism and Adjustment Among Cuban Americans." In *Acculturation: Theory, Models and Some New Findings,* edited by Amado M. Padilla, pp. 139–59. Boulder, Colo.: Westview Press, 1980.

Taussig, Michael. *The Devil and Commodity Fetishism in South America.* Chapel Hill: University of North Carolina Press, 1980.

Tilly, Charles. *The Vendée.* Cambridge: Harvard University Press, 1964.

_____. *From Mobilization to Revolution.* Reading, Mass.: Addison-Wesley, 1978.

Tilly, Charles, Louise Tilly, and Richard Tilly. *The Rebellious Century, 1830–1930.* Cambridge: Harvard University Press, 1975.

Touraine, Alain. *The Voice and the Eye.* Cambridge: Cambridge University Press, 1981.

_____. "An Introduction to the Study of Social Movements." *Social Research* 52, no. 4 (1985): 749–87.

_____. *Return of the Actor.* Minneapolis: University of Minnesota Press, 1988.

Touraine, Alain, Francois Dubet, Michael Wieviorka, and Jan Strzelecki. *Solidarity.* Cambridge: Cambridge University Press, 1983.

Treichler, Paula A. "AIDS, Homophobia, and Biomedical Discourse: An Epidemic of Signification." In *AIDS: Cultural Analysis/Cultural Criticism,* edited by Douglas Crimp, pp. 31–70. Cambridge: MIT Press, 1987.

Tuller, David. "AIDS Protesters Showing Signs of Movement's New Militancy." *San Francisco Chronicle,* October 27, 1988.

Turner, Ralph, ed. *Robert E. Park on Social Control and Collective Behavior.* Chicago: University of Chicago Press, 1967.

U.S. News & World Report. "The Artists' Diagnosis." March 27, 1989.

Van Velsen, Jaap. "Labour Migration as a Positive Factor in the Continuity of Tonga Tribal Society." In *Social Change in Modern Africa,* edited by Aidan Southall, pp. 230–41. London: Oxford University Press, 1961.

_____. *The Politics of Kinship.* Manchester: Manchester University Press, 1964.

_____. "The Extended Case Method and Situational Analysis." In *The Craft of Social Anthropology,* edited by A. L. Epstein, pp. 129–49. London: Tavistock, 1967.

Wallace, Steven. "Central American and Mexican Immigrant Characteristics and Economic Incorporation in California." *International Migration Review* 20 (1986): 657–71.

Waller, Willard. *The Sociology of Teaching.* New York: John Wiley, 1932.

Walter, Ingrid. "One Year After Arrival: The Adjustment of Indochinese Women in the United States (1979–1980)." *International Migration Review* 1981, pp. 129–52.

Watney, Simon. *Policing Desire: Pornography, AIDS and the Media*. Minneapolis: University of Minnesota Press, 1987.

Watson, William. *Tribal Cohesion in a Money Economy*. Manchester: Manchester University Press, 1958.

Watters, John K., John A. Newmeyer, Patrick Biernacki, and Harvey W. Feldman. "Street-Based AIDS Prevention for Intravenous Drug Users in San Francisco: Prospects, Options and Obstacles." In *Community Epidemiology Work Group Proceedings*, vol. 2, pp. 37–43. Washington D.C.: U.S. Department of Health and Human Services, 1986.

Weber, Max. *The Methodology of the Social Sciences*. Translated by Edward A. Shils and Henry A. Finch. New York: Free Press, 1949.

———. *The Protestant Ethic and the Spirit of Capitalism*. New York: Charles Scribner, 1958.

Weibel, W. W. "Combining Ethnographic and Epidemiological Methods in Targeted AIDS Interventions: The Chicago Model." In *Needle Sharing Among Intravenous Drug Abusers: National and International Perspectives*, edited by R. J. Battjes and R. W. Pickens, pp. 137–50. National Institute on Drug Abuse Research Monograph 80. DHHS Pub. No. (ADM) 88-1567. Washington, D.C.: U.S. Government Printing Office, 1988.

Weppner, R. S., ed. *Street Ethnography: Selected Studies of Crime and Drug Use in Natural Settings*. Beverly Hills: Sage Publications, 1977.

Whyte, William Foote. *Street Corner Society*. 2d ed. Chicago: University of Chicago Press, 1955.

Willis, Paul. *Learning to Labour*. Westmead, England: Saxon House, 1977.

Wilson, Thomas P. "Normative and Interpretive Paradigms in Sociology." In *Understanding Everyday Life*, edited by Jack Douglas, chap. 3. Chicago: Aldine, 1970.

Wilson, Kenneth L., and Alejandro Portes. "Immigrant Enclaves: An Analysis of the Labor Market Experiences of Cubans in Miami." *American Journal of Sociology* 86, no. 2 (1980): 295–319.

Winch, Peter. *The Idea of Social Science*. London: Routledge and Kegan Paul, 1958.

[Wisconsin] Legislative Reference Bureau. "Welfare Reform: A Look at Three States." Informational Bulletin 74-13-5, March 1974.

Zimmerman, Don H., and Melvin Pollner. "The Everyday World as a Phenomenon." In *Understanding Everyday Life*, edited by Jack Douglas, chap. 4. Chicago: Aldine, 1970.

Znaniecki, Florian. *The Method of Sociology*. New York: Octagon Books, 1968.

Zwerdling, Daniel. *Workplace Democracy: A Guide to Workplace Ownership, Participation, and Self-Management Experiments in the United States and Europe*. New York: Harper Torchbooks, 1978.

INDEX

Abortion politics, 75–76

ACT UP (activist group), 12; activities and goals of, 39, 40–42, 283; at baseball games, 31, 35, 54; boundary-crossing strategies of, 49–51; characteristics of, 41–43; and civil society, 32, 36–37; decision-making in, 41; and the enemy, 43, 46, 51; formation of, 39; and the state, 37, 287; theatrical protest strategy of, 31–32, 40, 41, 44, 46, 48–51

AIDS: and media, 40–43, 47–48; and pharmaceutical companies, 46; as plague, 35, 36, 46–47, 52, 53; social work and, 23–24; state and, 37, 40, 43, 45–46, 49, 51, 282, 287

"AIDS and Its Metaphors" (Sontag), 35

AIDS Coalition to Network, Organize and Win (activist group), 36

AIDS Coalition to Unleash Power. *See* ACT UP (activist group)

AIDS education, 223–24, 228, 259, 260; and distribution of condoms, 231–33, 238, 259; effectiveness of, 231, 233; ethnographic strategy of, 228–31, 241–42; funding of, 224, 231, 239–40, 243; goals of, 229, 240–42; 243–44; outreach workers in, 232–38, 243–44, 260; politics of, 231–32, 238, 239, 240–42, 243–44; state and, 227–28, 231–32, 237; state and restrictions on, 232, 241–42; and sterilization of

needles, 230–33, 238, 241–42, 259; subject interviews in, 237; tensions in, 236–38; treatment strategy of, 228–30, 241–42

AIDS political activism, 1, 8, 12, 35–36, 53, 287; vs. gay political activism, 42–43, 54–55; and wider social goals, 40, 42–43

Altman, Dennis, 40, 42

American Peace test (activist group), 58

Amigos (domestic workers cooperative), 139–40, 141–42; characteristics of, 143–45, 152–53, 155; compared with Choices, 146, 148, 150, 152–55; dealings of, with employers, 144, 153; and lack of English language skills, 144–45, 153–54; and lack of member training, 144–45

Anomalies, participant observation and, 9–11, 26–27, 36

Arato, Andrew, 72, 74

Autonomy, among ethnographers, 1, 25. *See also* Power

Bach, Robert L., 161

Baseball games, ACT UP at, 31, 35, 54

Bay Area Coalition against Operation Rescue (activist group), 75–76

Bay Area Peace Test (activist group), 13–14, 31; activities and goals of, 58–59, 60–61, 60–62; affinity groups in, 58, 68; and civil society, 59; decision-

Compositor: Auto-Graphics
Text: 10/12 Baskerville
Display: Baskerville
Printer and Binder: Edwards Brothers, Inc.